Women in the Resistance and in the Holocaust

Woman Crucified on Swastika, lithograph by Paul Colin. Courtesy of the Library of Congress.

Women in the Resistance and in the Holocaust

THE VOICES OF EYEWITNESSES

Edited and with an
Introduction by VERA LASKA

Foreword by Simon Wiesenthal

CONTRIBUTIONS IN WOMEN'S STUDIES, NUMBER 37
GREENWOOD PRESS
WESTPORT, CONNECTICUT • LONDON, ENGLAND

Library of Congress Cataloging in Publication Data
Main entry under title:

Women in the resistance and in the Holocaust.

(Contributions in women's studies, ISSN 0147-104X ; no. 37)
Bibliography: p.
Includes index.
1. Holocaust, Jewish (1939-1945)—Personal narratives.
2. World War, 1939-1945—Personal narratives.
3. World War, 1939-1945—Underground movements, Jewish.
4. World War, 1939-1945—Underground movements.
5. World War, 1939-1945—Participation, Female.
I. Laska, Vera, 1923- II. Series.
D810.J4W58 1983 940.53'15'042 82-12018
ISBN 0-313-23457-4 (lib. bdg.)

Library of Congress Catalog Card Number: 82-12018
ISBN: 0-313-23457-4
ISSN: 0147-104X

First published in 1983

Greenwood Press
A division of Congressional Information Service, Inc.
88 Post Road West
Westport, Connecticut 06881

Printed in the United States of America

10 9 8 7 6 5 4 3 2 1

To Andy, husband and friend,
who made the return from beyond
worthwhile

Contents

Illustrations

Foreword

When I read the manuscript of *Women in the Resistance and in the Holocaust,* my memory brought back a scene that had occurred in the concentration camp Lemberg–Janowska on July 5, 1943. It was early morning, and a group of women and girls led by armed guards to their execution passed me. One of the girls turned around and looked straight into my eyes. Her gaze penetrated into my soul and has remained with me for all these years. It meant a farewell, but it also conveyed a sacred message: do not forget!

Often when I face hurdles in my investigations of the criminals of the Holocaust, when it seems that everything is conspiring against me, I see the eyes of this girl before me, and they spur me on not to give up the search for the murderers of yesterday.

I do not know who the girl was, but her fate symbolizes to me the millions who perished in the Holocaust.

I witnessed many concentration camp selections by the SS. Children were immediately marched off to the gas chambers. The mothers sensed their destination, yet—in spite of being driven away by the SS guards—they pushed forward to accompany their children for those last few yards and into the gas chambers. At the price of their lives, in dying with these most innocent of all victims, they wanted to ease the children's anxieties and alleviate the boundless dread of death.

For the women life in the concentration camps and in the ghettos was often much harder to bear than for the men. In the camps they worked at hard labor; in the ghettos they additionally supported their families, and they had to comfort and encourage the desperate. And how do you measure the pain and anguish of a mother who has nothing to feed her children?

Too many horrible pictures haunt my memory while I write these lines. During the liquidations of ghettos or when concentration camps were overflowing with their victims, women were always the first to be selected for extermination, because to the Nazis they constituted less useful labor than did the men.

Women active in the underground movements were the bravest of the brave, ignoring every danger to reach their aim or to die in dignity. They knew well that the odds were against them, but they felt as much as the men the responsibility to resist the oppressors and to leave a message to those who came after them: life is worth living only when lived in freedom, and this freedom is worth dying for.

These were the women of the Holocaust.

May this volume stand as a memorial to the countless thousands of women who bravely fought barbarity in the resistance movements or bore heroically misery and torture to the bitter end with superhuman sufferance.

The role of women in all phases of the Holocaust has not been sufficiently documented on the pages of history. Vera Laska is in more ways than one highly qualified to speak about the abomination that was the Holocaust. Her book fills a much lamented need.

Women in the Resistance and in the Holocaust should find its way into every house, into every family.

SIMON WIESENTHAL

Preface

The word *Holocaust* has come to mean the mass extermination of Jews by Nazi Germany during World War II. This is an oversimplification.

It is true that anti-Semitism had a long history in Europe and with proper propaganda again became a best selling item under Nazism. Its pseudoscientific theories provided a "moral" umbrella for further criminal activities. In a perverted manner it came to sanctify the murder of millions of innocent men, women and children, whose only sin was that they or their forebears were Jewish.

Without the marketability and large public acceptance of anti-Semitism, the Holocaust could not have succeeded. However, there were additional incentives. Germany greatly profited from the elimination of the Jews, whose confiscated properties became the bounties of the Germans: real estate and severalties, businesses and homes, stocks and bonds, bank deposits and liquid assets, jewelry and art objects, even the clothes from the Jews' backs and the gold from their teeth. The people who did the extractions in Auschwitz testified in detail how the gold crowns and fillings were salvaged from the corpses on their way from the gas chambers to the crematoria. German racial propaganda repeatedly touched upon the economic power of the Jews (omitting their contributions). Thus, the largest mass robbery in history was glazed with lofty sounding theories and provided a "moral" excuse for criminal acts.

While the Jews were in the first place on the extermination list of the Nazis, the Nazis also intended to eradicate other so-called inferior races, Gypsies and Slavs. With the Gypsies they almost succeeded; with the Slavs less so, although the slaughter and losses in lives in Poland and in the occupied sections of the Soviet Union were devastating. Yet, certain Nazi practices contradicted their racial theories: children of "inferior races" were given to German families for adoption, to be raised as Germans, as long as they looked Germanic. More than this, Slavic and Jewish blood was transfused into the veins of German warriors. I saw it myself as blood was collected indiscriminately from unwilling concentration camp women for the army that by 1944 was bleeding more than the German blood supply could replace.

A great misconception has to do with those who paid the ultimate sacrifice in the Holocaust. The total number of the victims of Nazi atrocities has been estimated by most specialists in this sorrowful field of knowledge to have been very close to eleven million dead. Of this enormous number, larger than the populations of entire countries, six million were Jews, and the remaining five million were not. They were opponents of the Nazi regime, their family members and friends, in almost every European nation. They were prisoners of war from Great Britain, Canada, France and the Soviet Union, perhaps even from America. They were political prisoners from all nations of Europe, but also Turks, Chinese, Japanese and Americans. They were Gypsies, Jehovah's Witnesses and priests, ministers and nuns; they were homosexuals and so-called asocials, which could mean anybody from a prostitute to a Communist. They could also be innocent bystanders swept up in an insane whirlwind of hatred lashing out under fancy slogans. Rightfully, the Holocaust also includes them.

Simon Wiesenthal often points out that Jewish organizations after the war made a strategic mistake in reducing the Holocaust to a purely Jewish catastrophe. In so doing, they lost the support of many Christians in the quest for justice, that is, the search for the criminals responsible for the Holocaust.

Another misconception that obscures the truth is that the resistance movements were exclusively male undertakings. Until recently, history in general relegated women to oblivion, including the women in the struggle against Nazism. There were women on both sides of the fence, symbolically and literally. There were SS women at the concentration camps guarding and supervising female *Häftlings,* as prisoners were called. A large proportion of their charges behind the barbed wires were Jewesses, selected for a life of temporary slavery. But in addition, they were the women who before landing in the jails and concentration camps had been partisans, freedom fighters in the truest sense of that word; they were radio operators, code clerks, spies, double agents, messengers, smugglers of documents and people, yes, even secretaries, cooks and nurses, for the resistance.

These women fought and struggled alongside men or independently. They often were able to carry out missions that men could not. In addition to normal resistance activities, they could use as a cover for their clandestine missions the traditional images of females as innocent bystanders on the stage of such "male affairs" like politics or international intrigue. They matched their male counterparts in intelligence, courage and decisiveness. Risking their lives, they followed the dictates of patriotism and humanitarianism. The majority of women in the resistance of Central and Western Europe were not affiliated with political parties. In the line of their self-imposed duties, they not only sacrificed bodily comforts but also put their freedom and their very lives on the line.

There should be a double equality among the victims of the Holocaust, whether they were Jews, Christians or without any religious preference, and whether they were female or male. We must not discriminate against people who sacrificed years of their lives or against lives extinguished in front of a firing squad, in mass graves or in gas chambers.

The voices of the eyewitnesses that speak from the following pages are a testimonial to the roles women played in the various phases of the Holocaust. The introduction is meant to provide a framework, a minimum of information that every woman or man should know.

Women in the Resistance and in the Holocaust

Introduction

When I met the American liberators face to face on that glorious April day in 1945 near my last concentration camp in Germany, they were surprised to hear that women had also been in concentration camps, and equally incredulous to find out that women were also in the resistance, facing the same dangers, torture, execution or gas chambers as the men.

I vowed then that one day I shall bring the role of women in the cataclysm of World War II to the attention of the public. Mine is the story of but one woman. It was repeated in countless variations by others. That is the reason why I collected the memoirs of many women who all speak for themselves.

I am not an interpreter, or a psychologist, or a philosopher.

I am a gatherer of memories.

Resistance

Stories of invasions are not new to history. In 416 B.C. " 'the glory that was Athens' attacked and devastated the island of Melos, massacred the men, and sent into slavery the women and children," as Euripides tells us in his *Trojan Women.*[1]

In the conflagration of World War II, in which over fifty million people perished, the Nazi occupation often followed that pattern. Lidice in Czechoslovakia was but one village that was razed to the ground, the men shot and the women taken to concentration camps;[2] in Oradour-sur-Glane in France the women and children were also killed. Only Madame Marguerite Roufflance survived to bear witness. In both cases this outrage was perpetrated in retaliation for actions of the resistance.

This opposition to the totalitarianism of National Socialism started in 1933, the moment the Nazis came to power. One must remember that concentration camps were originally set up for political dissenters in Germany, the resisters who from the start opposed the regime. Dachau, Osthofen and

Moringen for women were all established in 1933, long before perverted minds came upon the idea of exterminating Jews or Gypsies.

Resistance or underground activities covered a wide range of actions, from passive resistance in not viewing a German film, to outright guerrilla warfare by partisans against the invaders. Americans should be familiar with partisan warfare; they had learned it so well from the Indians that they used it successfully against the British in the American Revolution (but forgot the "art" by the 1960s in Southeast Asia). There was considerable partisan fighting in World War II, with women participating in it, mostly in the Soviet Union and Yugoslavia, and corresponding maquis actions in France. Partisan statistics are usually inflated by both sides; still, partisans performed a valuable service for the Allies. The Soviet partisans claimed 500,000 operations against the invading German armies, who admitted less than half that number.[3] Most activities were directed against railroads and bridges to disrupt troop movements.

In Yugloslavia the partisans under Tito actually liberated the country, the women fighting alongside the men. Greek partisans twice blew up the Athens-Saloniki railroad viaducts, slowing down German troops at critical moments.[4] The Warsaw uprising of August 1944 (not to be confused with the Warsaw ghetto uprising in 1943), was doomed from the start because it was turned into a pawn on the chess board of the East-West power struggle. The Poles lost at least 150,000 people, every tenth of them a partisan man or woman; German casualties went over 10,000.[5] No wonder that the use of the word "partisan" was banned by the Germans for psychological reasons.[6] They usually substituted "bandits." The Slovak uprising of August 1944 was ill-timed and also had political overtones; the revolution in Prague in May 1945 was an urban rather than a strictly partisan uprising,[7] with the Allies *ante portas.* The former uprising failed, the latter succeeded.

The heroic French maquis struggle on the Vercours plateau near Grenoble was also premature, and hopes for Allied help did not materialize in time.[8] In general, partisan groups were underarmed and often suffered for reasons of political rivalry.[9] Many men joined their ranks to escape forced labor in Germany. Although we shall encounter women among the partisans on the following pages, traditionally there were fewer women than men among them. The lines cannot be drawn precisely; many resisters, including women, at times placed explosives under German tanks or carried out violent sabotage against the German war machine, without being partisans.

* * *

The activities of the resistance were infinite. Planning and carrying them out involved thousands of women, men and even children. Resisters came from all walks of life, from princes to paupers, and they served as messengers, couriers, typists, writers, editors, guides, chauffeurs, pilots, nurses, doctors, radio operators, cipher clerks, artists, photographers, saboteurs, experts on explosives, forgers of documents and ration coupons. Women on an equal footing with men collected military and economic information, and prepared films, photographs and microfilms to be sent to the Allies. They printed and disseminated information from the BBC, also from WRUL in Boston and WCBX in New York. They wrote, printed and distributed news releases, speeches, pamphlets and jokes about the occupiers, and instructions for sabotage of all degrees. Secretly, they put flowers on patriots' monuments, in defiance of German rules. They placed German leaflets with anti-Nazi propaganda into German newspapers, cars and mailboxes. They arranged classes when the universities were forcefully closed. They displayed at public places posters of bombed cities and crying children, of the burning of books or bombings of synagogues, all under the heading "German Culture."

They purloined German equipment, including arms. They sabotaged railways, blew up fuel depots, mined bridges and tunnels, cut telephone and telegraph wires. They placed explosives into barracks and under vehicles. They slashed tires. They dropped lice on German personnel. They blackmailed or talked the Germans into selling their insignia, belts, identification cards and even their guns.

Some resisters worked alone, others in small groups or in networks. One of the most spectacular networks was that of the French "Alliance," nicknamed by the Gestapo "Noah's Ark." Its chief was Marie-Madeleine Fourcade, known as "Hedgehog"; it cooperated with the Allies and consisted of about 3,000 agents, all under code names of animals. Some of this woman's exploits are detailed in Chapter 11, "The Woman in Charge of Noah's Ark." Another example of what a resistance network could accomplish is illustrated by the Czechs whose resistance groups maintained a connection with their central organ. ÚVOD (Ustřední vedení odboje domácího, or Central Leadership of Home Resistance). Between 1940 and 1942, they sent 20,000 telegrams over clandestine radio transmitters to the Allies. They supplied information about "Sea Lyon," the planned German invasion of Great Britain, about the date of the invasion of the USSR (which Stalin allegedly did not believe), and about the developments of the V-1 and V-2 rockets at Pennemünde.[10]

Humor was not lacking in these undertakings. An Italian priest's group transported Jews to safety in German army trucks, with a German driver, as "pilgrims."[11] All over occupied Europe it became the custom to turn around the arrows at highway crossings or switch street signs, creating utter confusion among the supermen of the German armies. Cooks placed laxatives into their food. The "Only for Germans" signs were removed from certain places of entertainment and hung from lampposts. The Danes invaded movie houses and replaced German films with the likes of "In Which We

Serve," the British war film.[12] They also distributed Danish cookbooks, but the last pages contained anti-Nazi recipes, urging German soldiers to desert (with one"s").

A most serious side of the resistance was the smuggling of people across closely watched borders to safety. Politicians, officers and young men intending to join the Allied armies, Jews, prisoners of war, or people who simply needed to escape the clutches of the totalitarian regime, were spirited away often under circumstances that put the best of sleuths to shame. This was a dangerous undertaking as smuggling people and aiding members of enemy armed forces carried the death penalty after December 7, 1941. Just like the underground railroad of the American Civil War era, these lines crossed several states, but in this case the frontiers were heavily guarded. One well-traveled line led from the Netherlands through Belgium, France, across the Pyrenees to Spain; another from Bohemia or Poland through Slovakia, Hungary, Yugoslavia and Greece to Lebanon. Women on the first line appear in Chapter 10, "Postman Across the Pyrenees," and those on the second line in "The French Connection" (Chapter 1) and "The Czech Connection" (Chapter 4). The organization of these lines was complex, involving messengers, guides and people at each safe-house or meeting point. Some of the best safe-houses were brothels and convents. There were countless women who risked their lives repeatedly to help others escape, and they went back to do it over and over again. Many were caught and perished in concentration camps.

In Denmark women and men, young and old, rich and poor were simply outraged when the Nazis wanted to deport the Jews. They spontaneously organized a network of boats and managed to get most Danish Jews across the sea to Sweden, as is documented in Chapter 2, "The Fishmonger and the Schoolteacher." In some cases resistance continued even in concentration camps and in the factories where camp prisoners were detailed. The extent of this resistance depended on the circumstances of time and place. There were political resistance cells in most camps, the strongest in Buchenwald. They usually aided the few attempts at escape. Only once did resistance succeed in sabotaging a crematorium in Auschwitz, and the members of the Sonderkommando (Special Detail) paid for it with their lives. Less spectacular sabotage went on in most places of work, slowing down production or causing damage. From my own experience I recall weakening hemp threads in the spinning factory of the Gross-Rosen concentration camp complex, or mismeasuring with a micrometer—as I did—the rings that went into the V-2 buzz-bombs, which were manufactured in the infamous tunnel at Nordhausen, next to the concentration camp Dora. It was gratifying after the war to hear Churchill acknowledge the value of our sabotage. Where there was a will, there always was a way to leave a window open overnight so pipes would freeze, or drop a wire among the ball-bearings. We were also alert, collecting evidence for future reference, observing the SS men and women in their treatment or mistreatment of prisoners.

* * *

It has been attested by no lesser authority than M.R.D. Foot that "women given the opportunity, were quite as good at sabotage as men." In the underground, "in the secret war against the Nazis, women without number played an invaluable part, participating on terms of perfect equality with men." He acknowledged that "in this field at least the cry for women's liberation was just." He pointed out that some of the most daring women were prostitutes in the service of the resistance, who could easily rifle the pockets of their German customers.[13]

Another well-known resistance leader, the Polish Jan Karski, paid tribute to women who according to him were better suited for undercover or conspiratorial work because they were quicker to perceive danger, more optimistic of the outcome, and could make themselves less conspicuous; they were more cautious and discreet, had more common sense and were less inclined to risky bluffing. He singled out for praise the "liaison women" or couriers, whose lot was the hardest, yet whose contributions were least rewarded. They were more exposed than the organizers, planners, or executors; they often carried incriminating materials or anti-Nazi literature for distribution. One of his couriers visited 240 places a week. She yearned for a sedantary job after the war, even if it meant being a matron in a ladies room![14]

As their fathers and brothers, husbands or lovers were being persecuted, arrested, tortured or executed, as their countries were totally exploited, the women did not lack tangible reasons to be motivated to enter the ranks of the resistance. Others joined to remain true to their beliefs in the principles of human decency, justice and democracy. Teenagers matured into women, mild-mannered women turned into Amazons, and many a time personal jealousies were cast aside in the interest of the cause.

Women, as well as men, in the resistance had to have courage and daring, nerves of steel and a quick wit; they had to possess endurance, a good memory and the rare gift of knowing how to remain silent. Speaking the native language in the place of operation always meant a multiple insurance for a successful mission. It was to the advantage of women that most of their adversaries were male, and women were less suspected of illegal activities by them—the old male underestimation of the power of a woman. This was especially true in feudalistic regions such as Hungary or the less progressive parts of Slovakia. A smile could often accomplish more than a bribe or a gun.

Women proved as inventive as men and often more imaginative. They played the roles of deception more convincingly. Only a woman could have talked her way out of the infamous Star prison of Szeged in Hungary, after having been arrested with two dozen or so foreign men whom she had been guiding toward the Yugoslav border (see Chapter 4, "The Czech Connection"). Only a woman could have had the nerve to slip into a German prison, contact her resistance chief, then convince his captors to release him for money and a promise of immunity after the war, as Christine Granville (the Countess Skarbek) did.[15]

At times girls or women were assigned by the underground to date Germans in order to pry information out of them. This carried an additional burden, for such females were ostracized by their friends in whom they could not confide. Unfortunately, some of them were "taught a lesson" by having their heads shaven the same way as the ones who truly fraternized with the occupiers.

One group of women has to be singled out here for special mention. They were volunteers for the British Special Operations Executive (SOE) in London. About one-third of the 10,000 people in SOE were women. They engaged in sabotage, subversion and escape operations in Belgium, Poland, Yugoslavia and elsewhere. Fifty of them were flown or parachuted into France. Of the fifty, fifteen fell into German hands. Ten were executed by shooting or injections of poison: four in Dachau, three in Natzweiler and three in Ravensbrück, the women's concentration camp. One each died in Ravensbrück and Bergen-Belsen; three survived Ravensbrück.[16] Among those shot at Dachau was Noor Inayat Khan, the wireless operator of the PHONO circuit of SOE, born in the Kremlin to an Indian prince and a cousin of Mary Baker Eddy. She had been betrayed for £500, and was kept in chains after she tried twice to escape. After having successfully organized escape routes between Budapest and Poland, Christine Granville also joined SOE in France. She lived through the maquis disaster at Vercours and caused the desertions of scores of soldiers from the German ranks. "She was certainly the bravest woman I have ever known," Major Peter J. F. Storr of SOE said of her.[17]

They were all heroes, these women of SOE, whether they were princesses, seamstresses or students, daring to do resistance work under false identities, using their minicameras, radio transmitters and compasses hidden in buttons, all under the noses of the Germans.

Women from many walks of life laid their lives on the line for freedom: Jana Feierabend spent three years in Ravensbrück for supporting her husband, a Czech cabinet member in exile. Dr. Milada Horáková, the fearless adversary of all totalitarianism, survived Ravensbrück only to be executed by the Communists. Young Electra Apostolou, involved in student resistance, was defenestrated from the Security Police headquarters in Athens; it was called a suicide. Barbara and Danuta Kolodziejska, the twin nurses with the Polish Home Army (AK)—whatever happened to them and to the thousands of their sisters whose names history no longer recalls?

Then there was Mary Lindell, Countesse de Milleville, "Marie-Claire" in the resistance, her World War I medals dangling from her old Red Cross uniform, majestically ordering about even the German police on her errands on behalf of her boys, the escaped Allied airmen and soldiers. She was determined to outrace death in Ravensbrück—and so she did, but she lost a son to the war.[18]

Beautiful, witty and multilingual Amy Thorpe of Minneapolis, "Cynthia" to the resistance in several countries, a magnetic personality with feline instincts, charmed the Vichy and the Italian naval codes out of the enemy, claiming that there was no rule of thumb for patriotism. "Ashamed? Not in the least," she commented, "my superiors told me that the results of my work saved thousands of British and American lives. Even one would have made it worthwhile."[19]

* * *

In most countries, the lines were not always clearly drawn between political resisters and Jews. The rape of their country and hatred toward the same Nazi foe created a common cause. There were Jews in the resistance movements from France to the USSR, from Denmark to Yugoslavia. They ran a double risk if caught. There were gentiles aiding Jews to hide and escape.

There were also separate Jewish resistance and partisan groups.[20] Agents from Palestine infiltrated enemy-occupied territories. In each of these cases women were participating, as did Hannah Senesh, the brave radio-operator parachuted into Hungary. (See Chapter 3, "The Anguish of a Mother.")

It is generally believed that the Jews did not fight back. It seems as if there had been a blackout on Jewish resistance since the time of Masada in A.D. 73 to the Warsaw ghetto uprising between April 19 and May 16, 1943. On that Passover morning in April, the fighting leadership of the 60,000 Jews left in the ghetto (over 300,000 had already been shipped out to the east and annihilation at Treblinka) launched an energetic revolt. According to at least one source, a fifteen-year-old girl hurled the first grenade from a balcony. The men and women fought valiantly, with primitive and insufficient arms, against the flame-throwers, machine guns, tanks and planes. The ghetto kept calling for help, but the cry was not answered.

Already in 1942 "Veronika," the writer Sophia Kossak-Szczucka, and "Alina," wife of the former Polish ambassador to the United States Filipowicz, together with other women in the Polish Catholic resistance, had urged organized support for the Jewish Fighters' Organization (ZOB) in the Warsaw ghetto; food, arms, money and false documents were needed. At the time of the ghetto uprising, the AK had hundreds of machine guns, thousands of rifles and pistols, and 30,000 grenades, much of this in Warsaw, according to the report of the Polish Military Attaché in Washington to the Allied High Command.[21] The little and late support coming from the Polish resistance is one of the saddest chapters of the Holocaust, and is outside the scope of the women's participation in it. Among the leaders of the uprising were many women, and several survived to bear testimony of the fierce, desperate fighting and of the merciless heartlessness of man to man. Zivia Lubetkin, Wanda Rothenberg, Masha Glytman, Hela Schipper and Feigele Peltel (who writes under the name of Vladka Meed) were among the eyewitnesses and participants of one of the greatest tragedies within the cataclysm of the Holocaust. One gets the taste of Nazi behavior from the case of a young girl found in the rubble months after the fighting was over. She was burned and barely alive. The Gestapo was so surprised that they nursed her and gave her decent clothes. After a few weeks of this charity they took her back to the ruins and shot her.[22]

"Little Wanda with the Braids," Niuta Teitelboim, was a self-appointed executioner. She walked into the Gestapo office, shot an officer and walked out with a smile. She repeated it in another Gestapo officer's house, shooting him in bed. In the ghetto she organized the women, teaching them how to use weapons. She smuggled hand grenades and people in and out of the ghetto. She joined the Polish underground, participating in bank robberies and bombings of German coffee houses. She was eventually captured and killed.[23]

It is a myth that the Jews gave in to slaughter without protest or fight. They revolted in five extermination camps, including Treblinka and Auschwitz. It was a Jewish girl, Rosa Robota, who smuggled in the explosives that blew up the Auschwitz crematorium.[24] In Sobibor, where as many as 15,000 Jewish bodies were burned a day at the height of the "production" in 1943, Soviet officer Alexander Pechersky led 600 prisoners in a breakout that put an end to that camp.[25] There were revolts in the ghettos of Czestochowa, Vilno, Bialystok, Minsk, Lachwa and several others. Considerable smuggling of people, food, medicines and arms went on in the ghettos. Babies were drugged with sleeping pills and carried out in coffins. Inventiveness to outsmart the Nazis and death was almost limitless, but unfortunately could not be applied on a large scale.

In Berlin the Jewish Baum Group of men and women operated from 1937 to 1942; they once blew up one of Goebbels' propaganda exhibits. Jewish resistance groups also functioned in Paris and other European cities. "Jews held leadership positions in over 200 partisan detachments" in the Soviet Union.[26] There is no lack of evidence that the Jews fought back.

The Jews also organized their own underground railroad that tried to rescue Jews and take them to Palestine. Ruth Klüger was the only female of a ten-member underground cell that operated the line in Rumania. She was fearless and resourceful; she had to be, dealing with corrupt ship owners, drunk captains and crew, and often unruly passengers on the one hand, and with shifting political intrigue and informers on the other. She sacrificed her marriage and her love, and years of her life for the cause.[27] Another illegal line under William Perl performed similar services in Central Europe. The gentile Lore Rolling married him secretly in order to share his fate and ended up in Ravensbrück. Lola Bernstein, a British subject, joined them as messenger. They defied Nazis and Britons, and while some of their boats sank with great loss of lives, they managed to get 40,000 people out of the Holocaust and to Palestine.[28] These rescues in often leaky boats were among the most traumatic and tragic ones of the war. The main trouble was that they could not accomplish more without massive assistance from abroad.

The least is known about the resistance activities of the other racial group persecuted by the Nazis. Perhaps because so many of them were illiterate at the time, the Gypsies, properly called Romanies, have hardly any chroniclers. We know from a Belgian co-opted into a Gypsy family that both Gypsy men and women took part in the Western European resistance movement, successfully hiding and transporting resistance fighters and fugitives from German justice. One of their safe-houses was a Catholic convent in Paris, where the Mother Superior and the nuns supported the resistance.[29]

Last but not least a few words about resistance among German women, who were, after all, the first victims of the "night and fog" that was descending over Europe. Antifeminism was a subspecies of racism. If a German judge in 1930 said that Jews were not human beings,[30] that could be explained by the lunacy of Nazism. But it seems that Goebbels also placed women outside the human race, when he proclaimed that "the female bird pretties herself for her mate and hatches the eggs for him."[31] The women of Germany in the 1930s were between the devil and the deep blue sea. Hitler was pointing them back to the three k-s, Küche, Kirche, Kinder (kitchen, church, children). If they joined the opposition, much of which was leftist, they encountered the Marxist creed, which placed class liberation above women's liberation. That symbiosis was like the old English legal view of marriage: man and wife were one, and the man was the one; in this case it was Marxism.[32] Still, many resisters joined the Socialist or Communist resistance, and women started filling the jails and the Moringen concentration camp from 1933 on.

The introduction to Chapter 12, "Women in the German Resistance," deals with this subject in detail. Let it be said in summary here that German women inaugurated the march of women up the calvary of resistance against Nazism. Their numbers were relatively small because, politically speaking, both the temptations of rewards for conforming and the threats of punishments for opposing the regime were great. In later years, if a German woman was caught with a Pole, of an inferior race, she could not only have her head shaven bald for shame but also be sent off to Ravensbrück and a twenty-five lash welcome for *Rassenschande* (defiling the race). Even Himmler's own sister Olga did time in Ravensbrück for that very reason.[33] This crime was referred to as "Bett-Politik," bed politics.

It took exceptional moral backbone to stand up to that kind of pressure. Few equaled educator Elisabeth von Thadden, whose school was closed because she would not follow the party line; she was executed on trumped-up charges of treason in 1944, at the time of the mass executions after the coup against Hitler.[34]

The sporadic resistance activities, like that of the White Rose of Sophie and Hans Scholl in 1943 at the University of Munich, were the exception rather than the rule; they were "sucked up like grains of dust in a vacuum cleaner." Without counting Jews, 302,000 Germans were imprisoned in concentration camps for political reasons before the war.[35] It is not known what percentage of them were women.

The Final Solution and Auschwitz

The Nazis did not invent anti-Semitism; they only perfected it as a weapon of the state.

Anti-Semitism is as old as Christianity. It usually expelled Jews from the midst of Christian nations, as happened in Spain in 1492. Throughout history Jews have been degraded, humiliated, discriminated against, persecuted, tyrannized, chicaned, tortured, enclosed within walls and sporadically killed. One early Moslem ruler ordered Jews to wear yellow badges, and Jewish women one red and one black shoe and bells. "Kill a Jew and save your soul" became the Crusaders' slogan. In the 1880s and early twentieth century, Jews were subjected to pogroms in Russia and Poland. In general, anti-Semitism has been a traditional bestseller in Europe, as Yankee baiting in Latin America.

However, neither in the Dark Ages nor since did anti-Jewish hatred reach the depths of Hitler's systematic campaign of annihilation. According to the Nazi theorist Alfred Rosenberg, "the Jewish problem" of Europe could be solved only when no Jews would be left there. The Nazi plot to exterminate the Jews "was born out of a monstrous wedlock between lust for power and a perverted ideology which mocked the insights of religion and the conclusions of science."[36]

To cleanse the soul of the German people, this nation of Goethe and Schiller burned the books of Heine and Thomas Mann. Two years into power, in September 1935, the National Socialist regime's Nuremberg Laws stripped Jews of citizenship; one Jewish grandparent made a person Jewish. In a rehearsal of things to come, on November 9, 1938, the Nazis staged the *Kristallnacht,* the Night of the Broken Glass, their first big pogrom, carried out with the acquiescing silence of the German people.

According to Luther, this was long overdue, for he had envisaged it in 1543, when in his treatise "On the Jews and Their Lies" he enumerated the ways of dealing with "this depraved and damned people of the Jews": "First, to set fire to their synagogues or schools. . . . Second, I advise that their homes also be razed and destroyed. . . ." He also advised depriving the Jews of their prayer books, religious teachings, safe-conduct on highways, cash and treasurers, and "Seventh . . . Let whosoever can, throw brimstone and pitch upon them, so much the better . . . and if this be not enough, let them be driven like mad dogs out of the land."[37]

From Luther, via Hegel, Nietzsche and selected others, the road led to the *Kristallnacht*. Then came the more orderly, systematic eradication of the Jews. Just before the outbreak of the war in 1939, the Nazi hierarchy ordered a plan for a "Final Solution" of the Jewish "problem." It was delivered at the Wannsee Conference on January 20, 1942, sanctioned by Hitler himself. At the meeting, "followed by luncheon," SS Obergruppenführer (General) Reinhardt Heydrich, the "man of the iron heart," presided over a rogues' gallery bent upon the extermination of millions of men, women and children whom they did not acknowledge as their fellow human beings. The British Jews were optimistically included in the program, but had to wait their turn until the Nazi occupation of their isles. Present were four SS generals, party leaders and state secretaries representing various ministries. Toward the end of the list was one Adolf Eichmann, a mere SS Obersturmbannführer (Lieutenant Colonel) from the infamous IV B4 department of the Reichssicherheitshauptamt (RSHA), the Main Reich Security Office, who reaped the honor of becoming the chief executor of the monster plan.

Jews were to be evacuated gradually from the West to the East; Poland was to serve as a huge labor reservoir. Their numbers would "diminish" during labor. The rest would have to be "treated accordingly." This became the job of the Einsatzgruppen, the special details that practiced the "treatment" by shooting masses of naked men, women and children into graves they had to dig for themselves. Goebbels noted in his diary: "The procedure is a pretty barbaric one."

Certain Jews were to be placed in the ghetto in Terezín (Theresienstadt) near Prague: old German Jews who distinguished themselves in World War I, or other prominent Jews whose sudden disappearance might embarrass Germany. (See Chapter 19, "The Yellow Star of David.")

The mass killings by shooting proved cumbersome and expensive. Too many people were needed to shoot 33,711 Jews on September 29 and 30, 1941, at Babi Yar near Kiev. Eventually, close to 100,000 corpses filled that ravine, mostly of Jews, but also of partisans and saboteurs. The puppet theatre actress Dina Mironovna Promicheva escaped from the bloody pit of corpses and excrement, and went into hiding. Later, she bore witness at the

Ukrainian and the Darmstadt trials in 1946 and 1967–1968.[38] A related testimony of a woman who escaped from another mass grave appears in Chapter 23, "Arisen from the Grave."

Mass graves were a risky business; there was always the possibility of incriminating evidence. Solutions were sought in other quarters.

Euthanasia was the other avenue to mass killing. Much of these "mercy killings" took place at Castle Hartheim, a sixteenth-century Renaissance castle near Linz in Austria, conveniently close to Mauthausen. There were other euthanasia centers in Germany at Hadamar near Limburg, Sonnenstein in Saxony and Castle Grafenegg in Brandenburg. Wiesenthal calls these places "schools for murder."[39]

Thus were killed the German mentally retarded, insane, incurably sick, crippled, deformed, invalids, the senile, all "useless eaters" with "lives not worthy of living" (*lebensunwerte Leben*). It was also a much simplified welfare system.

These preparatory schools for murder offered the training course for the roughnecks who learned by killing thousands of Christian German and Austrian individual victims and, thus insensitized, graduated to the main task, which was to be the genocide of millions of Jews, and eventually of Gypsies, Poles, Russians, Czechs and other less worthy Slavs. The program was administered under Rudolf Hess and, after his departure, under Martin Borman. Medical supervision was under Werner Heyde, M.D., professor at the University of Würzburg; 100,000 people were dispatched this way. They experimented with various gasses and injections; they photographed the effect, clocked the speed of death by a stopwatch, filmed it in slow motion and then dissected the brain—all as an undergraduate course preparatory for genocide.

Thus were trained Captain Christian Wirth, chief of Hartheim, later in charge of the extermination camps at Belzec, Sobibor and Treblinka, and Gustav Wagner who also commanded Sobibor; they in turn taught other cadres of executioners.[40] In 1941, as a test run, 285 Jews from Dachau were killed under this program at the mental institution of Bernburg.[41] This and the mobile gas units were the last preludes to the Final Solution. Then Adolf Eichmann took over and put the extermination process on the assembly line.

The answer came with the invention of gas chambers. The first gassings took place in moving vans, as for instance in Chelmno (1941 and in the occupied parts of the USSR and Poland. By the spring of 1942, gas chambers were installed at several concentration camps in Poland: Belzec (March 1942), Sobibor (May 1942) and Treblinka (July 1942); Majdanek, a former prisoner-of-war camp near Lublin, was extended for Jews in 1941.[43]

In occupied Poland and the Ukraine, traditional hotbeds of anti-Semitism, the Nazi henchmen found willing helpers among the local population. But even in Vichy France the militia picked up where xenophobia left off and pursued with uncalled for energy anti-Jewish legislation. In Italy, Rumania, Bulgaria and even in Hungary until the German occupation in 1944, the authorities tried to contain German pressure to deport the Jews. Only in Denmark did the majority of the population, including the king, support the Jews, and the resistance managed to spirit most of them out to Sweden and safety.[43]

By far the largest camp, eventually with five gas chambers and crematoria, was Auschwitz near Cracow. It first started in May 1940 as a concentration camp for Polish political prisoners. By October of the following year, Auschwitz II-Birkenau (Oswiecim—Brzezinka in Polish) was established for the purpose of the Final Solution. Each day thousands of men, women and children were gassed there upon arrival. Commandant Rudolf Hoess made competitive sport of it, boasting that his new gas chambers could accommodate 2,000 people at one time, while Treblinka's could do away with only 200. (Still, Treblinka would not be outdone and turned "Jews into ashes at the rate of over 25,000 per day.")[44] The highest Auschwitz record allegedly was 34,000 Jews and others gassed within twenty-four hours during the "height of the season" in the summer of 1944, when 400,000 Hungarian Jews were annihilated.[45]

The camp of Auschwitz, as most camps, also functioned as a source of almost unlimited slave labor, both male and female, for German industries near and far. Yet, of the thousands of slave laborers, as of January 1, 1974, only 14,878 Jews received a total compensation of 51.9 million DM (when the DM stood at 36.9, or roughly 2.5 DM to the U.S. dollar). About half of this amount was paid by I. G. Farben, one of the largest employers of slave labor; one-fifth came from Krupp, which consistently denied legal liability and paid only "to heal wounds" of the war.[46] Can German Marks heal the wounds, physical and spiritual, of the 90,000 prisoners sent to slave at the concentration camp of Neuengamme—half of them died of tuberculosis, medical experiments, malnutrition or overwork—or the wounds of countless thousands who labored at Natzweiler, Stutthof, Flossenburg, Jasenovac—and the list is endless, even without mentioning the better known slave camps like Dachau, Buchenwald, Ravensbrück and of course Auschwitz, where men and women were dying like flies to support the perversion that was the Nazi system. Herr Krupp's faithful servants take a simplistic ethical view of these matters.

Among the first women in Auschwitz were German prostitutes and Jewish girls from Slovakia. These women were issued evening gowns in which they were forced to help build Auschwitz, in rain or snow. Of the hundreds only a handful survived by 1944.

Auschwitz means four million dead, over two million of them Jews. The rest were political prisoners, Russian prisoners of war, with a sprinkling of

French and British, religious objectors, Gypsies, homosexuals, asocials and professional criminals. Most were from Poland and Russia, but almost all nationalities of Europe were represented, and even a few Americans.

The mass murders by shooting and in the gas chambers of extermination camps, together with the hunger, exhaustion, torture, executions, diseases and medical experiments in countless prisons and concentration camps, accounted for a total of eleven million victims. Of these the "crime" of six million, 5,978,000 to be exact, was that they were Jewish. All this occurred under the most horrifying circumstances and while the civilized world looked on in unforgivable, naive disbelief.

A more detailed account of Auschwitz will be found in Chapter 13, "Auschwitz—A Factual Deposition."[47] The perversities at the women's camp of Ravensbrück will be unveiled in Chapters 16 to 18, "Night and Fog," "Middle Ages Nazi Style" and "The Stations of the Cross," and the horrors of Bergen-Belsen in Chapter 21, "Notes from the Camp of the Dead." While the concentration camps of Dachau and Buchenwald as prevalently male camps are outside the scope of this book, a few words about them should elucidate still other aspects of life and death in Nazi camps, especially as they touched upon women.

Dachau

The national *Völkischer Beobachter* on March 21, 1933, announced the official opening of Dachau as if it were a coming out party or the inauguration of a fair. Under the headline "A Concentration Camp for Political Prisoners" then police commissioner for Munich Heinrich Himmler, later the top police officer of the Reich, proudly announced that "On Wednesday near Dachau the first concentration camp will be opened."[48] Dachau became the prototype for other camps. Here Max Kögel, later commandant of the women's concentration camp at Ravensbrück, served his apprenticeship.

Dachau was built for 5,000 inmates. By 1945, a total of 200,000 people of thirty-eight nationalities had passed through its gates; among them were Chinese, Japanese, eleven Americans and close to 3,000 Catholic priests. Thousands of Soviet prisoners of war were shot there without being registered in the camp.

Dachau was not meant to hold women, but beginning in 1941 they were working in several of the sixteen subdivisions of the camp. A few dozen women were brought in from Ravensbrück to service the brothel for privileged prisoners. These women were recruited with promises of freedom after serving six months (about 2,000 services), which was never the case. Most of the women were Germans, Poles and Russians. Two female Jehovah's Witnesses were in the penal bunker in February 1945.[49]

Women were brought to Dachau for execution, without being registered on the camp lists. The most prominent were the four members of SOE: Yolande E. M. Beekman, Madeleine Damerment, Noor Inayat Khan and Eliane S. Plewman (see above under Resistance). On September 12, 1944, they were executed, "kneeling down and holding hands, by shooting through the back of the neck."[50] Their bodies were immediately cremated. All four were posthumously awarded the Croix de Guerre avec Etoile Vermeil; Damerment in addition received the medal of the Légion d'Honneur, Inayat Khan the George Cross and M.B.E. All were between twenty-seven and thirty-three years of age. Their heroism is commemorated by a tablet attached to the wall next to the crematorium ovens where they were burned; its inscription intones the hope for eternity: "But the souls of the righteous are in the hand of God, and there shall no torment touch them."

Toward the end of the war, hundreds of men and women were transferred to Dachau in the confusion of concentration camp evacuations between two collapsing fronts.[51] An American soldier who entered Dachau with the liberators on April 29, 1945, saw the skeletal figures and viewed the fifty boxcars that had brought additional prisoners. Of all those people only one was alive. He later commented: "Suddenly we all understood what we had been fighting for."[52]

Buchenwald

The statistics of Buchenwald speak for themselves: according to German registrations, over 238,000 men, women and children entered, and 56,000 of them died there. Among the many nationalities murdered were the martyred thirty-four British and Canadian pilots and 8,483 Soviet prisoners of war.[53]

Buchenwald was established near Goethe's Weimar in July 1937, after the closing of Lichtenburg and Sachsenburg (not to be confused with Sachsenhausen) concentration camps. It was to be called Ettersberg, but since that mountain used to be the poet's favored spot, the SS with delicacy named it simply Buchenwald, Beech Forest. It was the training ground for many an eminent commandant of other camps. Its first chief was the infamous SS Colonel Karl Koch, a sadist and crook, later transferred to Lublin. He stands out among the rest of his equals as having been executed for corrupt scandals by the very SS on March 4, 1945!

His wife Ilse Koch, a vicious and brazenly promiscuous female, had caused the sufferings and deaths of countless inmates through her clout as the commandant's spouse.[54] While she did not originate the idea, she enjoyed the lamp shades and other objects made of the skins of inmates. These gory "souvenirs," knife holsters, book covers, and hundreds of pictures drawn on human skin, also shrunken heads of inmates, were handed out to visitors and to the SS personnel serving at Buchenwald. The fame of the specialty spread, and requests came from other camps. On December 4, 1944 (Christmas season!), 142 pieces were dispatched by courier to the concentration camp Sachsenhausen.[55] An especially neat curio was the lamp with the human skin lamp shade mounted on a human shinbone, turned on by a white button at the small toe bone; this masterpiece was presented by the head pathologist of the camp, Dr. Müller, to commandant Koch for his birthday. Some pieces were handed over to the American intelligence unit in April 1945.[56]

Buchenwald had some of the most bizarre accoutrements found in any concentration camp. One was a falconry court, built with no expenses spared, for Hermann Goering who never set foot in it. At one time, former French premier Leon Blum and other "prominents" were housed there. Next to it was a zoo, with monkeys, bears, even a rhinoceros. "One of the satanic SS pastimes under the regime of Commandant Koch was to throw prisoners into the bears' cage to be torn limb from limb."[57] The animals were fed better than the prisoners, whose meagre meat rations were cut in order to nourish the beasts.

Frau Koch had to have her own riding ring, 300 feet long, its walls surfaced with mirrors, costing about 250,000 marks and thirty prisoners' lives.

Buchenwald was also the place for some four dozen celebrities, who were held, some with their maids, in isolation barracks. Besides former German political and industrial leaders like Social Democrat Rudolf Breitscheid and Fritz Thyssen, who had financed the Nazis until he saw the light, there were wives, children and family members of labor leaders and of the perpetrators of the 1944 plot against Hitler like the Stauffenbergs and Goerdelers. Here also were Maria Ruhnar of the Jehovah's Witnesses, and even Italian Princess Mafalde of Hesse, daughter of Italian King Victor Emmanuel.[58]

Gemma La Guardia Gluck, sister of the New York mayor, was a prisoner in the women's concentration camp of Ravensbrück and recalled the many "prominent" women there, among them artists, diplomats, nobility, politicians and wives and widows of high officials, including those of the July 20, 1944, plotters against Hitler.[59] More about Ravensbrück will be revealed in Chapter 16, "Night and Fog" and in Chapters 17 and 18, "Middle Ages Nazi Style" and "The Stations of the Cross."

Like Dachau, Buchenwald was a prevalently male concentration camp. Most women who entered it were there in transit to other camps or to their labor commando posts. Thus, for a large contingent of Soviet women who had arrived on their way to Ravensbrück and had not received any food or drink for four days, the male inmates "organized" from the SS larders bread, marmalade and cucumbers, at the risk of their lives.[60]

A typical large female labor detail was that of 2,300 women of mixed nationality that worked in the HASAG commando at Altenberg, a branch of Buchenwald, manufacturing ammunition. On twelve-hour shifts they received 225 grams of bread and ¾ liter of watery soup per day. They were subjected to camp commander Frötsch's exceptional "bestiality, blackmail and raping of female inmates."[61] Their female supervisor, Frau Rupert, trained in Auschwitz, outdid in her cruelty most SS men. Health supervisor Fräulein Bassal's sadism manifested itself, among other ways, in denying women medicine and sanitary napkins,[62] which women new to camp life still needed. Three women from this commando met with the displeasure of the SS and were given twenty-five blows by flogging; Sergeant-Major Sommer boasted that he gave one of them forty blows, and she still did not cry out. How could she? She was dead. His colleagues then made fun of Sommer, telling him that he had wasted his energies on a corpse. The same Sommer was later asked at his trial whether he had beaten women as brutally as men. "Naturally," he replied.[63]

One of the most miraculous events that happened in any concentration camp occurred in Buchenwald. The men managed to adopt, nourish and conceal an unregistered toddler, Josef Streich, brought in by his Polish Jewish father in a knapsack. He survived for two years until liberation, a smart little boy who "could hide like a mouse at the first glance of a uniform."[64]

After the liberation of the camp, the American officer in charge made a shrewd move that, unfortunately, was not duplicated in every camp. He ordered the population of Weimar to come and see the conditions under which Nazis forced human slaves to exist.[65]

Children

The Polish Red Cross estimated that over 40,000 babies born inside concentration and labor camps and prisons were taken away from their mothers, and most of them killed.

Children of many nationalities passed through the gates of concentration camps, only to disappear in the gas chambers as "useless eaters." Most of them were Jewish children, and others belonged to Gypsies or political prisoners. It is known that even the children of partisans and of resisters were executed as bandits by the Nazis.

A certain number of babies and small children—the number will never be determined—were sent out for adoption by German families. In spite of theories about pure race and a determination to eradicate inferior "races" like the Slavs, the Germans encouraged the adoption of non-Germanic children, male and female, if they were of the right Germanic appearance and young enough to forget their roots. Such children were to be collected from occupied countries "if necessary by robbing and stealing them," as Himmler said in 1944.[66] In Poland alone over 200,000 children were simply kidnapped from the streets, schools or their homes, and taken to centers where the selection of "valuable" children took place.[67] After a few months of Germanization, they were adopted by German families. The undesirable ones were simply "disposed of."

The children of Lidice, the Czech village leveled to the ground on June 10, 1942, in retaliation for the resistance's shooting of Heydrich, met this fate. Their fathers were shot, their mothers taken to concentration camps, and they were abducted. Of the ninety-one children, only a handful were located after the war in an extensive search by the Czechoslovak War Crimes Investigation Commission, and a few were reunited with their mothers under most dramatic circumstances.[68] The children spoke only German and did not understand their mothers. Hundreds of parents in many countries are still living today, clutching the pictures of their children kidnapped four decades ago.

The fate of Jewish children in the Holocaust has not been explored sufficiently. Were the cases of Janusz Korczak, M.D., of Warsaw or of Ernst Papanek of Austria unique? Korczak, the popular voice of the "Old Doctor of the Radio," was a pediatrician and director of an orphanage for about 200 children. He never left them and in August 1942 he died with them in the gas chamber. Papanek was in charge of a rescue operation that tried to save children from the Holocaust in Paris and southern France with considerable success.

An extraordinary story of goodness is that of the small village of Chambon-sur-Lignon, also in southern France. Its population banded together to rescue hundreds of Jewish children and adults, harboring them and aiding their escape to Switzerland.[69]

To bring the deeds of such heroism to the attention of the world is as important as to point out the atrocities. Mankind could learn from both.

Gypsies

Like the Jews, Gypsies were singled out by the Nazis for racial persecution and annihilation. They were "nonpersons," of "foreign blood," "labor-shy," and as such were termed asocials. To a degree, they shared the fate of the Jews in their ghettos, in the extermination camps, before firing squads, as medical guinea pigs, and being injected with lethal substances.

Ironically, the German writer Johann Christof Wagenseil claimed in 1697 that Gypsies stemmed from German Jews. A more contemporary Nazi theorist believed that "the Gypsy cannot, by reason of his inner and outer makeup (Konstruktion), be a useful member of the human community."[70]

The Nuremberg Laws of 1935 aimed at the Jews were soon amended to include the Gypsies. In 1937, they were classified as asocials, second-class citizens, subject to concentration camp imprisonment.[71] As early as 1936, some had been sent to camps. After 1939, Gypsies from Germany and from the German-occupied territories were shipped by the thousands first to Jewish ghettos in Poland at Warsaw, Lublin, Kielce, Rabka, Zary, Siedlce and others.[72] It is not known how many were killed by the Einsatzgruppen charged with speedy extermination by shooting. For the sake of efficiency Gypsies were also shot naked, facing their pre-dug graves. According to the Nazi experts, shooting Jews was easier, they stood still, "while the Gypsies cry out, howl, and move constantly, even when they are already standing on the shooting ground. Some of them even jumped into the ditch before the volley and pretended to be dead."[73] The first to go were the German Gypsies; 30,000 were deported East in three waves in 1939, 1941 and 1943. Those married to Germans were exempted but were sterilized, as were their children after the age of twelve.[74]

Just how were the Gypsies of Europe "expedited"? Adolf Eichmann, chief strategist of these diabolical logistics, supplied the answer in a telegram from Vienna to the Gestapo:

> Regarding transport of Gypsies be informed that on Friday, October 20, 1939, the first transport of Jews will depart Vienna. To this transport 3-4 cars of Gypsies are to be attached. Subsequent trains will depart from Vienna, Mährisch-Ostrau and Katowice [Poland]. The simplest method is to attach some carloads of Gypsies to each transport. Because these transports must follow schedule, a smooth execution of this matter is expected. Concerning a start in the Altreich [Germany proper] be informed that this will be coming in 3-4 weeks. Eichmann.[74]

Open season was declared on the Gypsies, too. For a while Himmler wished to exempt two tribes and "only" sterilize them, but by 1942 he signed the decree for all Gypsies to be shipped to Auschwitz.[76] There they were subjected to all that Auschwitz meant, including the medical experiments, before they were exterminated.

Gypsies perished in Dachau, Mauthausen, Ravensbrück and other camps. At Sachsenhausen they were subjected to special experiments that were to prove scientifically that their blood was different from that of the Germans. The doctors in charge of this "research" were the same ones who had practiced previously on black prisoners of war. Yet, for "racial reasons" they were found unsuitable for sea water experiments.[77] Gypsies were often accused of atrocities committed by others; they were blamed, for instance, for the looting of gold teeth from a hundred dead Jews abandoned on a Rumanian road.[78]

Gypsy women were forced to become guinea pigs in the hands of Nazi physicians. Among others they were sterilized as "unworthy of human reproduction" (*fortpflanzungsunwürdig*), only to be ultimately annihilated as not worthy of living. (See Chapter 18, "The Stations of the Cross.") Gypsies and Jews could have joined in the Polish resistance song: "When a German puts his foot down, the soil bleeds a hundred years."[79] At that, the Gypsies were the luckier ones; in Bulgaria, Greece, Denmark and Finland they were spared.[80]

For a while there was a Gypsy Family Camp in Auschwitz, but on August 6, 1944, it was liquidated. Some men and women were shipped to German factories as slave labor; the rest, about 3,000 women, children and old people, were gassed.[81]

No precise statistics exist about the extermination of European Gypsies. Some estimates place the number between 500,000 and 600,000, most of them gassed in Auschwitz.[82] Others indicate a more conservative 200,000 Gypsy victims of the Holocaust.[83]

Sex

A few remarks are in order about the various sex relationships in concentration camps. I start out with the homosexuals since they were accorded a special category among the inmates and "merited" a separate, pink triangle. The following color-coding was established for the triangles worn below the prisoners' numbers:

yellow—Jews	purple—religious offenders
red—political	pink—homosexuals
black—asocials	green—professional criminals

Very little has been written about the tens of thousands of homosexuals who were the damnedest of the damned, the outcasts among the outcasts in the concentration camps. There are really only estimates of figures. During the twelve years of Nazi rule, nearly 50,000 were convicted of the crime of homosexuality. The majority ended up in concentration camps, and virtually all of them perished.[84] According to a recent study, "at least 500,000 gays died in the Holocaust."[85] As Stefan Lorant observed in 1935, the homosexuals "lived in a dream," hoping that the heyday of gays in Germany of the 1920s would last forever. Their awakening was terrible.[86] Yet, the few survivors among them did not qualify for postwar restitution as the Jews or the politicals, because as homosexuals they were outside the law. By German law homosexuality was a crime. After prison sentences most homosexuals were automatically shipped to concentration camps. In 1935, a new law legalized the "compulsory sterilization (often in fact castration) of homosexuals."[87] A special section of the Gestapo dealt with them. Along with epileptics, schizophrenics and other "degenerates," they were being eliminated. Yet homosexuality was still so widespread that in 1942 the death penalty was imposed for it in the army and the SS.

In concentration camps, some pink triangles became concubines of male kapos or other men in supervisory positions among the inmates. They were known as doll boys;[88] this brought them certain protection while the love affair lasted. The pink triangles were constantly abused by the SS, camp officials and fellow prisoners. They were seldom called other names than arse-holes, shitty queers or bum-fuckers. They were allowed to talk only to each other, they had to sleep with the lights on and with hands above their blankets. These people were not child molesters; those were considered professional criminals, green triangles.

While men with pink triangles were given the hardest jobs and were being constantly abused for their admitted sexual preference, considerable numbers of "normal" men engaged in homosexual acts with impunity—that was an emergency outlet. This double standard was an additional psychological burden for the pink triangles.

The SS considered it great sport to taunt and torture the homosexuals. The camp commander at Flossenburg often ordered them flogged; as the victims were screaming, he "was panting with excitement, and masturbated wildly in his trousers until he came," unperturbed by the hundreds of onlookers.[89] A sixty-year-old gay priest was beaten over his sexual organs by the SS and told: "You randy old rat-bag, you can piss with your arsehole in the future." He could not, for he died the next day.[90] Eyewitnesses tell of homosexuals being tortured to death by tickling, by having their testicles immersed alternately into hot and icy water, by having a broomstick pushed into their anus.[91]

Himmler, who wanted to eradicate homosexuals "root and branch," had the idea to "cure" them by mandatory visits to the camp brothel at Flossenburg. Ten Ravensbrück women provided the services with little success. The women here also were told that they would go free after six months, but instead they were shipped to Auschwitz.[92]

The pink triangles worked in the clay pits of Sachsenhausen, the quarries of Buchenwald, Flossenburg and Mauthausen; they shoveled snow with their bare hands in Auschwitz and elsewhere; they were used as living targets at the firing range; they had the dirtiest jobs in all camps. Towards the end of the war, they were told that they would be released if they let themselves be castrated. The ones who agreed were shipped to the infamous Dirlewanger penal division on the Russian front.[93]

* * *

While homosexuals were treated in a manner that even within the concentration camp framework was ghastly, their female counterparts, the Lesbians, were seldom hunted down for special treatment. Lesbianism was not on the books as illegal. The Nazis were confident that they could handle females properly to keep them to their "kitchen, church, children." After all, the Führer told women that "emancipation of women is only an invention of the Jewish intellect."[94]

If there is hardly any documentation on male homosexuals in the camps, there is even less available on Lesbians. This will not change until a former inmate who was a Lesbian comes out of the closet and writes her memoirs. There were without doubt hundreds of Lesbian relationships in the camps, but they were difficult to identify and to distinguish from the numerous close friendships that developed among the women in each camp and block.

Stripped almost totally of male companionship by the division of sexes, women formed warm relationships with one another. Occasionally, these relationships developed into Lesbianism, especially if one partner was a bona fide Lesbian. If a women had a position of eminence in the camp hierarchy, such as a block senior or kapo, with separate quarters, chances were better for such friendships to evolve into a sexual relationship. Endless months or years of living without psychological or physical love, in the constant shadow of death where the slightest move could land one in the gas chamber, compelled many women to the only sexual outlet available to them, that is, an erotic tie with a person of their own sex. As in many prisons, in concentration camps women who would otherwise regard Lesbianism with abhorrence would gradually slide into the acceptance of such liaisons. This was again mostly true in the cases of couples where one of the lovers was in a privileged position, either as a camp trustee disposing with private quarters or working at a place like Canada in Auschwitz, where she was at the source of endless trading in goods—food, clothing, cigarettes or medicine, which served as an irresistible incentive for gaining a sexual partner. While such relationships were dangerous, they could provide a submissive partner with the means for survival and an influential protective arm that could place her in a better job, or exempt her from a death transport.

Survivors are often asked how they could exist without sex. The answer is simple. The instinct for survival, the primary concern for maintaining one's body alive by supplying it with food, took precedence over any other instinct, including the sexual one. The chemical added to the "soup" caused the cessation of menstruation in women and also dulled the senses. The only constantly present yearning was for food, a piece of bread, a potato peel, a rotten piece of vegetable, anything to fuel the body. The will to live manifested itself "in a total devaluation of anything that did not serve this exclusive interest."[95] Viktor E. Frankl, the psychiatrist-survivor, confirms what most former inmates will say, namely, that "everything that was not connected with the immediate task of keeping oneself and one's closest friends alive lost its value."[96] Moral values from the "outside" and conscience were shoved aside by pangs of hunger. An aristocratic and cultured British woman admitted after her liberation: "Nothing else counted but that I wanted to live. I could have stolen from husband, child, parent" just to get some food.[97] While I personally would not have gone that far, I know that hunger took absolute precedence over sex. "Sexual energies . . . were withdrawn in order to rescue the ego from an overpowering excitation. The ego, frustrated by the outer world to an almost unbearable extent, abandoned its genital claims."[98] In simpler language, women in concentration camps had one priority: eat to keep alive.

This also helps explain the fact that sexual relations were carried on almost exclusively among the camp elite, those who were in a position to "organize" food at their place of work, in the kitchens, in the Canada detail where the belongings of new arrivals were sorted, or in the field, wherever they could get their hands directly or indirectly on food. The ever-present fear of punishment and the lack of privacy for physical love making also dampened sexual desire.

Even individual masturbation or fleeting touches of bed partners inviting to sexual play were made difficult by the cramped conditions most prisoners encountered, sleeping as they did five or six on a double cot. The fear of being discovered, ridiculed or beaten up by bed partners prevented many attempts at Lesbian relations.

Because of the hushed up and often hypocritical attitude of society outside and inside the concentration camps at the time and until recently, very little is known about the sexual relations between persons of the same sex in concentration camps. Since the male homosexuals were branded with the pink triangles and were visible, there are at least references to their treatment in the camps. Women's memoirs say little on the subject, either because they considered the subject indelicate or because they chose to remain in the closet. The women who were Lesbians when they entered the camps or became so afterward are hidden behind a double veil of hypocrisy and silence.

* * *

Normal sexual relations among female and male inmates were also rare. The keepers of the camps made sure that there was no mingling of the sexes. In some camps female and male working details when passing had to look the other way. On the few occasions when male prisoners entered the women's camp for repairs, they came under guard. They could establish platonic relationships with a girl, even pass her a piece of bread or a note, but they were strictly forbidden to talk to her. Here and there at work in factories or in the field, sex could be possible but was highly dangerous, and given the nature of the sexual act, few women were willing to run the risk and get nothing out of it. Long-time inmates, toughened to camp life and in privileged positions, resorted to sex with their own gender or with members of the opposite sex usually of equally prominent status.

Occasional prostitution, paid in goods or favors, also existed among inmates of the opposite sex, and the "erotic availability became a coin of incommensurate worth, in return for which the chance of biological survival could be won."[99] But such situations were exceptional.

In a place like Auschwitz, a much talked about love affair might consist of two or three fleeting glances over the fence; in a factory it might consist of a piece of bread or a turnip passed stealthily to the "lover" of choice. While postwar marriages between survivors of similar traumatic experiences were not uncommon, few if any germinated inside a concentration camp.

It would take a highly trained and specialized psychiatrist to analyze Hitler's attitudes toward women and their treatment in concentration camps. If it is true that he was a masochist in his own sexual practices, allegedly gratified by young women urinating and defecating on his head,[100] and given the fact that the Reich encouraged the impregnation of unmarried females by the SS in specially provided homes for unwed mothers, then it is contradictory[101] that the SS in the camps—thank God—were so strictly forbidden to have intercourse with female inmates of any nationality. If the Führer feared the thinning of true German blood through Jewish or Slavic mothers, proverbial German efficiency could have certainly found ways of limiting the production of babies to the non-Jewish, non-Slavic women, even though the large proportion of the inmates were Jewish and Polish women. Was it an indication of little faith in the future of the thousand-year Reich that the Nazis did not plan ahead for more babies by potential German fathers serving in the concentration camps?

Considering the tens of thousands of women incarcerated in the camps, rape by the SS was relatively rare. While it is a fact that the SS could—and did—do as they pleased with any female inmate, raping them was not their preference. First of all, most of these women looked unattractive, without hair, dirty, smelly. Second, if caught in intercourse with an inmate, the SS were punished, usually by being shipped to the Russian front, and most SS cherished their camp job which was a sinecure with power. If caught in the act with a Jewess, they could be shot for defaming or defiling the master race. When the affair of SS doctor Rolf Rosenthal and the inmate nurse Gerda Quernheim was discovered in Ravensbrück, they were both confined to the punishment bunker.[102]

In some concentration camps the SS had brothels available, as did a few selected privileged male inmates. Most of all, however, the SS guards had a better selection of sexual partners among their own kind, the female SS guards, who were only too eager to oblige with sexual encounters, under conditions that were much more leisurely and less fraught with danger.

Some of the meanest female guards with bizarre sadism liked to use sex as a means of further tormenting the women in their charge. They paraded in front of the women lined up for rollcall with their boyfriends. They encouraged the men to fondle and paw them.[103] These were not so much cases of voyeurism in reverse, as acts of taunting helpless women whose loved ones were far away or had been murdered. At Ravensbrück chief SS supervisor Dorothea Binz, a former maid, a pretty blond of nineteen with a whip and a dog constantly with her, would come accompanied by Captain Edmund Bräuning to watch the floggings. They would stand arm in arm enjoying the show and "were often seen in a passionate embrace during or after this type of 'ceremony.' "[104] Anthropologist Germaine Tillion, who observed this in Ravensbrück, concluded—and so did others with similar experiences—that there was a close relationship between cruelty and debauchery among the SS of both sexes.[105]

It was also a primitive and perverted instinct that often brought the SS men to the women's showers. On the rare occasions that the women were marched to the real showers (rather than to the ones in the gas chambers), the grapevine somehow always reached the lewdest of the SS, who came to jeer, tease and taunt the defenseless women. Stripping the women naked was also practiced at times of camp selections, or on long and boring Sunday afternoons, when the SS had nothing better to do than to order a roll call and expose the powerless women to a cruel parade.

The situation was worst when Jewish transports arrived in Auschwitz. In that first phantasmagorical hour, the women were in utter shock. They had just been separated from their men; their children had been brutally torn from their arms (they could not know then that it saved their own lives). They were hit by a Babel of voices screaming at them. They smelled burning flesh and singed hair. They were pushed and shoved into the shower rooms, ordered to strip naked and line up to have all their hair shaved from their heads, underarms and pubic regions. In this pandemonium, as they stood quivering and huddling to hide their nakedness, their modesty was further violated by the SS men, who arrived for their bonus show. They made lewd remarks, pointed at them, commented on their shapes, made obscene suggestions, poked into their breasts with their riding crops and sicked their dogs on them. It was the most shocking of all the shocks, a deep blow to their very womanhood. They were petrified with panic, not knowing what to expect next. The depravity of the men, indulging themselves in this cheapest, basest and most disgusting of games, as much for the pleasure of seeing naked females as for the sport of frightening them out of their minds, was one of the cruelest tortures to which women were subjected in the concentration camps. Jaded old-timers stood up to their tormentors by ignoring them. But those newly arrived to these jaws of hell were crushed under the deluge of foul language, obscene gestures and the fact that they were paraded like cattle on the market in front of men. To many women it meant an unforgivable and never to be forgotten humiliation.

Pre-1945 Knowledge of the Holocaust

As a person deeply committed to the decency of democracy, and carrying on the retina of my mind forever the sharply focused pictures of Auschwitz, of the thousands on a slow march toward the gas chambers, with the sweetish stench of burning flesh still in my nostrils, I stare with utter incredulity at the pages of the American press during the war years. They spell out clearly and without any reasonable doubt what was happening to the Jews: annihilation, extermination.

There were early voices warning about the inhuman treatment of men and women in concentration camps. In 1934, a book was published just across the border from Germany in Karlsbad, Czechoslovakia, that appealed to the conscience of the world.[106] Journalist-author Stefan Lorant lifted his voice in an eloquent indictment of Nazi methods.[107] The German press talked openly about concentration camps but, of course, did not give the gory details. In August 1938, the *Manchester Guardian* and the *Rundschau über Politik, Wirtschaft und Arbeiterbewegung* of Basel, Switzerland, printed reports about the horrors and indiscriminate shootings of prisoners at Buchenwald, also mentioning Dachau.[108] These were not isolated cases of publicity about concentration camps. But they were news of atrocities "only" against German political prisoners, it was said, an internal affair of Germany.

In the United States, one of the few lonely voices spoke up. Black Congressman Arthur W. Mitchell (D, Ill.) wrote to President Roosevelt as a member of a minority concerned about another minority, the "Jewish people in this hour of sad calamity,"[109] and asked for help.

In October 1941, under the heading "Slaying of Jews in Galicia Depicted," the *New York Times* informed the public of the slaughter of nearly 15,000 Galician and Hungarian Jews by German soldiers and their Ukrainian "bandit" aides. The testimony came from a Hungarian officer who had witnessed the mass murders by machine guns. At Kamenec Podolsk alone, 2,500 Hungarian and 8,000 Galician Jews were massacred. Some groups were killed while at prayer in the synagogue. "Bodies floated down the Dniester," with nobody caring or daring to bury them.[110]

Rumors based on fact have been flying around like bats in the night. Yet human brains were unable to accept it as a fact that genocide on a large scale could be an actuality. But by the summer of 1942 both the British and the Americans knew what was going on.

In March of that year, the German *Neue Volkszeitung* of New York printed a lengthy article based on the report of a Polish eyewitness who had managed to get out of Auschwitz. It described the physical and mental tortures of the *Häftlings,* or inmates, at the hands of the SS, the dismal living conditions, the lack of hygiene and the contagious diseases, the inhuman demands for labor, such as working barefoot in the snow, pulling carts loaded with rocks at a run until the prisoners dropped dead and the shoving of a still living victim into the crematorium oven on top of two half-burned bodies. The article did not mention gas chambers, as it was based on the report of a man who had left the camp in November 1940, when Auschwitz was still in the initial stages and planned for a mere 40,000 inmates. But it did talk of "Mauthausen with its notorious quarry" and "floggings on daily order as in other concentration camps." Among the inmates it listed Jews, slated for extermination, Catholic priests, political prisoners and professional criminals.[111]

Under the headline "1,000,000 Jews slain by Nazis," the *New York Times* reported in June 1942 that the "Nazis had established a vast slaughterhouse for Jews in Eastern Europe," that so far one-sixth of European Jews were "wiped out," mostly from Germany, Austria, Poland, Czechoslovakia, the Netherlands, Rumania, Lithuania and German-occupied Russia, all according to Hitler's policy of "extermination."[112] A few days later the same paper offered details on the "extermination of Jews" since the summer of 1941, on Jews being forced to dig their own graves before men, women and children were being machine-gunned stark naked into them. Some were killed with hand grenades. A subheading read "Gas Chambers Are Used," giving particulars on numbers of Jewish victims at different locations and mentioning the "the massacre still continues." (Interestingly, the article also informed the public that "two thousand 'Gypsies' were gassed.")[113] The name Chelmno, the first of the predecessors of Auschwitz as an *extermination* camp, stares the reader in the face.

Toward the end of November 1942, the *New York Times* reported that "Himmler Program Kills Polish Jews," who under the excuse of resettlement in the East were shipped as many as 150 to a cattle car to annihilation centers; half of them arrived dead of suffocation or starvation. The places of extermination were named, and they were after Chelmno the next camps to carry out the Final Solution: Treblinka, Belzec, Sobibor and the crematoria at Auschwitz. There the first selections took place; fewer than 2 percent were selected for slave labor, and the rest liquidated. Of the nearly half a million Jews in the Warsaw ghetto in March 1942, only about 40,000 were left by October of the same year. The mayor of the ghetto, Adam Czerniakow, committed suicide when asked to prepare the deportation lists. At the same time Rabbi Stephen S. Wise, president of the American and of the World Jewish Congress, at a press conference in Washington declared that, while he had received his information about the murders of the Jews from European sources, the Department of State had confirmed that two million Jews had been "slain in an extermination campaign"; so also did President Roosevelt's representative recently back from Europe.

The paper also talked of mass murder, of gassing and of mass electrocutions at Belzec, where Jews were forced to stand on a metal floor that was then electrified, causing instant death. It was also made clear that Jews from other parts of Europe were shipped to the various Polish ghettos, especially Warsaw and Lodz, and from there to the extermination camps. Rabbi Wise supplied country-by-country statistics showing that from September 1939 to November 1942 at least 2,258,700 Jews had been killed.

This news was disseminated via the wire services. Rabbi Wise's press conference with all the information in it was thus also picked up by the *New York Herald Tribune* in a front page article. This paper quoted Rabbi Wise as having disclosed that "Hitler has ordered the extermination of all Jews in Nazi-ruled Europe in 1942"; that the Nazis processed the corpses into "war-vital commodities as soap, fats and fertilizer"; and that Nazi physicians could dispatch over one hundred people per hour per doctor by injecting air bubbles into veins.[114]

Just a few days later, under the headline "Two Thirds of Jews in Poland Held Slain, Only 1,250,000 Said to Survive of 3,500,000 Once There," the *Times* unveiled specifics such as the "German Vernichtungscolonnen" (extermination columns) and confirmed earlier reports of "mass gas poisoning, electrocuting and machine-gunning." Pompous resolutions and threats of postwar punishments could not stop the slaughter. The article then transmitted the "ardent appeal" from Poland for "immediate" help to save the survivors.[115]

In hindsight, one is amazed at the relative correctness of these news, considering that no American journalist had first-hand knowledge of the camps and that Germany kept its macabre secrets well guarded.

In the British Parliament, Foreign Secretary Anthony Eden on December 17, 1942, spoke openly about the Nazi extermination of the Jews, about their transportation to the East, about their mass executions. By 1943, if not sooner, the British knew of the massacres of most of the 3.3 million Polish Jews. But the dilemma of Palestine, aside from financial considerations connected with a possible resettlement of Jews from Rumania or Hungary, prevented the British from accepting them. The Balfour Declaration of 1917, promising a home for the Jews in Palestine, was ancient history by then, superseded by other documents, dictated by British needs to placate the Arabs.[116]

At the court of history, the British share the docks of the accused with the Americans. For various reasons but mostly because of apathy—if not latent anti-Semitism—both torchbearers of democracy failed to rescue the remnants of the persecuted, of the thousands "yearning to breathe free."

In March 1943 *Time*, one of America's largest circulation weeklies, under the heading "Total Murder" reported the appeal of the American Jewish Congress to save the Jews from the "slaughterhouse and from extermination," quoting Hitler's latest speech about "the extermination of Jewry in Europe." It concluded: "It is not enough to indict the murderers. It is time for America and the United Nations to act. Every hour sees the murder of more thousands. . . . All who will be allowed to perish will be an eternal badge of shame on the soul of mankind."[117]

The same month the *New York Times* also reported the plea of the Warsaw ghetto via the London representative of the Polish National Council and the suggestion of the Warsaw Jewish leadership to hold German prisoners of war as hostages for the safety of the Jews of Warsaw. "You must rouse the whole world to action," they cried. There was also a plea to the Pope to intervene before the "liquidation" of the ghetto.[118] A few days later, reporting on the Warsaw ghetto uprising, the news item again mentioned the gas chambers.[119]

This is just a small sample of publicity that the Holocaust received at a time when mankind still had a chance to prevent the slaughter of at least the remaining millions of Jews, as well as of Gypsies, political prisoners, homosexuals, Jehovah's Witnesses, asocials and even criminals, whose deaths eventually climbed to an additional five million.

The verdict is still not in on the role of Pope Pius XII and the Vatican in the Holocaust. Several authors have addressed themselves to this highly controversial subject. Thus far no one has uncovered a saving action by the Pope such as, for example, that by the Swedish Raoul Wallenberg in Budapest. One cardinal said that in order to avoid partiality the Pope "imposed upon himself, in word and deed, the most delicate reserve."[120] Indeed. While millions died.

The American Office of Strategic Services (OSS) did considerable work in Europe, but the whole question of concentration and extermination camps was not among its tasks. One member of its labor branch, Arthur Goldberg, discussed the matter with Szmuel Zygielbojm, the Jewish representative of the Polish National Council in London, who urged the Allies to bomb the gas chambers of the extermination camps or the railroad tracks leading to them. It became Goldberg's mournful task to inform Zygielbojm of the decision of the Allied higher-ups that "aircraft were not available for this purpose." The following day Zygielbojm committed suicide.[121] In his farewell note, dated May 12, 1943, he wrote: "By my death I wish to make my final protest against the passivity with which the world is looking on and permitting the extermination of the Jewish people. . . . Perhaps by my death I shall contribute to breaking down the indifference."[122]

He did not. The death machine rolled on, over men, women, children.

Eyewitnesses also reported to the outside world. Jan Kozielewski, a courier of the Polish underground, secretly visited the Warsaw ghetto and Belzec extermination camp. By November 1942, he reported in writing and in person to the press and to government officials in London, New York and Washington. He personally spoke with President Roosevelt. He conveyed the message of the Jewish leaders in Poland: they requested public executions of Germans in Allied lands, leaflets dropped over Germany threatening the systematic destruction of the German nation in retaliation for the killings of the Jews; they asked for an official Allied declaration of postwar mass reprisals if the genocide were not stopped; they suggested buying out the Jews; and a widespread sit-in and hunger strike of Jewish leaders in the free world at American and British government offices. The gist of their message was: "Let not a single leader of the United Nations be able to say that they did not know that we were being murdered in Poland and could not be helped except from the outside." The message was out in book form by the fall of 1944 for everyone to see.[123]

By March 1943, even the skeptical Slovak Jewish leader Gisi Fleischman informed Zionist organizations in Geneva of the Lublin and Auschwitz exterminations.[124] The following April 7, 1944, two Czechoslovakian Jewish young men miraculously escaped after two years in Auschwitz and notified Jewish and papal authorities about the facts and figures of the extermination.[125]

Jewish leaders in the West made various efforts to negotiate with the Nazis to buy out Jews, but their success was infinitesimal in comparison with the number of those exterminated, especially in Poland, and with the large wave of Hungarian Jews driven to the gas chambers in 1944. The efforts of the Swedish Raoul Wallenberg saved at least a fraction of the Budapest Jews.[126]

General Dwight D. Eisenhower, head of the Allied operations in Europe, ever so cautious and "following orders," did not choose to bomb the railroad to Auschwitz or the gas chambers, just as he did not dare to move the few miles from Pilsen to occupy Prague in 1945. The first action would have saved thousands of lives and lifted immeasurably the spirits of concentration camp inmates with all kinds of triangles; the second would have changed the history of a nation. John J. McCoy, assistant secretary of war, twice vetoed the bombing of Auschwitz as "of doubtful efficiency," thus playing God over the lives of thousands. Nobody can ever convince me that a few planes could not have been spared from the terrific arsenal of the Allied air forces to go on one mission. Just as the Russians let Warsaw bleed at the August 1944 uprising, the British and the Americans joined them in allowing the slaughter in Auschwitz to go on.[127]

The Western democracies knew. They were not conspiring against the Jews. But they are guilty by having done nothing. If anything, it was a conspiracy of silence.

As far as the Allies' official policy was concerned, they calmed their consciences by inserting a general statement into the declaration of the Moscow conference in October 1943 about the perpetrators of German atrocities: "The three Allied powers [the United States, United Kingdom, USSR] will pursue them to the uttermost ends of the earth and will deliver them to their accusors in order that justice may be done." Ironically, it was Germany that first proposed the investigation of war guilt in late 1918.[128]

The claim that the German people did not know what was going on in the concentration camps is sheer nonsense. In 1945, the Germans were hit by mass amnesia.

From the very start of the Final Solution, at the Wannsee conference in January 1942, numerous high offices were involved: the Main Reich Security Office (RSHA), the ministries of Justice, Interior, for the East, for the General Gouvernement (Poland), the Foreign Office, the NSDAP (Nationalsozialistische Deutsche Arbeiterpartei, that is, the Nazi Party) and the Reich chancelleries.[129] The chiefs and their staffs knew. So did the thousands of German men and women involved in carrying out the Holocaust and in liquidating politically or otherwise undesirable people: the army that assisted in rounding up and expediting prisoners to prisons and camps; the police; the railroad personnel and truck drivers; the bureaucrats who so pedantically recorded confiscated homes and properties; the bankers and jewelers who sorted out bank accounts and valuables; the good Germans who took over Jewish businesses, factories, homes, apartments, cars and furs. Luckily for them, few former owners turned up in 1945 to reclaim them.

The thousands of German personnel in the concentration and extermination camps, male and female, also knew. The people in the euthanasia centers knew. They took photographs of "life" and death in their place of work. They sent home mementoes of their careers in the camps, perhaps a nice picture drawn on human skin. But mostly they kept taking movies and photographs for their family albums. Some are in our hands now, the souvenirs that turned boomerangs on the erstwhile photographers. The thousands of civilian supervisors in the hundreds of factories knew. They saw us, Jewish and gentile women and men, with shaven heads, emaciated, eternally hungry, in thin prison garb, half naked in the snow, working up to fourteen hours a day, guarded by soldiers or the SS with machine guns and dogs, and all without pay. I know that they knew, for what they could not see with their own eyes, we who slaved under them, we who were kicked and abused by them, made it a point of telling them in minute detail.

Crimes Against Humanity

The survivors of the resistance, the Jews, and all victims yearn for justice.

The crimes of the Nazi system are immeasurable. One hundred deaths are a tragedy; millions of deaths are a statistic, for they are incomprehensible to the human mind, especially since the eleven million deaths were premeditated murder.

It is physically impossible to enumerate all crimes against the human race committed by the Nazis. The gassing of the Jews, Gypsies, political prisoners, prisoners of war and other groups; the dread of death, the constant anguish, night and day, day and night, of those kept alive in the concentration camps, who knew not which was their last moment on earth before going up the chimney; the backbreaking labor, the beatings, the hunger, the thirst, the cold and the endless varieties of torture.

Oh, and those long, endless, eternal roll calls, in rain, snow, sleet, wind or scorching sun, exposed to the elements half naked while the guards jeered from cover. The slightest grin or frown, glance or move, could bring them running, kicking, boxing, slapping and punishing. I got hit in the face with a military belt, and the buckle broke my teeth; I scrubbed floors with a toothbrush. The crude abuses of the bodies and the subtle torments of the soul;

the degradations of human dignity and the humiliation of womanhood, with or without rape!

The SS hung prisoners from hooks, hands chained, like sides of beef. In the Bucharest slaughterhouse Jewish bodies were butchered and cut up so that they no longer looked human. Ruth Klüger, the organizer of the escape boats to Palestine, saw this, including the body of a five-year old girl, hanging by its feet, her entire torso smeared with blood.[130]

Inmates were fed salted herrings and denied water. Women were kicked, choked, their nails torn out, their breasts deformed, their faces slapped without reason. There were blows to private parts, and there was rape. Victims who befouled themselves from fear were forced to swallow the feces. Babies were smashed against walls while the mothers had to look on. Human beings were beaten and trampled to death under SS boots and spiked heels of female supervisors. Dogs were sicked against hapless women. They were kept without food or drink in darkened underground dungeons. Some froze to the floor, and their sisters were ordered to tear their flesh to remove them.

The psychological tortures included cheating, raising false hopes and fooling the victims—all to the obvious hilarity of the SS. Inmates were encouraged: "Go, hang yourself!" They were counted aloud at roll calls as "pieces," like so many sheep. They were called all names under the sun, of which asshole, bitch, gang of pigs or dirty Jew were the milder ones. (Pigs lived better than we did in the camps.) Every move, every utterance was meant to strip the victims of human dignity. For details on this subject, see Chapter 17, "Middle Ages Nazi Style."

The gruesome medical experiments conducted under the guise of scientific research in Auschwitz, Ravensbrück, Dachau and elsewhere still cry to high heaven. Sterilization experiments sought to decrease the births of "inferior races" like Slavs; others, like Mengele's "research" on twins, aimed at the faster propagation of the "Germanic races." A sampling of the experiments is found in Chapter 18, "The Stations of the Cross."

François Bayle, the French naval physician, prepared a detailed study with photographs of these experiments, based on the Doctors' Trial at Nuremberg in 1946–1947.[131] He lists the experiments systematically under: 1. aeronautic, high altitudes, cold and sea water; 2. "medical," sterilizations, castrations, euthanasia, tuberculosis, collection of Jewish skeletons; 3. chemical and biological; 4. medical and chirurgical; 5. infectious diseases, typhus, malaria, jaundice, typhoid fever, influenza. In each of these categories men or women, be they Christians or Jews or believers of all shades, were used as guinea pigs, more often than not succumbing to the experiment or being dispatched by a lethal injection after their usefulness ended. Yet there were survivors to bear witness. They carry the telltale scars on their bodies and the invisible scars on their souls.

Many perpetrators escaped justice and the chance for the world to hear their admissions of participation in the greatest crimes of history. Hitler, governed by "inexplicable hallucinatory conceptions and petit-bourgeois inhibitions,"[132] the maniac with pathological delusions of grandeur in his "mission" on earth, self-destructed. So did the head of the SS, Heinrich Himmler. The only high official in the machinery of death "liquidated" by the resistance was Reinhardt Heydrich, creator of the Main Reich Security Office (RSHA), the "man with the iron heart," whose only weakness was his "ungovernable sexual appetite."[133] He was gunned down by the Czechoslovak underground in 1942.[134] Adolf Eichmann, the faithful famulus of evil, was brought to justice in 1961[135] thanks to the tireless efforts of Simon Wiesenthal and the Israeli secret service.

The torturers were brought to court—if they were apprehended. There were trials of war criminals of various camps, where only too often justice was meted out by the letter of the law, disregarding the moral law.

I am using the expression "war crime" and "war criminal" with a reservation, since it is a generally accepted technical term by now. Yet, war crimes refer to matters military, while crimes against unarmed Jews or concentration camp inmates were crimes against humanity.

Too many war criminals escaped through the well-prepared and well-oiled machinery of the ODESSA, the Organization of Former SS Members, some to the Middle East, some to South America. Several live in Germany and even in North America. Josef Mengele, the "Angel of Death" of the Auschwitz selections and medical experiments, is still at large, as are dozens of others. The arms of ODESSA can reach far. While vacationing at Bariloche, Argentina, in the winter of 1960, Nora Eldoc, who had been sterilized in Auschwitz by Mengele, came face to face with him. She disappeared, her battered body found in a ravine. Was that an accident?[136]

The Cold War placed a dampening effect on their prosecution. It is only in the last few years that interest in the Holocaust in general has been revived and with it the prosecution of the war criminals. The German Statute of Limitations on war crimes was lifted on July 3, 1979, and as of early 1982, the German government was preparing a law that would make the denial of the Holocaust a punishable crime.[137]

Still at the last Nazi war crime trial in Düsseldorf, ending after five and a half years on June 30, 1981, of the sixteen Majdanek extermination camp perpetrators who shot, gassed, drowned and bludgeoned their prey of 250,000 men, women and children, only one received a life sentence. That was a woman, Hermine Braunsteiner Ryan, the extradited New York housewife known in camp as the "Mare" for trampling women to death under her steel-studded boots. She was found guilty of "complicity in the death of more than 1,000 prisoners in the camp's gas chambers." SS guard Hildegard Lächert, "Bloody Brigitte," got twelve years for "conspiracy to commit murder," although witnesses testified that she drowned inmates in the latrine, beat others to death with a steel-tipped whip and sicked a vicious dog on a pregnant woman.

Among the accused were Johanna Zelle, the supervisor known to have lured children with candy in order to shoot them; Alice Orlowski, who had complained in a bar that to get a beer took longer than to kill Jews; Hermine Böttcher, Charlotte Meyer and Rosa Süss, all tormentors of hundreds of women. Yet all except Ryan and Lächert received lesser sentences. Some of the defendants escaped justice by dying, others were acquitted.[138]

Yet these were the supermen who in early November of 1943, in what they jovially termed a "Harvest Festival," with vodka flowing and music blaring, murdered over 17,000 men, women and children! The blood of their innocent victims cried out in the outraged voices in the courtroom as the verdict was brought in: "Scandal! Outrage!"

It is hard to leave this subject without singling out one of the hundreds of SS women, a sadist of first rank. Irma Grese, the "Blond Angel of Hell" of Auschwitz and Bergen-Belsen infamy. At twenty-two this beautiful but depraved creature was placed in charge over the lives and deaths of 18,000 women, some of whom she whipped to death. Former inmate Gisella Perl gave testimony in her book *I Was a Doctor in Auschwitz* that Grese cut women's breasts open with her whip; when the infected breasts had to be operated on—with no anesthetic available—Grese looked on transfixed, with flushed cheeks and salivating mouth, and swaying from side to side in a revealing rhythmical motion in a sexual paroxysm. At the Bergen-Belsen trial at Lüneburg in the Fall of 1945, Grese was one of the few who did receive her just due. She was dragged screaming to the gallows.

In the United States the Office of Special Investigations was established in 1979, to investigate war criminals in this country and to compile evidence if they had gained citizenship under false pretenses and should be denaturalized. The guard Fedor Fedorenko, for instance, who pushed women into gas chambers at Treblinka, was thus stripped of American citizenship in late 1980. Action is pending on several cases.[139] It would help matters if the United Nations War Crime Commission files would be opened to investigators.

Hundreds of sadistic tormentors and murderers of Jewish and gentile concentration camp inmates are unaccounted for. They melted into the crowds under different names, protected by a conspiracy of silence. Even Mengele visited his home town of Günzburg in 1959, and none of the townspeople reported him.[140] He is still at large somewhere in or near Paraguay.

Two people above all have devoted their lives to bringing these criminals to justice. The first, Simon Wiesenthal, is often called the "Nazi Hunter," an epithet he does not like, for he considers himself a seeker of justice. He is a globally known figure. The other one is a woman, Beate Klarsfeld, a German Christian married to a French survivor of the Holocaust. She is known more for having slapped German Chancellor Kurt-Georg Kiesinger's face in Berlin's Congress Palace in 1968, while shouting "Nazi, Nazi!" than for tracking down Klaus Barbie, the "Butcher of Lyon."[141] She is also a dynamo in her quest for justice.

Wiesenthal often says: "My work is a warning against the murderers of tomorrow." But is the world heeding the warning? What did the conscience of the world do lately against genocide in Uganda, Cambodia or East Timor? As Hitler said to Goering in 1939: "Who still talks nowadays of the extermination of the Armenians?"[142]

The end of the war did not mean an end to anti-Semitism or to totalitarianism. There are countries today that hold Jews and gentile opponents of their regimes against their wills, and yet restrict their freedom and their choice of careers. They lack a Moses who would order: "Let my people go!" In Poland during the Solidarity crisis of 1981, there were insinuations in the press that the Jews were to blame, although after the Holocaust and the pogrom at Kielce in 1946 only a few thousand Jews were left in Poland. There were anti-Semitic cases of vandalism in France and elsewhere.

In the United States in 1981 alone there were over 1,000 reported cases of anti-Semitic actions, from New York to Los Angeles, desecrations of cemeteries and synagogues and institutions of learning. The virulent ingredients of the Neo-Nazi activities in Skokie, Illinois, and the harangues of their publications bear dangerous similarities with the beginnings of Nazism in Germany.

Will humanity learn from its past mistakes?

We should be able to draw a lesson from German Protestant Pastor Martin Niemöller, submarine commander turned distinguished churchman, imprisoned for seven years in Nazi jails, Sachsenhausen and Dachau:

> First the Nazis came for the Communists, and I did not speak up,
> because I was not a Communist;
> then they came for the Jews, and I did not speak up,
> because I was not a Jew.
> When they came for the trade-unionists, I did not speak up,
> because I was not a trade-unionist;
> and when they came for the Catholics, I did not speak up,
> because I was a Protestant.
> Then they came for me, and by that time
> there was no one left to speak up for anyone.

Women in Hiding

The people in hiding, in our case the women, be they from the resistance or Jews, were the unsung heroines of the cataclysm of World War II. Perhaps because the word "hiding" carries a subconscious connotation of cowardice, little is said about them, except for Anne Frank, whose life in hiding was a breeze compared with many others. But to refuse to be deported or to lay low and hide in the hope of eventually rejoining the underground took a lot of courage.

The physical discomforts, the hunger and the cold, were the smaller parts of the sufferings for those who were in hiding. The persistent mental anguish every single moment of their days and nights was harder to bear. A knock on the door, any unusual sound, could mean a police check, discovery and the end. A neighbor suspecting an unregistered person in an apartment or a house could denounce it to the authorities, bringing disaster on host and guest alike. Being totally exposed to the mercy of the host was an additional burden. Often the people in hiding would be told to leave, as the situation became more dangerous; it was nearly impossible to find another hiding place. The fact that in 1942 there were an estimated 42,000 Jews in hiding but at the time of liberation there were only 7,000 left speaks for itself.[143]

It is hard to say what was more difficult: hiding under a false identity among the population or hiding literally, holed up in an attic or a pigsty (see Chapter 25, "A Refuge Above the Pigs"). Both carried infinite risks. Some women with false identification papers remained indoors, if they could afford it, or worked as maids indoors, and diminished the risk of being apprehended. Others kept working on the outside and were exposed to the danger of sudden police checks on streetcars, in factories or any public place. If their falsified documents did not stand up to scrutiny, such women reached the end of their journeys.

Several clever women realized that the best hiding place was inside Germany. With false papers they signed up for labor in German factories, where they had to face only the danger of death by bombings. Such a woman was Cyla Wiesenthal, whose reunion after the war with her "dead" husband reads like fiction. She volunteered for factory work in Germany under the name of Irena Kowalska, a gentile. She eventually heard that her husband had been killed in a concentration camp. Meanwhile, Simon Wiesenthal was told that she had perished when her entire street was bombed with no survivors left. They both returned from the dead. The tragic chapters of their lives ended in a comedy of errors and a happy ending, as he describes it in his memoirs, *The Murderers Among Us.* (See Chapter 27, "A Happy Ending.")

Other women carried on resistance work while in hiding under another identity, as did the Dutch girl in Chapter 5, "Keeping the Divers Alive." She was in double jeopardy, as a fugitive from the law as a Jew in hiding, and as a resistance worker.

There were scores of women in every occupied country, good people who risked their own safety and their very lives in order to harbor Jews or other refugees. Can the deeds of the Lithuanian Klimatis, leader of the cut-throat gangs who volunteered to kill in the service of the Nazis in the Baltic countries, be juxtaposed with that of his compatriot Anna Simaite whom we meet in "Their Brothers' and Sisters' Keepers" (Chapter 6) or the Ukrainian SS hoodlums by women from the East who snatched their victims from

Nazi clutches, as we see it in "The Avenue of the Righteous Gentiles" (Chapter 7)?

The last part of this anthology opens a new vista and offers a seldom seen insight into the unspeakable anguish of girls and women who had to suspend their lives, so to speak, and hide from evil. They went through some of the most traumatic experiences in their search for a place to exist, to conceal themselves from the ambush of malice, to become stowaways from life.

Compare their fates with those of two other young girls. One, Zofia Yamaika, a seventeen-year-old Jewish girl from Warsaw, escaped from the train to Treblinka and extermination. After wandering for days without a place to go, she was taken in by a woman who also provided her with false identity papers. She joined the underground, and with another Jewish girl she shot a gendarme, then escaped to a partisan group. She organized reconnaissance parties and participated in train derailments. She died fighting, covering with her machine gun the retreat of her unit.[144]

Contrast this life with that of Sophia Hausman, a Dutch nursing student from Rotterdam, who in the twenty-seven months between her seventeenth and nineteenth year went through eleven (eleven!) ghettos and concentration camps, among them Sobibor, Majdanek, Lublin, Auschwitz, Bergen-Belsen and Terezín[145]—I am sure a record.

Which girl's fate would you have chosen for yourself?

Memento to the Reader

We the survivors, ankle deep in memories, carry an unwilling legacy imprinted on the cells of our minds, embedded in each one of our heartbeats: talk of the unspeakable, spread the word about the unbelievable!

The survivors of the concentration camps were appointed by fate to be the chroniclers of men's and women's inhumanity to their fellow humans, of the endless variations of perverted physical tortures and the diabolical permutations of psychological torments. It was a human mind that invented the slow but sure death of thousands by squeezing over a hundred men, women and children into cattle cars covered with powdered quicklime, which in contact with human moisture burned away flesh and bones, causing agonizing deaths—at an economical price. Alas, it was a female of the species, Ilse Koch, who placed orders for lamp shades, book-covers and other "ornamental" objects to be prepared from the skins of concentration camp inmates.

There is never a déjà vu in Holocaust literature, unless you read the same book twice. All victims, fighting or hiding, resisting or captive, lived through their own individual purgatories and hells; all saw their torturers with their own eyes, felt the blows on their own skins. They hold up a mirror to mankind: *ecce homo.* They should be listened to, for they are the eyewitnesses, the "primary sources," and time is running out on them. The past MUST talk to the future. Their life experiences range from anguish to rage, from tragedy to wasted prayers, but behold! the instinct of resistance to evil, the indomitable human spirit, is always entwined in their sorrow.

We the women who speak to you from these pages have one goal: to tell it as it was, to leave behind a reminder that we were there and saw Satan's realm. We were exposed at times to risks even greater than our male comrades, yet we came through with spirits equally strong, if not stronger than men. We were there, alas, inside the prisons of every land under the scourge of the swastika, and inside the gates of Auschwitzes and Ravensbrücks and Doras and countless other camps, where resistance fighters and Jews and all other victims of Hitler's *furor germanicus* welded us into a sisterhood of angels in hell.

If the survivors have the spiritual strength to reach to the bottoms of their souls—not a painless task—and bring forth and relive the horrors, those, who by the grace of God or by a fortunate geographical chance were spared of them, should garner sufficient fortitude to read about them; for as Santayana said: "Those who can not remember the past, are condemned to repeat it."

Notes

1. Jacob Glatstein, et al., eds., *Anthology of Holocaust Literature* (New York: Atheneum, 1973), p. xviii.

2. It was this atrocity at Lidice that provided the Allies with the impetus to set up the International Military Tribunals for the war crime trials after the war. Cordell Hull, *Memoirs*, 2 vols. (New York: Macmillan, 1948), II, p. 1185.

3. Walter Laqueur, *Guerrilla: A Historical and Critical Study* (Boston: Little, Brown, 1976), p. 203.

4. M.R.D. Foot, *Resistance: European Resistance to Nazism, 1940–45* (New York: McGraw-Hill, 1977), pp. 180-81.

5. Laqueur, *Guerrilla*, pp. 222-23.

6. Ibid., p. 426.

7. Ibid., p. 205.

8. Michael Pearson, *Tears of Glory: The Betrayal of Vercours, 1944* (London: Macmillan, 1978).

9. Laqueur, *Guerrilla*, p. 230.

10. Henri Bernard, *Histoire de la résistance européenne* (Verviers, France: Gérard, 1968), p. 98.

11. Alexander Ramati, *The Assisi Underground* (London: Sphere Books, 1981), pp. 72-86.

12. Ronald Seth, *Noble Saboteurs* (New York: Hawthorne Books, 1966), p. 62.

13. Foot, *Resistance*, pp. 48, 13-14.

14. Jan Karski, *Story of a Secret State* (Boston: Houghton Mifflin, 1944), pp. 277, 281, 285.

15. Madeleine Masson, *Christine—A Search for Christine Granville* (London: Hamish-Hamilton, 1975), pp. 206-7.

16. M.R.D. Foot, *SOE in France* (London: HMSO, 1966), pp. 465-69.

17. Masson, *Christine*, pp. 213-14.

18. Barry Wynne, *The Story of Mary Lindell, Wartime Secret Agent* (Milton Keynes, England: Robin Clark, 1980).

19. H. Montgomery Hyde, *Cynthia, the Story of the Spy Who Changed the Course of the War* (New York: Farrar, Straus & Giroux, 1965).

20. Jack N. Porter, ed., *Jewish Partisans*, 2 vols. (Washington, D.C.: University Press of America, 1982).

21. Dan Kurzman, *The Bravest Battle, The Twenty-Eight Days of the Warsaw Ghetto Uprising* (New York: G. P. Putnam's Sons, 1976), p. 54.

22. Ibid., p. 336.

23. Yuri Suhl, ed., *They Fought Back* (New York: Crown, 1967), pp. 51-54.

24. Ibid., p. 2. See also Martin Gilbert, *The Holocaust, Maps and Photographs* (New York: Hill and Wang, 1978), pp. 42, 44.

25. Ibid., pp. 7-9.

26. Ibid., pp. 55-68, 3.

27. Ruth Klüger and Peggy Mann, *The Last Escape* (New York: Doubleday, 1973).

28. William R. Perl, *The Four-Front War, From the Holocaust to the Promised Land* (New York: Crown, 1979).

29. Jan Yoors, *Crossing, A Journal of Survival and Resistance in World War II* (New York: Simon & Schuster, 1971), pp. 33-35.

30. George L. Mosse, ed., *Nazi Culture, Intellectual, Cultural and Social Life in the Third Reich* (New York: Grosset & Dunlap, 1966), p. 336.

31. Ibid., p. 41.

32. Lydia Sargent, ed., *Women and Revolution* (Boston: South End Press, 1981), p. 2.

33. Gemma La Guardia Gluck, *My Story* (New York: David McKay, 1961), p. 53.

34. Irmgard von der Lühe, *Elisabeth von Thadden und das Dritte Reich* (Freiburg, Germany: Herder Verlag, 1980).

35. Henry Bernard, *L'Autre Allemagne* (Paris: La Renaissance du livre, 1976), p. 206.

36. Abba Eban, *My People: The Story of the Jews* (New York: Random House, 1968), pp. 137, 176, 390.

37. Robert G.L. Waite, *The Psychopathic God, Adolf Hitler* (New York: NAL, 1977), p. 302.

38. Anatoly Kuznetsov, *Babi Yar* (New York: Dell, 1966).

39. Simon Wiesenthal, *The Murderers Among Us* (New York: Bantam, 1967), pp. 310-12.

40. Ibid., p. 318.

41. Glenn B. Infield, *Skorzeny, Hitler's Commando* (New York: St. Martin's Press, 1981), p. 229.

42. Gilbert, *Holocaust*, p. 16.

43. Michael R. Marrus and Robert O. Paxton, *Vichy France and the Jews* (New York: Basic Books, 1981).

44. Benjamin Ferencz, *Less Than Slaves: Jewish Forced Labor and the Quest for Compensation* (Cambridge, Mass.: Harvard University Press, 1979), pp. 19-20. Suhl, *They Fought Back*, p. 7, indicates 15,000.

45. Rudolf Hoess, *Commandant of Auschwitz: The Autobiography of Rudolf Hoess* (Cleveland: World Publishing, 1959).

46. Ferencz, *Less Than Slaves,* p. 86.

47. The most concise and informative treatment of Auschwitz is Danuta Czech, et al., *Auschwitz, Nazi Extermination Camp* (Warsaw: Interpress, 1978). It is also available in Polish, French, German and Russian.

48. Paul Berben, *Dachau, 1933-1945, The Official History* (London: Comité international de Dachau, 1968, 1975), p. xvi.

49. Ibid., pp. 6-7.

50. Ibid., pp. 273-74.

51. Ibid., p. 10.

52. Radioman Ralph Rundquist from Assaria, Kansas, in an interview on the occasion of the International Liberators' Conference in Washington, D.C., *Boston Globe,* October 27, 1981, p. 5.

53. Jiří Žák, ed., *Buchenwald varuje: Dokumenty, vzpomínky, svědectví* [Buchenwald warns: Documents, Reminiscences, Testimonies] (Prague, Státní nakladatelství politické literatury, 1962), p. 625.

54. Ibid., p. 128. Ilse Koch was condemned to life imprisonment by the U.S. Military Tribunal but was pardoned after four years. In 1950 at the German Augsburg trial she received a life sentence. In 1967 she committed suicide.

55. Ibid., pp. 176-79, photographs # 38, 42-44 following page 672.

56. Ibid., pp. 176-78.

57. Eugen Kogon, *The Theory and Practice of Hell* (New York: Farrar, Straus & Co., 1950), p. 44.

58. Ibid., pp. 44-45.

59. Gluck, *My Story,* pp. 50-54.

60. Žák, *Buchenwald,* p. 469; no date or specific numbers are given.

61. Ibid., p. 278.

62. Women as a rule did not menstruate in concentration camps, as a chemical had been added to their food to prevent it. The above case is rather exceptional, due either to a number of newly arrived prisoners or to the lack of "proper" additives.

63. Žák, *Buchenwald,* p. 129.

64. Ibid., p. 432.

65. Ibid., p. 624.

66. Kiryl Sosnowski, *The Tragedy of Children Under Nazi Rule* (Warsaw: Western Press Agency, 1962), p. 49.

67. Marc Hillel and Clarissa Henry, *Of Pure Blood* (New York: McGraw-Hill, 1976), p. 176 ff.

68. The editor was executive secretary to this commission at the time of the search. See also John Bradley, *Lidice, Sacrificial Village* (New York: Ballantine, 1972) and Vladimir Konopka, *Zde stávaly Lidice* [Here Once Stood Lidice] (Prague: Naše vojsko, 1959).

69. For details, see Janusz Korczak, *Ghetto Diary* (New York: Holocaust Library, 1981); Ernst Papanek and Edward Linn, *Out of the Fire* (New York: William Morrow, 1975?; and Philip Hallie, *Lest Innocent Blood Be Shed* (New York: Harper & Row, 1980).

70. Raul Hilberg, *The Destruction of the European Jews* (Chicago: Quadrangle

Books, 1961), p. 641; quotation by Staatsrat Turner, chief of the civil administration in Serbia, October 26, 1941, in ibid., p. 438.

71. Donald Kenrick and Grattan Puxon, *Destiny of Europe's Gypsies* (New York: Basic Books, 1972), p. 72.

72. Yoors, *Crossing*, pp. 33-34.

73. Hilberg, *Destruction*, p. 439.

74. Růžena Bubeníčková, et al., *Tábory utrpení a smrti* [*Camps of Martyrdom and Death*] (Prague: Svoboda, 1969), pp. 189-90.

75. Wiesenthal, *Murderers*, pp. 237-38.

76. Kenrick, *Destiny*, pp. 88-90.

77. Hilberg, *Destruction*, pp. 608, 602; the doctors were Hornbeck and Werner Fischer.

78. Ibid., p. 489.

79. Julian E. Kulski, *Dying We Live* (New York: Holt, Rinehart & Winston, 1979), p. 106.

80. Kenrick, *Destiny*, p. 100.

81. Ota Kraus and Erich Kulka, *Továrna na smrt* [*Death Factory*] (Prague: Naše vojsko, 1957), p. 200.

82. Yoors, *Crossing*, p. 34; Bubeníčková, *Tábory*, p. 190.

83. Gilbert, *Holocaust*, p. 22; Kenrick, *Destiny*, p. 184.

84. Kogon, *Theory and Practice of Hell*, p. 38.

85. Frank Rector, *The Nazi Extermination of Homosexuals* (New York: Stein and Day, 1981), p. 116.

86. Stefan Lorant, *I Was Hitler's Prisoner* (New York: G. P. Putnam's Sons, 1935), p. 8.

87. Heinz Heger, *The Men with the Pink Triangle* (Boston: Alyson, 1980), p. 12. This is a unique memoir of an Austrian who spent six years in Sachsenhausen and Flossenburg, surviving as a lover of camp kapos, and ultimately as one of the very few kapos with a pink triangle.

88. Rector, *Nazi Extermination*, p. 144.

89. Heger, *Men*, p. 56.

90. Ibid., p. 42.

91. Ibid., p. 82-83.

92. Ibid., p. 96.

93. Ibid., p. 98.

94. *The Speeches of Adolf Hitler, April 1922–August 1939*, 2 vols. (London: Oxford University Press, 1942), II, p. 731.

95. Elie A. Cohen, *Human Behavior in the Concentration Camp* (New York: Grosset & Dunlap, 1953), p. 139.

96. Viktor E. Frankl, *From Death Camp to Existentialism* (Boston: Beacon Press, 1959), p. 49.

97. Cohen, *Human Behavior*, p. 136.

98. H. O. Blum, "How Did They Survive?" *American Journal of Psychotherapy* 2, No. 1 (1948): 12, quoted in Cohen, *Human Behavior*, p. 140.

99. Anna Pawelczynska, *Values and Violence in Auschwitz* (Berkeley, Calif.: University of California Press, 1979), p. 99.

100. Waite, *Psychopathic God*, p. 63.

101. Another contradiction was that Hitler never fully mobilized German women

for his war machine, yet had no scruples about employing women of other nationalities, mostly Slavs, by the hundreds of thousands in the German factories.

102. Germaine Tillion, *Ravensbrück* (Garden City, N.Y.: Doubleday, 1975), p. 73.

103. Ibid., pp. 62-63.

104. Ibid., pp. 58-59.

105. Ibid., p. 62.

106. *Konzentrationslager: Ein Appell an das Gewissen der Welt* (Karlsbad, Czechslovakia: Graphia, 1934).

107. Lorant, *I Was Hitler's Prisoner.*

108. *Manchester Guardian,* August 5, 1938; *Rundschau,* August 28, 1938.

109. Roselle Chartock and Jack Spencer, eds., *The Holocaust Years* (New York: Bantam, 1978), p. 168.

110. *New York Times,* October 26, 1941.

111. "Eine Statte des Grauens, Bericht aus dem Konzentrationslager Oswiecim (Auschwitz), Polnisch-Galizien," *Neue Volkszeitung,* New York, March 14, 1942.

112. *New York Times,* June 30, 1942.

113. *New York Times,* July 2, 1942.

114. *New York Times,* November 25, 26, 1942; *New York Herald Tribune,* November 25, 1942.

115. *New York Times,* December 4, 1942.

116. Bernard Wasserstein, *Great Britain and the Jews of Europe, 1939–1945* (New York: Oxford University Press, 1981) deals in great detail with this matter. A special section in the bibliography lists entries on the topic.

117. *Time,* March 8, 1943, pp. 29-30.

118. *New York Times,* March 19, 1943.

119. *New York Times,* May 22, 1943.

120. Eliezer Berkovits, *Faith After the Holocaust* (New York: KTAV, 1973), p. 15.

121. Walter Laqueur, *The Terrible Secret: Suppression of the Truth About Hitler's "Final Solution"* (Boston: Little, Brown, 1980), p. 96; R. Harris Smith, *OSS, The Secret History of America's First Central Intelligence Agency* (New York: Delta, 1972) is mute on the subject of concentration camps in general.

122. Arthur D. Morse, *While Six Million Died, A Chronicle of American Apathy* (New York: Random House, 1967), p. 58.

123. Jan Karski (Kozielewski), *Story of a Secret State* (Boston: Houghton Mifflin, 1944), pp. 323-28.

124. Laqueur, *Terrible Secret,* p. 146.

125. Rudolf Vrba and Alan Bestic, *I Cannot Forgive* (New York: Bantam, 1964).

126. John Bierman, *Righteous Gentile, The Story of Raoul Wallenberg, Missing Hero of the Holocaust* (New York: Viking Press, 1981).

127. Martin Gilbert, *Auschwitz and the Allies* (New York: Holt, Rinehart and Winston, 1981) sheds light on this subject.

128. Armin Rappaport, ed., *Sources in American Diplomacy* (New York: Macmillan, 1966), p. 275; Thomas G. Masaryk, *The Making of a State* (New York: F. A. Stokes, 1927), p. 361.

129. Hilberg, *Destruction,* p. 264.

130. Ibid., p. 489.

131. François Bayle, *Croix Gammée Contre Caducée* [Neustadt (Palatinat): L'imprimerie nationale, 1950], p. xxvii; 1521 pages, no index.

132. Walter Schellenberg, *The Labyrinth, Memoirs of Walter Schellenberg* (New York: Harper & Brothers, 1956), p. 93.

133. Ibid., p. 14.

134. Miroslav Ivanov, *Target: Heydrich* (New York: Macmillan, 1972).

135. Gideon Hausner, *Justice in Jerusalem* (New York: Herzl Press, 1978).

136. Wiesenthal, *Murderers*, p. 158.

137. *Christian Science Monitor*, January 19, 1982.

138. *Response*, Los Angeles, September, 1981, p. 2.

139. Ibid., p. 3.

140. Wiesenthal, *Murderers*, p. 161.

141. Beate Klarsfeld, *Wherever They May Be!* (New York: Vanguard, 1975), p. 56.

142. *New York Times*, July 6, 1980.

143. Hilberg, *Destruction*, p. 378.

144. Suhl, *They Fought Back*, pp. 77-81.

145. Martin Gilbert, *Final Journey, The Fate of the Jews in Nazi Europe* (New York: Mayflower Books, 1979), pp. 168-73.

I.

WOMEN IN THE RESISTANCE

O Germany, pale mother,
How you sit defiled
Among the peoples!

Bertold Brecht, 1933

The best justification for democracy
is the immortality of the human soul.

Thomas Garrigue Masaryk

1

The French Connection

After the defeat of France in June 1940, French prisoners of war were languishing in German camps, some of them in occupied Poland. Many managed to escape from behind the barbed wires. At the same time, south of Poland, "independent" Slovakia was ruled by the German collaborator Monsignor Jozef Tiso (who in 1947 was executed as a war criminal). Under his regime, the deportation of the Jews was put into motion long before the same fate befell the Jews in neighboring Hungary.

Thus two streams of people were fleeing from north to south: the escaped prisoners of war from Poland, through Slovakia to Hungary, and the Jews of Slovakia, also to Hungary. A few Czechs still managed to squeeze through the German noose from their occupied homeland to Slovakia, and continue the roundabout way to join the Allies in the West.

It was the Czechoslovak undergrond that facilitated this traffic by smuggling people across the various borders. Just for the record, this was a free service. It was a highly perilous undertaking, the guides risking their necks at each crossing in case of capture. There were hundreds of such ventures until the Germans occupied Hungary in the spring of 1944 and put that country out of bounds as a safe haven.

In "The French Connection," one of the guides recalls some of the more colorful episodes of these crossings from Slovakia to Hungary.

The underground railroad conveying French prisoners of war who had escaped from camps in German occupied Poland was running smoothly via Slovakia into Hungary. There the Vichy embassy in Budapest took charge of them and spirited them away via Lebanon to join the Free French. We received our passengers from one station before us and delivered them to the next one down the line. The less we knew of the entire chain, the better for all concerned. Part of the program was to ship food packages to French war prisoners, but aside from providing some contacts, I had little to do with that.

Our little group of never more than six people came from a score of friends and was utlilized where it could do most good. We were all youngsters, inconspicuous, and we knew the terrain well. We all spoke Czech and Slovak, German and Hungarian, and could pass for natives on either side of the frontiers. The fact that some of us were female served the goal even better, for in those days few people ever suspected women of being involved in clandestine activities, especially in feudal, chivalrous Hungary.

We were ardent patriots, brought up in democratic Czechoslovakia on Masaryk's humanitarian ideas of fairness and justice, believing his slogan that "Truth Shall Prevail" more than any other philosophical or religious teachings. We were not connected with any political party. We practiced democracy as a matter of course, instinctively. We came from various national and religious backgrounds and were held together by common interests. Before the war we went hiking, canoeing, skiing, and on long camping trips with our bicycles and tents. We danced, we had love affairs, we sang songs of many nations, and we knew that the future was ours in this best of all worlds. We loved poetry because we were sentimental, and attempted versifying because that was romantic. We lived the lives of carefree teenagers. Strangely enough, we all found the time to take our studies seriously, for we had a lust for life and a curiosity for knowledge.

Then the war came.

The Czech universities were forcibly closed by the Germans. Some of the student leaders were executed, hundreds of others dragged to the concentration camp of Sachsenhausen-Oranienburg near Berlin. I had left Prague in January of 1940 on the underground railroad, accompanying as a protective female cover a high ranking officer of the Czechoslovak army, who was fleeing for his life and was on his way to join the Free Czechoslovak forces in the West.

After considerable adventures in Hungary and Yugoslavia with the Czech undergound, I lived through the bombing of Belgrade, the open city, on Easter Sunday in 1941; then I returned to Košice and the circle of my high school friends. The city was now under Hungarian occupation, as was a

"The French Connection" is by Vera Laska.

goodly southern portion of Slovakia after the Munich and Vienna arbitrations.

For all official purposes I was engaged in giving private German lessons. I went to my pupils' homes; they were the offspring of Hungarian officials and military personnel; who else would have cared to learn German in those days? The information that I gathered from conversations with the parents were often much more valuable than my fees. The job provided me with financial support and a schedule flexible enough to enable me to join in the smuggling of people escaping Nazi persecution across the Slovak-Hungarian border.

We used forest trails and our own short cuts. Except for the danger involved, it could have been a routine operation. We were familiar with every path, brook and spring, with each cave and precipice. We knew the best spots for strawberries or blueberries, the isolated farms with orchards where we could "borrow" fruit without disturbing the owners, and the noisy dogs to be avoided.

The borders were heavily patrolled, but the border guards were no match for us, especially those hailing from flat Hungary. They were like fish out of the water in the mountainous terrain that we knew as the palms of our hands from years of camping and skiing. They got easily tired and lost; on skis they made a pretty ridiculous picture.

The trips with our charges were dangerous, for we were accompanying people not used to hiking or skiing. Some were not alert to the pitfalls of the undertaking, and certainly they were sitting ducks in case of detection. They did not have the proper identification papers. After all, what good would false papers be to an escaped French prisoner of war, who could speak only French? How would you justify the presence of an older Jewish couple in the middle of the night in the forest near the border papers or no papers? Many of them must have had gold, diamonds or dollars sewn into their clothing, which would have clearly incriminated them. Our "empty" return trips were a lark compared with that. We were youngsters on a camping trip, minding our own business. Papers? Certainly, they came out of the right or left pocket, depending on the side of the border.

In the winter the cold and the snow complicated matters. We were mobile on our skis, but few of our passengers could ski. Our efforts to put some of the French Pierres through a quickie ski course were hilarious. Five of us took a group out on the slopes, but with only myself speaking French of sorts, the teaching consisted mostly of "allez," "stop," and assorted onomatopoetic shouts on our part, the repeated "merde" from our pupils. The most we achieved with them was a respectable ability to use the "pants brake," sliding on their derrières in safe contact with firm ground. We were dreaming of snow shoes, but none were available, and the attempt to construct them ended in total fiasco. We dreaded broken bones. We had better luck with a prototype of a sled, just a curved light board under the behind with a rope attached for stirring or carrying this primitive invention. Many years and several lives later I stood stunned in an American toy shop: here was our "assled," in multicolored edition for the kiddies, selling for good money!

The mini-sled solved our problem of speed and efficiency with the young Frenchmen. Later on, as our charges were older and less athletic, mostly Jews fleeing from deportation, we could not risk using them. Some of the civilians also complicated the situation by lugging cumbersome suitcases, although they had been strictly admonished to carry only minimal luggage on their backs or shoulders, leaving hands free for an improvised cane or for holding on to trees. The only serious aggravation we had were these treasures that they could not live without. Yet they endangered the outcome of our missions and their very lives.

Once our trips started, we had to adhere to tight schedules, pass certain points exactly between the rounds of the border patrols and make it before it became light. We had to reach train stations after daybreak and in time for the local train, yet not too soon so we would have to linger, always a dangerous point in the vicinity of the frontier.

Oh, the treasures that were left behind on these crossings! Teddy bears and silver candelabra had to be coaxed away from some people, causing them grief and all of us loss of precious time. For suitcases with their contents, including labeled clothing, could not be simply left alongside our paths. They had to be safely buried or otherwise hidden. The silver candelabra and other silver stuff in that damned heavy leather suitcase ended up in a farmer's woodshed. Trusting his greed, we thought it was safer with him than if the border patrolmen chanced upon it, advertising our route.

We had many a close call and several mishaps, but lost only one man, who insisted on wandering off near the station and got himself arrested just as he ran to board the train. We almost froze to death when a border patrolman broke his leg, and his companion started blowing his whistle calling for help. Laying low in the snow for over an hour, we used up all our reserve time and made the train by the skin of our teeth. One lady almost drove us out of our minds when she had to stop to search her bag for an aspirin; then she had to relieve herself; after which she tried to make us return because she had left her glove while doing so. After that charming adventure we added to our list of "do and don'ts" that all had to go to the bathroom before we picked them up. One Frenchman boasted to us that he had a German revolver, which was strictly tabu, for being captured with a weapon placed us all in double jeopardy. The ensuing debate among the contingent was resounding dangerously in the quiet of the forest and woke some birds that started a concert of their own. Pierre would not give up the revolver, but agreed that one of our boys could carry it for him. After a mile or so it ended up in the hollow of a tree, and for all I know is still there, rusting peacefully.

These trips taught me amazing lessons about human psychology. Some people while fleeing for their lives would risk their necks, not to mention ours, for material possessions. This to us was incomprehensible. They had been briefed as to physical exertions to be expected and about the importance of timing. Yet they would make it harder on themselves and the group by burdening themselves with weight that they would discard after the first hour of climbing. As time went on, we learned by experience to carry a lightweight elongated hand shovel to dig deep holes for discarded materials; aspirin to keep the children sleepy; ropes with loops for a handhold; and most of all that one of us had to be last in the line to prevent discarded items from becoming the telltale signs of our passing.

Two of us could take a group of eight young, healthy people on one crossing, but every older person or child had to be counted for two for unforeseen complications. One trip had to be aborted because two women showed up in high heeled shoes; their men gave us a hard time. The same group had to wait for several weeks before we could accommodate them, but they showed up in proper footwear. The women carried the high heeled shoes in their knapsacks. I often wondered whether those ladies were dancing away the war in those silly shoes, or whether they ended up with them in Auschwitz.

* * *

Memories of dozens of incidents chase each other in my mind. The most frightening one was of a winter crossing, after my companion stayed behind in Hungary for a contact meeting, and I was returning alone on skis. It was an uneventful trek. I noticed two border guards passing in the distance, and crossed a few minutes later into safe territory. It was hours after midnight, yet daylight comes late on wintry mornings. The snow provided the only light. Not a sound around. Owls and rabbits whom I would encounter after daybreak were fast asleep. I stopped at the top of a small hill, overlooking the meadow before me. I was contemplating swooshing through its middle, rather than skirting it under the trees. I remember my yearning for a cigarette, but the rule was not to light a match in the dark. I reached into my pocket for a cube of sugar instead. As I popped it into my mouth, my hand almost froze in midair.

For in the distance of about a hundred yards, suddenly a light went on and off, as if somebody had flipped a lighter. No sound, just that one isolated flicker of light. I remained motionless as a salt column. I strained my eyes. Nothing was moving where the light came from. No glow from the end of a cigarette. It could not have been one of us with a warning, for we had set whistling signals for that. Border patrols? They went in pairs, and by now in the stillness of the night I would have overheard even a whisper. The sugar was slowly dissolving in my mouth, and I had to swallow the saliva. I did so smoothly, quietly. My eyes never left the place where I saw the light for that one second.

Little by little, as I focused on the spot, I seemed to make out a face, two dark eyes, and a large mustache under them. A hunter? At this hour of the night? Here? It never happened before. Nonsense. Hunters may stand still, but their faces move. Nobody could stand that still. I was riveted to the ground, with a tree behind me to lean against. As time went on, minutes? hours? I stood petrified, gazing into the near distance. The face gradually acquired a body, uniformly dressed, all the same nondescript color. I saw two legs slightly apart and something like a wide belt dividing the torso. No skis; in case of a run I would have the advantage. What if he had a gun? I can not outrun a bullet. That darker shadow on the side of the figure looked like a gun holster. What is he after? He could not be dead or he would topple over. Is he waiting for me to make a move? Does he know that I am here under the dark tree? I must be melted into its wide trunk. Did he see me arriving? How long have we been standing here, gazing, staring, leering, reconnoitering each other? Smuggler? Wrong time, wrong place. Besides, there was not much to smuggle these days, except people.

How do you measure eternity? It is relative, a vector of uncertainty and of fear. Did I say I was never afraid? Am I afraid right now? Will I ever admit to my companions that I had been afraid? I was deeply, totally afraid, of the man and of his intentions. He was in uniform, and that did not augur well for my kind.

Here was a chance for my favorite pastime, observing my surroundings and myself. All my nerves were on the alert, the shock of fright ebbing and flooding my brain, but constantly part of me. I was getting used to it like to pain, yet it did not let off in intensity as it pressed on my consciousness.

It must have taken hours until the curtain of night was pulled slowly aside by the first breath of light color on the horizon. Will I become an easy target for his gun? Should I try to move, before I become visible, should I back away and then run for it? How do you back up on skis between trees and without letting on that you are moving? I was way into eternity of time. Instead of blood, fear circulated in my veins, keeping me in cold sweat.

He still did not move. As the light of the day conspired to unveil him to me, he became elusive. I recalled our spiritualist seances. A ghost? I did not believe in ghosts. I was the one who on a dare dated in an abandoned cemetery and laughed when some found it spooky. The man with the mustache was receding into grayness. His legs were no longer visible, although I still clearly saw the holster where his right hip was just a moment ago. The eyes were still glaring. My eyes hurt from staring. I pressed my eyelids together to clear my vision. The eyes, the mustache, the belt, all there, but in rather disjointed fashion. The rest of the man was no longer visible. As daylight freed me of my uncertainty, I saw the roundish spots and under them a narrow and a wide dark stripe on a tree.

The phantom of the night dissolved into a few bare spaces on a snow covered tree trunk. The phantasmagorical figure was conceived by my overly developed vigilance and the phosphorescence of decaying matter. The roots of my hair still tingled as I realized that my feet were frozen and my stomach growling for its due.

That was the longest night of my life, at least up to then. It was a milestone in my growing up.

* * *

Turn the page in the memory book. A moonlit night in the foothills of the Carpathians. A glorious stretch of the trail under starlit, summer skies, the air permeated with the seductive aroma of wild thyme in bloom. You felt like singing and rolling in the grass just for the joy of being alive. It was one of the early trips with the Frenchmen. We had to await daylight before reaching the station. We picked our usual spot near a creek full of lovely clear water, under a high embankment with a meadow of tall grass and wild flowers above.

It was a chance to relax and reflect. We stretched out among the pebbles and the roots of the trees that were reaching thirstily toward the water. Some men took a nap, others chatted in low voices. There was a velvety breeze caressing the leaves into a rustle. Once in a while the water stumbled into a rock and gurgled mischievously. A bird chirped from its sleep, dreaming of tomorrow's worm, no doubt. Peace and quiet. To think of the war and of our involvement in it seemed ludicrous and absurd. The sanctity of nature around us made wars emerge as the unnatural, obscene acts that they were.

It was a balmy night. Viki and I were sitting with our backs against the embankment, chewing musingly on blades of grass. A few yards away one of the Frenchmen took off his shirt and sandals. Stepping gingerly over the stones, he reached the water near a bend. As we were watching, he removed the rest of his clothing and stepped into the cool playful waves. With hardly a sound, he scooped up the water and washed his face and then the rest of his body. Viki was gripping my hand and whispered to me that this Pierre looked just like her Joe. Joe was worlds away, and the magic was here and now. Pierre stood erect, stretching his arms above his head, his manhood alert and pointing outstretched like another arm calling for a mate. As a somnambulist Viki let go of my hand and started walking towards the man rising from the water. I did not try to stop her. Silently she approached him, and their hands reached out for each other tenderly. Then they disappeared beyond the bend of the creek, two lovers meeting in the night, both seeking what the other could bestow as a gift.

The beauty of the encounter touched me to the depths of my heart. For if it was the worst of times, at fleeting moments it could also be the best of times, when human beings shed their artificial barriers and bared their souls.

Viki never had to face her Joe; she went up the chimney at Auschwitz about a year later. Joe was shot down over the English Channel as a Czech pilot with the Allies. And Pierre? Wherever he is, I hope he still cherishes the memory of that night when the world stood still and time suspended for the bounties of love.

And that, my friends, was also part of the undergound.

2

The Fishmonger and the Schoolteacher

Field Marshal Montgomery called the Danish undergound "second to none." Of the four million Danish men and women (and children), about 50,000 belonged to the resistance movement against the German occupants. Nowhere was it more widespread, effective and life saving.

Their thousands of acts of sabotage greatly contributed to the defeat of the Nazi machine. They cooperated with the Royal Air Force and British intelligence, pinpointing military targets and Gestapo headquarters. They firebombed factories that manufactured components of the V-2 rockets and earned the gratitude of Eisenhower's Supreme Headquarters of Allied-European Forces for preventing the total destruction of London. They disrupted railroad transportation, thus delaying German troop movements. They maintained communication with the free world through neutral Sweden, smuggling out people in danger, including Jews and downed Allied pilots, and smuggling in arms, ammunition, explosives, mail, film and secret agents. They organized strikes, they liquidated traitors.

They printed twenty-six million issues of illegal newspapers, some in Braille. They published cookbooks that gave recipes for homemade bombs and sabotage techniques, and sold the Germans pocket diaries with tips on how to feign illness or induce fever. They collected evidence by filming German atrocities, even inside a concentration camp.

They exhibited cold blooded courage, a high code of ethics and not a small dash of humor, as when they celebrated the birth of a royal princess by twenty-one acts of sabotage.

The women were right there alongside their men. Some dared to defy the Germans by wearing the RAF insignia, others were waving Danish flags on top of barricades.

The momentum of the Danish resistance shifted into its highest gear when on the first day of October 1943 the German occupants embarked on rounding up the Jews for deportation to concentration camps. While the story that King Christian X wore a yellow star in sympathy with the Jews is apocryphal, the fact remains that the king, his government, including the police and frontier guards, and the Danes in general were so strongly resolved to save the Jews that hiding and spiriting them across the Kattegat Sound to Sweden became a spontaneous undertaking. The Gestapo managed to deport to Terezín (Theresienstadt) only 477 Jews, among them a 102-year-old woman. There twenty-four women and nineteen men died, only one was further deported to Auschwitz and, under Danish government pressure, most of the rest were relocated into Sweden shortly before the end of the war.

In the most heroic rescue operation in the history of World War II, nearly 8,000 Jews, half-Jews and spouses of Jews were smuggled to freedom in Sweden. Through Danish help, 98.5 percent of the Danish Jews and Jews who had found refuge there before the Nazi furor survived.

Among the ranks of this underground resistance were women from all walks of life, from the intelligentsia to simple fishmongers, fighting with spiritual weapons of anti-Nazi propaganda, in the women's corps, as code clerks and radio operators, couriers and spies, nurses and illegal welfare workers. It did not mean that these women suddenly became "politicized." They saw people in trouble, so they wanted to help. It was as simple as that and as logical. Some women initiated their own actions, others joined friends, neighbors, or fellow office workers. Some women fed and sheltered the Jews before they boarded the boats, or cared for the children. Other women served as guides to the boats. Each of these services was equally dangerous and carried heavy penalties, because each was an illegal act resisting German occupation policies.

Young Inge Barfeldt was instrumental in alerting the Jews in time of the impending roundup and deportations, planned for the Jewish New Year, October 1, 1943. She deliv-

ered the message to Rabbi Marcus Melchior, who announced it at the synagogue the day before the raids: "There will be no service this morning. . . by nightfall tonight we must all be in hiding."

Army nurse Helga von Seck was the key person in the stupendous stunt operation, in which the underground kidnapped air force Lieutenant Colonel Torben Ørum of the resistance intelligence from a military hospital where he had been held prisoner under the tightest German security.

Mrs. Edith Bonnesen, one of the Copenhagen resistance code clerks, was captured. In the short minute she was left alone, she simply got up and walked out of the Gestapo building, calmly passing the guards at the gate, most likely the only person ever to do so. She later emerged as the operator of the Danish radio station at the American consulate at Helsingborg in Sweden.

Ruth Philipson of Aarhus was less lucky. As secretary to one of the resistance leaders, she was arrested by the Gestapo and tortured. Before she would break and divulge her secrets, an RAF bombing raid demolished the Gestapo building, and her interrogators disappeared in the ruins. She escaped and was eventually rowed to safety in Sweden, carrying the courier bag for the resistance.

In Danish hospitals wounded saboteurs received medical care, with doctors and nurses cooperating in the highly risky clandestine harboring of these "enemies of the state." Jews were admitted under Christian names to avoid arrest and deportation.

In Copenhagen, the Bispebjerg hospital's chapel served as a gathering point for fake funerals: the mourners were Jews, dressed in black, hiding their faces while sobbing into their handkerchiefs. From the chapel covered trucks rushed them to the waiting boats and safety in Sweden. These "funerals" became so popular that the Jews had to wait their turns. Hundreds of them were accommodated in the nurses' quarters until they could be spirited away to the fishing boats and freedom. Head nurse Signe Jansen spoke for all doctors, nurses and hospital staff when she said of their actions: "I did not think of these people as Jews, but as fellow Danes who needed succor."

While millions in other countries were hiding their consciences and asking "what can I do?" the Danish women and men simply acted because they felt it was their duty to their fellow human beings.

The following two episodes illustrate the contributions of two courageous Christian women, a fishmonger and a schoolteacher.

In the town of Dragør, about eight miles south of Copenhagen, lived two women of widely disparate professions who were destined to become close friends because of a common interest: rescuing Danish Jews. They were Mrs. Ellen Nielsen, a fishmonger, and Miss Elise Schmidt-Petersen, a schoolteacher.

In 1941, Mrs. Nielsen's husband, a worker in a chemical factory, died. To support her six children, Mrs. Nielsen became a fishmonger on the Copenhagen docks, buying fish directly from the fishermen and hawking it to passers-by. She had no interest in politics.

During the first week of October 1943, while she was hawking fish on the docks, she was approached by two brothers. They were flower-vendors in the flower market adjacent to the fish market, and she knew them only because they would occasionally buy fish from her, and she, in turn, would sometimes purchase flowers from them.

"What will have today boys?" she asked. "The cod is very nice and I have some fresh shrimp."

"Mrs. Nielsen, we wonder if you could help us," said one of the brothers. "You know many fishermen. Perhaps you know one who would be willing to take us to Sweden. We would pay him two thousand kroner to take us across."

"But why would want to do that?" asked Mrs. Nielsen.

"Because we are Jewish, and the Germans have started arresting all Danish Jews."

This was the first knowledge Mrs. Nielsen had of the brothers being Jewish and the first she had heard of the German roundup of the Jews.

"But if the Germans are arresting the Jews, what are you boys doing walking around here? Shouldn't you be in hiding?"

"Yes, but we don't know where to hide," replied one of the brothers.

"You can stay at my house," said Mrs. Nielsen. "I'll close early today and you can come home with me. And while you're in my house, I'll ask among the fishermen I know whether any of them would be willing to take you to Sweden."

During the next few days, Mrs. Nielsen managed to find several fishermen willing to take the brothers to Sweden. Arrangements were made with one of them, and the flower-vendors were taken safely across the sound. Through the fisherman who had taken them, word reached the underground of what Mrs. Nielsen had done, and they contacted her to ask whether she would be willing to aid more refugees to escape from the Germans. Because her work put her in direct contact with the fishermen on the docks, she was in a position to be a perfect liaison between them and the

"The Fishmonger and the Schoolteacher" is from Harold Flender, *Rescue in Denmark* (New York: Holocaust Library, 1980), pp. 182-88. Reprinted with the permission of the publisher.

underground. Mrs. Nielsen agreed to do what she could and during the following weeks over a hundred refugees passed through her house on their way to Sweden. At one time, Mrs. Nielsen had over thirty refugees squeezed into her small house. Her children aided her in her work by helping to feed and care for the refugees, and in addition, her two eldest sons acted as guides, leading the refugees from the house to the boats in the harbor. After the refugees were safe in Sweden, Mrs. Nielsen continued to work for the underground by hiding saboteurs.

In December 1944, Mrs. Nielsen was caught by the Gestapo. For three months she was in Vestre Prison, where the Gestapo tried unsuccessfully to get her to reveal the names of her contacts. She was then sent to Frøslev Concentration Camp for another three months, and from there to Ravensbrück in Germany. Upon her arrival in Ravensbrück, she was summoned to the office of the camp commandant.

"Mrs. Nielsen," said the commandant, "we know that you have been involved in the illegal transportation of Jews from Denmark to Sweden."

Mrs. Nielsen remained silent.

"There is no point in denying it," said the commandant, "because he have proof. We know, for example, that you saved the lives of dozens of Jewish children. We even have some of their names."

There was no reply from Mrs. Nielsen.

"No matter," continued the commandant. "The point is that we feel that since you were involved with the transportation of Jewish children in Denmark, we should give you a job here in Ravensbrück that would use to advantage your previous experience and interests. We are therefore giving you a job similar to the one you had in Denmark—transporting Jewish children."

Mrs. Nielsen had no idea what the commandant meant. But she learned all too soon. Her assignment was to carry those Jewish infants too young to walk to the gas chambers where they were put to death. She was also made to carry them, after they were gassed, to the crematorium to be burned. When, after several weeks, she refused to continue at her macabre job, she was condemned to death, and she was herself placed three times on the line leading to the gas chamber. The first time she saved herself by bribing a guard with a bar of soap which she had received in a Danish Red Cross parcel. The second time she was able to do the same with the contents of another Danish parcel. The third time she had nothing left with which to bribe the guards. Waiting on the line, stripped naked, she was resigned to death. Suddenly she was approached by German guards who informed her that she had been saved.

Count Folke Bernadotte had made an agreement with Heinrich Himmler to have all surviving Danish concentration camp prisoners shipped to Sweden for internment.

* * *

Working closely with Mrs. Nielsen in hiding Jewish refugees in Dragør was her neighbor, Miss Elise Schmidt-Petersen, a schoolteacher. Like Mrs. Nielsen, Miss Petersen offered no opposition to the Germans until the start of the Jewish persecution. The extent of her political naïveté is shown by her reactions on the day of the German occupation. She was bicycling from her house in Dragør to her school in Copenhagen when she met a friend on the road who told her that the turnoff ahead was blocked because German planes were landing at nearby Kastrup Airport.

"What does that mean?" asked Mrs. Petersen.

"It means that the Germans have taken over the country."

Miss Petersen turned her bicycle around to take an alternate route to the school. She had no idea whether Germany's taking over the country was good or bad for Denmark. She would inquire, she thought, when she arrived at the school and spoke to some of the teachers. At the school the teachers were divided in their reaction to the German occupation. Very few were violently opposed to it. The general feeling was that, good or bad, nothing could be done about it.

During the second week of October 1943, Miss Petersen received a telephone call from Kaj Holbeck, the newspaper editor who had first introduced Pastor Poul Borchsenius to resistance activities. Miss Petersen had worked for Holbeck as a housemaid when she was a young girl, and, since becoming a teacher, had often asked Holbeck to visit her in Dragør. During the war years, Holbeck had consistently claimed that he was too busy to visit her, but she never pressed the issue because she knew from mutual friends that reason—he was one of the leaders of the underground.

"Is your invitation for me to come up to have tea with you still good?" asked Holbeck.

"Yes, of course," replied Miss Petersen. "When would you like to come?"

"Tonight. And, if it is all right with you, I would like to bring seven guests with me. I hope that you will have enough tea for all of us. Is it all right?"

Miss Petersen knew that if she answered in the affirmative it would mean getting involved in some sort of underground activity. "Yes," she replied, "of course you can come. And by all means bring your guests."

Holbeck's seven guests were Danish Jews. Among them was a six-month-old girl and two boys of eight and ten years of age. Holbeck explained that they were leaving that night, after midnight, from Dragør for Sweden. Miss Petersen offered them food and tea, but they were all too nervous to eat. The two young boys were particularly upset.

"Why must we keep waiting?" asked the ten-year-old. "Why can't we go now?"

"We must wait for a man to come and take us to the boat," explained the father.

"Can't you telephone this man?" asked the son.

"What should I tell him if I telephone him?"

"Tell him to come and take us now," said the son. "Tell him we can't wait any longer. Please."

Miss Petersen spoke to the boy and told him not to be afraid, that he would soon be in Sweden. Seeing how frightened the two boys were, seeing the terror of the baby's mother, Miss Petersen was glad that she had agreed to help Holbeck. She turned to him and said, "You can use my house for this type of thing any time you wish to."

At midnight a doctor arrived at the house and told them that their boat was ready, that they would soon be boarding it, and that, meanwhile, it was his job to administer injections to the three children.* The children received the injections, and Miss Petersen, watching them become unconscious, found the sight almost more than she could bear. A few minutes after the doctor departed, there was a knock on the door. When Miss Petersen opened it, she was frightened to see standing in the doorway a Danish policeman. He quickly explained that he was a member of the resistance and that he had come to lead the refugees to the boat. The three unconscious children were wrapped in rugs and carried down to the harbor.

After the seven refugees were safely on their way to Sweden, Holbeck asked Miss Petersen, "Did you mean what you said a little while ago about using your house any time we wanted to?"

"Yes," answered Miss Petersen. "Of course I meant it."

Miss Petersen's house in Dragør was tiny—two small rooms and a kitchen—but during the next few weeks she managed to hide over fifty refugees in it. She worked very closely with Mrs. Nielsen in this operation, often receiving the overflow from Mrs. Nielsen's house. Some of the refugees were hidden in her house for a few hours, but several stayed for as many as three or four days at a time. She housed one particular group of refugees for ten days. The underground supplied her with ration cards, but the money with which she purchased the food for the refugees was her own. "Money meant nothing when you had to help people at a time like that," explained Miss Petersen.

After the exodus of the refugees, she continued to work closely with Mrs. Nielsen in the hiding and transporting of saboteurs. One of the first of the saboteurs to be hidden in her house was Pastor Borchsenius.

In August 1944, Miss Petersen's role in the underground was discovered, and she had to go into hiding herself. Using a fictitious name and false identity papers, she moved from one friend's house to another until the end of the war.

Why did Miss Petersen help the Jews? "I thought it was my duty," she said.

*Children's cries endangered illegal crossings. Occasionally, babies were choked into unconsciousness to keep them still. The Czech resistance used sleeping pills to put small children out of commission for the duration of border crossings.

3

The Anguish of a Mother

In that grim summer of 1944, a determined group of six young people from Palestine parachuted into Nazi-controlled Hungary on a suicidal mission, with the intention of helping to prevent the Holocaust from being carried through there. Among the six was one girl, Hannah Senesh, the radio operator, aged twenty-three, formerly of Hungary.

The mission might seem impractical and hopeless from hindsight: six "invaders" against the safely entrenched Nazi might; but it expressed poignantly their idealism, dedication and self-sacrifice. Hannah was captured, tortured physically and mentally and tried for treason in Budapest. On November 7, 1944, while still awaiting sentencing, she was shot.

Hannah's letters and diary were published, as was her biography. Heroic as her life was, the anguish of her mother Catherine was more heartbreaking, for she had to witness her daughter's martyrdom. Believing that Hannah was safe in a kibbutz near Haifa, she was suddenly confronted with brutal reality: her daughter's battered body in the hands of the Budapest police.

Catherine survived the war and moved to Palestine, which became Israel in 1948.

Catherine was aghast at the information Rozsa had just given her:

> I felt as if the floor were giving away under me and clutched the edge of the table frantically with both hands. My eyes closed, and in a matter of seconds I felt everything—hope, faith, trust, the very meaning of life, everything I had ever believed in—collapse like a child's house of cards. I was completely shattered, physically and spiritually.
>
> The door opened. I turned, my back to the table, my body rigid.
>
> Four men led her in. Had I not known she was coming, perhaps in that first moment I would not have recognised the Hannah of five years ago. Her once soft wavy hair hung in a filthy tangle, her ravaged face reflected untold suffering, her large expressive eyes were blackened, and there were ugly welts on her cheeks and neck. That was my first glimpse of her.

Hannah, who under the tender caresses of the SS had been completing her course in martyrdom, found Catherine's reaction far more painful than the various beatings she had been receiving over the last few days. She completely broke down, somehow tore herself away from her captors and launched herself at Catherine, just as she had done as a child, following some scuffle with George or some childish panic. Hannah repeatedly asked Catherine to forgive her, whilst the others looked on as if they were watching a play. Somehow the situation *was* so dramatic that Catherine was objective enough to retain her self-control.

Rozsa then told Catherine to use her maternal influence and "convince her that she had better tell us everything, otherwise you'll never see each other again." This cryptic remark left Catherine in as much ignorance as she had been in before. All she could think of was two invisible questions: Why was Hannah in Budapest? How had Hannah got from Palestine to Budapest? Rozsa then wanted to know why there was such a lack of conversation between mother and daughter. Catherine's voice was that of an automaton when she replied. "There is no need to repeat yourself. We both heard you."

Grudgingly Rozsa and his colleagues then left the room, leaving Hannah and Catherine facing each other. Only the detective remained, trying somehow to merge with the opposite wall.

Catherine was suddenly struck with the thought that Hannah had come to rescue her. Amazing as the thought seemed, somehow it appeared logical. She must have heard of the Jewish persecution in Palestine and come back on some impulsive and absurd rescue attempt. Catherine asked her,

"The Anguish of a Mother" is from Anthony Masters, *The Summer That Bled* (New York: St. Martin's Press, 1972), pp. 222-67. Catherine's Senesh's testimony is in Livia Rothkirchen, ed., *Yad Vashem Studies*, vols. VII-VIII (Jerusalem: Yad Vashem, 1968-1970). In the text, George was Catherine's son in Israel, Margit her Christian companion, Rozsa the Hungarian investigator and Seifert the Gestapo official. Reprinted with the permission of the publisher.

but Hannah immediately said no, she hadn't and that "You're not to blame for anything. Not anything at all." They talked for a moment of George and Hannah reassured Catherine about his safety. Catherine then noticed that one of Hannah's teeth was missing. "Of course your tooth was knocked out here," she stated, regardless of the detective who was still trying to melt into the wall.

But Hannah said, "No, not here." There was nothing else to say and they remained quiet, the silence like a warm, embracing quilt between them, covering them with an unspoken love that was more painful than speech.

Catherine then stroked Hannah's hands. She noticed that all her nails were broken and her skin was like sandpaper. As she leant over to kiss the purple-black bruises on Hannah's face, Rozsa and his four henchmen rushed in. He had obviously listened to every word spoken between mother and daughter, and being a good student of interrogation methods, had broken them up at the right psychological moment. He pushed them apart saying:

"Whispering is not allowed here! Anyway, that's enough for today."

Rozsa then said to Catherine: "I could detain you as well, but I'm taking your age into consideration. Go on home! If we have further need of you we'll telephone."

* * *

For the second time they took her away, but not before her friends had been scrutinised and nearly arrested, and a perfunctory search of the house had been made.

Seifert began inspecting the house, strolling from room to room, shouting out questions about the furniture, the contents of drawers and cupboards, finally demanding to know which of the rooms was mine.

Before they left, Seifert showed Catherine a photograph of Hannah, asking her if she recognised it. Hannah looked as she had looked that morning; the swellings made her virtually unrecognisable.

With a few sandwiches hurriedly packed by the caretaker, and leaving a message for Margit to phone her, Catherine left with Seifert. En route he made a slip that confirmed Catherine's impression that she would never return. Seifert had told her that she would be back before evening, but as they got into the car he asked why she was taking her front door key. Catherine remembers saying: "Didn't you say I would be back before evening?" "Of course, of course," he answered hastily, aware he had betrayed himself, "take the key."

The journey was not very long for the closed car soon pulled up at the goods entrance of the Budapest County Department of Justice, in which the German Police Prison was lodged. Once inside the interrogation began.

Presided over by Seifert the ritual was attended by a young SS officer with a Death's Head badge on his cap (a member of the Totenkopf SS, the unit responsible for the death camp atrocities) whose cadaverous appearance and arrogant manner immediately terrified Catherine, a young German soldier and a middle-aged civilian, who put Catherine's documents in a bag marked "very urgent," demanded her front door key and disappeared. It was now obvious that the home in Bimbó Street was to be the subject of a very thorough search. Catherine remembers:

> The young Death's Head man, whose face resembled his badge, took over. He asked for all my personal belongings, examined my handbag, turned it inside out. He confiscated my money, fountain pen, watch and wedding ring. He asked whether I had any more money. I wore a little bag around my neck in which I carried the maximum amount of money Jews were allowed. After an instant's hesitation, I handed it to him. The reward for the momentary delay was a powerful slap across my face.

Frail and weighing about nine stone,* the blow made Catherine spin around in a complete circle. Yet she hardly felt it for "after that morning's encounter with Hannah I felt nothing: as if a stranger had taken my place, or a mechanised puppet." She was then led away and after being searched by two women guards went numbly to Cell 528. There she met a number of Jewish women who had been in that particular cell for some time.

Amongst Catherine's cell-mates, there were a number of diverse personalities. There was the rich Baroness Hatvany; there was a widow, accused of collaborating with the Allies; there was the sister of a wealthy banker; there was Mrs. Eugene Vida, the wife of a former Jewish member of the Upper House; and there was Countess Zichy who was arrested whilst she was trying to hide some valuable paintings. There were many others, but Catherine knew that she could not—must not—confide in any of them. Some of them, like Baroness Hatvany, were rich Jewesses, others were poor. All had offended in some way or other and were waiting trial or more usually some different form of retribution. All activity in the cell was forbidden, yet this colony of women managed to pass their time playing bridge (out of fashioned cards) and draughts (out of numbered pieces of paper). These games had to be played furtively for often the Matron would check on them, to ensure that they demoralised themselves by sitting on the prescribed wooden benches doing the prescribed nothing at all from five in the morning until lights out. Equally furtive turns were taken lying on the beds but even in our dreams we heard footsteps, and automatically jumped up and ran to the table."

Catherine recalls some of her first impressions of that night:

*One stone is 14 pounds.

It was getting dark, and I had eaten nothing since the night before. I was famished. I found the sandwiches and bit into one of them. Twelve pairs of eyes fastened upon me. Hungry as I was, the mouthful caught in my throat: I handed the small packet of food to Boske [the baroness], who carefully divided it. She seemed to be the "officer in charge."

The next morning Catherine was told that she would probably be interrogated again on Sunday, the following day. So nervous was she that she confided in the baroness, who listened sympathetically and quietly. But even whilst she spoke Catherine was wondering if Hannah was alive. Somehow Catherine knew the Hannah would not break down, would not give the Germans whatever information they required and consequently her torture would be consistently stepped up. However, whilst Catherine was in prison there was a chance that they might be able to use her as a lever against Hannah's wall of silence.

Having realised this, Catherine took the only decision that she considered was logical. She would kill herself. Quietly and methodically she stole a razor blade from Countess Zichy and took it to bed with her. When it was dark and she thought the others were asleep, Catherine located the main artery in her wrist and slashed it

. . . and felt the blood flow—but it did not gush forth as I had expected. My neighbor sat up, and for a while I feigned sleep. Then, after a considerable interval, I tried once more. But again there was only a trickle of blood. Before I could bring myself to make another attempt, the prisoners began stirring.

As Catherine slashed again at her wrists, the baroness saw her, rushed over and grasped at her nervously working hands. She bound Catherine's wrists with handkerchiefs, told her how stupid her action was and how much trouble it would have caused for everyone in Cell 528. She also told Catherine to wear her long sleeved raincoat when she was taken for interrogation.

Faces to the wall and motionless, the other prisoners awaiting interrogation stood passively in the second-floor corridor of the building. Catherine joined them. Then, in an enormous police van, about forty prisoners were taken to the notorious Schwab Hill: the Budapest Gestapo Interrogation Centre. Swaying about in the windowless and crazily rocking van, crammed shoulder to shoulder with her fellow prisoners, Catherine noticed "postcards (previously written and addressed) were collected and slipped through the vents [the van had air-vents near the top] in the hope they would be picked up by people humane enough to forward them."

For the rest of that day Catherine sat awaiting her turn for interrogation. Nothing happened. That evening she was given a postcard and was told that this was her only opportunity to notify someone of where she was. She could also ask for food parcels, for clothes and for toilet articles. Packages, apparently, were accepted every other Wednesday, from ten until twelve in the morning. But at least they were immediately delivered to the prisoners. Anxious not to incriminate Margit, Catherine sent the postcard to her hairdresser with the covering instruction to give it to the "lady who lives in my house." The next Wednesday Catherine received her food parcel, complete with a bowl of still-steaming soup.

Still uninterrogated, Catherine stayed in prison throughout June and well into July. Prison life settled into a dreary round with the highlight of the day being a ten-minute exercise period around the prison yard.

> One soon came across forgotten acquaintances, and from day to day, as new prisoners arrived, friends and relatives one hoped had managed to escape joined the ranks. Gradually the number of inmates grew, and before long there were about twenty in our cell, which was not intended for more than six.

On June 23rd, both the Baroness Hatvany and Mrs. Vida were taken away. Nobody knew where they went, although rumour had it that there were "twice-weekly deportations, as well as twice-weekly selections for shipment to the Kistarcsa Internment Camp in the suburbs." As a result of this and to be ready for the worst, each prisoner packed a pathetic little bag of possessions each morning for directly a name was called that person had to leave immediately.

As the baroness and Mrs. Vida were driven away for the preliminary stages of what might turn out to be their journey to Auschwitz, Catherine was called up for interrogation. As she passed a younger prisoner scrubbing the floor, she learned something that suddenly gave her renewed hope. Hannah was here, and she was still alive.

* * *

Seifert, as an interrogator, was very different from Rozsa. He was sophisticated, courteous and bland. Because of this, and her slowly gathering confidence, Catherine asked him, half way through his detailed questions, what exactly had happened to Hannah and what the charge against her was.

Catherine remembers that he answered after a pause by saying: "According to my interpretation of Hungarian law, your daughter's life is in no danger. German laws are more stringent."

Immediately Catherine's confidence redoubled. That evening a trusty told Catherine to look across the yard (looking out of the window was generally forbidden). Catherine did so, and saw Hannah at a window exactly opposite hers. She was overjoyed and they immediately established contact by writing the outline of letters slowly in the air. One of Hannah's first questions concerned the Star of David, worn by Catherine and the other inmates of her cell. They told her why this was worn, and, in return, asked Hannah whether she was excused from wearing such a discriminating emblem. Hannah answered that "she was no longer a Hungarian citizen, thus not bound by such 'laws.' " Somebody else in Catherine's cell wrote in the air: "You're lucky not to be branded." In response, Hannah immediately drew a huge Star of David on her dust-coated window. Immediately after that she disappeared from view and did not reappear for the rest of the day, despite the fact that Catherine spent all her time watching for her. But the Star remained, ingrained in the dust, for weeks to come.

The next day, via the same trusty, a meeting was arranged between Catherine and Hannah in the bathroom. Catherine recalls:

> At last I could hold her close, kiss her. Hannah hastily explained that she was a Radio Officer in the British Army, and had volunteered for a mission which "unfortunately I could not complete." She continued, "I'm reconciled to my fate. But the thought that I've needlessly involved you in all this is unbearable."

Whilst Catherine tried to reassure Hannah, Hannah gazed back at her sadly. She looked better and had obviously not been recently maltreated. The swellings and marks of her beatings had healed, her hair was clean—and the only sign of change was the gap in her teeth that still upset Catherine so much. Hannah told Catherine about her arrest, about Kallos's suicide, about the finding of the earphones and so on. But all Catherine could think of was to what extent Hannah had been tortured. She remembers Hannah replying: "Believe me, compared to the mental and emotional anguish, the physical suffering is negligible."

At that stage they had to part, and over the next few weeks their meetings were rare. Hannah was taken daily to the Hill for interrogation and didn't return until nightfall. Sometimes she appeared in the early mornings at her window determinedly cutting out paper letters and holding them up to form words. Sometimes, in the few days when she was not being interrogated, Catherine would watch her walk in the yard; she was a lonely figure for, being in solitary confinement, she was officially not allowed to have contact or to have direct conversation with anyone.

One day, in the exercise yard she managed to snatch the first few words she had had with Catherine since their bathroom meeting. Immediately Hannah told Catherine that a few days after Catherine's first meeting with Rozsa he had wanted to question her again, and had phoned her home whilst Hannah had been in the office. Margit had answered and had told him that Catherine had simply disappeared. Furiously Rozsa banged down the phone. The same day the house was carefully searched by the Germans, neatly demonstrating, in Catherine's words, how "the Hungarian and German Nazis, distrustful of one another, spied on and double-crossed each other."

Meanwhile Hannah, still as Zionistically evangelical as ever, was becoming a teacher. Her window became an information and education centre, and from morning till evening prisoners looked towards it for news, much of which she, in turn, gleaned from guards and newly arrived prisoners she met in the vans. Opposite her cell window was that of some members of the Zionist Movement who had been arrested for undergound activities and were awaiting sentence. She encouraged them, gave them new heart.

Hannah consistently told officials of the SS and the Gestapo exactly what she thought of them, and also exactly what fate had in store for them. Her captors were slightly stunned by her self-confident predictions as to their approaching defeat. They had been taught—and it had been amply demonstrated to them—that Jews did not fight back. Here was an exception. Even the prison warden, totalitarian in his Nazi belief, occasionally visited her cell out of curiosity, and found himself the unwilling but immovable subject of a stream of criticism. He went away from her exhausted. Hannah had bullied him, and won.

* * *

July 17th was Hannah's birthday. Catherine sent her a jar of marmalade whilst the others in Catherine's cell sent her gifts gleaned from private and precious stores. That afternoon her thank-you letter arrived. Touchingly it was vintage Hannah. Catherine remembers:

> She said the marmalade particularly pleased her, not only because it was so good, but because it reminded her of Palestine. She continued that she had summed up and weighed the events of her life, and upon looking back over her twenty-three years decided they had been very colorful and eventful, her childhood happy and beautiful.

Next time Catherine met Hannah in the prison yard. Curiosity overcoming her Catherine asked Hannah about the mission for which she had volunteered. Hannah told Catherine that she couldn't tell her anything as the Mission was a military secret but "the war will soon be over and then you'll know everything." Hannah went on to say that even if she could tell her she wouldn't since it was much too difficult to maintain silence during interrogation anyway, and the less you knew the better off you were. In fact, it was best if you knew absolutely nothing.

Catherine said that she was sure that it was not her enthusiasm for the British that made her decide to volunteer for the army, there must be a Jewish cause somewhere. Hannah replied that Catherine was very much on the right track there, to which Catherine remembers herself retorting: "The only question is whether it's worth risking your life for your boundless fanaticism."

Hannah smiled and said that it was worth it to her. Besides, she had done nothing to harm Hungary. She went on to add that "what's considered a crime today will probably be considered a virtue in the near future, justified by coming events."

When they next met Hannah told Catherine that she had been naïvely trapped during her first interrogation. Unable to extract any kind of real information concerning the earphones they told her that "one of the boys has confessed and he'll be executed tomorrow." Hannah had risen immediately to the bait, saying that the "boy had absolutely nothing to do with the matter. The radio is mine." It had gone very hard with Hannah from then on, for despite the fact that she had deliberately left the radio code book behind on the train that took her to Budapest, she was intensively tortured in an attempt to force her to divulge her code.

But Hannah, once the self-indulgence of telling somebody was over, rarely discussed her interrogations and their subsequent torture with Catherine. Instead, during the course of a window conversation, she asked Catherine if she would like to learn Hebrew as Catherine would never have a better opportunity, considering all the time on her hands. Though Catherine was not exactly in the mood to study anything, she knew if she agreed Hannah would be pleased. From then on excellently organised and prepared lessons arrived daily.

A few days later Hannah covered an empty talcum powder tin with silver foil. In the holes at the top of the tin were placed white paper buds attached to twenty-five blades of straw pulled from her mattress. She glued a lace doiley to the bottom of the tin and sent these ingenious paper roses, via a trusty, in time for Catherine's silver wedding anniversary. With the flowers came another doll—this time a paper doll bride carrying a miniature bouquet of tissue paper roses. With the gift came a poem which Catherine was forced to destroy in the prison. But she remembers it as reading:

Memories, like paper flowers
Remain forever fresh.
One often longingly studies them,
The while forgetting
They are not alive.

Catherine retained one particularly photographic memory of Hannah. She recalls:

One exceptionally quiet and beautiful night I found it impossible to sleep, and had the distinct feeling Hannah was not sleeping either. I crept to the window, fearful I would wake someone in the still night. The moon was shining so brightly it was almost like daylight, and I clearly saw Hannah silhouetted against the half-opened window wearing her light blue dressing gown, her hair softly framing her lovely face. It seemed to me her soul was mirrored in her face at that instant. . . . Overwhelmed by infinite sadness, I returned to my bed, fell upon it, and buried my head in my arms to stifle my sobs. I was crying for my child, for her youth, for her cruel predicament and probably hopeless fate.

Then on the night of September 10th, the old horrors returned when the lights were suddenly turned on in each cell and all Catherine could hear was one unified moan of terror, as if some great animal was being awakened and shown its own death. It was the Polish prisoners being rounded up for deportation. The Hungarian authorities might protect their own but they certainly did not feel they were bound to protect the Poles, and Eichmann was quietly rooting out what he could without censure from Himmler. The Poles, the Czechs and all other Jewish refugees could be deported because they were not under the all-too-temporary Hungarian protection.

Catherine's door was abruptly opened by a solider and they could see groups of non-Hungarian refugees sobbing in the corridors. They took out a woman from Cracow, the same woman who had first told them of Auschwitz. Now, ironically, that was her destination. Meanwhile Hannah lay crying on her bed as the refugees were removed from her cell. The continuous feeling of failure—the total failure of her attempt to rescue the Jews—was thrown once again in her face.

On the morning of September 11th a trusty called Catherine to the door of her cell. She told her that Hannah had been taken away, to an undisclosed place. Catherine was inconsolable. She felt destroyed and utterly without hope.

4

The Czech Connection

At Munich in September 1938, France and Great Britian sold down the river the only true democracy in Central Europe. The pragmatic actions of "la douce France" and "treacherous Albion" caused a traumatic bitterness among the Czechoslovaks, those Yankees of Europe, whose existence was sacrificed to secure an illusionary peace. It lasted only until Hitler invaded Poland the next fall, thus proving the shortsightedness of French and British diplomacy at Munich.

Czechoslovakia was eventually split into a Czech and Moravian Protectorate under direct Nazi rule, and an "independent" Slovakia, a puppet catering to the Germans. Hungary, which never had much love lost for Czechs and Slovaks, was under pressure a silent partner of Germany; Yugoslavia was still free, passionately anti-German and sympathetic to the cause of freedom.

After the war broke out in September 1939, the Czech underground went into high gear. Its well-organized freedom line ran an underground railroad from occupied Prague through Slovakia and Hungary to Yugoslavia. On this illegal track hundreds of political opponents of the Nazis fled persecution, and thousands of young volunteers reached the free Czechoslovak armed forces fighting on the Allied side.

Traveling couples were less conspicuous than single males, especially in the neighborhood of frontiers. Because of my fluency in the languages concerned (Czech, Slovak, German and Hungarian), I was chosen to accompany a high ranking officer across the first two borders. Then I remained at the Czech underground center in Budapest, until my cover was blown. Next came Yugoslavia, where I lived through the bombing of the open city of Belgrade on Easter Sunday, 1941, before returning to "independent" Slovakia to carry on.

Those border crossings were full of adventures. In retrospect, stripped of the element of fear, they seem almost amusing, but they were hair raising when we lived through them.

It was the winter of 1939–1940 and bitter cold. In Moravská Ostrava, the courier with the password had been delayed, thus we arrived before the password did. The first shock came when we reached the address given to us in Prague and discovered that the first floor of the building housed the offices of the Gestapo! I had long known the Czech proverb that "under the candle the darkness is the deepest," but this was carrying the Schweik-like philosophy a bit too far. Yet—it was midnight, and no other place to go. We climbed to the third floor and roused our contact:

"Do you still have that small rocking horse?" we asked.

The woman at the door did not even take the safety chain down.

"What rocking horse? You must have the wrong address."

Shuffling feet, and her husband was looking us over. He did not know anything about a rocking horse either. We had to show our colors.

"Uncle Skála sent us, he said you could put us up for the night."

The door opened and we were welcome, although unannounced. We were fed and bedded down. Exhausted by the long train ride and the excitement, we fell asleep. Suddenly the sharp ringing of the doorbell woke me. I heard voices whispering in the hallway. Were we being betrayed? Did they call the Gestapo and we shall be arrested? The landlord stuck his head into the room:

"All is well. The courier with the password just arrived. He had a flat on his bicycle and was delayed. Sleep tight." We did.

The next morning a short train ride to Frýdek. Here we were joined by a medical student, who carried a huge Bible in his knapsack. "When Comenius* fled the country three hundred years ago, he also carried a Bible," he said. The three of us were steadily plodding on the snow-covered trail to Salajka, the forester's lodge. We reached it toward the evening. Here they did have the password, and all went well. We ate our last meal on home grounds. The forester treated us to good home-made slivovitz and to even better fireside tales. Shortly after midnight, we started out on our crossing from the Protectorate into Slovakia.

The forester's wife came along as an alibi for her husband. In case we ran into a German border patrol, he would claim that he was just taking a stroll with her. We proceeded among the trees, single file, trying to step into the same footprints in the deep snow. After about an hour, we heard short whistles. We stopped in our tracks, motionless. Above us on the trail two

"The Czech Connection" is by Vera Laska.

*Jan Amos Komenský or Comenius (1592-1670), father of modern education who recommended among other things equal education of women, was the last bishop of the Unity of Brethren before being forced to flee Bohemia during the Counter Reformation.

figures passed swiftly in the opposite direction. The picture is engraved on my mind like a snapshot. The collars of their overcoats raised, their soft hats pulled over their eyes, their legs moving in unison, like two black apparitions from an Al Capone movie. The word passed from the forester: all clear, they were just smugglers going about their business. But he liked to avoid them. No use in getting caught in each other's nets, in case the Germans were around. But the Germans were warming their hides with hot rum between their rounds, and the forester knew their schedules well.

On the very border the Slovak contact awaited us with bad news.

"You will not run into a single border patrol here, because they are all at the house where you were supposed to spend the night, helping celebrate a birthday." A brief conference. Abort the trip? The following night other fugitives were expected, and we could not overcrowd the line of the underground railroad. Instead we went on to the next village, to the farm indicated by our guide. We played the lost tourists and asked for a night's lodgings. They would not take us in. I "fainted." They took us in. It turned out that they were expecting smuggled horses and did not want strangers around as witnesses. What a brisk scenario all in one night on the dark border!

Next morning we were shown the way to the station. I purchased our tickets to Nitra, in Slovakia, where we found the Lutheran teacher. Late that night we were taken by car near the Slovak-Hungarian border. A little boy of ten guided us from then on. We crossed through vineyards and walked on to the village inside Hungary. By now it was daylight. I bought our train tickets to Budapest. As we were waiting for the train, a Hungarian gendarme appeared. I engaged him in conversation in Hungarian, while my two companions made themselves scarce in the men's room. The train arrived, and I saw with horror that instead of following me, my dear student was climbing into the wagon coming from Slovakia and subject to passport control. Sure enough, he was caught and returned to Slovakia. With exceptional luck and the help of the Yugoslav consulate, he reached the Hungarian capital in two days.

In Budapest the Czech underground functioned in the building of the French embassy. This was the Vichy embassy, under the shadow of the Nazis, yet its officials helped the Allied cause. Here was the center of a network where Czech and Slovak patriots were provided with food and lodging and were sent on the next leg of the underground railroad to Belgrade in Yugoslavia. Room and board were secured in Hungarian homes on a strictly business basis. The landlords were told that their tenants were Polish. This was less risky, as Hungary and Poland, the two remnants of feudalism in Europe, felt some affinity toward each other.

I accompanied the fugitive men from the French embassy to their various lodgings, ran errands for them, negotiated with landlords and visited the apartments where our men were staying. In one apartment I overheard the owners planning to double the rent or else report our suspicious group to the police. We cleared that billet in a hurry. At one particular place the landlady sentimentally insisted on hearing the Polish national anthem. We obliged by singing an old street song entitled "The fairy tale of youth shall never return," standing at attention with solemn faces. The lady was near tears.

At times I not only purchased the men's railroad tickets to Szeged near the Yugoslav border, but also accompanied them. On one occasion we were betrayed by a chauffeur and were surrounded by police the moment we arrived. The men claimed they never saw me before. Eventually they were thrown out of the country, luckily toward Yugoslavia.

I was interrogated for hours in the infamous Star Prison of Szeged. There I received the first slaps in the face; they stung like the paprika for which Szeged is famous. I spent the night in jail with a bunch of prostitutes who demanded my underwear and silk stockings—or else. I handed them over; I did not want to be scratched or beaten or forcibly infected with their specialties. Next morning I kept insisting that I came to Szeged to inquire about the university, as all Czech universities had been forcibly closed by the Nazis. My interrogators were not buying the story. Their chief, by the name of Mr. Virág (meaning flower), took me to the university for a confrontation. There I must have said the right things because they were willing to admit me for the fall semester. For good measure I haggled over the transfer of credits. Mr. Virág took me back to the prison. He seemed to be satisfied and said that he would release me if I promised that I would return to the town where I was born. That was formerly in Czechoslovakia but now under Hungarian occupation. I agreed.

I was put on the train with a secret service escort, who was supposed to deliver me to the police for "supervised residency." That was not a healthy outlook. When we were changing trains in Budapest, I asked to go to the ladies' room. This was my only chance. I shed my winter coat, tied my scarf around my waist as an apron, grabbed a broom and a pail, and exited through the window. I found myself in a tiny space with large garbage bins and only one door, leading to the restuarant. I walked calmly through it, placed the broom and pail at the street exit, removed my handbag from the pail, wound the scarf around my shoulders and hailed the first taxi. I was afraid to go to the French embassy, so I directed the cab to the Yugoslav one; from there I called my people.

At a meeting that night it was decided that my usefulness in Budapest had ended, and I took the next transport of men to Yugoslavia. This time it was the line through a place called Kiskunhalas, since the Szeged line had been compromised. From the station a number of sleighs took us through the Hungarian flatlands southward. There were close to thirty of us, all men except myself and another girl. It was a freezing night; I never knew that cold could hurt so much. Many of us ended up with frozen extremities. My right foot took over a year to heal, and I would feel the pain for years to come. After several hours in the sleighs, our hired guide pointed to the dark line on the horizon:

"Those woods are Yugoslavia." The sleighs turned back.

We started walking in the deep snow. Next to me was trudging Karel, a fellow student from Prague, also bound for the Czech army. We ran into each other in Budapest; now we supported each other. Perhaps because of the bitter cold no Hungarian border guards were in sight. Finally, the woods. We were exhilarated. Two men climbed up on a watchtower and hollered into the icy night:

"Hey, Yugoslavs, come and get us!"

We clambered under some barbed wires and continued southwards among the trees. In a while there was another set of barbed wires. After almost an hour, suddenly a towering figure blocked our way. A huge hunk of a man, in a uniform overcoat down to his ankles, with a fur hat, and a gun lifted high above his head by both arms, boomed at us:

"Stoj. Tu bratska Jugoslavija," "Stop. This is brotherly Yugoslavia." He hugged and kissed us. We reached freedom. He and his comrades were expecting us, as they had been expecting every Czech transport twice a week. They all welcomed us with open arms. We were given hot tea well laced with rakija, the Serbian vodka, bread and sausages, and warm bunks on which to lay our weary bones. The soldiers covered us with woolen blankets as if we were their babies. They called us brother Czechs and juicily cursed the Germans. The giant homeguard who first had met us discovered that we were misled by the Hungarian guide. The woods were not the frontier. The watchtower and the first set of barbed wires were still inside Hungary. The son of a bitch of a paid guide just did not want to risk his neck for the last few miles. On the other hand, the second set of wires was connected to a bell that rang at the Yugoslav border patrol, so they knew exactly when to go out and get us in from the cold before we went astray. Brotherly Yugoslavia indeed.

Next morning we were in Belgrade, where our welcome by the natives and the Czechoslovak ethnics was equally warm. We were lodged at the Czechoslovak House, a cultural center with library, gymnasium, theatre and a good kitchen. The men spent two or three days there, sleeping on mattresses in the auditorium, before they were sent on their way through Greece to Beirut in Lebanon. From there they sailed to Agde, France, and joined the armed forces fighting the Germans.

About two dozen Czech women in exile lived in the attic of the house, helping with the chores of cooking, sewing, office work and all that was connected with expediting the transports. The undertaking was financed through the generosity and patriotism of the Czechoslovak ethnics living in

Yugoslavia. The nerve center was under the management of the Czech underground. The Yugoslav authorities knew well what was going on but closed both eyes to it.

Twice weekly there were unforgettable sentimental moments. The men were already soldiers, having gone through their physical and having passed their security checks. After a hearty dinner, with the women sitting among the men, we sang songs that tie young people together even if they hardly knew each other; we lived for the same cause. There was always somebody who played the piano, guitar or banjo. At ten it was time to part. The girls started in on the well-known Czech song "Long winding is the road to the West," and hardly an eye remained dry. We all felt the solemnity of the moment, as our men shook hands; some kissed us good-bye. How many would never return from that long road that led them through half of Europe and across the Mediterranean, so they could join in the struggle for the liberation of their beloved country?

Important government officials and high ranking officers passed this way, among them cabinet ministers and generals. Jan Smudek, who shot two Gestapo men and was hunted under a German warrant for his arrest, also came through here. But most were young men who wanted to fight for their country. They had been prevented from doing so before Munich by the pusillanimous and blind foreign policy of France and England. Now they risked their necks several times over before they could even join the fighting forces against the occupiers of their homes.

Photographs were not allowed, so they remained only in the eyes of my memory. My friend Karel was among the lucky ones who made it back from the wars, richer by a British war bride. The old Slovak farmer, himself a guide on our line, came through just a few days after his sons did. Two boys, so young that they were offered a chance to remain in Belgrade and finish high school first. But poet Jan Machálek and his sixteen-year-old pal Pepík Holub were so insistent that they were allowed to meet their fate; they both gave their lives for freedom. I forwarded Jan's last poems to his girl back home. I recall old Pop Vavřinec, the caretaker of the Czechoslovak House, with his steel-rimmed spectacles sliding down his nose, his curly moustachio, his rattling bundle of keys, as he shuffled like Saint Peter toward the inner sanctum of the wine cellar, to ration out the *crno vino* on special occasions. Twice a week he shed his tears for our boys. "Just as our legionnaires in the first war," he kept saying, "those also had to fight the Germans east and west."

Thus the weeks passed and turned into months. Fewer men were able to escape, and our activities were winding down. The women were moved out of the capital under German diplomatic pressure. Only Martha B. and I remained. For a while I was moonlighting as a nightclub singer. Then Martha and I were given jobs at the local branch of the Škoda Works, the Yugoškoda. That was a precarious situation, because one German executive most likely was a plant from the Gestapo, ordered to watch over those Slavic Schweiks. There was talk of a German attack on Yugoslavia. The Czech women were evacuated to the Middle East and later to North Africa. A few joined their husbands and brothers in England.

Under pressure the Yugoslav government signed a pact with Germany. But within a couple of days the popular outcry against it led to the military overthrow of regent Paul. On March 27, 1941, young king Peter II was carried on his people's shoulders in the streets. Masses shouted in unison: "Bolje rat nego pakt," "Rather war than the pact." Then for a few days all was quiet. But it was the same quiet I had experienced after the Prague demonstrations at the funeral of the martyred student Jan Opletal in 1939, just before our universities were forcibly closed and hundreds of our students shot and taken to concentration camps. Belgrade was proclaimed an open city. People by the thousands were streaming in with their children, understanding that open cities would not be bombed.

Saturday evening, April 5, I was walking with friends in Kalemegdan Park, overlooking the joining of the Danube with the Sava. The waters were rolling lazily as they had for hundreds of years. Flowers were in bloom, and blue skies were smiling on lovers walking arm in arm. We had dinner at the Kazbek, where the food was good and the music even better. Well past midnight, on our way home, we saw army columns marching out of the city. One of us recognized a lieutenant:

"Where are you going?" we asked.

"We are evacuating the city," he replied. "We are the last ones. There is not a soldier left in Belgrade."

The Yugoslavs complied with the rules of an open city. As I was sinking into an uneasy sleep, I wondered whether the Germans could be trusted to play fair and by the law.

Next morning, Easter Sunday, I was awakened before 7:00 A.M. by bombs raining upon us. From my balcony I saw swarms of planes circling and dropping their deadly cargo on the open city. More and more were approaching. One block in front of me a bomb hit the headquarters of the newspaper *Politika.* The ground was shaking, the sirens were wailing and the planes were emitting an eerie screeching noise that made the blood freeze in my veins. But there was no defense action, for it was an open city.

My roommate and I huddled in the basement with the rest of the tenants. The waves of planes were coming toward us, the sounds of their motors and their screamers in a crescendo louder and louder. The corner of our house was shaved off by a hit. I felt a tremendous pain shooting into my ear and it was bleeding. We were covered with falling debris. Nobody who did not live through it can have an idea of what it feels like to sit helplessly and wait to be blasted apart. This "carpet bombing" continued for over an hour. My friend Michael from the Yugoškoda and his wife Rose appeared from nowhere in the midst of this inferno, and together we started on the obstacle course out of the city. Bombs were still falling as we clambered over tons of broken glass, next to dead people and burning houses, among the stream of humanity fleeing for life. It took us the whole day to cover three miles.

That Easter Sunday I saw sights that seemed the fantasies of a deranged mind. The front of a building was denuded, like a toy house. In an upper room a woman sat playing the harp, with a peaceful smile on her face, singing. Two legs were sticking out of a bathtub; death is not choosy, it will take you anywhere. A man was thrown by the blast from the sixth floor, made a few cartwheels and started running; but after a few steps he collapsed dead. A mother kissing the fingers of her dead baby; a father hitting his youngster because he would not let go of his bicycle, a useless burden in streets strewn with broken glass. A new wave of planes. We are running opposite their direction. The bombs fall behind us. We are hurled to the ground by air pressure. When the dust clears, everything is white. White? Are we out of our minds? A warehouse of flour exploded. Confusion, bewilderment, chaos. Crying, shouting, screaming, wailing. Pieces of bodies all over the place, trunks without heads. A horse with a bleeding neck is running straight at us. And still another wave of planes with their deadly manna in our wilderness, the harvest of man's inhumanity to man.

In that year there was no spring. Spring was canceled in 1941.

King Peter did not have a long reign. He and his government joined the Free Czechoslovak, Belgian, Dutch, Norwegian, Danish and other governments in exile in London.

I headed north, back to Slovakia, to see if there was anything I could do there. Life is stranger than the most unlikely fiction. Crossing the Danube near the Hungarian border at Novi Sad on a makeshift pontoon bridge, I faced the Hungarian authorities. They were in a hurry to carve a chunk out of prostrated Yugoslavia. As I started into my prefabricated story about having lost all my documents in the bombing, a man pulled me out of the line. Mr. Virág, whose agent I had escaped at the Budapest station! I was a dead duck. His hands were grabbing my arm like a noose.

"Don't be afraid and don't talk," was all he said. He took me across the new border into Hungarian-occupied territory and deposited me at an inn. I was told not to leave it. I tried, but it was swarming with uniforms and secret police. At dawn Mr. Virág came to my small room. I was sure he wanted to rape me. I knew I would fight and he would shoot me. Who would give a damn? I was an illegal without papers, and he was the big boss of all those men at the inn and at the border crossings. He handed me a sandwich instead. He took my coat and said:

"Hurry. Pretend we are old friends. Do not contradict anything I say."

We entered an official car with two civilians already there. We drove through the night. At the frontier Mr. Virág just rolled down the window, said "me and three," the guards saluted, and we were on our way. Just before Szeged the car stopped, and Mr. Virág bid me adieu in a gracious manner. I never saw him again. I have no idea why he helped me. Perhaps I was to be his insurance in case his side lost the war. After the war I tried to get in touch with him. My letters were returned marked "addressee unknown." Perhaps Virág was his cover name.

5

Keeping the Divers Alive

The Dutch resistance movement was a complex organization. Its various sections engaged in different anti-Nazi activities. They eliminated German collaborators or liberated political prisoners; they received agents, arms and ammunition from Great Britain and broadcast information on German troop movements to the Allies; they carried out sabotage against German targets.

*A large group was in charge of the divers (*onderduikers *or people who dove under, that is, went into hiding). Divers could be Jews or people persecuted for political reasons, resistance members whose covers had been "blown," or men and women who refused to be cornered for forced labor in Germany. The National Organization for Assistance to Divers (LO) was founded in 1942 by a housewife, Mrs. H. Th. Kuipers-Rietberg, a mother of five who eventually was deported and died in Ravensbrück, and the Calvinist minister F. Slomp. A special unit, the National Action Group (LKP), was assigned the task of procuring and distributing false identification papers and ration coupons for the divers. They often had to raid government offices for the blanks or make up their own with falsified seals, stamps and forms.*

Leesha Bos, a Jewish girl just out of high school, herself with false Aryan papers, was one of the 1,500 members of this section. She was a nurse in Heemstede, a Haarlem suburb. When her LKP supervisor, Fritz van Dongen, was arrested (and later tortured to death in prison), she was called upon to take over his dangerous job. She rode and pushed her bicycle in pouring rain twenty miles to get to Leiden, arriving "drenched, exhausted, frozen and hungry" to the place of Eddy, her contact.

Leesha Bos' parents and brother Jackie were murdered in Auschwitz, her brother Paul in Sobibor. Soon after the war she married Canadian Captain Isaac B. Rose. For many

Eddy stood up and introduced me: "I sent for Leesha Bos to come here immediately. I had originally put her in Heemstede where she has been our contact in the region and where she had fulfilled her duties fearlessly and effectively. She worked closely with Fritz and knew him very well. Now, Leesha, Victor will tell you what we have in mind for you."

It was obvious that Victor was the leader of the group. Subsequently I learned that he was called *Zwarte* (Black) Vic, since he was dark-complexioned and he always wore black boots and a black leather jacket. He stood up, began pacing up and down the room, and then spoke to me in a direct, authoritarian manner:

"Fritz, and now we will call him by his real name. Reinier van Kampenhout, and his wife, were picked up yesterday when the Germans raided his home. They found stolen ration cards, underground news bulletins, short-wave radios, and many guns. It was a stroke of bad luck for him and devastating for all of us. We will find out where the Nazis are keeping him and then we will try to get him out to freedom. I am sure of one thing. They will not get any information out of him. He is strong; Leesha, you know that.

"He was responsible for the needs of nearly two hundred hidden Jews and non-Jews. He provided them with food, ration cards, payments for their lodgings, and even supplementary food rations. His capture is a lamentable loss for us.

"Leesha, we asked you to come here to fill the void left by Reinier. We know your abilities, you must take his place. We will help you and give you full cooperation, but we must tell you that there is no existing list of people he took care of. He was so concerned not to carry incriminating information with him that he kept everything in his head. We have only a few names that we know for sure. You will have the difficult task of proceeding very carefully to find the other hidden people and to reconstruct the list.

"We don't know the contacts yet; you cannot trust anyone. But somehow the people who take care of the 'hidden' will find you, since they cannot exist without your help. It will be very dangerous work on your part, and we wish you good luck. Here are the six names we have. Look up these people tomorrow. I'm sure more will follow in no time at all."

I sat there, listening to him, overwhelmed. How could I possibly do all that Reinier had done? How will I ever discover the names and addresses of the hidden people and get food and money to them in time?

Vic said: "Don't worry, you'll do all right. You'll start right away in the morning. Do you have a bicycle?"

When he heard that my bike had one wooden tire he promised to get me

"Keeping the Divers Alive" is from Leesha Rose, *The Tulips are Red* (South Brunswick, N.J. and New York: A. S. Barnes, 1979), pp. 207-18. Reprinted with the permission of Oak Tree Publications, San Diego, Calif.

one with rubber tires. Then he informed me that he might need me for special activities in his LKP. . . .

Everything had happened so fast. So much had occurred since the long and trying trip from Heemstede, and now a new and heavy responsibility was suddenly resting on my shoulders. I was nervous and perturbed.

Vic waited for me at the corner while I got my suitcase and bicycle, and we left for my next base of operations: the house of the Kruizingas on the Endegeesterstraat weg in Oegstgeest, a little suburb town and an extension of Leiden.

It was a little house almost at the end of a street that connected with the highway. Tom Kruizinga was a psychiatric orderly in the mental hospital down the road. Ada, his wife, who was much younger than her husband, took care of their small daughter. Miep, and a number of people hidden in their house, which was also used as a meeting place for some of the Resistance workers. In the attic, six people were hidden and more could be brought in an emergency.

From the moment I met Ada, I felt so much more at ease. She was a sweet and friendly person, tall and blond, with a ready smile on her face. Nothing bothered her, and she took everything in stride. After Vic left, Ada showed me to a small studylike room in the front that faced the street.

"This is where you'll sleep, on the couch. You can use part of the closet. Please join us now in the family room. You have time to unpack."

The large table in the center of the family room was used for meals, for preparing food, for work, and for conferences. It was the only room that had a heating stove and where an oil lamp burned at night. The house itself usually buzzed with activity, with young people coming and going through the back door. I was introduced to everyone but no one revealed anything about his underground activities. We belonged to the same group, each one had a different task to perform, and it was far wiser for everyone not to know too much.

When Tom Kruizinga came home from work at the mental hospital, we went to my room and talked about the mission that lay before me. He had the greatest admiration for Reinier, and he, too, was apprehensive about the consequences of his capture:

"The Nazis had known exactly where to look and they found a lot of incriminating evidence. It could have been a betrayal from close by—Leesha, I have my suspicions. Please, be careful! Reinier was very popular as a leader. It could have been some rival who betrayed him. It is a tightrope we are walking on, working in the Resistance and exposing ourselves to danger every minute of the day and night. We are deeply involved and we have to wait and watch for the next move. Let's hope it was not a traitor from within our organization, because then nobody will be safe. In the meantime we have to go on with our tasks."

After listening to my doubts about the delicate detective work ahead of me, he assured me:

"Look, you can only do your very best. Go easy, that way you will not arouse suspicion. I am sure that within a few weeks you will have added even more *onderduikers* [hidden people] to your care than Reinier had. I will help you with information and in every possible way. Leesha, I am glad you are here. Welcome to our house."

I felt so much better. Tom and Ada Kruizinga were exactly the kind of people I needed at that moment: trustworthy, strong, and friendly. They had no way of knowing the impact and depth of my friendship with Reinier. I felt lost without him, as if a safe protective membrane had been brutally torn away from me, and I had been left raw and exposed. But there was no time for such thoughts now.

We joined the others in the family room just as Black Vic came in with Hans and Phil. They were all so excited. They had just executed a daring mission. Under the cover of darkness they had broken into Reinier's house and rescued from the hidden part of the cellar a small transmitter, more weapons, and radios. This was a terrific coup, and they had already brought the items to various hiding places.

"That's a good sign, Leesha," he said. "At least the Nazis won't get their dirty hands on these treasures."

Later that night in my bed all alone and half-frozen with cold, I listened to the howling wind outside. Each little noise startled me but I did not move, trying to preserve the little warmth generated by my body. I forced myself to sleep. I needed it so badly. . . .

* * *

Tom Kruizinga was right. It did not take three weeks, and I had recovered the names of about one hundred and fifty hidden Jewish and Gentile people whom I took under my care. It started very slowly with the six names I got from Vic. I went to visit them right away, and when they realized who I was their gratefulness and relief were so intense that I was almost embarrassed by their expressions of thanks. They had been petrified lest they be forgotten and unattended. All the Gentile people who were hiding Jews in their homes knew someone else who was also hiding Jews or knew someone who could lead me to the right person.

I could not find a moment's rest for myself, as I worked at my job relentlessly. The idea that someone might be in need, and I could not reach him, drove me on to increasing activity. It weighed heavily on my conscience and left me no peace of mind. I started talking to shopkeepers, grocers or bakers and the florists about Reinier. My questions about what had actually happened there, whether anyone had ever heard from him since he was imprisoned, brought forth various reactions. Very often the shopkeeper would tell me that many people were suffering because of his capture. That was a sign for me and the following day I would go to him when he was alone and very delicately persuade him to reveal where I could find the hidden people in need of help.

My *onderduikers*—the hidden people I took care of—were eagerly looking forward to seeing me. Very often I was the only outside person whom they saw in their isolation. I brought them news and stories from the outside. I supplied them with food ration cards, by special arrangements with Vic. Sometimes I brought them extra food that the Resistance requisitioned by raiding farms or other storage areas, to supplement their meager rations.

I was shocked to see the pitiful condition of most of the people in hiding. The starvation diet of less than five-hundred calories a day had left them skinny, weak, and without resistance to sickness. They looked grey and waxen from being shut in and shabby in their old torn clothes, and they smelled unwashed as a result of their lack of soap and laundry detergent.

People started eating strange dishes never intended for human consumption: sugar beets, fodder beets, tulip bulbs, spinach, and other vegetable seeds. None of these foods satisfied the pangs of hunger, whereas they caused terrible gas pains. Small babies and the very old suffered most from hunger and underfeeding. The icy and freezing winter weather intensified their suffering. The death toll rose at an alarming rate. Wood for coffins was scarce, and the dead were often buried in cardboard boxes or blankets.

One morning I was confronted with a tragic problem. When I came to see an aged couple, the grocer in whose attic they were hidden informed me that the old man had died during the night. The interment had to be done clandestinely after curfew. The grocer was distressed:

"What shall I do? He cannot be buried at the Christian cemetery; one must have a plot. It's also too dangerous. People know me and they will ask questions. I'm so glad you came today, Leesha. What do you advise me to do?"

"First, let's talk to his wife. She has to be informed of whatever we intend to do," I said.

The little old Jewish lady was grief-stricken. I tried to calm her, and together with the grocer we decided that there was really no other way but to bury him temporarily somewhere on the outskirts of Oegstgeest. After the war she could reinter him wherever she wished. She cried bitterly.

"Even in death the Nazis rob us of our dignity!"

I promised to be present that night at the burial, even though it meant breaking curfew and being subject to search by the German nightly patrol.

A storm was raging in full force as I walked by myself to the appointed place on the edge of a meadow. I had to cross a narrow moat in order to join the grocer and his two sons at the tree that marked the place of burial. They took turns digging the grave, working quietly but with great speed. The rain turned the fertile Dutch soil into a clinging paste, making their labor doubly difficult. Finally the hole was large enough to slide in the body, wrapped in a sack. They had carried the dead man from the house, since there was no wagon available for transportation.

That nightmare, my first burial, became symbolic of our deteriorating and hopeless situation.

Would we survive this blackness that was gradually choking off our last breath of life?

It was so dark I could hardly make out the contours of the men as they left. I followed them guided by the sound of their steps. Suddenly I felt no ground under me. Panic went through me as I was sinking up to my shoulders in the icy water of the moat. The men heard my cry and reached down to pull me out. For my protection the grocer wrapped around me the same blanket that had been used for the dead man. Nevertheless the rain and the freezing wind were biting through me, and by the time I got home, a half hour later, my body was shaking, my teeth chattering, and my clothes were frozen wet around me.

To judge from Ada Kruizinga's reaction I must have looked like a ghost. I wanted to say something, but I could not coordinate my words. She put me to bed right away, and everything went blank. Afterwards I recollected feeling fiery heat that alternated with shivering iciness while I battled frightening images.

When I opened my eyes, I saw Ada. "Hi, sleepyhead," she greeted me. "Did you have a good rest for two days?" You have had a serious attack of the flu, and we called Dr. Hogenholz to see you. What a nice man he is, he didn't even want to charge anything for his visit. He is known to be very helpful to the Underground Resistance."

I was so grateful to Ada for taking care of me. When I started to thank her, she made me stop. But something bothered me and I had to ask her.

"Ada, when I was delirious, did I give away all my secrets?," I joked with her. She answered lightly:

"You mumbled nonsense. I couldn't make any sense out of it. Don't worry about it!" She avoided my eyes.

Did she find out I was Jewish? I was sure it was safe with her for she said I should not worry about it. As soon as I could stand on my feet I got back to my work, still shaky and coughing, but I had to help my people—they were counting on me.

Gradually I became accepted as an integral part of the Resistance group located at the Kruizingas and led by Black Vic. I kept him informed of my progress and shared all my problems with him. He was obviously relieved that I felt so responsible about detecting all the hidden people and providing them with the necessary care.

"Leesha. I told you that you would succeed because you have the right personality to do this kind of work. I have other important things to do," he added impatiently. . . .

He continued: "Three weeks ago we blew up the railway tracks at Warmond when a convoy of V-1 missile weapons was being transported. That was something! The raids on the distribution offices have to be executed regularly to keep you and the other workers supplied with food ration cards for your hidden people. And then the raids we carried out on farms of the NSB*-Nazi sympathizers who still have meats, fats, potatoes, and vegetables, for distribution to the hidden people. Do you know, now that the railway men are unemployed, we must feed them too? We have enough problems, believe me—and the end of the war is still not in sight."

"Vic, you never told me about it, but did you ever find out anything about the whereabouts of Reinier? You mentioned on that first night that we met about raiding the police station or the prison."

He got up and started his usual nervous pacing: "That's a sad story and I didn't want to make you feel worse than you do already; I know how closely you worked together. Unfortunately, we can't track him down. The Nazis transported him from one prison to another in quick succession. The Germans know they caught in important Resistance leader, and the security around him has been very tight. But I am still trying."

He looked at me more intently and asked: "Would you like to assist us in some 'event' soon? I need you. Your face is not known around Leiden. It will be right to use you." I agreed, and he said he would let me know.

A few nights later Vic, Hans, and Phil came into the house and talked around the table long after everyone had retired. I heard the rustling of papers through the sliding doors that partitioned off my small front room from the living room.

I heard instructions being given. I caught words like guard, door, window, vault; names of people and street names. The men sounded very excited. I wondered whether they were preparing the action in which I would be involved, too. Would Vic call on me? I knew that any raid the LKP performed would be dangerous. It could mean that any or all of us could be caught if something went wrong.

But I felt as if something beyond my control was driving me to become part of every action that would mean resistance to the long years of oppression. This, in spite of the demoralizing hunger and the increasing danger of betrayal. For the Germans encouraged the NSB-Dutch Nazis to report any suspicious persons in return for money or extra rations. I did not fear exposing myself to serious danger. My firm intention of defying the enemy drove me to take any risk, a feeling that increased even after what I had heard about the atrocities in the concentration camps.

I had closed my mind to thinking about my family, but I could not block out my subconscious. Many nights I woke up crying and my body shook

*National Socialistische Beweging on National Socialist Movement, the Dutch Nazi Party under Anton Mussert.

with feelings of anguish, longing, and love for my family. My heart cried out:

"Oh God, hear me, help me. Please . . . I am ready to bring any sacrifice but let them live. Please let them all return . . . I beg You . . . let them return . . . ," and I would cry myself to sleep.

* * *

The following day Vic was very nervous. He paced back and forth and did not eat a thing. When Tom Kruizinga pointed out to him that it was a pity and a sin not to eat the food, Vic said:

"Tomorrow something big is coming up. I won't sleep here tonight." On the way out he said to me:

"Stay here tomorrow morning. You'll hear from me."

At about 9:00 A.M. Hans brought a message from Vic, and we went together to yet another meeting place of Black Vic and the LKP group. There were about twelve young men plus Julie* and myself in the room.

The foul-smelling ersatz "black-grass" cigarettes made it difficult to breathe in the room. Vic had just finished explaining something to the others. He turned to me:

"Leesha, it's good that you are here. The news is that we are going to raid the Rotterdamse Bank on the Rapenburg at around twelve noon. By that time the people in charge of the soup kitchen will have deposited their day's receipts in the bank. We need that money desperately for our unemployed railway men.

"You and Julie will stand across the street from the bank and be on the lookout for either the police or the Nazis. Our action won't take more than ten minutes. We have it all figured out and very well organized and coordinated with the help of an employee of the bank. Hans will stand at the entrance outside the bank. You and Julie will make-believe that you are talking to each other. If you see either a policeman or a Nazi, wave your hand and call out: 'Yoohoo,' as if you see someone and you want to say hello.

"Hans will give the alarm sign to us, inside. That's all you two girls will have to do. When the raid is over and you see us come out, leave the scene as fast as you can and head for a safe place. Understand?"

We waited until everyone had left one by one on their bikes, which had been leaning against the wall of the house. Finally, Julie and I left separately.

It was a cold but clear day, and I peddled against the wind until I got to the Rapenburg, right across from the Rotterdamse Bank. Julie arrived, and we positioned ourselves facing each other, making believe we were talking

*Another member of the group, often used as a messenger.

and holding on to our bikes while we scrutinized the street. Soon we saw our men going in, one by one, with Hans remaining outside the entrance.

Julie and I were nervously talking to each other: "No, nobody. I see no one. . . . I see no sign of police. I hope everything will go alright. Vic is O.K. He researched everything meticulously. Oh God, let no Nazi come now! I hope the boys make out alright, so that no one will get hurt!"

After what seemed like ages, but in reality was only minutes, the boys came out two and three at a time, some of them with briefcases. Everything had gone O.K.!

Julie and I jumped on our bicycles and raced away in opposite directions. As I came to the Oude Singel, I saw two big green German vans standing on either side of the canal. The soldiers had cordoned off the street and everyone passing on foot or on bicycle was asked to show identity papers and was frisked for weapons or black market food.

Oh, I was in trouble! I had a small gun in my belt, about fifty ration cards rolled up in my bra, and two blank identity cards. Such evidence of illegality would incriminate me without a question.

I spotted the danger but I saw no way out, not even an alleyway I could turn into. I quickly made a complete U-turn and started to race against the traffic. One of the German soldiers saw me and started yelling: "Halt! Halt!" he grabbed a bicycle and raced after me.

I was desperate. If he caught up with me it would be the end of me. Who could help me now? Like a flash I got an idea and began to whistle the first four notes of Beethoven's *Fifth Symphony* in C minor. This was a whistle we used in the underground: if there was a friend nearby he would answer me with the second part of the phrase: "bum bum bum bum."

As if from heaven I heard a whistle answering me and then a crash of bicycles, shouting angry voices and cursing in German:

"*Verfluchte leute!*" Damned people!"

The oncoming cyclists kept to the right of the road leaving me a path. I raced against traffic and as I turned the corner I looked behind and saw a pile-up of bicycles with the pursuing German caught in the middle.

I ducked in and out of side streets till I reached the home of the Kruizingas. When I finally caught my breath again, I related my adventure of the day to Ada. I could not get over my miraculous escape. Ada was so happy:

"You see, Leesha, there are some wonderful people in this world. You have to keep on believing."

That night Vic was the hero of the hour, as he told the story of the raid on the branch of the Rotterdamse Bank on the Rapenburg and how he had planned for whole procedure:

"When our twelve LKP men entered the bank, one by one, I went over to a little man guarding the vault and I said to him: 'In the name of the Prince of Orange raise your hands' and I stuck a gun in his ribs. The frightened little man put up his hands and started singing: *"Oranje boven"* —"The House of Orange* I hold high."

"When the cashier saw two of us approaching his window, he threw everything down and fled. Then we confronted the bank director with two guns under his nose, and he had to hand over the money. We pushed all the people in the bank, including the employees, into the vault, while we quickly packed away fl. 95,000 into our briefcases. After we finished, we let the director and the rest of the people out of the vault. We assembled them against the wall, and I said to them:

"Gentlemen, this is not a theft or a burglary. This is a raid executed by the Underground Resistance movement. This money, instead of going to the Nazis, will be given to people in hiding whose lives we are saving and to the railway people who are now unemployed. Long live the Queen."

We could not stop discussing the exciting events. We were making so much noise that Tom Kruizinga sent one of our group to be on guard around the house, for he was afraid we might attract unwelcome visitors. Then he took out a bottle, and we each drank a glass of wine. He said:

"Boys and girls, I am still saving a bottle of real Dutch 'Bols' gin to celebrate the end of the war and the end of the Nazi occupation and persecution."

We fell quiet, each one filled in his own thoughts. We almost heard the unspoken question: "When?"

*The House of Orange is the ruling dynasty in the Netherlands.

6

Their Brothers' and Sisters' Keepers

On November 6, 1957, the Anti-Defamation League of B'nai B'rith in New York dedicated a bronze plaque to commemorate the "Christian Heroes who helped their Jewish brethren escape the Nazi terror." It was unveiled most appropriately by a woman, who as a member of the French resistance had helped Jesuit Father Pierre Chaillet save hundreds of Jewish children. She was Madame Marie Helene Lefaucheux, member of the Légion d'Honneur and French delegate to the United Nations.

At the same ceremony the book Their Brothers' Keepers *was presented to the guests, among them many survivors and their Christian rescuers. Ten years in preparation, the book is based on interviews with eyewitnesses in several countries; its documentation is especially rich on further sources. The following selection is its chapter dealing with women of various nationalities in the resistance movements against the Nazis.*

The hymn to the heroic non-Jewish women who risked their lives for the victims of Nazi barbarism is yet to be written and the song is yet to be sung. It would require more than can be told in the pages of one book to call the roll of the women of many nations, political persuasions, and varying social strata who gave their time, their wealth, even their lives for those who had been marked by Hitler for extermination. Behind each proud name cited in these chapters stand the nameless, anonymous legions of women whose inspiring acts will live as long as the conscience of mankind is disturbed by the remembrance of the murderous Hitler era.

Anna Simaite was a Lithuanian, rather on the stout side, with a broad peasant face, and flaxen hair which she parted in the middle and braided into a coil to crown her head. In her early childhood Anna had many Jewish friends and classmates. Among her favorite authors was the famous Polish writer Eliza Orzeszkowa, who wrote a number of stories about Jews and whose distinguished novel *Meir Ezofowicz* treated the Jew with compassion and love. Her grandfather, a liberal, broad-minded man, taught the girl to consider the Jews objectively and not through the distorted vision of bigotry and anti-Semitism. When Anna entered high school in Riga, she joined a Social Revolutionary underground organization aimed at destroying the tsarist regime that spread its tentacles from faraway St. Petersburg. Later, she studied at the Teachers' Seminary in Moscow, and after graduation became completely absorbed in the plight of the underprivileged, choosing to devote her life to the children of the poor.

But soon after the outbreak of World War II, we find Anna Simaite in charge of the cataloguing department of the old and famed Vilna University. She was counted among the best literary critics in Lithuania; her position and reputation were secure if she chose to remain silent. But Anna Simaite chose to fight. Ten years later, after the guns had been stilled and weeds had grown high over the shattered brick and mortar of the walled-in ghettos, Anna explained her compulsion to act. "When the Germans forced Jews of Vilna into a ghetto, I could no longer go on with my work. I could not remain in my study. I could not eat. I was ashamed that I was not Jewish myself. I had to do something. I realized the danger involved, but it could not be helped. A force much stronger than myself was at work."

Obsessed with the notion that only by helping the Jews could she fulfill herself as a human being. Anna Simaite turned toward the ghetto. Non-Jews were prohibited from entering this reservation where the Jews of Vilna had been immured to suffer briefly before they were exterminated. Anna, the non-Jew, was determined to breach the ghetto walls, to offer her services, to declare her oneness with the sufferers. She appeared before the German authorities and presented them with a singularly innocent plan. In

"Their Brothers' and Sisters' Keepers" is from Philip Friedman, *Their Brothers' Keepers* (New York: Holocaust Library, 1978), pp. 21-32. Reprinted with the permission of the publisher.

the ghetto were books that had been borrowed from the University library some time before by Jewish students. Would the Germans permit her, a conscientious librarian, to go behind the barbed wires and high walls in order to rescue the priceless volumes? The Germans granted her request, and for a few weeks Anna enjoyed a limited immunity. She prowled among the crowded hovels of the ghetto, which had been the slum area of Vilna before the war, offering her aid to the hapless Jews. When the Germans declared that she was taking too much time reclaiming her valuable books, Anna contrived new schemes. As time went on, she became completely absorbed by the feverish life of the ghetto. She visited friends, ran to amateur theatricals and concerts, attended lectures, art exhibits, and teas. She could not get over the fact that the Jews, whom the occupying power had sentenced to death by starvation, torture, and deportation, spent all their waking hours celebrating life.

As Anna went back and forth, she got in touch with people in the Aryan part of the city, people who might risk taking in an old friend languishing in the ghetto. There were those who nodded quick assent, and others who wavered while Anna pleaded with them and tried to infuse them with the courage she possessed in such abundance. And there were those who spat in her face. But she was not to be insulted, intimidated, or diverted from her mission. She sought out hiding places for Jewish children whom she later helped spirit out of the ghetto. She obtained forged Aryan papers for Jews who determined to scale the ghetto walls. She proudly enlisted as a courier, smuggling letters from the leaders of the ghetto Underground to their compatriots outside, letters that could not under any circumstances be sent through the mails. Assisted by a small, valiant group of friends, among them the well-known Lithuanian poet Baruta, Anna carried food to the starving Jews. For those among the decimated ghetto-dwellers who resolved to make a last stand against the enemy, she brought small arms and ammunition. It goes without saying that each article Anna smuggled inside the reservation, she carried at the risk of her life, were it a small gun hidden on her person, or a bouquet of roses for some beauty-starved woman of the desolate ghetto. She came always laden with things and thus did she leave, carrying precious archives, rare books, documents, and scraps of diaries of the martyrdom of the walled-in people to be preserved for another time. She hid the precious objects in the vaults of the Seminar for Lithuanistics at the University.

In April of 1942, Jacob Gens, the commander of the Vilna ghetto, cautioned Anna Simaite that the Gestapo was becoming suspicious of her activities. This warning came at the time when the Germans were launching their campaign for total extermination of the ghetto-dwellers. Anna scorned the commander's warning: her own fate seemed inconsequential in the face of the disaster threatening the Jews. She organized a rescue group in the Aryan sector of the city, determined to save as many Jewish children as possible. She worked tirelessly, bribing guards, wheedling, cajoling, her life as much in danger as the lives of the skeleton children she snatched from the ghetto to hide among non-Jews. For a short time she evaded the Gestapo net by taking shelter among members of the Underground, but in the summer of 1944 the inevitable happened: Anna was seized by the Gestapo. Threatened, beaten, starved, still she betrayed no secrets. Finally she was sentenced to death.

Without Anna's knowledge, the University interceded on her behalf, bribing a high Nazi official. The death sentence was commuted, and Anna was deported to the notorious Dachau concentration camp and later transferred to a camp in Southern France, where the Allied armies found her barely clinging to life. Following the Liberation, she went to Toulouse, penniless, her health shattered. After a period of convalescence in a hospital, Anna found a job as dishwasher in a small restaurant. Despite the fact that she lived the withdrawn life of a refugee, word mysteriously got around that Anna Simaite was in France and in need of help. Messages with offers of aid began to arrive at her flat. The offers came from organizations like the Union of Lithuanian Jews of America, and from individuals to whom her name had become a legend. Determined to earn her own livelihood, Anna Simaite declined the aid. When the job as dishwasher came to an abrupt end, she went to Paris and found employment first in a laundry, then as a doll seamstress, and finally as a librarian.

Anna might have remained in Paris to live out the rest of her days if the news of her survival had not reached some of her former "children." Letters began to arrive from many parts of the world. All of her "children" implored her to come and live with them. One of the most persistent correspondents was Tania Wachsman, a mother of two children, who lived in a *kibbutz* in Israel. "My dear Mother," Tania began each letter, "when will you finally come to us?" Anna hesitated—she did not want to be a burden—but in the end yielded to Tania's pleas.

She arrived in Israel in the spring of 1953. Everywhere in the new republic she was received with flowers and applause. She was feted by the Association of Lithuanian Jews and by the editorial staff of the largest Hebrew daily newspaper, *Davar.* The government of Israel granted her a pension, an honor she refused but eventually agreed to accept. What impressed Anna more than the receptions, flowers, and emoluments was the welcome accorded her by the "children" whom she had helped to survive the ghetto. "It is not possible for me to tell you how much I appreciate this warmhearted reception," she said. "I have not the words. I am here . . . among my kin."

And there she lives, among her "children," in a place called Petah Tikvah —the woman with the peasant face, her gray hair parted smoothly in the center—writing essays, memoirs and articles.

"For me, as a Lithuanian," she says, "it is a very sad thing to admit that not all of my co-nationals, during the years of the Jewish ordeal, showed compassion for the victims. To my great sorrow, it must be admitted that some elements among the Lithuanians even collaborated in the extermination of the Jews." As for the Vilna ghetto where she virtually lived in those terrible days, she has this to say: "How the Jews stood it, I do not know. The Jews of the Vilna ghetto and all other ghettos were great heroes, even if they themselves did not realize it."

It is not possible to call to memory the Vilna ghetto without also invoking the name of Anna Simaite, who stormed its walls, clutching a gun for resistance and a crushed flower for the comfort of some beauty-starved soul.

* * *

The small nunnery was located not far from the Vilna Colony railroad station. During the German occupation there were only seven sisters in this Benedictine convent, all from Cracow. The Mother Superior, a graduate of Cracow University, was a comparatively young woman of thirty-five at the time when the Jews were driven from their homes. Although the convent was too far removed from the ghetto for her to hear the cries of a tortured people, the Mother Superior seemed always to be gazing in that direction, as though she were waiting for a summons. She found it hard to keep her mind on the work which had previously claimed all her time and love, the ministering to the poor and the miserable.

One day she decided that the time had come to act. She summoned the other nuns and, after prayer, they discussed the subject of the ghetto. Not long afterward, as a result of this conversation, a few of the sisters appeared before the gate of the ghetto. The guards did not suspect the nuns of any conspiratorial designs. Eventually contact was established between the convent and the Vilna ghetto, and an underground railroad was formed. The seven nuns became experts in getting Jews out of the ghetto and hiding them at the convent and in other places. At one period it seemed as if the small nunnery were bulging with nuns, some with features unmistakably masculine.

Among those hidden in the convent were several Jewish writers and leaders of the ghetto Underground: Abraham Sutzkever, Abba Kovner, Edek Boraks, and Arie Wilner. Some stayed a long time; others returned to the ghetto to fight and die. When, in the winter of 1941, the Jewish Fighters' Organization was formed, the Mother Superior became an indispensable ally. The Fighters needed arms, and the Mother Superior undertook to supply them. Assisted by the other nuns, she roamed the countryside in search of knives, daggers, bayonets, pistols, guns, grenades. The hands accustomed to the touch of rosary beads became expert with explosives. The first four grenades received gratefully by the Fighters were the gift of the Mother Superior, who instructed Abba Kovner in their proper use, as they were of a special brand unfamiliar to him. She later supplied other weapons. Although she worked selflessly, tirelessly, she felt not enough was being done. "I wish to come to the ghetto," she said to Abba Kovner, "to fight by your side, to die, if necessary. Your fight is a holy one. You are a noble people. Despite the fact that you are a Marxist [Kovner was a member of *Hashomer Hatzair*] and have no religion, you are closer to God than I." Her ardent wish to enter the ghetto to fight and, in the end, to die the martyred death of the Jews was not realized. She was too valuable an ally, and was prevailed upon to remain on the Aryan side. In addition to supplying arms, she also acted as a liaison between the Jewish Fighters' Organization inside the ghetto and the Polish Underground with which they were desperately trying to establish a military partnership. The partnership was never achieved, but this failure was not her fault. And although the battle was lost, she was not the loser. Her heroism was enshrined in the hearts of those who would remember.

* * *

Janina Bucholc-Bukolska was employed in the small firm of Rybczynski on Miodowa Street in Warsaw. The tiny office, which specialized in translations, was always overcrowded. Papers and documents were piled on desks, shelves, and cabinets. The papers were not even remotely connected with translations; they were, in fact, birth certificates, marriage records, school diplomas, food ration cards, letters of recommendation from employers, and all manner of documents and forms. Mrs. Bukolska was a large woman, awkward in movement. Wearing the thick glasses she depended on, she sat calmly in the midst of this chaos of papers and attended busily to her work. Her work, among other things, consisted of supplying false identification cards to Jews. A German policeman would sometimes pass outside the window and gaze curiously at the picture of industry and prosperity inside. Customers were always coming and going. The males among Bukolska's clients invariably wore bushy mustaches and the women displayed peroxide-blonde hair. In fact, not one person entered the office who did not have a Nordic appearance save Mrs. Bukolska herself, and she was the only Gentile in the crowd. All the others had been Aryanized, in appearance at least, before they came to her. They brought with them photographs, fingerprints, and other pertinent information, most of it spurious. Janina Bukolska then had the Aryan identity papers known as *Kennkarten* made up by an expert.

The customers entered her office as Jews and left as Gentiles. But they seldom went out without consulting with Bukolska about a possible place to hide in the Aryan sector. She took down their names. Finding places for the new Aryans to live was one of Bukolska's occupations. This was far from easy, as the Germans offered ten pounds of sugar and a pint of vodka as a reward for surrendering a Jew hiding in the Aryan sector of the city. The punishment for hiding a Jew or helping one to find a place to hide was death.

Mrs. Bukolska shrugged off all obstacles placed in her way. After a busy day at the overcrowded office, she spent her evenings visiting around, ringing doorbells, inquiring whether the good people of Warsaw would consider giving shelter to one of her new Aryans. On occasion she met with a bit of good luck, as she did when Dr. Jan Zabinski, director of the Warsaw zoo, offered her clients some cages vacated by animals that had perished for lack of food. But in most instances she met with reticence, refusal, and abuse; often she was threatened with the Gestapo. Her labors continued, however, and her "business" prospered until the last ghetto hovel had been put to the torch by the Nazis and the last Jew murdered. And even then Pani Janina carried on, for her work was not finished. It came to an end only when the Hitler hordes were driven out of her beloved country.

* * *

A roll call of heroic women who risked their lives to help a cause that appeared lost would not be complete without the mention of Sophia Debicka, Jadzia Duniec, Irena Adamowicz, Janina Plawczynska, and Rena Laterner. Sophia Debicka came from a family of Polish intellectuals and was related to the veteran Socialist leader, Stephanie Sempolowska. She hid several Jewish women in her house, camouflaging them as nurse, seamstress, cook and maid. She seized a little Jewish girl from a transport, declaring the child was her daughter. Her home became an operational base for the Jewish Fighters' Organization of Warsaw. She alerted her friends in the Postmaster's office who examined letters addressed to the Gestapo, to intercept those containing tips from informers about Jews hiding in the Christian sector.

Jadzia Duniec, a Catholic girl of Vilna, did not leave behind a long record of deeds which would memorialize her. She died too young. But for a brief period before the Gestapo captured and executed her, Jadzia served as a courier and liaison between Jewish underground organizations and the outer world. She supplied weapons to the Szeinbaum fighting group in Vilna, and she was often sent to Kaunas and Shavli on errands for the Fighters. She died as she lived, courageously. Her name deserves to be remembered, for she was one of a small, valiant group.

Irena Adamowicz belonged to the same small group. Irena was not so young as Jadzia. She came of a pious, aristocratic Polish family, and before the war she was an executive of the Polish Girl Scouts. During the German occupation she became a courier between the ghettos of Warsaw, Vilna, Kaunas, Shavli, Bialystok, and other cities. Along with several other Christian women, she volunteered for this work that meant certain death if she were captured. Among her co-workers, though Irena probably never met them, were two wrinkled old ladies, Janina Plawczynska and Rena Laterner. Both these venerable ladies were in their seventies. They carried messages between the Fighters and the Polish Underground in Warsaw. After the collapse of the ghetto uprising, they sheltered ten Fighters in a bunker they erected. They perished with the ten Jews.

* * *

Mother Maria of Paris was a Russian woman, born Elizabeth Pilenko. Her grandfather was a Don Cossack general; her grandmother a descendant of a French officer in Napoleon's army. The first woman to be graduated from the Theological Seminary in Russia, Elizabeth became a distinguished poetess and an active Socialist. Soon after her graduation she married, but her married life was tragic. A little daughter died at the age of four, and later the marriage ended in divorce. Elizabeth's second husband was D. E. Skobtzoff, a writer, by whom she had a son, Yuri. After the Bolshevik Revolution the Skobtzoffs left their native Russia and went to live in Paris. In 1932 Elizabeth divorced her second husband and became a nun, taking the name Maria.

She was no longer a young woman when the Nazis overwhelmed France. She was fifty, past the age when one joins with conspirators and those who imperil their lives for one cause or another. But she enlisted readily, out of a strong inner need to help those in greatest jeopardy, the Jews. The reflective poetess, the nun who not long before had withdrawn from the storms and stresses of the world, was in a short time transformed into an exalted partisan of a cause. As she joined the battle, she was certain beyond any doubt that the path she now chose would eventually bring her closer to her God. She took command of a clandestine organization of Greek Orthodox priests for rescuing Jews, particularly children. A small convent in Paris became the headquarters of the group. Liaison was established with the Catholic Underground headed by the Jesuit Father Pierre Chaillet. Food and clothing were collected at the convent and sent to the Jews in the Drancy concentration camp. A hidden mill inside the convent turned out identification papers and German documents for Jews who were still at large. Scores of Jews were given temporary shelter in the Little Cloister until more secure and permanent hiding places could be found for them. In the midst of these feverish activities Mother Maria, who was in full charge, found time to indulge in an old passion, the writing of verse. After the Germans had foisted the Jewish badge on the French, Mother Maria wrote a poem brimming with anger and defiance; the Jewish badge intended by the Nazis as a symbol of humiliation, she cried, was in fact a mark of distinction. Widely circulated among those who read Russian, the poem stirred the Nazis no less than it did its Russian-speaking readers, though for different reasons.

In the early morning of February 7, 1943, a Gestapo man by the name of Hofman came with several guards to the convent on Rue de Lourmel. He demanded to see Mother Maria, and was told he would have to come another time—Mother Maria was out, in the country. The Germans left, but not without taking along Mother Maria's young son Yuri as a hostage. Alarmed by the arrest, Mother Maria returned, and was immediately summoned to Gestapo headquarters. She demanded the release of her son, who was in no way involved in any of her activities.

During the angry interrogation, Hofman turned to the nun's mother, who accompanied her: "You educated your daughter very stupidly," he shouted. "She helps Jews only."

"This is not true," the old woman replied, "She is a Christian who helps those in need. She would even help *you*, if you were in trouble."

"You will never see your daughter again," the Nazi said, by way of concluding the interview.

Mother Maria was arrested and taken to Romainville. Yuri was sent to the Compiègne concentration camp and later to Buchenwald where he was tortured to death. On April 24, 1943, Mother Maria was transferred to the notorious Ravensbrück camp. There were 2,500 women in the cell block where she lived, most of them infested with vermin and suffering from dysentery and typhus. She helped where she could, with a morsel of food, a kind word, a prayer. Weakened as her body was by the ravages of hunger, disease, and torture, she continued to minister to the women, moving about in the filthy, tightly packed barracks like a disembodied shadow. She was a tight-lipped, grim witness to Nazi barbarism. Daily she watched the guards come to fetch Jewish women, whom they dragged to the crematoria for the greater glory of the Reich. And she waited for her turn to take the final walk. But the Gestapo seemed to be in no hurry. Mother Maria, "criminal" though she was, possessed Aryan papers; there were a great many Jewish women still to be exterminated.

Her turn finally came. She was last seen alive on March 31, 1945, one month and a few days before the collapse of the Thousand-Year Reich. It is said that she committed one last saintly act—exchanging, with a Jewish woman chosen for the gas chamber, her precious Aryan card. But she was not quite strong enough to walk to her execution upright; the guards carried her.

7

The Avenue of the Righteous Gentiles

There were millions who either looked on or looked away as their fellow men and women were being dragged away from their homes and killed, but few were those who rose in indignation and risked their lives to help the persecuted. The more they deserve the gratitude of humanity, for they were the ones who were their brothers' and sisters' keepers, the true Christians loving their neighbors. They rescued resistance workers and they rescued Jews, to deliver them from the forces of evil. Ultimately, they were the ones who kept alive the torch of humaneness in the hours of deepest darkness that mankind had ever known.

Some smuggled fugitives from Nazism across borders; others hid them in their homes, in each case with full knowledge that detection by the Gestapo or the SS—or by informers—could mean death for them and their families. Many ended up in concentration camps; many never returned.

Those who saved the lives of resistance members, fed them, clothed them and offered them refuge in their hours of need are commemorated in many countries. Those non-Jewish humanitarians who harbored and otherwise aided Jews have a memorial in Israel. Yad Vashem, the Heroes' and Martyrs' Remembrance Authority in Jerusalem, established an Avenue of the Righteous, where a carob tree is planted for each gentile who helped Jews during the Holocaust; about half of them were women. Over three thousand trees have been planted already, and their number is still growing.

Below are the stories of a few of these righteous women on the "Roll of Honor." All belonged to resistance movements, and in the course of their activities they also hid Jews and spirited them away to safety. One continued to support them even behind barbed wires.

Anna Christensen, Denmark

Forty Jewish children owe their lives to Anna.

Until the outbreak of the Second World War, there had been few links between Danes and Jews, but the German occupation of Denmark [in 1940] changed things overnight. As early as the 1930s, after Hitler came to power, Jewish refugees from Germany and Austria had begun to enter the country and were welcomed with open arms and warm hospitality. . . . Long active in the pacifist Women's International League for Peace and Freedom, Anna regarded the German invaders as enemies, both of her own Danish folk and of universal humanity and liberty.

At first she enrolled the refugee children openly in the local Nyborg school; but after the German invasion, the authorities were too frightened to allow it, so she turned her cellar into a classroom for forty pupils, herself teaching the general subjects, the group leaders taking care of the Jewish syllabus. As long as a man is alive, she insisted, he must study. When the hunt for the Jews was on [after October 1, 1943], she "billeted" the children among her friends in the neighborhood. One of the survivors, I.R. of Haifa today, records this of her:

> She made sure, to start with, that every Jewish child was in the care of a Danish family. She inspected the homes to which each was sent meticulously; if one did not come up to her standards, she searched unwearingly until she found something better.
>
> Thus under her personal supervision and vigilance, the children were housed by Danish peasants and could undergo agricultural training before their departure for Palestine; she disclosed the hiding places to the Danish resistance, so that in the event of danger or of her own arrest, the children might be warned or removed to safety.
>
> But she did not give up the weekly get-togethers at her own home, ignoring the near presence of Germans and disdaining all risks, for these comforting and educational occasions were vital for the children's morale and, apart from that, enabled her to discern each child's weaknesses and fears and thus help and hearten it in any crisis.

Another survivor, A.H., also of Haifa, says:

"I was one of these children and for a year and a half attended the meetings at Anna's home. We were very much aware of her warmth toward us and have remained attached to her. She revitalized in us a little of our belief in humanity and encouraged our determination to emigrate to Palestine."

Especially memorable were the get-togethers during the holidays, with discussions on pertinent themes. At the end of the fast on the Day of Atonement, Anna would cook a meal for the children; on other holidays she would prepare traditional Jewish dishes. She took care of their spiritual as

"The Avenue of the Righteous Gentiles" is from Ariel L. Bauminger, *Roll of Honour* (Tel Aviv, Israel: Hamenora Publishing House, 1971), pp. 25-86. Based on depositions in the Yad Vashem Archives, Jerusalem.

well as of their bodily needs. She did not want her wards to be untutored or unknowledgeable. As the meetings ended, she would hand out books for reading in their hiding places.

Since October, 1943 the Germans had been deporting Jews from Denmark to extermination camps in Eastern Europe. Anna warned the children to stay securely hidden and not to budge without permission from her or from the resistance. When those days of terror had passed, she was able with the help of Danish partisans to get most of them to the coast, to embark in small craft for Sweden and safety.

I.A. of Haifa says: "I especially remember my own rescue. One terrible night I had undergone an operation at the municipal hospital. I felt that nothing in the world could prevent the Germans from capturing me. But one day Anna came to visit me: I was not to worry, she would get me out. I did not believe it could be possible; but soon Pastor Jeppensen, a member of the resistance, came to my bedside and explained to me my escape. He arranged for documents certifying that I was mentally ill, and I was transferred to a mental hospital in Middlefart, where I spent several weeks and was then taken to Sweden."

Anna has forgotten none of her wards. . . . Her dream had always been to visit Israel, and in 1966 it came true. The beloved guest of her erstwhile "eaglets," Anna was graced by the double guerdon of a Righteous Gentile: a medallion of gratitude and a tree on the noble Avenue of the Righteous that would bear her proud name for ever.

* * *

Olga and Dragica Bartulović, Yugoslavia

When in April of 1941 Hitler invaded Yugoslavia, a resistance movement sprang up . . . against the Nazi incubus. It was headed by Josip Broz, known among the partisans as Tito. His army grew from month to month and soon numbered hundreds of thousands of fighting men and women. . . .

Yugoslav partisans fought the Germans, the Fascists and the Ustachis* at the fronts and in the rear as well. In the hinterland, they tried to help the Jews in different and devious ways, and women partisans could act there much more easily than men.

Olga Bartulović and her sister-in-law Dragica risked everything to save the Nachmias family, Samuel, Erna and their three children, of Banja Luka in Croatia. . . . All five of them fled to Split in July,to enjoy briefly the kindliness which the Jews were shown by the local Italians and the garrison. But in September, 1943 the Italians were forced out, and within an hour of their entry, the Germans had placarded the town with warnings that any-

*Fascist separatist group in Croatia, collaborating with the Nazis.

one found harboring Jews was liable to the death penalty. The next day posters ordered all Jews in the town to register at the police station.

In the house where the Nachmias family lived, there was a partisan girl, Olga Bartulović, who became friendly with the children. She advised the family not to register and urged them to escape or hide until things quieted down. But the family had nowhere to go and knew of no safe hiding place. Olga came up with the idea of the Marian convent. She managed to get hold of a set of forged identity papers. At the convent, Erna presented herself as an orthodox Christian married to a Jewish merchant, and the nuns seemed to accept the story. She and her husband were treated well and with courtesy. Yet in spite of that, and Olga's visits and reassurances notwithstanding, they lived in constant fear. At times the Germans searched the convent; German attacks on Jews in the town were frequent.

Olga now offered to help the family escape into the region liberated by the partisans. To play it safe, she first took Samuel alone, traveling tortuously through the mountains to Trogir, which was held by the partisans. Next she brought Erna to a friendly home. Erna writes: "I was hiding there for over a month. The women did not ask me for anything. Like Olga, they did not help for the sake of money."

Two months later Olga came for the son, Lazar, and led him to safety in partisan territory; then the other son Joseph and the daughter Mary. Finally the sister-in-law, Dragica, delivered Erna out of the German infested area.

Erna ends her testimony with these words: "Olga Bartulović and her sister-in-law Dragica were prompted in their actions by purely humane considerations, deriving no personal benefit or gain. In doing what they did, they exposed themselves to mortal danger, for it is certain that had they been caught by the Germans in the act of saving Jews, they would have paid for it with their lives. The husbands of both Olga and Dragica were active partisans, and Olga's brother lost his life in battle against the German invaders."

* * *

Kleopatra Minos and Maria Choleva, Greece

On 29 April 1941, three Jewish soldiers from Palestine, serving in the British Army, were captured by the Germans. After a fortnight in a prisoner-of-war camp, they, together with a number of British captives, were transported in cattle-trucks to Germany. The three of them—Aharon Yerushalmi, Asher Shwartz and Moshe Weinbaum—realized the dreadful end that would await them in Germany, and so jointly deciding to jump the train, made good their escape one night near the town of Darniza on the northern frontier of Greece. There they established contact with a Greek peasant, who took them to the Barba Leonida family in the village of Kalotronion not far away. In Kalotronion and the neighbouring villages searches for escaped British prisoners-of-war were being pursued by the Germans and their Greek lackeys, and the villagers had been threatened that if they hid the runaways in their homes, their homes would be burnt down. But none of this dismayed the Leonida family, and for three months the Jewish soldiers were cared for securely, clothed and fed.

In the summer of 1941, Kleopatra Minos and two of her friends came from Athens on a visit to Kalotronion. The three Jews asked them what was the shortest and safest route to Palestine. Kleopatra suggested that they first come to her home in Athens. By winding ways and paths, and with the guidance of the Leonida family, they reached the apartment of Kleopatra's sister Maria Choleva, a dentist. At the time food in Athens was rationed, yet the sisters often gave up their last crust so that the soldiers might eat; Kleopatra and Maria had to take particular care of Aharon Yerushalmi, who had a stomach ulcer and needed a special diet. It later turned out that the sisters were members of "Homeros," the Greek resistance, which, besides manifold other anti-German operations, was energetically engaged in the rescue of Jews.

A skilled dental surgeon, Maria could live a quiet and sheltered life, as did many of the Greek intelligentsia, more particularly since her patients included officers of the German occupation forces. But as a serving partisan, to whom the Nazis were anathema, she looked upon Jewish soldiers in the British Army as champions in the fight against Greece's oppressors and had no compunction about offering them help, though doing so might well have jeopardized not only her professional status, her freedom and family, but the very security of the Greek underground itself.

She had a German sister-in-law, who often came to see her and the visits were nerve-wracking experiences to the sisters and to the hidden Jewish soldiers, lest she took a fancy to explore the courtyard hideaway.

When the soldiers began to realize that the Germans were hot on their trail and that their long presence in Maria's house might have disastrous consequences, they decided to embark for Egypt and thence make for Palestine. With Maria's help, they found a vessel that was about to sail for Egypt. Kleopatra did her utmost to dissuade them from attempting the risky voyage. They did not heed her; but her fears proved to be only too well founded, for after only a short spell at sea, they were re-captured and taken to the notorious Averoff prison in Athens.

Yerushalmi managed to convey a note to Kleopatra through a Greek warder, and she commenced sending him food parcels. This, too, was a hazardous thing to do, but disregarding their family's warning, the two sisters kept in touch with the three Jews in their cell. With the outbreak of the war on the Russian front, in June 1941, Greek hatred of the German conquerers had mounted, and this led to intensification of the Nazi policy of local suppression. German, Italian and also Greek spies were constantly hunting the hundreds of British prisoners-of-war in hiding in Greek towns and villages. But never for a moment did Maria and Kleopatra, who were now much more prominent in the underground, withhold their aid from British soldiers in general or from the three Palestinians in particular. The German Secret Police seem to have suspected them of partisan activity, because during the interrogation of Yerushalmi—who tried to pose as a Greek soldier by the name of Vasilai Papadopoulos—his German inquisitor asked him: "But do you remember Kleopatra and her sister Maria Choleva?" Yerushalmi surmised that the officer had information enough, as it was, on the two sisters, and therefore admitted that he knew them, having become acquainted with them as would any foreign soldier with a local girl. But he did not divulge ever visiting their home and said that he even suspected them of collaborating with the Gestapo.

The few pleasant days that Yerushalmi passed in the Averoff prison were those when greeting cards came from the sisters, on Christmas or New Year, or food parcels arrived by a circuitous route.

In June 1942, in Salonika, Yerushalmi escaped from the Germans for the second time, intending to get to Palestine through Athens. He wrote to Kleopatra, and she replied at once, with a sum of money and an invitation to come forthwith.

In 1943, the two sisters were arrested for helping a Jew called Alex Korlanski. They were imprisoned for six months, suffering harshly at the hands of the Gestapo, but by a miracle were left alive.

* * *

Ingebjorg Sletten Fostyedt, Norway

The Nazi occupation of Norway was no bed of roses for the invaders. The hardy Norwegians fought them tooth and nail, in a resistance that waged its own war on two fronts—against the Germans as such and against Quisling's* Nazi Party. The Germans made public announcements in Norwegian that anyone extending aid to Jews, in the way either of clothing, food or shelter, would be liable to execution, together with his family. But Norwegians like Inge were undeterred, and several hundred defiant patriots were interned in the Grini concentration camp. It was there that Inge met her future husband, Fostyedt.

On the night of 25 November 1942, Mrs. Henriette Samuel, wife of the Chief Rabbi** of Norway, had a telephone call from her neighbour in Oslo, Inge Sletten. The message was: "The night is very cold. I suggest that you wrap your children up well." Inge, a young woman of 25, member of the

*The fascist Vidkun Quisling was the Nazi puppet premier of Norway during the occupation; he was shot as a war criminal in 1945. From his name comes the word *quisling*, meaning traitor.

**Rabbi Julius Samuel had been arrested on September 2, 1942, in a roundup and was never seen again.

Norwegian resistance, had to use this cryptic phrasing, as the telephone lines were tapped by the Gestapo. Mrs. Samuel understood it, not least because her husband had been arrested by the Gestapo almost three months earlier, and taken to the Grini concentration camp near Oslo. She woke her children and dressed them warmly. Within an hour, Inge arrived and took all four, together with Mrs. Samuel's sister-in-law and her two children, to the home of friends. The danger was grave that the neighbors' children might in innocent chatter reveal that "there are Jews staying with us" and jeopardize the gentile family which had agreed to succour the fugitives; so Inge took upon herself the exacting surveillance of the youngsters. Eventually she transferred the two women and the five children to an empty villa on the outskirts of Oslo and alternating with other members of the underground, brought them food and clothing each day.

On the night of 3 December, Mrs. Samuel and her family were part of a group of forty Jews who were taken in two trucks to the Swedish frontier.

As the trucks were officially meant to be carrying potatoes, the escapees had to simulate tubers covered by tarpaulins and to keep strictest silence lest the Germans discover them in routine searches along the way. The children were given sleeping-pills, the adults forbidden to speak. The last lap of the transit was impassable to trucks and had to be undertaken on foot, with the temperature down to 20° below freezing. Thanks to the brilliant organization of the Norwegian resistance and the exemplary behaviour of the group, the Swedish border was safely crossed. In like manner, eight hundred and fifty other Jews were smuggled out to sanctuary by the Norwegian underground. . . .*

Fostyedt had saved Mrs. Samuel's brother-in-law, convalescing in an Oslo hospital after an operation. When the resistance learned that a scheme was afoot also to remove the Jewish patients and murder them, Fostyedt managed to extricate this man, whom he did not know at all, and conveyed him in a long trek to the Swedish frontier.

There was a home in Oslo for the children of Viennese refugees, of whom Inge took special care. When the Norwegian underground was apprised that they were to be deported to Eastern European death camps, Inge managed to get fourteen of them out of the country and to safety in Sweden. In 1943, she sensed that the Germans were dangerously close on her tracks, and she too, fled to that safety.

* * *

Dr. Anna Binderová, Czechoslovakia

Anni was born in 1912 in České Budějovice, a small town in Bohemia, the daughter of poor German-Czech parents who had not the means to let her

*After the German occupation of Norway in 1940, 770 of the 1,700 Norwegian Jews were sent to be gassed in Auschwitz; the resistance spirited away 930 to Sweden.

attend university, and she had to earn her living by giving private language lessons. In 1936, her knowledge of English, French and Italian, on top of Czech and German, got her a job in the Czech Foreign Office, but she was dismissed in the political turmoil of 1938 and, after the German conquest, kept herself by again giving private lessons in Prague—this time to Jews who were about the emigrate. So she learned at first hand about the tragic plight of the Jewish refugees from the provinces. Till then, her main interests had been philology, music and art, but now, in a calamitous Czechoslovakia, her outlook upon the world was transformed, her attitudes were boldly defined. She began to proffer every possible aid to the Jews and put her diplomatic passport at the disposal of the underground, as well as the certificate testifying to her ancient lineage, which she had procured for this very use. She helped in hiding Jewish property and transferring it abroad, and when, at the end of 1938, she smuggled out to Switzerland jewelry belonging to one of her Jewish students, she and her sister were arrested by the Economic Police. In 1941, she was arrested once again, this time by the Gestapo, together with Dr. Harry Epstein, now her husband, on a charge of anti-Fascist activity: Dr. Epstein after detention in one camp after another, was liberated from Buchenwald at the end of the war; Anni was sent to the Ravensbrück camp for women.

At the end of March 1942, she was dragooned into the first transport of a thousand women shifted from Ravensbrück to Auschwitz, where a new women's camp was to be established. The SS selected the administrative staff from the tiny minority of political prisoners, and Anni was one. At first she was registrar of the new entrants, Jewish women from Slovakia, but after a few weeks became secretary to Dr. Caesar,* and he told her to find suitable German-speaking prisoners to staff the rubber-plant experimental station and laboratory. As Ra'ya Kagan put it: "Anni found two biologists and a chemist in our number; there was actually no need for a chemist but Anni wanted to save her life. We came to Auschwitz in 1942 with the first transport of Jewish women from France. Within a few weeks the physical condition of most of the women, who were instantly assigned to hard labor out in the open, was so bad that those chosen by Anni Binder to work in the laboratory believed that they had been saved from certain death. But, of all the group, only one biologist, Claudette Bloch-Kennedy, managed to survive; she now lives in Cambridge, England."

Claudette Kennedy has this to say:

> Anna was of a great help to the Jews during the time that we were at Auschwitz. Thanks to her, three women from my transport, Anni Litwak, Ella Schluesser and I, were transfered to the Plant Cultivation Commando, where working conditions were less difficult than elsewhere.

*SS Obersturmbannführer (Major) Joachim Caesar was head of the agricultural section of Auschwitz.

That was in 1942, and had it not been for Anna's intervention, no Jews who knew no German could have been employed there. There can be no doubt that for her, an Aryan, giving recommendations to Jews was a dangerous matter. . . . She always took the Jews' side. By her devising, we were transferred in winter 1943 from the Birkenau camp to the Stabsgebäude* and quartered inside the buildings. Anna also gave us moral comfort, which at that time was no less important than material help. When we were not at work, she made us preserve our human image and not let the SS-men humiliate us, as they usually did Jewish women. This she did in an intellectual way: she gave us lessons in German, biology and philosophy, which kept up our morale. In all these circumstances, Anna was a friend to the Jews, which in the Auschwitz camp, under the thumb of the SS, implied extraordinary courage and emotional fortitude. Personally, I owe her my life.

In a similar way, Anni managed to save four other biologists from the second transport that arrived from France in January 1943. . . .

Not content with giving counsel and moral comfort to the Jewish prisoners, she gathered around her all who had not resigned themselves to the reign of terror. By organizing lectures and talks, by teaching the women languages, she made them for a brief moment forget their suffering and humiliation and gave them hope of a brighter future. Her behaviour affected the other Aryan women, too, so that she became the leader of a group of Czech, French and Polish prisoners. In the autumn of 1942, when the women's camp was moved from Auschwitz to Birkenau, the administration decided that all the women doing office work should be kept in Auschwitz lest they carry rampant infection to the SS-men in Birkenau. By Anni's intervention, all of them—Aryans and Jewesses alike—were housed in the cellar of the Stabsgebäude.

In 1943, Ra'ya Kagan was transferred from the Plant Cultivation Commando to the Political Department of the Camp, right opposite the gas chambers, where it was her duty to record the dead. "This work left me no illusions whatsoever regarding our situation and our future. I knew that Anni, the Aryan, had a chance of getting out of the camp alive. I therefore decided, although this was strictly forbidden, to tell her what was going on in our office, which was the headquarters of the SS-men in charge of the extermination plan, in the hope that she might be able to tell it to the world. We met daily and passed on the news."

In autumn 1943 Lilly Topler, a young Jewess from Slovakia who was working in the Political Department, was arrested on a charge of corresponding with a Polish prisoner. Anni mustered up courage to ask Dr. Caesar to intervene, but he advised her to stop defending the Jews, especially in such serious cases. Lilly was shot dead by Obsturmfueher** Buger of the Political Department.

Shortly after, Anni's position weakened. Her widespread activities on

*Birkenau was Auschwitz II: Stabsgebäude means headquarters.

**Lieutenant.

behalf of the Jewish prisoners aroused the suspicion of the SS and, in a surprise search, an SS supervisor found a cigarette-lighter among her effects; she was called before the Chief Inspector of the SS and given seven days of solitary confinement. At the beginning of 1944, Dr. Caesar was replaced by a director who worked in close cooperation with the Chief Inspector and took on a new secretary. In January, when preparing presents and letters for the prisoners working in the Plant Cultivation Commando, Anni was surprised by the new director, who discovered the names of her collaborators, including her friends from the Political Department and the Commando. It was clear that this endangered all the women on the list and, indeed, the existence of the Commando. Now it was that Anni manifested her full greatness and nobility. She went to her office manager and suggested that he keep the whole matter quiet on condition that she herself would go to Birkenau. He agreed, but before she left, she found a chance to take leave of the Jewish women whom she had taken care of and tell them of the deal that she had made: they were to keep up their spirits and not abandon hope.

Early in 1944, she was sent to the Penal Labour Commando and made to pave roads in the vicinity of Birkenau, out in the mud and snow. When she fell ill as a result and was taken to the Birkenau hospital, her friends working there took special care of her and contrived to get her out of the Commando into employment as a clerk. On 1 August 1944, however, she was transferred to Ravensbrück, and a few months later to Graslitz in Northern Bohemia. She made her escape in the end and returned to Prague, where she met her old friend, Dr. Epstein, himself back at last from concentration camp. They married, and she is now the mother of three children and a lecturer in philosophy and modern philology at the University of Prague.

8

Death at the Firing Squad

After the carpet bombing of the open city of Belgrade, capital of Yugoslavia, on Easter Sunday, April 6, 1941, the German campaign for the conquest of the Balkans rolled on to Greece. The situation in that erstwhile cradle of democracy was complex.

The king and his entourage fled and tried to influence the resistance from Cairo and London. The exiled politicians and the resistance were united only on one thing: free Greece. But there were factions in both groups.

Most resisters hoped for a Greek republic after the war. In September 1941, the Communists founded the National Liberation Front (EAM); their recruiting for this resistance group was so widespread that only one in ten of their members was actually Communist. They had a partisan branch about 20,000 strong, called the Greek Popular Liberation Army (ELAS). Their main resistance rival was the National Republican Greek League (EDES), with about 5,000 partisans. EAM looked for support to the Soviet Union, and EDES to the West.

Men and women in these and still other resistance groups harassed the Nazi occupiers a great deal. Aside from hundreds of acts of sabotage, twice they managed to blow up the viaducts of the Athens-Saloniki railroad, thereby slowing German troop movements at critical times. Yet it was the British Special Operations Executive (SOE) on Crete that carried off the most spectacular coup of the resistance. In April 1944, they kidnapped a German general in his own car and spirited him across numerous German check points to the seashore and via submarine to Cairo! W. Stanley Moss, one of the commandos participating in this daring nocturnal undertaking, entitled his memoirs Ill Met By Moonlight.

The women of the Greek resistance played a significant role in rescuing, hiding, and conducting to freedom Allied soldiers, a number of whom had been stranded in Greece at the time of the German invasion. Some of their stories are told above in Chapter 7, "The Avenue of the Righteous Gentiles." Only one rescue operation was unsuccessful for a quite unexpected reason: a British submarine came to pick up two Australians, conducted to a cave on the seashore by the resistance. They were into their cups, their arms around good-looking Greek girls and in words unfit to print refused to be rescued!

But the story that follows has to do with another side of the resistance in Greece, which dealt with illegal publications, black markets and informers.

The economic situation in Greece was desperate. The Germans were busy with the Russian front and could not care less about feeding the country they occupied. They requisitioned everything they could lay their hands on and "paid" in worthless scrip, called "baloony marks."

The New York Times *reported in detail on October 26, 1941 (p. 8): "An orgy of looting by individual German officers and soldiers . . . . German troops in Greece receive a free rein to rob and abuse the people," partly to keep the soldiery's morale up.*

The report continues: "If the means by which the Germans looted Greece of nearly everything portable, including the bulk of its food supplies, automobiles, ordinary merchandise and the country's stock of raw cotton which forced Greek textile mills to close, were contemptible, their methods of obtaining big loot must evoke the admiration of every big-time gangster and every pirate in big or little business. They reduce Al Capone's most grandoise [sic] exploits to the level of stealing pennies from children."

Under threats from the Gestapo, Greek companies were forced to sell their output below cost to the Germans or be "bought out." So much of Greek industry was taken over that the Greeks suspected that this was part of a major operation directed from Berlin for the personal enrichment of party, army and government high officials.

Meanwhile, the population was literally

starving. Farmers were producing less, yet they had to account for everything to the occupiers. They had to feed their own families, often also the partisans. There was little they could spare for the black market in the urban areas, and that was sold mostly in barter for gold and jewelry.

This then is the framework in which an extraordinary young woman by the name of Maro enters our story.

I was a little girl that fateful spring of 1941, when Hitler's armies attacked Greece. Yet the memory of the day as well as of the years of occupation that followed, remain vividly in my mind.

One event of those tragic times that has haunted me more than any other was the murder of a most courageous woman, a close friend of the family, and one who had greatly influenced my thinking.

Her name was Maro Mastraka. According to my mother's recollections, she was born around the turn of the century in Constantinople of Greek parents. Her father, Andreas Mastrakas, was from Corinth; her mother, whose family name was Mitsotaki, came from the island of Crete. It was a well-to-do family, and Maro received an excellent education. She graduated from the "Megale tou genous schole," a famous Greek school of higher learning in Constantinople, majoring in literature. It was not common for Greek women of those days to pursue higher education, especially not in the milieu of Asia Minor. Maro was, however, far from the ordinary. She was their only child, exceptionally intelligent, and her parents had high hopes for her.

After the first world war Maro entered the Sorbonne in Paris. Here she came into contact with the elite of the French literary world. Both in France and upon her return to Athens, she was most comfortable among bohemians, engaging forever in literary and political discussions. While vehemently debating the political problems of her nation, she had never been involved in practical politics.

It was upon Maro's return from Paris that she met my parents who had been just married. My mother was only sixteen, and Maro was hired to teach her French literature, as used to be proper for a well brought up young lady. After about a year, Maro became such a close friend of the family, that she refused to accept a fee for the lessons. She continued her tutoring for many years, even after I was born. My fondness of her was boosted by the many little art treasurers that she so generously transferred from her collection to us. A few of these are still my cherished possessions.

Maro did not need to work; she was satisfied enjoying a leisurely cultural life.

Things changed drastically with the Nazi occupation of Greece.

The whole world was turned upside down. The king and his government fled the country. The Greek people, who had fought so valiantly to stop the invasion, were helpless against the raging Nazi hordes.

Hundreds of thousands of Greeks died of starvation during the first year of occupation. The nation was led with mathematical precision toward destruction and extinction. The economic resources of the country came under the control of the conquerors who monopolized mining, oil and all

"Death at the Firing Squad" is by Dr. Beata Panagopoulos, Professor of Art, California State University at San José.

industries. Food supplies in government warehouses were confiscated, and so was agricultural production. Farmers managed at times to hide some of their produce to feed their families. A few of them succumbed to the temptation of the black market and sold food at exorbitant prices.

Urban areas were hit hardest and had no means of survival. Currency lost all value; savings of people who had put money away in banks for the proverbial rainy day were wiped out. The occupation forces printed their own money with which they "paid" for confiscated goods. The only stable currency was the British gold pound, demanded in all dealings on the black market. Under these conditions many Greeks were forced to live on roots, St. John's bread, dandelion greens and similar plants.

The first efforts of organized resistance came in the middle of July, 1941. Anti-Nazi slogans appeared on the walls. Demonstrations took place, especially when Greek men were to be mobilized for the German army. As a result of mass protests, at least that calamity was averted.

Maro Mastraka had now taken a job. She was working in the library of the Association of Architects and Engineers (Technikon Epimeleterion). Here she became actively involved in the Greek resistance. In the basement of her office was a clandestine printing machine. Here she printed and with the help of others distributed a bulletin of news received from Allied broadcasts. The bulletins also disseminated information on the illegal activities of the Nazis; in their editorials, they called for moral and material resistance. Maro was dedicated to this work body and soul.

In the spring of 1942, scraping the bottom of the barrel, Maro decided to sell a ring, a valuable family heirloom. One of her fellow workers, by the name of Xythalis, offered to sell it for her. She trusted him and handed him the ring. She waited for weeks on end for the money, but received only excuses from Xythalis. Her financial situation was growing worse. Her father died, and she became the sole supporter of her mother. Xythalis admitted that he had sold the ring, but still did not come up with the money. Exasperated by endless postponements, Maro decided to act. On payday, she stood next to Xythalis at the bursar's window and asked that his salary be handed over to her as payment for the ring.

The incident proved fatal for Maro.

Xythalis vowed revenge for his damaged male ego. Since he knew of the printing machine in Maro's office, he went directly to the German authorities and denounced her.

She was arrested that same night.

She was first taken to the detention prison on Victoria Square and interrogated by the infamous director of the Greek Security Police, Vassilis Lambros. She was subjected to torture. After a month of this she was transferred to the Hadjicosta prison in Athens. Here she was pressed to sign a statement condemning her patriotic activities and to agree to collaborate with the Nazis.

She flatly refused.

Instead, she started organizing her fellow prisoners. She was tireless as she talked to the other women, informing them of the latest progress of the Allies, encouraging them to keep faith in the ultimate victory and the return of freedom to Greece. She raised their consciousness as patriots and their spirits as human beings. She kept the fires of hope burning in their darkest hours.

Unfortunately, Maro was equally open and enthusiastic about the victory of democracy when she was talking to the prison physician, whom she had known as a brother-in-law of a close friend. Little did she know that this doctor had turned informer to the Nazis, a Judas who for pay reported the prisoners' activities and statements to the Gestapo. He repeated verbatim what Maro trustingly had told him about the deserved defeat of the bestial Nazis.

She was immediately taken to another prison, Haidari, on the outskirts of Athens. From here prisoners were usually sent either to concentration camps or to the execution block.

Maro's situation thus went from bad to worse. All efforts of my parents and of her numerous friends to save her from the clutches of the Nazis seemed in vain. My father got up the courage to see the German ambassador to Greece, von Erbach. Perhaps because my father's doctorate was from the University of Berlin, the ambassador received him. My father informed the ambassador of Maro's troubles, about the denunciation caused by Xythalis' greed. Von Erbach thought it a minor offense connected with the black market. But once he asked for Maro's file, his attitude changed. He read the prison doctor's report, the story of the printing press in Maro's office, and the illegal activities Maro participated in. He told my father in a cold and detached way:

"Your friend is a very intelligent woman but also a very dangerous one." He washed his hands of any connection with such a "traitor."

Father came home shaken. There was little he or anybody else could do now.

Soon thereafter word came from Maro that according to prison rumors she would be soon deported to a concentration camp. At that critical moment my mother heard of a Greek woman, an interpreter for the Germans, who might have some influence. She had connections among the high and mighty Nazis. In order to pull some strings with her German officer friend, she demanded one hundred British gold pounds.

Dealing in gold was in itself a dangerous business for it was strictly forbidden. Bribing a German or his collaborator was equally risky. Either might take the gold and simply do nothing; or they might do a complete turn-about and accuse the petitioner of attempted bribery. In either case there was no recourse to any higher authority.

My parents were desperate to help Maro, but they did not have the gold. Mother went to see Maro's mother, but she did not have the gold pounds either. However, she handed my mother a small chest filled with jewelry, remaining from her better days. Mother took the jewels to a reputable jeweler; he lent her the hundred gold pounds and kept only one of a pair of earrings as a token.

Now came the problem of getting the money to the interpreter without being seen. She lived in the Nea Smyrne district, quite far from us. Mother, accompanied by Maro's friend Lily Iacovidou, the well known author, dared the German curfew after dark. They managed to avoid the German sentries and finally arrived at the woman's place. They handed over the one hundred gold pounds and received lots of promises.

And promises they remained. The woman either did not have any intentions to help in the first place, or she did not succeed.

On the first of May, 1943, Maro and two hundred other prisoners from Haidari prison were taken to Kaissariani, at the foot of Mount Hymetus, and there summarily shot to death.

The names of those executed were not made public. But a few days after the killings mother went to Haidari prison to visit Maro as she had before. Only this time she was told that she could not see the prisoner. Instead, she was handed a little bundle with Maro's belongings.

For a while nobody could find out whether Maro was among those executed on May first or deported to a concentration camp. Mother was told that she had been transferred to a German prison. Maro's mother died believing that her daughter was in a Nazi prison, somewhere in Germany.

It was not until the war ended, and the Germans pulled out of Greece, that light was shed on the tragedy of Maro Mastraka.

A year and a half after her martyrdom, mother as Maro's closest surviving friend was called in by the police to identify the body. After the executions in 1943, all two hundred corpses were buried in a mass grave in a nearby ditch. But Greek guards had cut small pieces of material from the victims' clothes and pinned them to the garments they had been executed in. With the help of these little pieces of cloth Maro's remains were identified.

Maro was then reburied in her own grave, where she sleeps her eternal sleep, an honor to all the women of the Greek resistance. She was a woman of courage who refused to compromise her deepest beliefs in justice and freedom.

Xythalis, after having denounced Maro, continued collaborating with the Germans and with the Greek quisling police. He betrayed other Greeks, too. In 1945, after the liberation of Greece, he suffered either from remorse or from fear of retaliation. Back in his birthplace of Mani he killed his mother, then hung himself from a tree.

Lambros, the collaborating prison director, and the physician informer were brought to trial after the war; but they got off with easier sentences than their crimes should have warranted. They caused unspeakable anguish, suffering and the deaths of some of the best people of Greece, among them my unforgettable mentor and friend Maro Mastraka, a courageous woman of the resistance.

9

Intrigue in Oslo

Norway was occupied by Nazi Germany the same day as Denmark, on April 9, 1940. Like the Danes, the Norwegians managed to smuggle almost half of the 2,000 Jews to Sweden; many were hidden inside the country. Aside from the usual anti-Nazi propaganda, continuous sabotage and acts of defiance, the Norwegian underground performed the additional service of coast watching and reporting to the Allies on German naval movements along the North Sea and the Skagerrak. The fabulous "Shetland Bus" provided almost regular connection with England, with two-way traffic of agents, material and refugees.

Nine Norwegian resisters carried out one of the greatest acts of sabotage of the war, when in February 1943 they blew up the Norsk Hydro heavy water plant near Oslo, thus slowing down German atomic research. Norwegian history teachers, male and female, refused to teach the revised version of their history, dictated by the German-imposed puppet Vidkun Quisling, whose name has enriched the language with a synonym for traitor. The history teachers were arrested. Rather than sign up for a political union, 12,000 of the 14,000 teachers resigned; schools were closed for half a year. On the whole, the three million Norwegians were such a thorn in the Germans' side that they had to keep seventeen divisions there, when they were desperately needed elsewhere, especially during the last winter of the war.

One of the countless resistance fighters was Helen Astrup. She was the British widow of a Norwegian sea captain, whose ship was sunk by the Nazis. Living in Oslo with her eight-year-old daughter Kirsti, she became involved in a mesh of hair-raising intrigues concerning Nazi gold smugglers, the "Joessings," or resistance fighters, and refugees. She harbored Joessings before they set out to kill a collaborator and saw them slain before her eyes. She had to spy on her friends suspected of double dealings. She missed by a hair being arrested by the Gestapo meeting an alleged British agent.

One assignment she received from her underground contact Nils Berg was to claim the "body" of her neighbor Mrs. Hirschfeldt from the hospital morgue. The catch, however, was that the woman was not dead. She was being smuggled out from the hospital, in the dead of night, enclosed in a coffin together with her little daughter Sara, to a safe-house in Oslo on their way to Sweden. The false death certificate would put a stop to further German investigation in the case. Eventually the whole family reached Sweden.

Helen Astrup's role in this rescue took only a couple of hours, but they must have been the longest hours of her life.

Eventually I heard the sound of a heavy box being pushed over wood into the back of the truck, and the driver came round and climbed up. We moved out of the hospital yard, past the policeman and the German soldiers. . . . We were on our way and Fru Hirshfeldt and Sara were safe in the back!

My thoughts went to her there, lying quietly with her daughter. They were probably wrapped in each other's arms, dreading—as I was—the sound of the engine slacking and the truck stopping to answer questions flung in harsh German. "You are bound to be stopped," Nils had said.

We drove down Kirkeveien, turned sharp left at Majorstuen into Bogstadveien, and no sound broke the night except the hum of the engine and the crunch of the freezing snow. Then on the corner of Holtegaten by Uranienborg Kirke a voice cried, *"Halte!"* The driver's expression did not change as he brought the truck to a standstill. A soldier opened the door and I saw that his rifle was pointed up at us over the floor boards. The driver had a little book of papers ready which he casually handed to the German, who examined them with his flashlight. He handed the pass back and slammed the door without a glance at me.

The driver changed gears, down the hill and away toward our destination, which was somewhere near Grefsen. This was all I knew. We had been traveling now about fourteen minutes and I knew that the journey should take twenty-five. We were halfway there and my job would soon be done.

"Halte"—this time it was a German staff car. A lot of German troops were standing in the road by a garage, and we were surrounded.

A lieutennant questioned the driver, then said in German to him, "Get out." And almost immediately, "Get *out!*" he screamed, *"Schnell!"* The driver moved like a man shot from a gun. A Nazi pulled me out by the leg. German soldiers came out of the garage and began to climb into the back of the truck. The business was so sudden and so horrible I burst into tears, and this, strangely enough, was our salvation. . . .

It turned out that the lieutennant only wanted to get to some other place as quickly as possible. He had dismissed his transportation when he made a raid on the garage. Our driver told him that I was next of kin to a body which I was taking home for burial.

The lieutennant turned to me and saluted. Like most Germans, he was very correct. *"Gnädige Frau,"** he said, "accept my regrets, I personally will see that you have your transportation back in half an hour at the most. I must move my men swiftly. I will leave you with a sergeant and two men to protect you. *Heil Hitler!"*

"Intrigue in Oslo" is from Helen Astrup and B. L. Jacot, *Oslo Intrigue, A Woman's Memoir of the Norwegian Resistance* (New York: McGraw-Hill, 1954), pp. 43-51. Reprinted with the permission of the publisher.

*"Gracious lady," the polite address toward a married woman.

The coffin was lifted from the truck and placed on the ground in front of the pumps on the concrete of the garage yard. Silent beside it stood the sergeant and his two thugs. The driver and I stood apart under the shelter, protected against the wind-driven snow. I was thinking of Fru Hirschfeldt and her little girl. If they moved! If the child cried out! I could not bear to think of it, but meanwhile I thought of the cold for them there under the drifting snow.

Once or twice, as we waited for the return of the truck, in absolute silence, the Germans turned to look at me. I did not like the way the sergeant was eyeing me. He had a pistol in his holster, and we had all heard of what happened to girls who found a pistol held against them and a dark alley—or a garage—close at hand.

But the worst was yet to come—the thing that stood to betray us. After a while some sixth sense seemed to warn me that there was something wrong with the coffin. I stared in the half-darkness but could see nothing amiss. The district seemed empty of life. The gaping street stretched away into the darkness. Nothing was moving and somehow the impression came that we—the little group in the garage forecourt—were the only people in existence. I cannot explain the weird feeling. It was just there.

The scene is as clear in my memory today as it was when it happened. The forecourt of the garage was white with finely powdered snow which showed like a linen cloth in the thin light. Only our footsteps broke its glistening surface. Grouped by the pumps were figures like something unmoving out a dream. No one spoke and no one moved. Then suddenly I saw that everything was white *except the coffin.*

I realized then what was wrong. The snow was melting as it fell on the wooden box. Around the coffin, too, was an edging clear of snow. The heat of the bodies in the coffin was betraying their presence. I pictured the two lying there, holding on to each other, terrified out of their wits by this sudden and unexpected hitch in their plans. I knew I had to do something before anyone noticed, but all I could do was to say rather stupidly, "I suppose the truck will be back soon and we shall be on our way again. It's cold."

I wanted Fru Hirschfeldt to hear and to be reassured.

The German sergeant turned his head to took at me. His face was not intelligent—but he was sharp enough, no doubt, to notice sooner or later that there was something warm and living inside the box. "You are ill?" he asked.

I expect I looked it, standing there shaking in every limb. "I do not feel well," I told him. "The cold—and the—"

"I understand. It was—a near relation?"

"My husband," I said. Then the idea came, suggested as is so often the case by what is actually happening around you at the moment. "I think I shall have to sit down." I stumbled over the snow and sat on the coffin itself. There was nowhere else to sit.

"It is bad to lose one's man," the German said. He offered me a cigarette and I took one from the packet and put it in my mouth with a hand that shook. The boy flicked a lighter, hiding the flame in his cupped hands because of the blackout. "That is better now, *nicht?*"

"Thank you," I answered. He stepped two paces back to where he had been standing with his companions, and silence fell over us again.

I cannot think of that scene even now without a shudder. There was nothing I could do but wait—wait for the scrunching of tires over the snow that would herald the return of the truck.

If only someone would move! If only I could do something! I saw the driven snow collect on the greatcoats of the Germans, emphasizing the folds and the surfaces against the wind. In times like this you tend to notice unimportant things.

And now suddenly, while I was watching the emptiness of the road outside the garage, I heard a soft sound in the snow and someone sat beside me on the coffin. "With your permission, *gnädige Frau,*" a German voice said, and I feared its softness more than the command of the officer when he yelled at our driver to get down from his seat in the truck.

For a while I remained stiffly as I was, looking along the road. I was telling myself that this was how it started. If you are pleasant, that makes it easy—and conventional. Of course, if you are difficult, there is always the threat of the pistol.

I looked around and saw it was the sergeant. His eyes were moving over my hair—fair Nordic hair. He was looking as if searching for something. If I had ever known panic before, it was nothing like what this turned out to be in hard-fact. I was not imagining this in the night when I knew I was really safe in bed. *This was happening.* Here on a wooden box in a snow-blown yard with no help near.

I looked for our driver. He was watching me neutrally. He did not seem interested, or alive to the danger. Maybe the other Germans would soon settle him if he tried to interfere.

"I thought you looked lonely and cold all by yourself, *gnädige Frau,*" the sergeant said.

"I *am* cold," was all I could think of to answer him. Then an idea came to me that I suppose was essentially a woman's idea. I argued that if I made myself sympathetic, he would like me a little and I would have that amount of edge on the situation, anyway. "It was nice of you to come and sit by me." This made the business a gesture of courtesy, a masculine and chivalrous act of consideration.

The German moved closer to me, which made it all the better for an explanation of the melting snow—so I told myself. He was not bad-looking. He could not have been much more than twenty. Nevertheless, almost before I had time to think of what next to say. I found my hand in his hand, being gently rubbed.

"You will get frostbite, *gnädige Frau.* And that is not nice! Let me tell you that I was in Poland and there the hair freezes over your head if you take your cap off."

He was beginning to tell me about himself and to boast, which was all to the good and in the time-honored pattern of the male. But I wanted my hand back before he began to tell me I must not get frostbite in my shoulder, or perhaps around the waist. "You're not very blond for a good German," I teased him. "Let me see your hair. It won't freeze in Norway."

"Not as blond as you—but blond. See! He shook his hair, which indeed was tow-colored and very thick and grinned impudently. Then he replaced his cap.

"I would like another cigarette please."

He took a cigarette and lit it for me, offering it to my lips with his fingers. It was a gesture of the night clubs and no doubt he was very proud of it. I saw that our driver was looking daggers at me now.

"*Gnädige Frau*! I would like to show you what we did to the pigs who own this garage."

"They—they were shot?"

"They were not here so we wrecked the place. They have been helping the Joessings, so we stood and turned our automatic weapons up and down the rows of cars. Come, I will show you."

Not for anything now would I have left that box. I clung to it as to a plank in a shipwreck. "I'm too cold to move," I said. "Not just now."

He sat for a while scuffing his heavy boots in the snow. "You should not live in a place like this. You should live in Germany. The world belongs to us now. In a few weeks we shall be in England. I shall be in London. I shall like that. They say the English girls are fair, like the Danes. I like the Danish girls."

I said to him, "I expect you like all the girls."

"Some," he admitted. His arm moved over the lid of the box and came up on the other side of my waist. It drew me closer to him. *"Herr Leutnant!"* I said, flattering his rank, "The others!"

"What do they count? *Gnädige—"*

"They count to me!"

"Well, come and I will show you what we did to those cars in the back."

I got up from the box. I had to, but I had no idea in my mind as to what I should do next. He was good-tempered and smiling now, but I knew all that could change in a flash. He was watching me expectantly.

"Well, Fru Norsk?"

I shook my head. Let him do what he wanted about my lack of sympathy, but let him do it here, out in the open. When I looked up his hand was on my arm and his eyes were different. They had a look that seemed to say I already belonged to him. "It is not always polite to refuse a well-meant invitation."

"It is not always possible to accept it, *Herr Leutnant."*

I felt my arm jerked roughly as he came closer up behind me, but at that moment the sound of a car approaching reached the others and they began to move out into the road. One of the men called to the sergeant and I felt his hand drop away from my arm. The sensation of relief that came over me was actually like a wave. I felt it surge through me and then it drained away, taking the strength from my limbs. It is all very well to be strong and courageous in theory. Every woman has imagined situations like this, but living through one of them is a very different matter.

The truck swept into the garage and a corporal who was driving jumped out and saluted me. Speaking German, he gave me the officer's compliments, then they all helped to raise the coffin and slide it into the back. It was all I could do to climb back into the cab.

The corporal gave another smart salute—the German military salute with a snapping of the heels that always reminds me of the springing of a rat-trap—and the sudden noise of it in the blanketing silence brought a little scream to my lips. The driver looked at me cautiously. I said something but he did not answer as he shifted his gears and bumped out of the garage. We were on the road again, and away!

"Is it far?" I asked, but the driver stared, unresponsive, ahead. He was not impressed with the way I had been fraternizing with Nazis. But, *he* did not know what was inside the coffin. We turned sharp right down a side street and the truck drove into a yard beside a big building. The driver switched off the engine and disappeared without a word to me. Soon I heard the scrape of the box being pulled out of the truck. I climbed down and a harsh voice said, "Get back!" Footsteps faded.

After a time the door opened and I saw the face of the driver. He stared at me with his face contorted into a sneer, then spat out *"Din fordoemte Quisling!"** He slammed the door and *his* footsteps faded. I felt very cold and miserable as I waited.

Then: *"Kom, kjaere deg!"*** a voice in the pitch-darkness said. I did not recognize it, but I climbed down and walked beside someone—a big man—until we reached the end of the yard. In the doorway Nils was waiting and he smiled down at me, saying *"Du har vaert enestaaende!**** You delivered them both safe and sound."

I tried to speak, but something in my throat prevented me. The nervous strain of the last hour had taken a toll of me and my legs were far from steady.

"There was some incident, I hear? What happened?"

I told him about being stopped by the patrol. I told him about sitting on the coffin and talking aloud to reassure Fru Hirschfeldt.

"She heard you and knew everything was going to be all right."

*"You damned Quisling!"

**"Come, my dear!"

***"You have been great!"

10

Postman Across the Pyrenees

Over 7,000 British and American airmen were rescued and returned to combat by male and female operatives from the Netherlands, Belgium and France during World War II. The price of this cloak and dagger game came high. The rescuers had to outwit not only the Gestapo, but also the local police and the swarms of undercover agents in German pay. Of the 12,000 resistance workers involved, over 500 were executed or perished under torture and in various concentration camps.

The rescue missions started spontaneously after Dunkirk in 1940 and continued throughout the war as Allied fliers had to bail out over occupied territories and prisoners of war kept escaping from the camps.

After 1942 "Room 900," a combined American and British military intelligence group in London, started supporting the action of the various guides, couriers, forgers of identification papers and the people who housed and fed the escapees.

The lines of these clandestine routes went from the Netherlands through Belgium and France and over the Pyrenees to Spain; others led to ports and rescue by sea or to improvised airfields for a risky airlift over the English Channel.

Many women followed the early example of Edith Cavell, the British nurse who was executed by the Germans in 1915 in Brussels for aiding British soldiers to escape to Holland. Some of these women will forever remain nameless, among them nuns who often sheltered fugitive airmen in convents. One pilot, camouflaged in a nun's habit, started flirting with a pretty nun, who must have given him the shock of his life with "her" answer:

"Don't be a bloody fool, I've been here since Dunkirk!"

The story might be apocryphal, yet it is indicative of the helping hand the Sisters offered to the resistance.

Without any doubt the most colorful among

the women in this sector of the resistance was Mary Lindell, a British nurse living in France and mother of three children. She paraded around in a Red Cross uniform, her World War I decorations aglitter. She often presented herself as a countess, exhibiting a haughty personality to match. She was fearless, marching into German headquarters, demanding travel permits and gasoline to go with them, so she could escort her Allied fliers in style! She acted with such self-assurance that for a long time the Nazis did not catch her. Under her power of persuasion, a Nazi judge reduced her sentence from ten years to nine months. She survived Ravensbrück.

The saddest case was that of Dutch Beatrix Terwindt, who was dropped in February 1943 from England behind enemy lines in her country—directly into the arms of the Germans, who had not only penetrated the Dutch underground during the infamous "Englandspiel," but actually operated over a dozen captured radio sets broadcasting in the name of the resistance to London. She never saw action except in Ravensbrück and Mauthausen.

The woman who had accomplished most in this line of work was a wisp of a girl, Andrée de Jongh, code name "Dédée." As the war engulfed Belgium, she left her nursing job and created the Comet Line which in its three years of existence spirited away over eight hundred Allied airmen and soldiers to safety and to a second chance to fight the Nazis. Her father, a school principal, paid with his life for helping her, and her sister Suzanne was incarcerated since 1942 at Mauthausen and Ravensbrück. Dédée herself was eventually captured and served time at Ravensbrück. Yet so well was her line organized that it continued without her.

After the war Dédée set aside her George Medal, the highest award Great Britain can award a civilian, and followed in the footsteps of her countryman Father Damien, the man who aided the lepers on Molokai. She served as a nurse in the Belgian Congo, in a leper hospital in Addis Ababa, and more recently in Senegal.

Her wartime British contact and biographer, Airey Neave, called her "a phantom of delight" and "Little Cyclone." In the following selection, he tells her story.

The story began with her arrival with two young Belgians and a British soldier, a survivor of St. Valery, in August 1941, at the British Consulate in Bilbao. They had come from Brussels and crossed the Pyrénées on foot with a Basque guide.

The Consul had been astonished at the sight of this slight figure. He could hardly believe that such an innocent-looking girl had really crossed the mountains. It was an arduous journey from the foothills of St. Jean-de-Luz, made only by smugglers.

She gave her name as Andrée de Jongh, aged twenty-five, living with her parents at 73, Avenue Emile Verhaeren in the Schaerbeek district of Brussels. Her father, Frédéric de Jongh, she told the Consul, was a schoolmaster. She had been helping British soldiers and airmen in Brussels since 1940, but at first did not tell her family. In 1941 she was forced to leave Belgium, and her father took her place there. They had together planned a chain of "safe-houses" in Brussels, Paris and the frontier zone. Their object was to establish an escape line to Spain. . . .

In writing his report to "Monday"* the Consul concluded with a hint of caution. It was always possible she might have been sent by the Germans, but he did not himself believe this. The appearance of this intriguing girl at Bilbao produced a flow of telegrams, reports and minutes lasting several weeks. Her file included the M.I.9** interrogations of those who had made the crossing with her. They spoke of her incomparable courage and firmness.

She reappeared at Bilbao on October 17, 1941, when she met "Monday," a big genial member of the British Embassy staff. . . . "Monday" gave her the code name "Postman."

The arrival of valuable aircrew dispelled any doubts about her. Only our chief at the War Office continued to make dark hints. But even he was forced to change his mind. Each time she reached San Sebastian or Bilbao, admiration for her exploits grew. In her talks with "Monday," she insisted that the line should remain in Belgian hands and although M.I.9 (and the Belgian Government in exile) should provide funds, they should not control it.

When I arrived at Room 900, Dédée and her line had been in operation for ten months. I could see that, brilliant and daring as she was, she could not continue without serious risk to her father and herself. There was no direct communication with her except the meetings with "Monday" on Spanish territory. She had so far refused to allow a wireless operator to be

"Postman Across the Pyrenees" is from Airey Neave, *The Escape Room* (Garden City, N.Y.: Doubleday & Co., 1970), pp. 126-38. Reprinted with the permission of the publisher.

*An agent of the military intelligence at the British embassy in Madrid.

**Section of British military intelligence in charge of escapes.

sent to Brussels so that Room 900 could maintain contact with her father.

She relied on the couriers to carry messages up and down the line between Brussels and St. Jean-de-Luz. It was an informal, even high-spirited escape line and she wanted it that way. She did not like to be regarded as a spy. Her youthful, but nonetheless effective methods were difficult for a previous generation to understand. . . .

A successful system made it essential that guides escorting the airmen by train should be inconspicuous. Dédée chose young men and women who would pass unnoticed at railway station controls and be able to explain the presence of passengers of Anglo-Saxon appearance who spoke no French. The girls in her organisation were quietly dressed and modest in appearance, but self-possessed. Their looks belied their toughness and resource. The evaders, survivors of air combat, followed them without question.

Between July and October 1942, this slim girl, and her Basque guide, Florentinò Giocoechea, personally escorted fifty-four men over the Pyrénées. Her fame grew and with it the morale of the R.A.F.

Dédée became a symbol of courage and defiance during her extraordinary career. Her lively charm and energy won over the most faint-hearted. At the great Central Hotel, when airmen on their return spoke of her exploits, their eyes filled with tears. I could understand that in these fighting men she inspired not only respect, but also deep affection. They knew that she had saved their lives, and they were afraid for her. So were all those who knew what terrible risks she ran. But Dédée, always determined and independent, kept her own rules. She showed little interest in our admiration. She was possessed by some inner strength. And to the last, she made her own decisions.

Throughout the war, the line was organised by Belgian leaders at every stage of the journey from Brussels. Belgian pride in its independence was jealously guarded. It was not until 1943 that Room 900 provided radio links and trained agents were sent from London to reinforce it, some of whom were French.

Before the war, Dédée had thought of being an artist, had designed posters and later trained to be a nurse. When war came to Belgium in 1940, she worked in a hospital among wounded British soldiers. Their helplessness moved her to action. Early in 1941, she began to gather friends around her to hide young Belgians and British soldiers who wished to escape to England to fight. Her headquarters were the house at No. 73 Avenue Emile Verhaeren in Brussels where she lived with her father, and here she made plans to establish a route through to Spain.

She was helped by her mother, her aunt and her elder sister, Suzanne Wittek, but her most ardent supporter was her father, Frédéric de Jongh. He could remember the day in 1915 when Edith Cavell was shot for hiding British soldiers. He was a man of great purpose and principle and his country's surrender in 1940 had shocked him deeply. Although a liberal in politics and a hater of violence, he was determined to atone for his sense of shame. At fifty-eight, a bowed and scholarly man, rather shortsighted but, with a resolute chin and mouth, he became a fanatic in his daughter's cause.

When Dédée paid her first visit to the British Consulate in Bilbao in 1941, her father received an unwelcome visit from the Gestapo and the Secret Police of the Luftwaffe* at No. 73. The Germans sat in the demure living-room overlooking the street. They wore the regulation long dark mackintoshes and kept their hats on their heads while they fired questions at him:

"Where is your daughter, Andrée?"

Her father shrugged his shoulders.

"She left here months ago. Young girls—you understand," he sighed. "Nowadays one can't keep track of what young people do."

It seemed that the Gestapo had a full description of her, though it is possible they were then looking for Andrée Dumon (Nadine), one of the guides to Paris and a girl of similar height and appearance to Dédée.

They asked Frédéric de Jongh his occupation.

"I am headmaster of the primary school for boys in the Place Gaucheret."

"Do you go there every day?"

The questioning dragged on, as the German voices grated in his ears. Frédéric de Jongh must have wondered where his admiration for youth and adventure would lead him. All his life he had been a man of peace.

In his headmaster's desk at the Place Gaucheret there were stacks of false identity and ration cards.

But the Gestapo got nothing from him. They smiled sardonically, and left the house.

"We shall be back."

Their grey Opel car sped down the street.

Dédée warned "Monday" on one of her visits to Spain, and new plans were made. The headquarters were moved from No. 73 and they remained in Brussels at the school in the Place Gaucheret until February 1942. In that month, the Secret Police of the Luftwaffe, incensed by reports of the number of airmen returning to Britain, began a further search for Dédée. They arrested her elder sister.

German Commanders-in-Chief in France and Belgium had published orders which made hiding or otherwise assisting Allied prisoners-of-war punishable by death. From this time, the Gestapo and Abwehr** launched their determined campaign against the escape lines. It was to be a grim combat which cost many lives. The intervention of the Luftwaffe was significant. It is known that Goering realised the existence of secret escape organi-

*German Air Force.

**Intelligence service of the German army.

sations for recovery of R.A.F. pilots and crews. He must have known its value to the Allied Air Forces. He gave orders that it was to be crushed. Dédée's father was at Valenciennes in February 1942 reorganising the systems of guides to Paris. On his return to Brussels, he too narrowly escaped arrest. The price on his head was a million Belgian francs. On April 30th, he left Brussels for ever and fled to Paris to continue operating from there.

Six days later, three of his principal lieutenants in Brussels were arrested. It was the end of the pioneer organisation formed by Dédée and her father in Belgium.

At first, it seemed to me that the Brussels organisation would collapse. But out of the confusion appeared a new chief, the Baron Jean Greindl. Since the early part of the year, he had been the Director of a canteen run by the Swedish Red Cross to provide food and clothes for poor children in Brussels. . . .

This new system brought splendid results for Dédée until the end of 1942. He also recruited a new series of guides to take the men by train to Paris.

In the early days of the escape line, Dédée and her French friend, Elvire Morelle, had taken the men direct from Brussels to Bayonne without a halt in Paris. But by 1942, the controls had grown stricter at Quiévrain, the Belgian frontier post, but they could still cross the Somme by boat. Five names appeared regularly in M.I.9 interrogation reports until the end of the year. They were Peggy van Lier, Count Georges, and Count Edouard d'Oultremont, Baron Albert Greindl, younger brother of "Nemo" of the Swedish Canteen, and Jean Ingels. In the spring, they replaced other guides who had been forced to flee from Belgium or who were already in German hands. Among these was the other Andrée—Andrée Dumon, alias Nadine—a nineteen-year-old girl who took twenty men to Paris before her arrest in the summer. She was the "Andrée" whom, it is believed, the Gestapo mistook for Dédée. Andrée Dumon survived Ravensbrück, but her father, who worked for Frédéric de Jongh, disappeared for ever in the programme of mass extermination. His younger daughter, Micheline Dumon, alias "Michou" became one of the line's most successful operators in 1943-44. After several hairbreadth escapes, she reached London safely in May 1944.

As I sat in box-like Room 900, I tried to visualize this new group under Jean Greindl. They were none of them, except their chief, over twenty-five. Even in the wooden English of interrogation reports, I could feel their high spirits and gaiety. They were not professional agents, but as guardians for bewildered airmen they were superb. I had reason to hope that with the strong personality of Jean Greindl in Brussels, the line would revive.

But these were the days before the storm. I was less happy about the Paris section of the line. After his hurried departure from Brussels, Frédéric de Jongh was reunited with his daughter. Dédée, too, was unable to return to Brussels and travelled continually with parties of airmen between Paris and Spain. She had not seen her father since January, when she had paid a daring visit to Brussels and escaped through the back garden of her home seconds before two officers of the Secret Field Police invaded the house.

Frédéric de Jongh refused all his daughter's entreaties to escape to England. He was determined to continue. As Dédée told me afterwards, he could not bear to leave. His wife and elder daughter were in danger in Brussels, and it would seem like desertion. He stayed in Paris till the end.

The Paris organisation had rented a huge, ugly villa at St. Maur to hide airmen before their transport to the south. In charge of it, as housekeeper and cook, was Elvire Morelle. This brave French girl had made one crossing of the Pyrénées with Dédée in February 1942. With Florentino, their Basque guide, they had begun the return journey from San Sebastian to France on February 6th, in driving snow. Elvire slipped in the darkness and fell, fracturing her leg. Florentinò, quick to appreciate the danger, for it was getting light, went off in search of a mule from one of the mountain farms. Elvire, in great pain, was mounted on it and taken back down slippery ways to a farmhouse near Renteria. But thanks to the skill of a Basque doctor from San Sebastian, she recovered and returned to Paris.

Dédée and her father now searched for a suitable flat and found one on the fourth floor of a modern block at No. 10 rue Oudinot, where they made their headquarters and prepared false papers. Jongh organised the hiding of more and more airmen as the months went by. The pressures on the organisation grew. Through "Monday," I sent money to them, but I began to make plans to equip the line with trained agents. I still hoped that Dédée and her father would escape to Britain before it was too late.

Two courageous French assistants of the line were René Coache and his wife Raymonde, of Asnières, a northern suburb of Paris. Raymonde Coache organised food and civilian clothes for the evaders. She and her husband hid no less than thirty men in 1941 and 1942 in their small apartment at Asnières. They still live there today. The rooms are modest and the furniture unchanged from those dangerous months. Their flat on the second floor is reached by a winding stone staircase. There is no way of escape. How often must they have listened for the tread of the Gestapo at their door. Here the Coaches lived their finest hours. They were both to suffer terrible hardships for their service. Madame Coache was arrested at Lille in 1943 and emerged thin and starved from a concentration camp two years later. . . .

The organisation in the south was controlled by an indomitable Belgian lady, Madame Elvire de Greef, known as "Tante Go" after her deceased pet dog [named Go Go]. . . .

From the earliest days, Madame de Greef worked closely with Dédée. When the airmen reached the frontier zone, she made all the arrangements for hiding them in St. Jean-de-Luz before their journey to Spain. She was involved in numerous black market operations to obtain the best possible food, and by these activities lulled suspicion of her real work. She knew all the local smugglers and undercover agents in the bistros of Bayonne and St. Jean-de-Luz and on more than one occasion she blackmailed German officers by threatening to reveal their possession of black market goods and thus escaped arrest.

Her husband, Fernand de Greef, worked as interpreter at the German Kommandantur in Anglet. He had access to official stamps and supplied his wife with blank identity cards and special passes for the Forbidden Zone along the Atlantic coast. Her son Freddy acted as her courier, and her pretty eighteen-year-old daughter, Janine, escorted the men from the station at St. Jean-de-Luz to safe houses in the town. . . .

No less than 337 airmen and soldiers of all the Allies passed through their hands before reaching Spain. With Dédée and Micheline Dumon ("Michou"), Madame de Greef received the George Medal after the war.

The image of Madame de Greef and the deep impression which she made on the evaders became a source of wonderment to me, chairborne in London. I could only marvel at her resource and daring. A photograph of her came into my possession at this time. I forget how it reached me. Not every airman had been trained in security, and one might have brought it as a souvenir. She was slight, with a round face and high cheekbones. Her eyes were prominent, grey tinged with green, and she had short, dark hair. Even from this photograph I could understand the impression of energy and dedication which she gave. In this she was like the other Belgian and French women who worked under the leadership of Dédée, but far more ruthless.

It was some years before I met her in Brussels, when she gave me an account of her exploits in her brisk and unemotional way. She is an extraordinary woman. She was a match for the Gestapo over three years of continuous underground activity. She bribed, cajoled and threatened the Germans and deceived them to the end. Her contribution to victory was tremendous. She is now a widow living in Brussels, but still keeps her air of mystery and resource. She was one of the most skillful and dangerous enemies the Germans ever had. Like Dédée and Michou, who survived these endless dangers, she is strikingly untouched by time. All three of them have kept their vitality and good looks, despite their perilous and often heartbreaking experiences. They are wonderful examples of the triumph of will power and feminine subtlety.

11

The Woman in Charge of Noah's Ark

Women played a significant role in the French resistance. One of the first resistance groups, which emerged around the Musée de l'Homme, was considerably strengthened when anthropologist Germaine Tillion (see Chapter 16, "Night and Fog" below) linked it with military experts. Among these "learned plotters" were the head librarian Yvonne Oddon, secretary Marie-Louise Joubier and typist Jacqueline Bordelet. Historian Agnès Humbert, from another museum, joined the Musée de l'Homme group with her own team that published the first underground paper, Résistance. *Two women from the American embassy, Josie Meyer and Penelope Royall, cooperated. Their letter drop was the religious book store of Madame Templier in Auteuil; the military plans were prepared in the office of Espérance Blain, who otherwise specialized in false identification papers; her coterie of old ladies were experts in pilfering ration cards from the Paris City Hall.*

One of the most effective resistance groups was the trio of women in Béthune: garage owner Sylvette Leleu, café owner Angèle Tardiveau, and a nun, Sister Marie-Laurence (from County Cork). One of the safe-houses on the underground route to Spain belonged to the Countess Elisabeth de la Panouse. One of the operatives was "Mimi la Blonde," a waitress.

There were countless women in the many resistance groups and among the maquis, the partisans. There is no doubt, however, that the greatest French resistance heroine of World War II was Marie-Madeline Fourcade, an enchanting Parisian in her thirties, mother of two and executive secretary in a publishing firm. She was the only woman who headed a major resistance network, the Alliance, dealing mostly with espionage for the Allies. Starting in 1940 in southern France, her network of over 3,000 operatives eventually covered all of France. Her story surpasses all fiction about beautiful spies.

The Germans referred to the Alliance as Noah's Ark because its members took code names of animals. Madame Fourcade was Hedgehog; her bodyguard Ant; a female messenger Chinchilla; two gunrunners Ram and Great Dane. One of her most valuable operatives was a seamstress inside the German submarine base at Brest; whenever the Nazis had their Mae Wests (life jackets) checked, she reported the preparations to Hedgehog.

It was to the advantage of Noah's Ark to have a woman chief. Few suspected a woman in that position. Not even the British knew at first that they were dealing with a woman. When a double agent was discovered in the Ark and was to be liquidated, he gallantly warned Hedgehog of the impending German invasion of the heretofore unoccupied part of France, in November 1942. Chances are that he would not have done this for a man.

The network supplied the British and later the Americans with details of German military installations, arsenals, troop movements and the best detailed map of the coast for the 1944 invasion of Europe. The British in turn provided transmitters, radios, food, money and arms, dropped by parachutes or flown in at secret landing fields.

Hedgehog had her agent in the huge German naval base at Keroman in Brittany; it was her operative Jeanne Rousseau who first alerted the Allies about the research at Peenemünde on the V-1 rockets, Hitler's secret weapons. The network had underground routes to Spain, Monaco and England, and cooperated with the Belgian resistance group called Dame Blanche (White Lady). It was Hedgehog's réseau *that spirited French general Henri Giraud* to the submarine that took him to Algiers in North Africa, no small task, considering the general's delusions of grandeur (he demanded two subs and an American crew on a British sub; he got one sub and one American officer).*

The ranks of Noah's Ark were often decimated by arrests. Its members were tortured beyond imagination; one had burning papers

*The Allies at the time preferred Giraud to de Gaulle as leader of the French in North Africa.

passed all over his naked body. Many were dragged to concentration camps and executed.

Hedgehog's exploits would put Homer to the test. She never for a moment lost faith in the ultimate victory of freedom and justice. While she was eternally vigilant and circumspect, she considered patience "an absurd virtue fit for a thin-blooded Diogenes," for only "an ass seeks no vengeance." "I looked into my heart," she said, "my hostility remained undiminished and I boiled with a desire for revenge."

Her survival borders on the miraculous. In the fall of 1941, she was smuggled to a conference in Spain in a diplomatic pouch; she almost froze to death on the nine-hour trip. At one point she had to be airlifted to London for safety, but she insisted on returning and carrying on the struggle.

She had dozens of close calls with the enemy. Once she was arrested with several of her men, but the French police inspector transporting them to jail was Alpaca of her own Ark! They were freed, and in turn she provided for all policemen involved to be flown out to England to join the Free French.

Her other arrest occurred in July of 1944 near Marseille, shortly after her return from London. The police were after Grand Duke (Night Owl) who had been in charge in the south of France during her absence. He had just dropped off numerous messages at her place, including one on the plan of the German generals to assassinate Hitler. What transpired at her arrest and after is best told in her own words.

After the war, Marie-Madeleine Fourcade was rewarded for her services with a membership in the Légion d'Honneur and the Order of the British Empire; she received countless honors from organizations and cities. She became an author and a member of the European Parliament. Her faithful companion and secretary all these years has been Josette Fournal Desaintfuscien, the code clerk, Aigrette (Egret) of the resistance.

"German police! Open!". . . .

The wave surged in. There were two dozen of them, almost all in grey-green uniform. Among them were four civilians, one obviously a North African. "Where's the man? Where's the man?" they screamed into my face, digging their revolvers into my chest. The soldiers carrying sub-machine guns gathered in a circle round me.

"What man?" I asked, putting on a bewildered look. "I'm a woman and I'm on my own."

"He went that way," the North African said, pointing to the courtyard.

I flared up. "There are other flats in the house. If you're looking for someone, why do you imagine he's in the first one you come to?"

"That's true," said another civilian, who seemed to be in charge. "We're wasting time. Let's go and see. You, watch her," he said to a little soldier, who leaned against the mantelpiece and trained his gun on me. I heard the doors banging on the other landings and people shouting and protesting. In the half-light the grids of my messages glimmered on the table in the centre of the drawing room. It was a miracle that in their excitement they had noticed nothing. Under the watchdog's vigilant gaze I went back to the table and quickly piled up the papers spread over it. Then pretending to blow my nose noisily I backed towards the divan in the alcove, and, slipping out of my guard's line of sight for a second, I threw the whole lot as far as possible underneath.

"What are you doing?" barked the watchdog.

"I'm blowing my nose," I said gravely, walking over to him.

"In this heat!" he commiserated. Seeing that he was ready to chat, I asked him who they were looking for. "A man who is causing us a lot of trouble, a terrorist."

This was my cue and I picked it up at once. "Someone from the maquis?" I asked, pretending to be frightened.

"*Jawohl!* Someone from the maquis. He came into this house about three-quarters of an hour ago. We were sent to get him."

"What does he look like?" I asked in a dead voice.

"Tall and fair, apparently. The Gestapo chiefs call him Grand Duke."

At that moment the Gestapo chiefs themselves came back, still shouting.

"He's not up there; he's got away. This woman is lying to us; she wanted to gain time," they told the North African.

"Why did you push against the door when we wanted to come in?" shouted the leader, grabbing me by the shoulders.

"Put yourself in my place. You gave me a fine old fright. I thought you

"The Woman in Charge of Noah's Ark" is from Marie-Madeleine Fourcade, *Noah's Ark, A Memoir of Struggle and Resistance* (New York: E. P. Dutton, 1974), pp. 328-38.

were terrorists from the maquis. I stopped as soon as I heard you shout German police."

"That's right," he said, withdrawing his claws. "What are you doing here by yourself?"

I let fly. I told them I was getting away from the bombing in Toulon, as the raids were driving me mad. I hated the war and I'd come to Aix to get some peace and quiet. It was a deliberate decision. "Can't you go about things a bit more gently?" I added, going over to the offensive. "I've always heard the Germans were courteous. If I'd known that you were the Gestapo I'd have opened the door right away."

Meanwhile the soldiers and civilians had been searching the flat, turning up the mattresses and easy chairs, rummaging through the cupboards, the suitcases and the fireplaces. "What are you hoping to find?" I went on, to keep the atmosphere relaxed.

The leader described Grand Duke, going into details about his importance, and a big network that they had not yet been able to smash, the "Alliance." My blood froze. So it was *us* they were after, not me. But what then? I must go on and spin out my yarn. I blundered on, making myself seem as stupid as I possibly could.

"You see how right I was to be afraid of the man from the maquis. I heartily approve of your hunting them down. Is there any way I can help?"

The ferrets returned empty-handed. "Nothing suspicious, chief," said the North African.

Now completely mollified, the leader lowered his revolver: "Here's the address of our office. If the man I've described comes back here, let me know at once."

"Are you sure he lives here? What's his name?"

"We don't know. We only know his alias. He may have come in under the porch to throw his pursuers off the scent and then got away while these idiots were raising the alarm instead of shooting him on sight."

Once again they split up and looked through the flat. Suddenly they pointed to the pile of cigarettes on a corner of one of the pieces of furniture. "I see you smoke Gauloises. You've got a lot. Cigarettes are rationed."

I began to curse my vice. Why ever had I started smoking again? "I made a swap on the black market," I said brazening it out. "Some people would rather have butter."

I offered them the Made-in-England Gauloises and lit one myself. They seemed to be in no hurry and went on standing around and smoking. Then, after a few brief orders, the soldiers picked up their weapons and moved towards the door. My heart gave a leap. I had won, they *were* going. The civilians began to say goodbye, repeating their request. I gave a silent whoop of joy. Bells rang in my ears. "They've gone, they've gone."

Before passing through the drawing-room door, one of them suddenly went down on all fours and looked under the divan. I saw his arm shoot underneath. Carefully he pulled out the grids, looked at them and with a triumphant gesture thrust them under his colleagues' noses.

That was that. My turn had come. I tried to think only of those who had gone before me: Navarre, Eagle, Swift, Schaerrer. The glorious band gathered round me and sustained me. It was perfectly normal; it was bound to happen to me as well. Anything else would have been unfair.

* * *

Hurling abuse at me in a way that convinced me it would be better not to make a dash for it, the Gestapo began to smash the furniture with their rifle butts. They shoved me violently aside so that they could get at a pretty desk. I was swept by a terrible rage.

"Stop! Nothing here is mine, this isn't my home. The owner hasn't the least idea who I am and has locked her cupboards. Wait until tomorrow and she'll open them for you. Anyway, you're surely not going to smash up old furniture just for the sake of smashing it up!"

"But who are *you*?" asked the leader, shaking me like a plum tree.

I looked at him and his sweaty face with withering contempt. "You're much too unimportant for me to tell you."

"You're British?"

"No, French."

"When did you arrive?"

"A few days ago, parachuted in the dark, not far away."

"Who is the man who came here just now?"

"It was the first time I'd seen him. I don't know his name any more than you do."

"What did he come for?"

"To arrange to meet me at noon tomorrow in the Place du Marché, to introduce me to someone who's to take me somewhere else."

"Where?"

"I don't know. I do as I'm told. I just carry out orders."

"Who is this person?"

"One of the network's agents."

"How will you recognize him?"

"*He* will recognize *me*, by a scarf that I shall wear." I must gain time, yes, gain time by saying anything false but plausible. . . .

In kicking up the carpets, the soldiers had burst open my little hassocks. The reports in them flew out like a swarm of butterflies, spread all over the room and were passed quickly from hand to hand. They had found some cognac, and they made the most of it. Their voices rose as anger overcame them. An NCO explained to the men the meaning of the plans and schedules at which they were goggling: *"Ach so! Geheim! Sehr geheim!"* (So! Secret!

Top Secret!") they growled. "They're going to lynch me," I thought. Giving way to indignation, several of them rushed at me, itching to shoot." "Halt!" ordered the leader and, not without some difficulty and the help of his acolytes, he restored order by punching and threatening his men. Then he dragged me off sheepishly into a corner of the room.

"You don't look scared," he said.

"I've nothing to reproach myself with."

"Exactly!" he said and lowered his voice. "That's what I'm beginning to think. If you're in the same business as I am we could both do ourselves a bit of good."

"That takes the biscuit," I thought to myself. Then it dawned on me. "He takes me for a double agent and he's offering to go shares."

"I don't understand what business you want to talk about," I hedged. "Mine only concerns me."

"That's not helpful," he insisted. "At least tell me who you are."

"I'll only tell the big Gestapo chief who I am. I haven't the right to tell you. Once again, you're too unimportant."

He snapped an order to the North African, who ran off and then, trying his luck again, asked me about the rendezvous at the Place du Marché. "If we take you to this rendezvous, will you be helpful and allow yourself to be accosted by your agent? God help you if you're lying. You've been leading us up the garden path for two hours. We have ways of making you talk and beg for mercy."

"Tomorrow? Of course!"

I must gain time, I must gain time. The blood was pounding in my head. I saw the North African coming back, still running, like a figure in a nightmare. The civilians went into a huddle.

"You're lucky," the leader said to me. "The regional boss will be in Aix tomorrow at nine. He's willing to see you."

"You bet he is," I thought. "Considering the time he's been after me, he's going to have a very pleasant surprise."

"Meanwhile we're going to get you out of here. Pack your case."

They were going to put me in prison. How could I raise the alarm? Grand Duke was going to arrive at eight next morning and would walk into the trap. "I must escape tonight," I thought, throwing a few toilet articles into my big bag. Toothbrush, toothpaste, soap, comb and a change of dress. "I must escape to save Grand Duke, Weevil and the others. I haven't come back to France to be caught. I must save them."

"Get a move on," shouted the Gestapo man on guard outside the dressing room. I groped for and found the poison. If I had not discovered a solution by tomorrow. . . .

"I'm ready," I said, and I was bundled down the stairs and into a black car that drove off with a strong escort.

"You certainly took us in, madame, you never betrayed the slightest sign of emotion, except perhaps a trembling of your fingertips; but we were quite convinced that we were on the wrong track."

"Then why did you look under the bed?"

"An old professional reflex. But what about you? After all you're not the Queen of the Netherlands. I don't see why you refuse to tell us your name."

"Perhaps I'm another queen," I said, trying to put on a haughty voice.

I had heard the words "Miollis barracks." So I was going to be put into a barracks. Would it be to shoot me at once? We did in fact draw up at the entrance to a barracks and I was taken through the guard room, at the back of which was the classic "punishment cell" for recalcitrant soldiers. There were a few men in it, but they were promptly kicked out and I took their place in a suffocating fug of stale urine, sweat and German tobacco. The Gestapo man gallantly put my traveling bag at the foot of the bed, which was covered with a thick, greyish blanket.

"There you are. I'll be back at nine tomorrow to see the chief. Do you want me to leave the light on?"

"No, I mean to sleep."

"A cigarette?"

"Why not, if it's one of mine."

He laughed as he held out the packet. "You're not going to commit suicide?" he asked, suddenly seized by suspicion.

"Why should I?"

"Because all British spies commit suicide as soon as they're left alone."

"But I'm neither a spy nor British and I've no reason to commit suicide."

"Then I needn't worry?" he asked stupidly.

"Not in the least."

These people were incredible. They arrested you so that they could kill you and then they asked you to put their minds at rest!

* * *

The door was heavily bolted and the light hanging from the middle of the ceiling went out. I felt my way towards the right-hand corner of the window like a lost dog and was overtaken by a horrible fit of vomiting. If the oily Gestapo thugs had only known how mortally afraid I was! The tremendous effort I made to face up to this ordeal left me gasping, limp and exhausted and my head was as empty as a nutshell. "You'd do better to go to sleep, old girl," I chided myself, flopping onto the bed in spite of its stench, compounded of squashed bedbugs and leather badly maintained with ersatz soap. "You'll have to sleep so as to stand up to tomorrow's interrogation."

A Gestapo interrogation! Arrest, the possibility of being shot or of having my throat slit had been with me too long to cause me fear; but in a few hours they would open the door and they would say: "Marie-Madeleine," —for they would have discovered my real name during the night from the captured mail—"we've got you. Tell us what's going on in your network. Tell us what it did in the past, the inexplicable things still happening, because in spite of the hundreds of arrests, we can't wipe you out. Now we've got *you,* the most important one of all. Where is Grand Duke? Where are all the others?"

I would have no choice but to say nothing, grit my teeth, endure the beatings, the humiliations, the tortures. I should have to resist. Resisting torture was undoubtedly what Resistance meant.

The Chief's chivalrous offer came back to my mind: "If they arrest you, my dear, tell them that I sent you to France to watch the Communist Party. They won't dare touch you." How was I to tell them that and make them believe it when they had captured me with all that material! And the grids beneath the bed! They would read the first grid written out in clear and I should be implicated in the plot against Hitler: that was the only thing that would interest them. I knew them; they would want to drag the names of the conspirators out of me. Everything became as clear as day; their haste to get me away and out of sight, to bring in the head of the Gestapo, their pretence of friendliness. I was becoming the centre piece of a diabolical game of chess that could bring them great honour and great fortune.

To save Hitler. Better to die here and now. I sprang to my feet and rushed to find my bag. Where was it? It had fallen on the ground near the window. I opened it and felt for the pills. Should I take them now or tomorrow, when they came in? No! Before taking that irrevocable step I must try everything. . . . Escape! The idea that had been uppermost in my mind from the beginning took hold of me. Escape! Escape! Every other thought was paralysed.

I looked at my watch. It was midnight. . . .

I had five hours left in which to escape.

I lay down again on the bed. I was stupid; it was impossible; it would be better to go to sleep. I could not close my eyes. A faint gleam of light came from the window. I was suffocating. "You must breathe, old girl, you're going mad." I got up and went over to the window, a big, ordinary kind of opening, probably overlooking the street by which we had arrived. A thick wooden board screwed into the frame blocked four-fifths of it. It had undoubtedly been put there to prevent soldiers under punishment from communicating with the world outside while at the same time allowing the air, as well as a little light, to come in. But this meant that they must have removed the glass. There was, in fact, no proper window at all, only bars dimly outlined against the night.

I pushed the bed under the window, put the sanitary receptable (a sort of big zinc washing-up bowl) upside down upon it, took off my shoes, climbed up and found I was level with the opening. I avidly gulped in the soft night air. I tried the bars with my forehead. They were not prison bars; simply the bars that are found on all ground floor windows the world over, strong and proud in their protective role. Without proper tools it was pointless to think of moving one from the uprights or of tearing down the wooden board. The problem was to slip somehow between the board and the bars and, once there, to push to get out. . . .

What a pity I hadn't brought Turtle Dove's olive oil. I would have smeared it all over my body like those Indo-Chinese burglars who, according to my father's stories, used to break into houses at night, their naked bodies covered with fat or grease so that they would slip more easily through the hands of anyone trying to catch them. They went about the job stark naked. I must go naked like them, to be as thin as possible. I took off my clothes and practised holding the little batik dress in my teeth and a few banknotes in my hand. The main thing was not to take anything that might make a noise if it dropped.

My watch showed three o'clock and, as I expected, there was a change of guard. The men coming in got into bed without a word and the light went out. Those men were really tired, as their snores immediately confirmed. I waited a few minutes, then got back into my batik dress and banged on my door. . . . No response but snores.

I undressed again and began my climb to freedom. Steadying myself at the top of the window opening and plunging feet first between the wooden plant and the bars was less difficult than I had feared; but I lost almost all my bank notes in the process. I immediately stopped trying to push my head between the bars that were set into the stonework on both sides of the frame, for only iron is likely to give. Methodically, I tried the rest of them. To my great surprise one gap seemed big enough to take my head provided I was prepared to push hard. I tried them all again. I was right; only one was big enough for me to get through. I returned to it and pushed with all my strength. My head went through.

At that precise moment a motor convoy swirled into the street from the left and drew up with a screech of brakes. It stopped opposite my window and I quickly withdrew my head, so sharply that I thought I had torn off my ears. The Gestapo were returning. They would find me, naked and pinned like a beetle against this board that scrapped my back. What an idiot I was to have waited so long! The NCO in charge of the convoy began to shout: the raucous voice of a sentry posted a few yards to the right answered. I hadn't seen him! And I was counting on fleeing in that direction. . . . A dialogue started. The convoy had missed its way; it turned and went back. It was not the Gestapo. As it went by I saw that it was a unit that we had told London was being sent to reinforce the Normandy front. The trucks disappeared, their headlights glowing like cats' eyes, just above ground level.

Pushing my head through again was even more painful than the first time, but the pain and the fear of failure made me perspire profusely, which helped my skin to slip against the iron. After my neck I got one shoulder through, then my right leg. Squeezing my hips through was sheer agony.

The pain was appalling but I knew that once the head is through the rest of the body will go, while the pain I felt would be nothing compared with what would be in store for me with the Gestapo.

I suddenly found myself down on the pavement, but the slight thud of my feet as I dropped to the ground had attracted the sentry's attention. I wrapped my dress round my neck and crouched down. *"Wer da?"* The soldier flashed his torch and its beam swept the darkness. I lay flat on the ground. I must get away quickly! Summoning up all my remaining energy I crossed the square on all fours and began to move as fast as my legs would let me, first straight ahead, then dodging from side to side, out into the vague open space that I could just make out. I ran on, stumbling into the potholes and tearing my skin on the brambles. At last, no longer hearing any sounds behind me, I put on my dress. I was free! Free! But if the sentry had raised the alarm, they would send dogs after me and I should be found in no time.

* * *

The whitish outlines of the stone crosses in a cemetery caught my eye. Here there was safety. I could hide in one of the chapels. In the morning I could be sure of finding a priest who would help me, or a grave digger who would take pity on me. I plunged into the cemetery and sat down on a tombstone to rest.

The thought of the dogs and how to escape them obsessed me. But an episode in a childhood book came back to mind; the story of an escaping officer who had put the dogs off the scent by washing his hands for a long time in a stream. But no river flowed through Aix, except a stream that skirted the city to the east—the Torse. The road that I was now following ran due east, so, rolling, and tumbling down a stony bank, I eventually found the Torse—a thin thread of water, but big enough for me to wash in. I began with my feet and then washed my raw, badly skinned face for a long time.

Which direction must I take to get to Grand Duke's farm? It looked in fact as if I had to start all over again and go back through the town. The very idea terrified me. If need be I could go to the radio operator, Weevil, but would he have time to warn everybody? At half-past seven Grand Duke would leave his farm and go to pick me up at the flat on the Rue Granet and he would walk into the trap. I was ashamed of my hesitations.

So I retraced my steps. In the dawning light that in Provence spreads swiftly in an immense haze of gold and birdsong. I found myself close to the barracks once more. Everywhere was quiet; the sentry was lost in his own thoughts and saw me appear without interest. How could the German suspect that the person coming by was the prisoner who had escaped? I walked past him, proud and dignified, but panic seized me once I had turned the corner. I ran feverishly up a path that looked like an Arab street and went into a garden where I crouched down among the hollyhocks. It was too much; I could not move.

Then the thought of Grand Duke being arrested because of my cowardice drove me on. I dashed up to a very simple little house and began to hammer on the shutters. After a long delay a woman opened them. She was altogether unpleasant—dishevelled, rheumy-eyed and stinking of garlic. I mumbled that I was fleeing from the bombing and had lost my way in the curfew.

"Clear off! If you don't go away and let us sleep, I'll call the police," she barked, threatening me with a broom. With that she barricaded herself in.

I set off again, my legs trembling. In the barracks the bugle would soon be sounding reveille. In ten minutes time they would be opening my cell to take in some food.

By a miracle I came out in the centre of the town. A woman in deep mourning was clearly on her way to mass. I went up to her and said: "Madame, I lost my way during the curfew. I'm looking for the Vauvenargues road."

"Come with me, I'm going that way."

She started walking again, not too quickly, so that I could pad along barefoot behind her. "Would you like to lean on me?" she asked. "You seem to be in pain."

I leaned on her arm. The city was awake and passers-by looked at me in surprise. The woman in mourning appeared to me like a marvellous bulwark against the dogs I could hear barking in the distance and the armoured cars dashing across the square. That was it! They had discovered my escape. They were going to close the roads out of the town. I saw with horror that we were heading for the very street where I had been staying. We crossed one square, then another, and when we reached the corner of the Sainte-Marie-Madeleine church, my protectors parted from me.

"Go straight on. Past the convent you'll find the Vauvenargues road. Cross the Torse". . . .

How was I going to cross the bridge over the Torse? It was bound to have been guarded since my escape had been discovered. I crept through terraces and leapt over piles of stones and found myself in a field in which some old peasant women were busy gleaning. I began to do the same, picking up ears of corn and bits of dandelion. Out of the corner of my eye I could see the German soldiers setting up road blocks, striding up and down the bridge, stopping all the women who went over it and checking their papers. But they paid not the slightest attention to the gleaners below. I moved forward, bending double and finally came out on the road a long way beyond the soldiers.

Seven o'clock. I should be in time to warn Grand Duke. One, two, three bends. Where was the farm? They all looked alike in their setting of olives and cypresses. At last I saw it, a cool oasis nestling among its geraniums. One more hill, a stream to cross, two bends. The front door was unlocked —how careless Grand Duke and Marie-Sol were! I went into the hall, I called out and pushed open their bedroom door. They were up and on their feet in a flash, naked, healthy and beautiful, their wide staring eyes brimming over with loyalty as I heard myself saying: "I've just escaped. I've saved your lives." Then everything around me became confused and I collapsed.

12

Women in the German Resistance

Heinrich Mann once said that one of the most horrid things about Nazism was the immense silence in Germany; while the regime made so much noise, the Germans themselves were mute. What Hitler perpetrated on his own people remained a deep secret.

After the end of the war, some of this deep secret started emerging into view. Still, the English speaking public is hardly aware of the fact that there had been resistance inside the Reich aside from the July 20, 1944, attempt against Hitler's life. Even less is it known that a considerable role in this resistance, such as it could be, was played by women.

Proportionately to its population, Germany produced less resistance against Nazism than other countries. Resistance within Germany was more difficult than in the occupied countries, where it was sanctified by the struggle against the foreign invaders. It is easy to state with hindsight that the Germans had more reasons to resist Nazism than anybody else, as in the long run it presaged their own doom. One must keep in mind that after the humiliation of Versailles, for the majority of Germans Hitler offered an acceptable way out of economic misery and a psychologically greatly ego-inflating ideology, garnished with slogans of their own superiority. "Deutschland über alles" was a potent tonic, a panacea for all that ailed them and a sedative to hush up unwelcome pangs of conscience.

Much of the German resistance was radically "cleaned up" between 1933 and 1939, eradicated to a great extent by executioners. With the start of the war, the Nazi terror intensified, resistance became even more dangerous and less likely to succeed. Relatively few German men and women resisters were found still alive in prisons and concentration camps by the end of the war.

Since the Gestapo and SS destroyed a great deal of their files, it is impossible to reconstruct the total picture of women's participation in the German resistance. A now rare book, published before the war by the Union of Law and Freedom in Prague, Czechoslovakia, under the title Deutsche Frauenschicksale *(London: Malik Publishing House, 1937), listed for the years 1935 and 1936 alone close to 300 names of German women* known *to have been convicted for political reasons. More recently, Hanna Elling offers a list of 271 German women who were executed or died as a result of political activities and persecution under Nazism, emphasizing that the list is by far not all encompassing.*

Who were the female resisters? Most were single women, not in the public eye, although a few had been members of state and local governments. They were homemakers, secretaries, sales ladies, seamstresses, students, teachers, newspaper women, writers, nurses, nuns, governesses, laborers, also artists, actresses, dancers, singers; a few were university professors and physicians. In age they ranged from teenagers to women in their seventies. Maria Ehrlich, a Munich teacher, was executed at the age of eighty-one for "defeatist utterances"; Liesel Plücker of Düsseldorf, aged sixty-five, was let go after five years of prison, only to be gassed in Auschwitz as too old and hence "unworthy of life."

They were politically aware women, especially those who had belonged to labor movements and to the outlawed Communist and Socialist parties; these formed a large proportion of the German resistance. Some of them also drew the longest sentences and after their prison terms were shipped "for indefinite periods" to concentration camps. Thus, for instance, socialist Anna Stiegler spent eleven years, Communist Käthe Popall twelve years, and Communist Erika Buchman ten years in various prisons and concentration camps. Unlike many criminals, asocials and some others, they demonstrated, as most politicals did, exemplary solidarity and discipline during their incarcerations.

In one respect, the Nazis did not discriminate against women: when caught in the resis-

tance, they were subjected just as the men were to hunger and thirst, torture and chicanery; they were jailed, sent on to forced labor, to concentration camps, shot, hanged and decapitated.

Women who were mothers often sent their children away partly to be free for resistance activities, partly to keep the children out of harm. They were farmed out to relatives or friends in the countryside or sent abroad to Sweden or Switzerland.

A few German women, like Emma Gumz of Berlin, hid Jews because they felt compassion for them. A few thousand Jews were saved this way. In Berlin, for instance, where there were 160,000 Jews before the war, 5,000 survived, but even this number included those who were protected by marriage to a non-Jew.

German women worked actively against the Nazi regime writing, printing and distributing anti-Nazi and later antiwar literature, serving as messengers maintaining contact within and outside of Germany, arranging illegal meetings at their homes, disseminating news from Allied broadcasts, collecting money, food and clothing for the families of the persecuted, hiding illegals, cooperating with the French underground, and furnishing information to the USSR. A few were captured as parachuists, like Erna Eifler, who was shot without a trial at Ravensbrück on June 7, 1944.

Some worked independently, like Hiltgunt Zassenhaus, who as an interpreter stumbled into the chance to help Scandinavian prisoners of war. She did so spiritually and materially under the very noses of the Nazis, repeatedly risking her life. Now a physician in the United States, she was decorated by the governments of Denmark, Norway and West Germany. A television documentary about her life and work, entitled "It Mattered to Me," has been aired in Europe.

Others belonged to organized resistance groups like that of Harro Schulze-Boysen, in which at least ten women were executed during 1942-1943, among them Libertas Schulze-Boysen; or the "White Rose," one of whose legendary leaders, Sophie Scholl, twenty-two, was executed in Munich on February 22, 1943. There were women in the "Red Orchestra" network, in the Schlotterbeck group and several others.

Hundreds of women were denounced by informers or watchful Nazis. The regime eliminated them "in self-defense." Thus, the Reich felt threatened by sixty-one-year-old Paula Billstein, a Krefeld knitter and former Communist. For expressing anti-fascist sentiments in a letter to her convicted son, she was thrown into the concentration camp Lichtenburg; she was released shortly before her death on July 4, 1938. Anne Meier, forty-six, a Catholic social worker from the Saar, was sent to Ravensbrück in 1942 for declining to join the NSDAP (National Socialist German Workers' Party or Nazi Party). Deaconess Ehrengard Frank-Schultz, fifty-nine, expressed regret that the attack on Hitler failed; she was summarily executed, as was the young nurse Gertrud Seele, whose comment that collecting old newspapers only prolonged the war was interpreted as aiding the enemy.

Still other victims were relatives and friends of resisters, caught in the net of the Gestapo, like Elisabeth Kusnitzky, sixty-six, of Berlin, mother of a person implicated in the July 20, 1944, plot against Hitler; she was executed on November 30, 1944, in Berlin-Plötzensee.

A large group of female resistance members came from the Jehovah's Witnesses, referred to in Germany as Bibleforscher, *or Bible researchers. Many ended up in concentration camps and several were executed, as for instance, Frieda Metzen, thirty-two, a servant from Dörpling, for spreading news of foreign broadcasts, or Helene Gotthold, forty-eight, from Herne, for trying to dissuade young men from military service.*

Over 400 nuns from various religious orders are known *to have fallen victims to the Nazi furor in Germany and the lands occupied by them. Their "martyrology," as Pope John Paul II called it, has been recorded recently* but only in part; for never will it be known how*

*Benedicta Maria Kempner, *Nonnen unter dem Hakenkreuz* (Würzburg, Germany: Nauman Verlag, 1979).

many more risked their lives for their patriotic and humanitarian convictions. For aiding and harboring persecuted Christians and Jews they also suffered and died in prisons and concentration camps.

They also saved dozens of feeble minded and crippled people under their care, preventing their gassing under the Nazi euthanasia program to which about 100,000 men, women and children fell victims. Unfortunately, most of the time they had to "stand by silently like martyrs," in the words of one Mother Superior, while their patients were dragged to their deaths.

The fingers of hatred also reached inside the convents, claiming as their due nuns converted from Judaism. Thus perished, for instance, the philosopher Edmund Husserl's former assistant, the Carmelite Sister Theresa Benedicta from Breslau (Dr. Edith Stein, fifty-one). She was arrested in her convent and gassed upon arrival in Auschwitz on August 9, 1942 with several other nuns and monks. Franciscan Sister Restituta (Helene Kafka, forty-eight), an operating room nurse, was beheaded for treason. The charge: she duplicated an anti-Nazi poem, "Soldiers' Song."

The early resistance of German women is demonstrated by the fact that, long before Ravensbrück, the first female concentration camp was established in Moringen in October 1933, the year Hitler came to power. By March 1938, it proved to be too small, and the inmates were transferred to the concentration camp of Lichtenburg, from which the male inmates were sent to Buchenwald. The surviving 860 German and 7 Austrian women were then shipped to Ravensbrück on May 18, 1939.

The following testimony of Luise Mauer affords us a glimpse into the activities and the fate of a woman in the German resistance. After serving her four years in prison, she was not released but as an "unreliable element" was sent with sixteen other women to Ravensbrück, where she spent another four years.

I was born on February 26, 1906 in Hochheim am Main. I grew up in a small-town, not to say bourgeois, milieu. My parents owned a ceramics factory. I was the seventh child. In my third year I lost my mother through an accident. Soon afterwards my father remarried.

In 1923 I met my future husband. We got married in 1927. By this time we were both already members of the KPD [Communist Party of Germany]. In 1930 my husband, who was member of the Opel factory council, was arrested for the first time during the strike of the Opel workers. This fact spurred me on even more to fight against the bourgeoisie and the beginning trends to turn Germany into a fascist state. Shortly after this my husband had been elected to the legislature of Hessen. Now we saw each other seldom, because we each had our political work.

At the end of February, 1933—the Reichstag was burning*—my husband went underground. During the night before the national election, from March 4th to the 5th, 1933, a few comrades and myself prepared flyers, in which we urged the population to join our struggle against fascism. [We stated that] it was highest time to do so; its rule would lead to the suppression of the wide majority of the masses, and then it would take a long time until we could live again as free people. The distribution of the leaflets was done in the following way: we divided Raunheim, where we lived at that time, into districts, and stuck the leaflets during the night into mailboxes. Raunheim at that time had 5,000 inhabitants.

The next morning 38 people were arrested, I among them. I was remanded into custody of Darmstadt. In spite of being abused during the interrogations, no confession could be forced out of any of the arrested, and thus in September of 1933 I was released. After that I was under constant police surveillance, so that it became impossible for me to carry on further political activities where I had done so up till then. Besides there was the probability that I could be arrested again, should they notice the slightest illegal activity on my part; therefore the party sent me abroad to support from there the illegal anti-fascist work. First I went to Switzerland. From here I covered Southern Germany, renewed broken contacts, organized new contacts and distributed anti-fascist literature that I imported from Switzerland.

"Women in the German Resistance" is from Hanna Elling, *Frauen im deutschen Widerstand 1933-1945* (Frankfurt am Main, Germany: Röderberg Verlag, 1981), pp. 120-23. Translation copyright by Vera Laska. Reprinted with the kind permission of the publisher.

*On February 27, 1933, the Reichstag (Lower House of Parliament) in Berlin burned down. Hitler, chancellor since January 1933, accused the Communists of arson and outlawed the party. Dutch Marinus van der Lubbe was beheaded for the crime; some evidence pointed to Hermann Goering as initiator of the fire. The truncated Reichstag, without the eighty-one expelled Communists, voted Hitler dictatorial powers on March 23, 1933; the following year the Reichstag was abolished.

In Stuttgart I looked up a woman whose husband had been remanded into custody. Naturally, it was dangerous, but we had to start somewhere. She was very kind and referred me to three other friends whom I looked up and asked whether they would be ready to distribute anti-fascist leaflets and periodicals that I would bring them. A few declared that they were ready. Then I returned illegally [to Switzerland] near Lörrach, across the so-called Green Border that had been pointed out to me. I picked up the leaflets and crossed the border the same way, disguised as a tourist, with my backpack; in Lörrach I took the train to Stuttgart. I went to those friends, handed over the leaflets that called upon the population to beware of fascism and to be united because Hitler meant war. Then I returned the same illegal way. I brought over materials this way four or five times.

Then I went to the Saar region, where my husband worked as a trade unionist, and placed myself at the disposal of the KPD. I was, however, referred to the IAH (International Workmen's Aid) and carried on agitation work for it. In the towns of the Saar we arranged lectures with slides, we organized transports of children or comrades in danger to France and to Luxemburg. I took part in three such transports; each time I took about 20 children and after three weeks accompanied them back. All children were guests in private homes.

When the Saar district was annexed to fascist Germany in January of 1935, I went through Forback to Strassburg. There I received orders to go to Prague. First I visited once more my child in Switzerland. . . .

In Prague I received a Czech passport and took the train via Annaberg to Köln [Cologne] to get an endangered female comrade out of the Saar. Near Saarlouis I crossed with my passport to the Saar. There I already had my contacts since my previous work. The next morning the comrade showed up. We took the train and got without any trouble to the Czech border. There we were met and passed on illegally.

All that had to be prepared down to minute details. Everything had been agreed upon beforehand in Prague; besides, we had comrades at the border who could have advised us and who would have facilitated the connection to Prague, had not all gone well. But everything clicked down to the minute.

Now I got a new order: I was to carry illegal political literature to Leipzig. But I did not take this illegal material across the border; that was done by a so-called border-man, who was not in the KPD, but who was an anti-fascist. He handed over the package to me at a prearranged place in Annaberg. . . . I took it and went by train to Leipzig. In the bundle were issues of the *Rote Fahne* [Red Flag], which was the central organ of the Communist Party, and leaflets for workers in factories, trade unions and on the railroads. All went well. I rushed to my destination at the place of a comrade whose husband was then in jail. He was serving six years in the penitentiary, so that it was reasonable to assume that she was reliable. I also had additional addresses where I could have delivered the materials. I stayed overnight at the place of another comrade, whose husband was in illegal work in Prague. Naturally, she herself was in danger, so for me this was not a reliable place to stay. But this was the time of the fair, so she could register me as a visitor to the fair. And so this worked well twice. Within 14 days I went twice back and forth.

But after the second time I was arrested at the Café Felche together with another comrade. I saw right away that something was wrong, because too many Gestapo looking men were sitting all over the place. I said to the comrade: "Watch out, do not pay my bill, do not take the leaflets that I meant to give you, refuse the package, get up abruptly, pay your bill and say that you do not want to have anything to do with me. Say that we have once known each other and I used that to give you [illegal] materials." That stuff was next to me, so I had no way out. The comrade did as told. Then I saw how four men got up, followed him, and arrested him on the steps. I still ordered another coffee and cake, thinking that it might be the last time. Then I also got up and was arrested the same way on the steps. Below there stood three cars with Gestapo people. They took me to the prison in Wächter Street in Leipzig for questioning.

That was on August 18, 1935. I sat in that prison for a whole year. In August of 1936 I was tried at the Superior Court in Dresden and given four years in the penitentiary. The comrades who were tried and convicted in the same case with me, fared pretty well. Three were acquitted and two received two years each. The border-man got two years, a Jewish comrade the same. From Dresden I was shifted to Waldheim where I had to serve my four years. First I was in solitary confinement; after four weeks I was placed on a cell block. There good friends immediately welcomed me. Word spread quickly, so they knew that another political prisoner had arrived. We established solidarity right away. Those who were in for over a year and were on their best behavior could get each month a pound of sugar and a quarter of butter; that was always shared among us.

We also had a chance to get together on Sundays with women from other cell blocks. Sunday was church day. Most women went to church; we politicals [here meaning Marxists] stayed behind. Since there were only three or four of us left on each cell block, we were herded into one cell block and thus had the good fortune to be together. Besides, we had a female guard who was somewhat human. We could also talk of political affairs. A few had newspapers, so we could discuss the political situation.

I would like to relate briefly one episode from the penitentiary. Once we got spinach which was sour. When we got the next day the same spinach, the political prisoners refused to eat it. The following day we received the same spinach, and then the asocials and the criminals also refused to eat it. When that happened, we were taken to task, from each cell block one that was suspected of rebellion. We were taken to an official of justice, one at a time, and we were asked how come that we were stirring up the cell blocks not to eat the spinach. We said: "The spinach was sour." Each of us said the same thing, and so the affair was finished.

We did not have any official leadership, but there was solidarity from block to block among the politicals. When one was in need, the others jumped in to help. Had we not had solidarity in the penitentiary and in concentration camp, many of us would not have survived, myself among them.

1a. Vera Keršovan of Yugoslavia at the age of fifteen, before her mistaken deportation to Auschwitz, Gross-Rosen, Nordhausen-Dora and Mauthausen.

1b. Vera Keršovan, 1981, in her home in Ljub - ljana, Yugoslavia. Photo Bogo Leskovic.

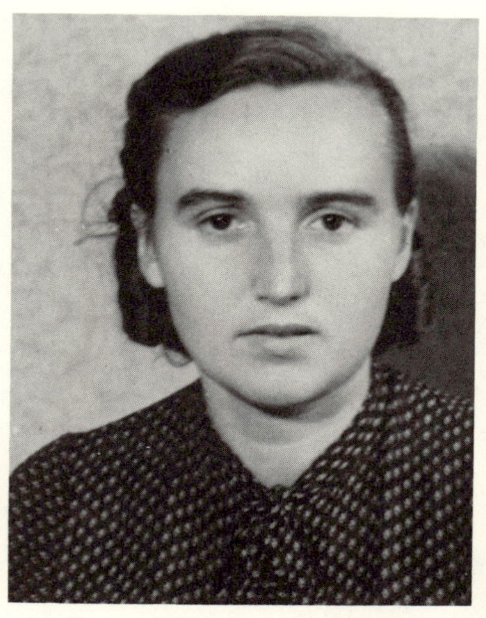

2a. Dagmar Hájková of Czechoslovakia in 1945, at the time of her liberation after almost five years in the women's concentration camp of Ravensbrück as a political prisoner.

2b. Dagmar Hájková, 1979, in Prague, Czechoslovakia.

3. Zdenka Morsel of Prague in 1940, before her deportation to Terezín (Theresienstadt).

4. Franciscan Sister Restituta (Helen Kafka from Husovice, Moravia), aged forty-eight, an operation room nurse in Mödling near Vienna, beheaded on March 30, 1943, for duplicating an anti-Nazi poem.

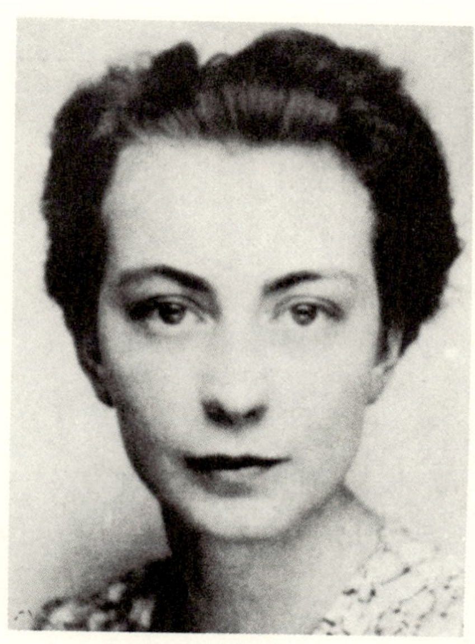

5. Andrée de Jongh of Belgium, 1941, when she organized the Comet Line as "Dédée" or the "Postman Across the Pyrenees," saving hundreds of Allied flyers. Photo by Airey Neave.

6. Hiltgunt Margret Zassenhaus, the German resistance worker aiding Danish and Norwegian POWs in Germany, now an M.D. in Baltimore, Maryland.

7. Madame Marie-Madeleine Fourcade, "Hedgehog" in charge of "Noah's Ark," the large French resistance network during the war, later member of the European Parliament, in her Paris home with the author, May 1981. Photo by Josette Fournal, the former "Egret" of "Noah's Ark."

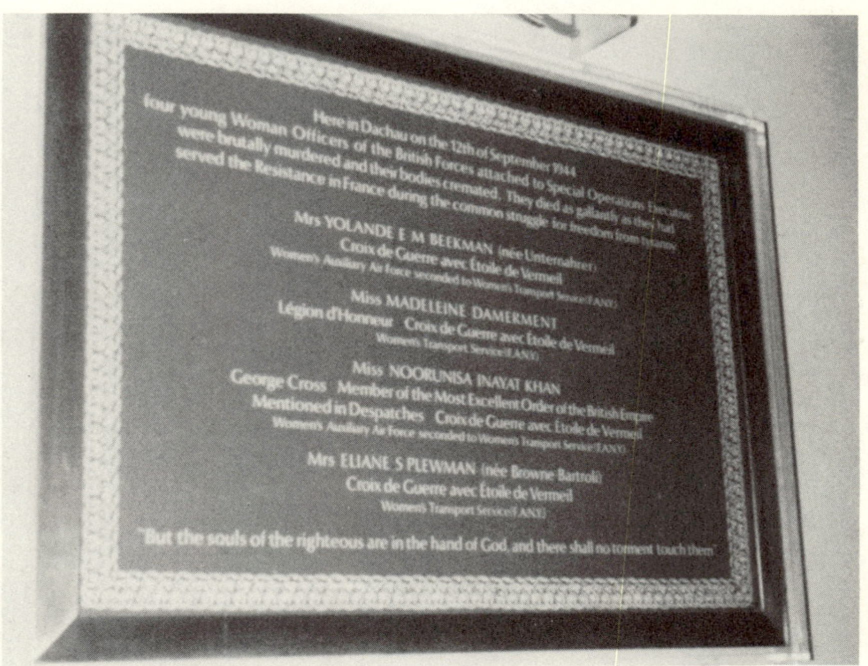

8. Memorial tablet at the Dachau crematorium to the four women executed at Dachau on September 12, 1944, as members of the British Special Operations Executive (SOE). Photo by Vera Laska.

9. Captured Freedom Fighters from the Warsaw Ghetto uprising in 1943. Nuremburg Trial Collection, National Archives. Photo taken by Nazi soldier.

10. Naked women with their children lined up for mass execution by the Special Squads (*Einsatzgruppen*) at Mizocz in the Ukraine in 1941. Among the murdered thousands of Jews were also an American woman and an American man, killed on August 2, 1941, in the roundup near Kaunas, Lithuania. Photo courtesy of Photo Archives, Yad Vashem, Jerusalem.

11. Beate Klarsfeld, the German non-Jewess dedicated to bringing war criminals to justice. Photo Le Républicain Lorrain, Nancy, France.

12. Simon Wiesenthal, who had forsaken an architectural career to devote his life to the pursuit of justice, in his office at the Dokumentationszentrum in Vienna, with the author, May 1981. Photo by Andrew J. Laska.

II.

WOMEN IN CONCENTRATION CAMPS

O the chimneys
On the ingeniously devised habitations of death
When Israel's body drifted as smoke
Through the air

Nelly Sachs

S.S. Gretchen: . . . Arbeit macht frei!
I: Auch Wahrheit macht frei.
S.S. Gretchen: Scheisse, du Schweinhund, kein fressen heute!

13

Auschwitz—A Factual Deposition

The crime of the assassins, who so proudly adorned themselves with skulls and crossbones and gathered under the hooked crosses of the swastika, stands alone in the history of mankind. Nothing ever has approached the thoroughness of the premeditated, deliberate and systematic genocide of eleven million men, women and children. The most frightening thing about the Holocaust was that it was carried out not by savage tribes, but by members of one of the most cultured nations. The concept of this modern annihilation was born in the sick minds of politicans self-drugged with the idea of supremacy and carried out often under the supervision of equally perverted physicians. The thoroughness and the brutality at times stunned even the SS men new to the job, but devout followers that they were, they adjusted to the tempo.

Auschwitz was a giant factory, where the end product was genocide; the byproduct was free labor for the Nazi war machine. Here Christians and Jews, believers and agnostics, were funnelled into the gaping jaws of gas chambers, some right upon arrival, others later, after the last drop of energy was pressed out of their bodies.

In Auschwitz, this place of the starkest, most absolute evil, all the vestiges of civilization were stripped away from guards and prisoners alike, and naked existence fought for survival in a dance macabre of a diabolic scenario.

In Auschwitz values changed, and morals took a nose dive into the bottomless abyss of nothingness. To steal meant to live, and to steal from Germans was a virtue. Auschwitz was also the great equalizer, where past accomplishments, status, richness or power meant zero. Women from high society turned into experts at billingsgate, modest violets into tigresses in order to survive. Here formerly strong people turned into weaklings and wasted away, and nobody ever came up with an answer why.

My testimony is based on my own experiences in Auschwitz and on those of my fellow prisoners, hundreds of whom gave depositions under oath at the Czechoslovak War Crimes Investigation Commission of which I was the executive secretary.

Nowhere did the Nazi supermen reveal their colors as clearly and as ruthlessly as in the annihilation camp *(Vernichtungslager)* of Auschwitz near Cracow. This death factory accounted for more than one-third of the eleven million victims.

Of all the concentration camps, of all the extermination camps, Auschwitz was the crown of perverted imagination, the feather in the cap of the master builders bound on efficient extermination, with an assembly line leading from freight trains through gas chambers to crematoria going full blast night and day, in sun and fog. Production was kept up in order to transform human beings from "parasitic consumers" into consumer goods. Human hair, bones and gold teeth served the German economy well. Ground bonemeal was sold for the manufacturing of superphosphates. Flesh reduced to ashes took up no living space (*Lebensraum*). Whether in some cases ashes were used for fertilizer, I am not sure. They were used as ground fill, and they were also indiscriminately stuffed into urns and sold as the remains of their loved ones to the families of political prisoners; not so the ashes of Jews—there were hardly any loved ones left. Political prisoners often arrived with the marking R. U. (*Rückkehr unerwünscht*), return undesirable. The thousands of SS men and SS women with their whips and vicious dogs saw to it that such orders were carried out.

The fires of the crematoria soared without letup twenty-four hours a day. At times the chimneys cracked from overheating and had to be reinforced with steel bands. Inside, their walls were covered with human fat inches deep. When the going was so good that the gas chambers and crematoria could not handle the volume, people had to dig their own graves, undress—for clothing should not be wasted—and be machine gunned; or bodies were tossed from the gas chambers into ditches and incinerated on pyres in the open air, permeating our nostrils with the stench of burning flesh and bones. The soot from the chimneys was constantly covering us, as a last caress by those who had gone before us. The flames of the crematoria were shooting high into the air, covering the night sky with a constant glow. The sun was often obscured by the thick, choking smoke that spread a depressing cover over the already gray surroundings: our gray sack dresses, gray blocks, gray dust, turning with the rain into gray mud under our wooden clogs.

The application of science and technology in the service of perversity was so perfected that it would have made Genghis Khan blush. SS commandant of the crematoria Moll improved the outside incineration by ordering canals dug under the pyres, thus collecting the dripping human fat. This was then ladled over the corpses to accelerate the burning. *"Mach schnell,"* which can be interpreted as "get going" or "move your ass," was one of the main

"Auschwitz—A Factual Deposition" is by Vera Laska.

mottoes of Auschwitz and of the SS vocabulary, with or without the additive of *"Schweinhund,"* literally swine-dog but rather approximating "son of a bitch." Moll was a temperate man, he did not drink or smoke; but he was an addict to his duties. He declared that if the Führer ordered it, he would burn his own wife and child. He kissed babies, treated them to chocolate, then took them from their mothers' arms and threw them into the sizzling human fat. After doing this several times, he declared:

"I did enough for the fatherland today."

He would save ammunition by trying to shoot up to five people with one bullet. He held up children by the hair and shot them. He was probably the only SS man who, when the work load was heavy, rolled up his sleeves and helped the inmates throw corpses into the fire. He was a hard working SS man, for Führer and country, and he was not the only one. Hundreds of people have witnessed SS men throwing children into the pyres or the ovens. I saw a baby swung by its feet and smashed against a wall by an SS man, its brains splattering in all directions.

Those condemned to temporary life and labor in the selections became slaves forced to oil the wheels of the German war machinery. Concentration camps were usually located next to factories and vice versa. Auschwitz itself was a complex conglomeration of thirty-nine branches. The nerve center was the administration and Gestapo headquarters. The gas chambers and crematoria with multiple ovens were in the Birkenau section (Brzezinka in Polish, meaning a birch grove). Here were most of the 9 x 40 meter (27 x 120 feet) barracks or blocks that were built for 500 to 800 prisoners, but held more often 1,200 each in three- or four-storied bunks. My block "housed" 1,450 women. In the lower bunks you could only lie, on the top one there was space to sit up. The third section of Auschwitz was Buna, the gigantic factory complex that manufactured ammunition and other war matériel. Here they also tried to produce synthetic rubber and gasoline but without success. In this section alone 15,000 slaves labored for various German concerns, among them I. G. Farben, the chemical conglomerate. In 1943, there were sixty-three chemical laboratories in Buna. According to some witnesses, Buna was bombed in the summer of 1944 by the Americans. But the gas chambers and the railroad leading to Auschwitz never were. Every time we heard the sound of an airplane, we all wished the Allies would drop bombs and put the gas chambers out of commission. Being instantly killed by a bomb was certainly an advantage over being gassed, and oh, the satisfaction that we could have cheated our torturers out of our lives! But the Allies did not oblige.

The entire Auschwitz complex covered forty square kilometers, that is about twenty-five square miles. It was good business for the SS, who rented out the prisoners for 4-6 DM per day to I. G. Farben, Hermann Göring Werke, Krupp's Weichsel Union Metallwerke and numerous other companies. It cost them only half a DM per day to keep a prisoner alive. Worn out slaves were discarded into the gas chambers and replaced by new ones free of charge to the industries. Incidentally, the cyclon B gas used in the gas chambers was produced and sold to the SS by DEGESCH (Deutsche Gesellschaft für Schadlingsbekampfung), owned 42.5 percent by the very same I. G. Farben. The initial investment for this slave labor was slight, just the cost of transportation to Auschwitz. It was more than a thousand times compensated by the prisoners' properties that were simply stolen.

The personal belongings of new arrivals, whether dead or alive, were gathered from the cattle cars by hundreds of prisoners of the Canada detail, so-called because of the bounties they were dealing with. Clothing, food, liquor, medicine, jewelry, foreign currencies—all were hauled to the Canada blocks, where they were sorted and shipped to Germany. One list of such shipments, stamped "Secret," shows the contents of over 700 railroad wagons full of men's, women's and children's clothing, table and bed linen, all meticulously itemized. Among others, there is an entry for one wagon or 3,000 kilograms (6,600 pounds) of women's hair. After the liberation of Auschwitz, seven tons of women's hair were found there. It was estimated that it was cut from the heads of 140,000 women. Gold was extracted from the teeth of gassed victims before they were shoved into the ovens. One witness, a dental technician, declared that up to the fall of 1944 his detail melted down two tons of gold from teeth alone. I think of my mother's gold fillings and still shudder.

Auschwitz was established in May of 1940 by experts trained in the concentration camp of Sachsenhausen. Among the early arrivals were not only political and criminal offenders, but also Russian prisoners of war. Of the 12,000 in October 1941, there were only 450 left six months later, and 100 half a year after that.

The women's camp was started in March 1942 with a thousand German women, many of them prostitutes, transferred from Ravensbrück. Soon Jewish women from Slovakia arrived. They were issued evening gowns and thus attired they helped build the camp. In spite of high mortality, by the summer there were 12,000 women jammed into limited space. Therefore, in August 4,000 were gassed, and the rest were moved to the swampy Birkenau section. At the height of productivity, there were nearly 100,000 women there, living on borrowed time in this abominable Babel of all European nations.

It is simplistic to date the birth of the German "final solution of the Jewish problem" to the January 20, 1942, conference at Wannsee near Berlin. It is known that gassing with carbon monoxide—slow, messy, very inefficient! —had been carried out in German-occupied eastern territories before that date. More interesting is the fact that the blueprints of the I. A. Topf & Sons Company of Erfurt, according to which the Birkenau crematoria with the gas chambers were being constructed, bore the date of 1937. The blueprints were secured in 1944 by a Czech woman architect, Věra Foltýn, who worked as an inmate at the camp construction office. On the plans the gas chambers were with extraordinary delicacy marked as "Bath for special purposes." Of course, Jews were not the only ones being gassed; so were thousands of political prisoners and other undesirables. The long-range plans called for the elimination of all "inferior races," especially Slavs.

The first gas chambers started functioning in Birkenau in the summer of 1942. Herr Himmler in person attended the inauguration. Instead of Diesel exhausts, the more effective pesticide hydrogen cyanide, called cyclon B, was used in pellet form, one milligram per one kilogram of body weight. It worked within two to four minutes. The cans of cyclon B were always delivered by a Red Cross truck; how else? The pellets as by magic created pink corpses with green spots. The buildings had elevators and chutes for corpses and also an execution chamber for individuals and smaller groups. The Sonderkommandos, prisoners who serviced the whole operation and were periodically also liquidated, lived up in the attic. Some saw their own families entering the gas chambers. Two thousand people could be gassed in one chamber; the capacity of the crematoria was 12,000 bodies, each cycle taking about twenty minutes.

Six million European Jews were exterminated by the Nazis, the largest numbers of these in Auschwitz. According to the various War Crime Investigation Commissions, around four million men, women and children, Jews and non-Jews, perished in Auschwitz alone. Of these, 2.3 million came from Poland and Russia, and between 400,000 and 450,000 from Hungary (including the occupied parts of Czechoslovakia and Rumania). The international death invoice of this genocide also lists 250,000 Germans, 150,000 each French and Czechoslovaks, and down the line Dutch, Greek, Belgian, Yugoslav, Italian, Norwegian and also British and American victims.

Most arrivals to Auschwitz went directly to the gas chambers. The camp lists indicate 398,000 *Häftlings* or prisoners admitted and tattooed with numbers on the forearm (and there were additional thousands not tattooed and not listed). Of these, about 30,000 were actually transferred to other camps in the Reich in 1944, a miracle in which I was lucky to have been included. In January 1945, at the time of the last roll call or *Appell,* there were about 50,000 *Häftlings* alive. The missing 318,000 are easily accounted for: they perished in Auschwitz. The Greeks and Italians were dying like flies in the cold, foggy climate and swampy environment. The Poles were the sturdiest, perhaps because they were on home grounds and so numerous. The Czechs were somewhere in between living by their wits and will power, with a dash of Schweik in many of us.

The last gassing took place on October 28, 1944, when most of the 2,000 Jews from the Terezín ghetto went up the chimney, with the additional cruel twist of irony, certainly known to the torturers, that being the Czechoslovak national holiday equal to the American Fourth of July. From then on, Auschwitz was being feverishly evacuated toward the West. Two crematoria were dismantled and blown up in November. Of the last 50,000 evacuated prisoners, one-third perished through hunger, freezing, beating or shooting during the death marches. The Russians liberated what was left of Auschwitz on January 27, 1945. They found the crematoria blown up, most Canada blocks burned to the ground and a few hundred dying wretches among the ruins.

* * *

Vignettes from the mosaic of memories. Nightmares follow one another. The eyes register but the brain resists belief. Cattle cars fit for eight animals jammed with a hundred people. No water. Food, yes all smells melting into one nauseating wave that engulfs me. My precious orange peel is overcome by garlic. A little window, nailed shut with pine boards. Laboriously I split away part of one with my fingers. Air. I see the name of a station. Polish. Days glide into nights. Three? Four? I am with people I do not know. We are the result of emptied jails and ghettos and police stations. The woman next to me is dead. Now she takes up two spaces. I have to stretch over her toward the slit in the window.

The stench of excrement is overpowering. The woman on the floor emits a putrid smell. There are over a dozen corpses by now in the wagon. They are taken off, thrown on the platform. A bucketful of water is hurled in, cooling those at the middle. Perhaps they were able to swallow a mouthful. Most of the precious liquid drips down through the floorboards. It only intensifies the stench of human waste and vomit. Women cry, shriek, tear their hair. One is hysterically laughing. I will myself to think of ice and snow melting in my mouth, but my palate is dry, my tongue glued to the roof of my mouth. I repeat to myself: *cogito ergo sum;* as long as I think, I still exist. But thoughts are becoming hazy. Perhaps I am not even here. But I am hanging on to the large hook over the window, not high enough to hang myself. No, I have no intention to oblige the unleashed demons of bestiality and do away with myself.

Dawn, the bleakest, most wretched, shocking, mortifying dawn of my life. The apocalypse of a doomsday where forlorn souls loom against the reddish glow. The long train comes to a screeching halt, the doors are being opened. Pandemonium. The living stepping on the dead to get out. Air, breathe deeply, air, as much as you want, air.

A gray factory town. Several tracks run parallel with ours. Flames from factory chimneys shooting upward and licking with blazing red and orange tongues the awakening sky. How can red flames spit black smoke? But logic is excused here and now. Strange smells. Stranger people.

Men dressed in gray and blue striped pajamas, like zebras, whispering emphatic but incomprehensible words in several languages: *rechts, vpravo, jobbra,* to the right. Give the children to the old folks and go to the right.

What are you? Czech? Look snappy like a Sokol and GO TO THE RIGHT! Where am I? In Auschwitz, you stupid bitch, for letting them catch you. Go to the right, to the left you go up the chimney.

Masses of people. The stream divides as if sliced through by a knife, an SS uniform with a riding stick, pointing to the left and to the right. I go right with my head high as if it were my own decision. I avoid contact with Mengele's stick. A long march. Foul stench of burning flesh—a childhood memory of a lamb turning on a spit; also the smell of scorched hair and rotting carcasses. Zebras behind fences. Throw me your watch, you will not need it. Throw me your ring, your bread, your anything.

A long corridor with pegs on the walls. SS men with dogs straining their leashes and baring their teeth. Strip down to the skin. Zebras shave off all hair, top, bottom and middle, whispering strange tidings. SS men looking on with blasé expressions or shaking with laughter, the newer ones glaring at naked females as if judging a contest of ugliness. Each of their degrading glances is an obscenity. A menstruating woman is kicked for messing up the floor. Be sure all your stuff is on the same peg. Remember the number under the peg. Showers, dozens of showers in one huge room, real water coming from the ceiling. One second it is hot, scorching, then cold, freezing, then it stops. Cursing it, I do not realize that at the same time in another shower room gas is pouring from those shower heads in the ceiling, exterminating those who went left.

Disinfecting, delousing, smarting eyes. A gray shirt reaching to the knees, clogs for the feet. I still remember that number under the peg. I am now officially a *Häftling,* initiated as number 31,979.

March. First view from behind the wires. Grayness. All is gray. I am melting into it. Faces are gray. No color in sight except for the zebras and soldiers who are grayish-green or black, and the white of their dogs' teeth. It is raining. Clogs get stuck in the mud. *Mach schnell,* hurry, get going, move your ass, you scum of the earth. A few slaps in the face or kicks in the rear for the stragglers.

The block. Dark. We are pushed inside and fall over each other into the gaping hole. The *Blockälteste* is standing at the entrance and encouraging us with her stick. We are numbers condemned to life. My eyes are getting used to the dark. It is an inferno, no, not Dante's, that is poetic, this is our own. Shaven heads look all the same. I climb on a bunk where the stream of bodies pushes me, but I cannot sit up. I climb higher; on the top bunk I can sit. Women are still being driven into the block in an unending stream. We end up six to two bunks. All straw is gone from the mattress, there is only dust, and soon to be discovered and very ambitious lice.

Food is coming in huge cauldrons. A darkish liquid that once upon a time was warm. Nothing in it. At times it would be called coffee or tea. If some potato peels and barley or turnips floated in it, it was called soup. We drank it from smelly bowls, for there were no spoons. A slice of dark, military bread that tastes like sawdust, with a pat of fat on it. Women are already fighting over it, and it crumbles. Others are picking up the crumbs. A phantasmagorical scene etched on the brain with the acid of reality. Stripped of civilization, the human animal emerges with astounding speed. An indelible image, forever.

A civilian woman is walking between the bunks. A figment of the imagination? Edita, with hair, a dress and normal shoes. I call out to her. She turns toward me, and after a searching glance she recognizes me. She remembers me from the high school volley ball team. The mild-mannered girl of our former lives who once spoke with respect to upperclassmen now screams at me:

"You should have hidden up to your nose in shit rather than come here!" She was one of the few Slovak girls who survived from the 1942 transports and was working at Canada. She told us the facts of life in Auschwitz. She was a hardened *Häftling.* All who went to the left were gassed and are now burning. Watch out for the numbers with green triangles—professional criminals, murderers, thieves, cheats, although a different triangle is no guarantee that the bearer is not a murderer, thief, cheat. The law of the jungle prevails. Its only imperative: don't get caught by the wrong people. The greens are the kapos and other supervisors. Shut your mouth. Do not complain. Do not stand out in any crowd. Lay low. Eat all the food immediately. Never trade food away. Do not be sick or you go up the chimney. Don't eat your heart out over the past or it will break you. Think of today and what you can organize, get by hook or crook. Think of staying alive as long as you can. Hate "them," it gives you moral support. All good, valuable advice. As time went on, I added will power to her recipe for survival.

The latrines, about forty holes in two rows. A Russian woman parading on top of the bench with the holes, swooshing her stick on bare behinds and having fun. At the entrance a small, slender Italian woman singing an aria, a former opera soprano. There is no time to lose inhibitions gradually. We left them behind in one abrupt trauma, when they shaved our hair or when we entered the blocks. Some girls are constipated and with bulging eyes are coaxing their bowels to move. Others are cursed with diarrhea and are making natural noises without bothering who hears them. There is no toilet paper. The bottoms of dresses are used in the hope that the water from the only faucet will still be dripping on our way out, and the garment can be rinsed. The polish of civilization receded as the snows of yesteryear.

In the block 1,450 lungs are contending for the same air. The six bodies on our double bunk are turning in unison. We experiment to sleep three and three in an upside down pattern, but cold feet are kicking noses and toes gouging out eyes. Eventually we learn and perfect our positions to an art, better than any in a French manual of lovemaking. The lice start in early; the rats come later, big as racoons, with their fat bellies and long tails, winding after them as snakes, whipping me over my face. I wonder if they would make a good stew? But there is no way to catch the insidious beasts.

The night is short, for at five is the first roll call. If once upon a time sunrises were symphonies, now they are dirges. We are standing in rows of five, shivering in the single garment. The SS woman counts, pointing her riding crop: 5 Stück, 10 Stück, and so on. We are not human, we are "pieces," and she makes sure that we hear it. We stand *Appell* for hours, morning and night. Our shaven skulls blister in the scorching sun or are chilled by icy rains. Our bodies fester with boils, the result of avitaminosis. Flakes of soot settle in the green and yellow puss. *Schweinhunde,* you dirty swine, and we are hosed down with freezing water and stand wet until dozens of us fall and are carted away. The rest do not move. Only Lily the half-wit grins and dances between the rows and makes the SS woman laugh.

Work details go out at six and return at five, if all goes well. At the gate a female orchestra is playing, conductor and all. Some of the melodies are familiar and fill us with a confusing mixture of joy and painful nostalgia. How could my mother's song survive her? Or is it a belated dirge for her?

The days pass as the falling leaves of a calendar, but we lose all track of time. The outside world is dead. Rumors abound, especially around the latrines, the news centers. As an experiment we started a rumor that a famous movie actress arrived. We got it back a few days later: she was brought in by her lover, an SS man, who shot her in front of the crematorium.

I find it hard to think systematically; my thoughts are wandering in all directions. The bromide mixed in the soup had a double effect on women: they stopped menstruating and they were sedated. I concentrated on observing and remembering every detail. What the hell for? We shall never have the chance to tell what we have seen, for we shall sooner or later all go up the chimney.

Frames of the laterna magica of my mind: a pregnant girl pulled out at *Appell;* we never see her again. Pregnancy for *Häftlings* is verboten. A woman ran to the electric fence and is hanging there by her fingers cramped by death. The SS in the guard tower does not even bother to shoot. Latrine rumors: the Americans invaded Europe; this months before and after the fact. *Lagersperre,* nobody allowed out of the blocks, sirens blowing, an inmate escaped. We wish her luck, in vain. Few ever escaped from Auschwitz. A group of Yugoslav partisan women did, but that was in earlier days.

The most romantic escape story that became a legend in Auschwitz also ended in tragedy. Let their names stand here, for few remember by now: Mally Zimetbaum and Edward Galinski. Their memory should live forever. They were # 19,880 and # 531, simply known as Mala and Edek. They escaped together and managed to evade capture parties for several days. The SS were raging mad. Two escapees looked bad on the record. Inmates stood *Appells* for hours, and blows were raining on them with even greater frequency. But in vain did thousands of prisoners rejoice. Mala and Edek were brought in and hanged separately while the inmates were ordered to look on.

We are getting slimmer and slimmer. I lost almost half of my weight. Yet we are not Musulmans yet, those apparitions of skin and bone without any will to live, who were the choice candidates for the gas chambers. (Their photographs in the German press showed them as victims of British rule in India.)

A late afternoon after work. SS doctors with a group of inmate assistants closed off the yard between two blocks. They caught a woman and took her blood, then another and still another. Many were Jewish, but it did not seem to matter. The Nazis needed blood for their soldiers so badly that they set aside their theories about pure races. They were chasing indiscriminately after everybody, Russian, Czech, Jew or Gypsy. The women are running from them, like chickens when the fox gets into the chicken coop. I move strategically from corner to corner, slowly, not making visible waves by running. I'll be damned to contribute my life blood to the gangsters.

A long *Appell.* We stand in our rows of fives for hours. Other blocks are also lined up, waiting. Finally the SS women come with their dogs and two male deathheads. They order the fallen bodies thrown on the cart collecting the corpses. One is still alive; it does not matter, the flames in the ovens do not discriminate. *Achtung!* Look snappy, stand at attention. The camps are overcrowded, and this is selection time. As the masters of life and death pass from row to row, we freeze, and the very fear straightens our sagging backs. The delegation of judges playing God is nearing my row. The SS Brunhilde points to a woman with gray stubs of hair and nudges her with a stick to the group of women already selected and standing aside. Everybody knows what is going on. They know that we know. Yet there is absolute silence. The SS men do not like disturbances and noise, they silence it with their revolvers. Fate is standing in front of me. I lift my chin and look at her. My brain tells me to smile confidently, and I feel like a moral prostitute for it. But before my face can obey or refuse my brain, she passes on to the next row, and the selection continues. Several hundred women are taken away to the gas chambers. Life, such as it is, goes on, where permitted to do so by supermen and superwomen.

And the skies with their wandering clouds look on, going about their business as usual. Where are you Gods invoked in all languages? Are you deaf? Only the grimy soot keeps falling on us like black snowflakes of mourning, memento mori, memento mori. . . .

Another day. An SS man enters the block. *Achtung.* We stand at attention. Slowly he unwraps the package under his arm and starts tossing slices of bread high into the air, one to the right, one to the left. Women rush to catch the bread. A human zoo, and a spectator is amused by the animals.

The women fight, they holler, they scratch, they elbow their way through the twisted masses of arms and legs, they roll on the floor in search of the food. The SS man is enjoying the game. He is standing with his legs apart, his head thrown back, and his hearty laugh is heard over the din of the desperate, starving packs of women. After a while he rolls the empty paper into a ball and tosses it into the face of the *Blockälteste,* a green triangle. She catches the ball, and they both exit laughing. Most of the bread ended up in crumbs on the floor. Some cover the motionless bodies trampled to death. The rats will again have a field day tonight.

One day I managed a few minutes of conversation with the older women in the next block. To my amazement they were the wives and mothers from Lidice. This village next to Prague had been totally razed to the ground in June 1942, as retribution for the assassination by the underground of Reinhardt Heydrich, the brutal police general and then acting Protector of Bohemia and Moravia. All men and dogs were shot on the spot. The children were packed off for "reeducation"; many were adopted by Germans and never seen again. It was a moving moment even in the atmosphere devoid of sentimentality to meet these women in Auschwitz.

Among the thousands of poignant chapters in the Holocaust, there is one in particular to which a woman added a heroic finale in Auschwitz. In 1943, through the mediation of the actress Katerina Horowitzová, about 2,000 Polish Jews purchased American passports and exit permits from the SS for millions of dollars. These people were kept aboard a ship in Hamburg while their families were further blackmailed. Then they were told that they were being sent to Switzerland to be exchanged as Americans for German prisoners of war. The train, however, delivered them to the gas chambers of Auschwitz, together with Horowitzová. When she was ordered by SS man Josef Schillinger to remove also her brassiere before entering the "shower," she whipped off her garment and startled him by hitting him with it in his eyes. While he was blinded by pain, she grabbed his revolver and shot him and another guard. Some SS men fled the scene, but others with pistols drawn ordered the Sonderkommando to herd the "Americans" into the gas chamber.

The hospital, or Revier, in Block 10 usually had around 400 inmates. Here the infamous doctor Josef Mengele and his colleagues were carrying out their medical experiments in the interest of Nazi science. Mengele's speciality were twins, dwarfs and Gypsies. Two sets of twin girls came visiting in our block and related the details of the goings on in Block 10 and in the other medical blocks.

Under controlled conditions, the twins were forced into intercourse to see whether their offspring would also be twins. "We will never get out of here alive, we know too much," they said, "you have at least one chance in a million, so you must know." They told us of fenol and chloroform injections in the hearts of the victims, of human flesh being excised for bacteriological cultures, of surgeons practicing on healthy victims, butchering most of them. One doctor bet that he could perform ten hysterectomies in one afternoon and won; the women who were his guinea pigs lost.

One of the most important medical projects was the sterilization of women "unworthy of reproduction" *(fortpflanzungsunwürdige Frauen).* This was done by overdoses of X-rays. The physician in charge was gynecology professor Karl Clauberg from Königshütte, who functioned in Ravensbrück before coming to Auschwitz in 1942. He used as his guinea pigs women in their twenties, and between him and his colleague, Horst Schumann, they sterilized thousands of women. In other experiments, women's organs were gradually injected with jodipin, a substance called F 12a and citobarium diluted with water. Block 10 resounded with the constant screams of these women. Many had one or both ovaries removed; these organs were shipped to Berlin for further research. The women's blood was frequently taken, including that of Jewish women. Other experiments consisted of the castration of males and the artificial insemination of females. The main purpose of this research was to find the fastest ways of limiting and eventually exterminating "inferior races," and to raise the birth rates of the "pure" Nordic race. The directives came from Heinrich Himmler, head of the SS. By the summer of 1943, Clauberg could proudly notify Himmler that the time was near when with ten assistants he could sterilize "several hundred, possibly a thousand women in a single day." His rival Schumann raised the ante to 3,000-4,000 per day. All these experiments and others were fully corroborated and documented by former prisoners—physicians who had been witnessing them over the years.

Sex in concentration camps? Without any doubt whatsoever, the survival instinct for food was primary and ever present and took absolute precedence over everything else. Few even among the sexiest *Häftlings* were concerned with sex. I know from others that some women were gang raped but that was not routine. Why should the SS risk their necks for intercourse with dirty, unattractive females, without hair and in a gray shirt, when they had all they could handle among the SS women? There was a better chance for sex among the kapos and other prominents, or among the Canada detail, but not among the run of the mill *Häftlings.*

I know that in Auschwitz there was a bordello of forty rooms in Block 24 for the black triangles, German inmates and a few select sycophants with green triangles. Tickets were handed out as a reward by the SS to this "Puff Haus." The madam was called the "Puff Mutter." The girls worked a two-hour day and three times a week. With German thoroughness the Puff Mother rang the bell each twenty minutes (same time as the burning shift in the ovens!). In an orderly society even fun and games had to be rationed.

By the summer of 1944, Auschwitz was filled to capacity, and transports were still coming in day and night. Selections were more frequent. At times even the efficient SS miscalculated, as with the 2,000 women squeezed and locked into Block 25, who had to be kept there for ten days before they could be accommodated in the gas chambers. By then one-third of them were dead. It saved gas.

To prevent resistance, entire blocks were told that volunteers were needed for factory work in Germany. Most of the volunteers ended up in the gas chambers. So did the Czech transport from Terezín that had been kept alive for half a year in the exceptional family blocks. The SS used them for propaganda, or just loved to play cat and mouse games. These unfortunate people were packed off on Masaryk's birthday, March 7, and were told that they were being moved to another work camp. The following night they were all gassed. They entered the gas chambers singing the national anthem. Their postcards, an especially cruel Nazi custom, were postdated March 25, and arrived at Terezín postmarked from Dachau, stating that all was well. This was supposed to keep further transports from Terezín calm.

In another Terezín group, the women had a chance to be sent to work camps in the Reich. But mothers would not leave their children and in July 1944 accompanied them into the gas. One of the 15,000 children in Terezín had written in a poem: "I never saw another butterfly." Few ever did. Barely one hundred of them survived.

These were the darkest days in Auschwitz. Gassing took longer, for there was a lack of cyclon B, which could be stored for only three months. As the German fronts were collapsing, the SS was becoming nervous. At the next call for volunteers for labor in Germany, I decided to take the chance. Should I go up the chimney, better now than suffer through the winter. Half of our block volunteered. We stood in two groups in the yard, and for hours we were not sure which group would go and which would stay. It was my birthday. Will I die on my own anniversary? By the count of probability there was a small chance for that. By the perverse chances of this place, this inferno and insane asylum rolled into one, all statistics and all logic were off. Yes or no.

After endless hours our column was moved. Right or left? To the right was the famous gate with the greatest joke ever known emblazoned on it: "'*Arbeit macht frei,*" "Work liberates." Next to it the only female orchestra in hell was playing. Slowly our column approached the crossroads. The sadistic SS bitch stopped and faced us with her ironical smile. "*Was nun?*" "What now?" she asked. We all wished we could tell her what we truly wanted now: tear her to pieces as a farewell to this place, for all her physical and mental torments, for the extended *Appells,* for the slaps and kicks and blows with her stick, but mostly for her ironic style that elevated abuse to sublime heights of pleasure for her. This was her last chance, to torture us just once more, keeping us perched on the edge of life and death. Then an SS car came careening around the corner. "*Los, Mensch, los,*" the driver shouted at her, get them going, and the SS Brunhilde's last pleasure was cut off before she could reach her orgasm. She turned toward the gate, and we followed, totally dredged by her sadism, but still stepping friskily to the music of the orchestra. It was doubly my birthday.

On our way to the railway station we passed another transport moving in the opposite direction. Hundreds of Gypsies were marching toward the chimneys. One girl had a white angora bolero. Her deep brown eyes seemed to ask what to expect ahead. How could I tell her: everything and nothing.

My friend risked her life by stepping out of the column and making a grab for the tufts of grass struggling for life alongside the road. All she managed were two blades of precious, smooth, green grass. She handed them to me, the loveliest birthday bouquet I have ever received. I ate them.

* * *

After Auschwitz everything was anticlimactic. Our transport ended up in Zillerthal as part of the labor force of the Gross-Rosen concentration camp We worked in a spinning mill, where it was warm. We found out that the Allies did land indeed, weeks ago, on the west of Fortress Europe. We could tell the state of the war reasonably well from the barometer of the German civilians' behavior. When they were winning, the kicks rained pretty systematically. When they were losing, they desisted from pestering us. My supervisor left an unguarded little apple on my machine; was she taking out insurance, with her God or the victors? We were still very hungry, and it was at that factory that I gobbled down a small rotten potato swimming in the trough of oily refuse.

It was also in this *Spinnerei* that Verice got her fingers caught in the steel combs for flax, and we were terror stricken that she would be taken away and gassed. It was from organized blond flax that my barrack mates knitted me a sweater, with a row of stars appliquéd in green wool that came from a ripped glove.

We had some exceptional breaks here. In the factory the toilets had doors on them. There were only forty of us to each barrack, and one to a bunk. There were few long *Appells.* We could scrounge up pieces of wood under the snow. The food was still barely a thousand calories a day, but it arrived with regularity, potatoes and beets, beets and potatoes, and once in a while something called salami. We ate everything. The bread was almost fit for human consumption. We even had a table and benches.

We sat on our bunks in the evenings and listened for hours to stories true and made-up, to lovely poetry and songs of many lands and mainly to tales about food. The best cook was a former teacher who described with incredible detail the color scheme of a meatloaf or the direction the rivulets of butter took winding their way among the breadcrumbs on a well-sculpted apricot dumpling. What feasts that Lucullus would have envied she provided for us! A Michaelangelo painting heavenly images with her culinary brush.

It was her sister-in-law who had managed to camouflage her pregnancy by wrapping herself in tight bandages made of rags. We were all hoping that her baby would be stillborn. There was talk about killing it the moment it would arrive, to save the mother's life. One Monday dawn, on the bunk just below mine, she gave birth to a tiny baby. That day she did not march with us to the factory. By the time we got back, she and her baby were gone.

By January 1945, the Russian front was nearing from the East. Some nights we thought we could hear the cannonade. We woke each other to listen to the lovely sounds. But we were saved from the enemy and evacuated to central Germany, near Nordhausen. We were lodged in Gross Werther village, in an auditorium, sleeping on the floor. We were transported daily to the Tunnel, where thousands of French war prisoners had their barracks above, and a factory of several stories was working full blast underground. Whole trains could enter into the Tunnel, it was so huge. It was an international slave center, with French, Belgian, Czech, Polish, Hungarian and other nationalities laboring. Among other war materials, the V-2 missiles were manufactured there. My detail was assigned the task of measuring with micrometers the diameters of small duraluminum rings. We measured and mismeasured millions of them. Churchill once acknowledged that the sabotage of prisoners prevented many V-2 missiles from exploding over London.

In the last days of March, as the Allies were pressing on from both East and West, we were taken on a hunger march toward Mauthausen. This concentration camp was to gather in as many *Häftlings* as possible and then be blown up. From the disorganization of the transport it was evident that the Germans had admitted to themselves that they were losing the war. Still they stubbornly kept us under machine guns and armed guards. We slept in barns if we were lucky, or along the highways strewn with abandoned carts of fleeing people, dead soldiers and horses. Among them lay the corpses of prisoners, shot because they could not keep up with their columns or tried to escape. Some days the SS requisitioned a few turnips or potatoes for us, but mostly there was no food.

In a village the name of which I no longer know, I used the general confusion around a bin of potatoes and of broken ranks to make my move. I vaulted over a fence and I landed on the other side on a heap of manure. I listened. No whistles, no shooting. I looked around and ran into a double barn and up a ladder into the piled up straw. I shoved the ladder to the opposite side. Male voices, encouraging a dog: *"Such, Sonia, such,"* "Search, Sonia, search." Sonia was barking at the foot of the ladder. Somebody climbed up and poked around the straw with a pitchfork. I held my breath until he climbed down, and they all left. I stayed in that straw almost motionless for four and a half days. Sonia never came back. I heard guns most of the time from all sides.

Then, on the fifth day, a voice from below shouted in broken German: "Woman, out, goddamned Germans *kaput,* war *kaput.*" It was a Ukrainian forced laborer on the farm, who had seen me make a run for it five days ago. His name was Anatol, and he said Stalin was no good, and he was not returning to Mother Russia. It was a revelation to me. There was still sporadic shooting. We ran, and I never saw him again.

Behind the village I saw tanks and cars with white stars painted on them. The stars had five points: Russians. I started out towards them and was immediately surrounded by a dozen soldiers with guns pointed at me. To be shot by mistake after the war was over would have been the most frustrating experience. "*Voda,*" I managed to say, hoping that it is the same word in Russian as in Czech for water. They took me to a house. They spoke English. They were Americans. Why the hell did they paint Communist stars on their vehicles? With my short hair and straw sticking out of my outlandish clothing I scared them. An officer asked me my name and was surprised that I was female. He did not know that females were also imprisoned by the Germans. I have never forgotten his ignorance. Without a word I grabbed the red apple he was eating and wolfed it down.

They fed me, they requisitioned a room for me, they posted a guard to protect me. I started working for the American Military Government. Somewhere along the line I shook hands with General Eisenhower. I made contact with liberated Czech political prisoners from Camp Dora. Jan Češpiva, a physician from Prague, and his friends organized an automobile, had it painted on top with a huge red cross, the sides proclaiming for all to see in English and Czech "Czechoslovak Red Cross," self-appointed, naturally. In the trunk were the prisoners' lists and correspondence of Camp Dora.

All American check points let us pass. Only the Russians, at our own borders, gave us trouble, suspicious of our American identification papers. Finally, we were let go, poorer by a bottle of whiskey.

Next day we saw once more the hundreds of golden spires of Prague, dressed in the finery of an ocean of Allied flags. With us arrived safely the first documents for the files of the Czechoslovak War Crimes Investigation Commission.

14

The Bread Box

Women in the concentration camps were stripped of all possessions, including all their hair. They were issued gray sacks for dresses and wrong size shoes or clogs. The slop called coffee one day and tea the next was the same mud-hued dishwater; with luck, it was warm. The daily ration of hard bread, with an occasional pat of margarine or marmalade, made all the difference between life and death. Humans turned into animals when it came to the defense of this slice of life. As I have already said, I have seen with my own eyes in Auschwitz an SS man enter the barracks of 1,450 women, throw chunks of bread into their midst and then step back in a fit of laughter as hundreds of women pushed and shoved, clawed and fought for the crumbs. Within minutes three women were trampled to death and dozens injured. Panem et circenses? *The SS man provided the bread, the screaming women the games for his pleasure.*

The selection below illustrates the dehumanized mentality of a woman after two months in Auschwitz. The scene takes place in the concentration camp Revier or hospital left for the night under the supervision of a few female prisoner wardens.

The night does not bring peace. Strange, tinny voices are heard from above and from below, like voices in the radio, deformed by imperfect reception. Some ringing, trembling sounds, resembling human speech, but blurred and indistinct. Words are not intelligible, one does not distinguish the language they belong to; they might be Hungarian or Dutch or Greek. Nobody understands them and nobody listens to them. There is no receiving station that would want to catch them, no earphones are used—ears are deaf to them.

Who cares to listen to these voices? They sound in the void of several hundreds of human beings. They come from the third tier of bunks, from the second, too, but mostly from the ground floor. This is the safest place to be in. Urine flows straight on the earthen floor, nobody swears or gives a beating. . . .

The night brings no peace. But it brings moments of independence. The masters make their appearance but rarely at night. It is not pleasant or safe for them to walk about at night in this camp full of sleepless and tough slaves who are, after all, free to give up some moments of their all too short sleep. It is hardly possible to sleep in this resounding stillness, full of tinny sounds, especially when one is lying in one bunk with two other feverish and emaciated bodies.

Wikta cannot sleep. The stove is nearby and the night warden is throwing coals into its open maw. The open door of the stove emits strong light which falls upon some figures diffidently standing around it. The figures are thin, so thin that one could hardly believe human beings so emaciated would be able to move and to live. Both from under the incredible rags and the elegant silk shifts stolen from the prisoners' property store, there appear the same thin shanks in wooden clogs. The skulls are shaven and bare like bullets, some have a several months' old growth of unruly hair on them, resembling the mane of a horse. Long shadows follow these creatures whose eyes glitter feverishly, the hungry, cunning, shifty eyes of prisoners.

The women are grasping small pots of half a litre in their hands. These pots contain a veritable treasure—water or soup, not the camp soup, but one containing a couple of potatoes, salted water and a bit of margarine. The most fervent wish of the waiting women is to be able to cook this wonderful soup at the fire, but in order to do so one must beg the night warden to be granted this utmost distinction—the permission to cook it. Then one would be able to drink the clear, boiling hot water instead of the lukewarm bitter herbs. To be able to eat soup which did not contain turnips and the horrid Awo powder that makes the gullet burn! To be able to taste a whole, well-cooked potato! The women continue to stand, undiscouraged, patiently waiting for their turn; they will stand long. Theirs is the night. Should the warden at the gate rush in shouting that a camp kapo or a Ger-

"The Bread Box" is by Maria Elzbieta Jezierska in Kazimierz Smolen, et al., eds., *Reminiscences of Former Auschwitz Prisoners* (Auschwitz: State Museum of Auschwitz, 1963), pp. 37-48. Translated by Krystyna Michalik. Reprinted with the kind permission of the publisher and the author.

man was approaching, they would disperse and vanish, but as soon as the danger is over, they will return and wait on with a stubbornness that would put to shame the persistence of gold prospectors who tried to get gold from the mythical lakes of Eldorado. Gold is lifeless but a pot of soup is life itself. The very core of life.

But Wikta is not standing at the fire with a pot in her hand. She is looking on, her eyes filled with a horrible, devouring, murderous envy. To kill but to possess a pot! That is not all, however. One still has to bribe the night warden who wouldn't otherwise allow you to put the pot on the fire. The night warden risks much by doing so. She risks being sent to the penal company in Block 25, she risks loosing her privileged position and becoming a hard working superpariah with a red-white circle, which makes one so conspicuous that all "organizing" is out of the question.

The night warden is the championess of "organizing." She couldn't be bribed by trifles. The piece of bread, Witka's only treasure within 24 hours, means nothing to the warden. She can easily have many ordinary bread rations from the prisoners every day, just for letting them boil some water at the fire. Those suffering of typhus or malaria would gladly part with their bread rations, with margarine and even with the bit of horse sausage, just to get one mug of boiling hot water.

Witka is unable to avert her eyes from the pot. She continues to look at it and she seems to feel the taste of a sip of the wonderful hot soup. She senses how it would taste on her tongue, her lips, she thinks of the potatoes with the fat, the onions, the vegetables. Oh, to think that one ate such soups without even noticing, when one was free, to think that one could have had several helpings without limitation, taking as much as one wished!

Wikta swallows hard. The thick, sticky saliva of those, who take too little liquids, gathers in her mouth. But thinking of the soup makes her saliva flow as freely as it did in the times when she could eat and drink her fill.

Wikta notices how the night warden takes the pot from the fire and walks down the aisle among the bunks. Wikta knows where she is going; it is just opposite, the second tier bunk, placed crosswise and occupied by a lucky woman who is getting food parcels almost every day! The food parcels weigh only one pound but—a pound! My God, what an amount of bacon, onions, garlic, bread from home, sugar, delicacies!

Wikta feels such a surge of implacable hatred and of a pauper's overbearing envy that looking on is no longer bearable. She violently turns to the wall, the damp wooden wall covered with the glittering white of frost. The cold penetrates easily through the edge of one blanket shared by three. She had for the moment forgotten that there were three of them in the bunk. But now she again feels the other two hot and sweating and repulsive bodies, struck with typhus and thrown together with her upon a bunk that is just wide enough for one. She raises her head and looks at them with repulsion, her hatred transferred upon the nearest objects:

"May you die soon!"

She was ill, just as they are, some weeks ago. She also talked deliriously all night through, in that reedy, groaning voice. Sweat and urine were freely flowing from her body, she was a helpless victim of the lice. But she would at least lose consciousness. And they won't, the mean creatures! What use is food to them? But they guard it as if they were completely healthy. When Wikta was ill, her food was taken by her neighbors who were as hungry then as she is now. And these vile creatures won't let her have it. Particularly that Janczak woman.

Wikta is looking with morbid rage at Mrs. Janczak's sharp nose which sticks out unnaturally upwards as if in a dead woman's face. Mrs. Janczak has a box which she had begged from somebody who was getting food parcels, and this box is securely hidden under the pallet. She collects bread in this box. And she eats her soup, though Wikta warned her she shouldn't. But she persists in eating it in spite of her diarrhoea and then she will foul the bed.

Wikta has been in camp since September; it is November now. But she is already aware what it means to eat the camp soup when one had typhus. That means that Mrs. Janczak is going to die. She has diarrhoea, she will die soon. Her box. . . .

Nobody can imagine what it means to be hungry, unless one had recovered after typhus. The fever has barely subsided when she has felt a tremendous appetite and has been ready to eat anything eatable, even horse meat bones in the soup which someone else had already chewed; they have such a tasty flavor when you suck the tiny crevices where nerves and sinews once had been, yes, even the pulp that seems to have completely gone in cooking. . . . There is the taste of the marrow, the wonderful taste of fat and meat, a taste remembered from her days of freedom!

To fill the emptiness of one's guts with anything! To satisfy the sucking of the empty stomach! To be full, just once! To eat as much as one can, to eat one's fill, as much as one would want to, to devour big, thick, generous slices of bread, the ordinary bread one could get in abundance from bakeries before the war. . . . The smell of bread. . . . The golden crust . . . . Its softness and elasticity. . . . To eat to one's full capacity, to sink the teeth into it, to masticate, to feel the taste of the soft mass on the tongue and to swallow, to swallow. . . .

In spite of the cold penetrating from the wall, Wikta raised herself up and looked at the woman beside her. She dimly saw the profile of her; her dirty feet were just under Wikta's armpits. Mrs. Janczak's breath was turning into a rattle.

Wikta has been looking at her like that for the last ten days, ever since she became conscious again and had gasped the fact that the other was hoarding her bread in the box. She kept looking at her neighbor watchfully and greedily. Every night she expected . . . perhaps now? Mrs. Janczak was growing weaker and weaker. It was out of the question for her to get up and use the bucket. Wikta tried to shove the chamber pot under the woman, because she wanted to salvage their common pallet from being wetted and fouled by excrements. But Mrs. Janczak was no longer able to raise herself up. There was one thing, however, she was still able to do—to hide her bread ration in her box. She did it regularly, her eyes glittering feverishly. In spite of her illness she fully realized what bread meant to her. She was conscious of the fact that her bread would mean life to her, once she had recovered from typhus.

But this day Wikta heard a different note in the delirious ramblings of Mrs. Janczak. This was not the usual reedy tone, it was something new.

"Will she die at last?" she whispered.

And all at once she felt certain that the box was going to be hers. She would make sure no one else got it. Besides, who else was there to get it? The women nearby were weak and unconscious. Only she. . . . Yes, the bread was going to be hers. And then she would eat, she would have her fill. . . .

But as dawn came, Mrs. Janczak was still alive. There was the roll-call, the doctor's visit, which was to decide who was to leave the hospital and get back to the camp, who was "well;" thirty-five typhus patients were waiting for admission to the hospital and only twenty-two had died during the preceding night.

Wikta was trembling in her bed; it was both the cold from the wall as the night had been frosty, and the fear of being sent away to work in the fields, in the frost and muck, and she still so weak, barely able to drag her feet along. Nobody would try to protect her, she had no backing, no influential friends. And with greedy eyes she was waiting for the morning herb tea. To eat, to eat.

And Mrs. Janczak was still alive, damn her. When would she die at last? But all at once Wikta realized it was just as well that her neighbor hadn't died last night. That meant another bread ration that day. And it would be Wikta's bread. No, let her live a little longer, till the evening—then only two of them would spend the night in the bunk which was meant for one person only.

And Mrs. Janczak was sure to die. Her eyes had sunk back into their sockets.

But when the bread rations were brought, those eyes came to life again, they glittered, and a hand, resembling a rusty root, snatched at the bread, took it, folding it to the bosom as fondly as a mother would a child, and kept it there as securely as a hawk would keep its prey in its talons. Wikta was looking at the bread which was not hers, as if bewitched; she was unable to avert her eyes from it all day long.

It was for the first time that Mrs. Janczak did not put away the bread in her box. She had no strength left to do so. But she folded it to her bosom with passionate greed. Wikta was sitting still and full of envy she kept her eyes glued upon the talons grasping the bread.

Evening had come and early twilight had darkened the tiny windows high up in the barracks. The lamp was lit but it was throwing its light upon the stove, while the bunk underneath was in deep shadow. Wikta did not see the bread any longer, it was too dark. And Mrs. Janczak had not died yet.

Wikta rapidly looked around her. No, nobody was looking that way. She quietly moved toward Mrs. Janczak and listened. . . . No, she certainly was not conscious any longer. Her head was lolling backwards more and more all day long.

Very, very carefully Wikta touched the bread and tried to take it from the dying woman's hand. But the fingers of Mrs. Janczak had closed upon it so securely in her death spasm that it was impossible to snatch the slice of bread away from their grasp. Wikta was trembling with excitement; she was swearing profanely as she violently struggled to grab the bread from the rigid hand which in the moment of death had still obeyed life's instinct. The dying woman did not let go of her bread. Wikta was shaking all over as if rocked with fever. There was bread close to her fingers! Bread in her hand! Madness descended upon her. To grab it, to grab it at all cost! Darkness enveloped the cavern of the third tier.

Wikta was eating, swallowing greedily, ravenously, She felt the body next to her getting cold and stiff. At last! She got the bread at last. And now she had to get hold of the box before calling the night warden who might take it away together with the corpse.

"Night warden! Night warden!"

"What are you shouting for, damn you!"

"She is dead."

"Are your sure?"

"Quite sure. She got cold already."

"God damn you all to hell, the damned work and you and the whole pissing camp. It's the sixteenth cadaver and the roll-call only just over. The sixteenth! There are sure to be fifty of them till the morning. I haven't got time to haul them all away. She is a bitch of a corpse, so heavy! She must have been in camp a short time to be so stout! What?"

"Maybe. I didn't know her."

"Oh, yes, hers is an October number. These autumn transports die like flies. Typhus finishes them off."

Thus talking the night warden threw the corpse's arms and legs over the edge of the bunk and then dragged the body to the floor. It was almost naked, clad only in a man's shirt, and it fell to the earthern floor with a thud, the head bobbing up and down. But Wikta did not stop to have a look at the astonishingly thin shanks or the swollen, distended body of the corpse which the night warden was dragging along the floor. She could barely wait for her to go away. At last!

She plunged for the box and opened it with shaking fingers. She moved it toward the narrow streak of light visible in the aisle between the two rows of bunks. Yes, she was not mistaken, there were twelve rations of bread.

Twelve rations, three whole loaves, a fortune in the barter money of the camp. You could get a whole outfit of civilian clothes for it, if you thought of a getaway from camp. Gold perhaps? But Wikta was not interested in wealth or the treasures of the prisoners' property store or clothes or even the chance of escaping. For her bread was tangible and real, and there were three loaves of it, there was the chance of surfeit even, at last! Now she could eat till she had her fill.

But what was this? These whitish traces . . . Oh, God, God! This ration was mouldy in places. Yes, it stunk of mould . . . My God, the bread! The bread and mouldy! She had to examine it in full light.

Wikta got out of the bunk. She hid the box underneath the pallet and moved towards the light with some of the suspected rations, a groan on her lips. Damn that Janczak woman to hell! She hadn't eaten it and wouldn't let anybody have it and now nobody would be able to eat it. The bread had lain for twelve days underneath the damp pallet, close to the hoary wall, not far from the wet earthen floor. That ration was good for nothing. Even when broken into halves, it showed green mould inside. What about the next ration? It was mouldy on the outside but perhaps it was all right inside. . . . No, that one was mouldy right through too. Such a quantity of bread and spoilt. "No, I can't throw it all away, I must cut out the good pieces, save some of it at least! It is bread, after all. Somewhat mouldy, yes, but no matter. It can be eaten. I must start with the first, the oldest ration. And I needn't keep it for days, as I had planned to do." She had visualized several days of appeased hunger, but it was not to be. No, better not lose all of it. Better eat today as much as she could, it might get completely mouldy and spoilt by tomorrow.

Wikta took her only treasured possession, a small penknife she had once grabbed from a woman who had died in the bunk next to her. She started cutting the mould away from the pieces of bread. Her hand shook lest she cut out too much. She only wanted to remove what was really uneatable, completely green with mould. She would save something from the middle of the bread. . . . well, one little piece had to be removed, but only a very little one. One more slice, thin as paper, had still to be removed. Then she tried to eat the bread, but she couldn't, not this ration . . . it was no good. She looked at it with tears in her eyes—a whole ration! Her ration, her bread, and she unable to eat it! But it stunk of mould so much that she nearly vomited.

And the next ration? She started to cut out the mouldy parts again and then ate some of it. The other rations were in a much better state. A lot of the bread had proved to be eatable after all.

And now to eat, to eat. . . .

Wikta died after two days of horrible pain, vomiting and diarrhoea. Her last conscious thought was full of hatred, her last conscious feeling was that of a sickish sucking in her empty stomach.

Her neighbors found a box under her pallet, a box full of bread rations. That bread was not mouldy.

The news that delousing was to take place in our hospital barrack was to us like a thunderbolt out of the blue. Very early, at 4 a.m., we had to leave our beds, our illness and fever notwithstanding. I was unable to get up all by myself, but Wanda and Mrs. Ula helped me down, as usual. That was not all, however. We had to undress completely, and the mornings at Auschwitz were foggy and cold. I was trembling all over, and my teeth kept chattering as if in fever. My case was not the worst, however. There were others, lying with high temperature, yet they had to be deloused, too. All furniture was removed from the barrack, and the beds were scrubbed. We sat upon the stove till 7 a.m., then were taken outside. I was carried outdoors by two nurses who put me down behind the barrack. The sun was still rather low in the sky, and the cold was terrible. I was not strong enough to stand about, so I sat down on the gravel which penetrated into my bare body or rather into the skin with which my bones were covered. When the sun rose higher, it grew so hot at noon that one could not bear the heat. Some women had fainted, they were so weak. I lay down upon the gravel, and the sharp pebbles made my skin bleed. Our doctor was just passing by; when she saw me and examined my pulse, she had me carried into the shade, but there again were sharp cinders.

The barrack was being fumigated meanwhile, and so were the pallets and the blankets. It was already 4 p.m. when the convalescents were driven to the baths, while we who were seriously ill were carried into the barrack one by one. But we were not put into our beds, not yet. An SS doctor was standing and watching the procedure of thorough delousing. We were carried into the lavatory and there they put us into tubs with icy water, tinted with some bluish fluid. Some 15 Jewesses, all seriously ill, had been put into the same tub before me, some of them were delirious with fever. The one before me had scabies, and her flesh was rotting away due to illness and to lying in bed long. If I only hadn't seen her, but I was brought in just at the moment when her emaciated body, covered all over with sores, had been taken out of the tub. My heart stopped beating for a moment. That would be the last blow, to get scabies on top of everything else! My entreaties remained unheard, I was immersed in the cold water till I gasped. They did not keep us in the cold water long, it was not a question of washing us, not at all. Nobody cared about that, it was just a formality. Thanks to the influence of friends I had my hair wetted under the tap, not in the tub. Then they carried me outside again into the "garden" to let me dry in the sun. My legs felt like cotton wool. My God, would I be able to survive all this? After an hour they let us go inside, and we lay down on beds from which the pallets and blankets had been removed. Naked bodies upon bare boards. But I ceased to feel anything. And then I had fever for several days. I didn't even

"Delousing" is by Wanda Koprowska in Kazimierz Smolen, et al., eds., *Reminiscences of Former Auschwitz Prisoners* (Auschwitz: State Museum of Auschwitz, 1963), pp. 49-57. Translated by Krystyna Michalik. Reprinted with the kind permission of the publisher and the author.

realize who it was who gave me a pallet or who covered me with a blanket. Marysia, for sure. . . .

We lie only two of us in one bed, Henia and I. Thanks to Marysia, of course. Other beds are occupied by three, even four women. The sight of their half naked bodies is repulsive. They all keep scratching themselves incessantly. The bodies of some of them are literally covered with rotting scabies sores. Nothing but scabies and lice all around us. We also have lice, of course. Delousing had only irritated the insects which were attacking the more fiercely after it. I kept removing them not only from under my nightgown but also from my bed sores. I was happy only when I had high temperature, then I wouldn't feel lice biting me. I still ran a temperature when "my number was due" to write a letter home. I was too weak to write it myself, so one of my neighbors did it for me. I don't know whether my dear ones at home ever got that letter, but if they did, they must have thought I had gone crazy. I asked them in that letter to send me wine and fruits instead of bread and sausage. This request was the result of the fever which was undermining my organism. All I wanted was to drink, to quench my thirst. I used to give away my food parcels in exchange for some sips of water. One day I felt like eating a fresh cucumber. Marysia somehow got it for me, and I peeled it myself not to lose any of it. I ate it so greedily. . . . A pity it was so small. Then I fell asleep and when I awoke, I felt much better.

Next day Marysia gave me again part of a cucumber. But this time it disagreed with me, and I got diarrhoea. I was in despair. The doctor only shrugged. I was again threatened to be transferred to another barrack, but Marysia once more intervened, and I was able to stay on.

I consumed masses of carbon tablets—they were my exclusive diet. I have felt better for the last few days and I have begun to care about my appearance. I am given a bowl of water and I wash my body. I have also begun to get up, with the help of Wanda. I walk in a strange way. I feel dizzy, stars keep dancing before my eyes, and my legs, from the knees downwards, seem to be made of rubber. I have a feeling of putting one foot upon the ceiling and the other upon the ground. . . . And the fleas. . . . The legs are black with them after a few steps. To walk longer is impossible. I am too weak, my forehead is bathed with perspiration.

It is three months since I have been in the hospital, thanks to friendly backing, of course. I am getting a rest now in the full sense of the word. I am no longer ill, but my weakness is extreme. Having been bedridden for a long time has weakened me so much. But one had to lie in bed since this is a hospital. There is no roll-call here, or at least we don't go outside to be counted. The room warden counts the patients twice a day and that is all. But we are wakened here with the first whistling of the siren, just as in camp. Then the morning herb tea is brought, and we can't sleep any more though it is in the morning that one would like to get some sleep. There is too much noise in the evening and at night when one ceaselessly hears the cries: "Night warden, chamber pot!" I usually wake up properly only after the second whistle when the roll-call in camp is over and people have gone out to work.

Being now a convalescent I can observe what is going on in the hospital. The death rate is alarming, the amount of corpses is terrifying. . . . And the corpses are not left in peace, not even they. Rats gnaw them before they get cremated. The rats in Birkenau are a veritable calamity. They are as big as cats, fattened upon dead bodies. But they do attack the living, too. A corpse lying on its right side would be completely gnawed clean at the other side—cheeks, neck, breast—all fleshy parts are devoured by the rats, and nobody bothers to disturb them when they are at work on a corpse. The nurses are afraid to come near them as they won't run away, not even when threatened with sticks. Whole families of them will pass by, and one has to step back and let them pass, they are so bold.

Special squads were assigned the task of carting the corpses away; they were called in German "Leichen—or Himmelkommando."* They consisted of Jewish women and were easily recognizable by the leather gloves they used to wear. They came with stretchers made of boards and covered with a dirty and stinking bit of cloth with which they used to cover the corpse. If the dead body lay on the ground floor bunks, the procedure was simple, but if it was the second or third tier, the spectacle was gruesome. One of the women used to climb up to the bunk and then threw the body right down upon the floor, so that its head would strike the floor with a thud. The body was then put upon the stretcher and carried to the mortuary, from where lorries conveyed the corpses to the crematorium. But only bare skeletons were leaving the mortuary, the rest having been gnawed away by the rats. Whole truck loads of bones—the flesh was eaten by the rats. One might say: "What does it matter, it is a corpse only." But I don't think anybody who saw it happen would say so. I have no words to describe what I saw. The dead were always given a decent burial everywhere. Nobody thought to do it here. All corpses were cremated together.

Not all women prisoners, however, felt the horror of these things. Our barrack authorities, for example. They were immune to emotions of that kind. Was one of the women dying? Well, what of it? It can't be helped, can it? There is perhaps a birthday celebrated at the moment, and everybody is shouting in chorus: "Many happy returns of the day!" As it is August 15th, Marysia is celebrating hers, particularly since no SS men are about. The dying woman does not hear all that noise, maybe, but what about the sick? Don't they need some quiet?

When I had completely recovered, I used to get down from my bunk and it was then that I met Mrs. Chlebosz who had been here for the last 13 days only. She used to live in Starachowice before she got arrested. This was the time when General Sikorski died and Italy had capitulated. I must say we were always greatly interested in political matters and in the problems of

*Corpse or Heaven Squad.

our country, in spite of our illnesses. I often sat deep into the night with Mrs. Chlebosz discussing problems which interested us. People expected some change in politics just then, at least they used to talk much in the camp on that subject, but they were doomed to be disappointed. We were getting all sorts of news, and they varied according to the source they came from. Men used to comfort us always with the words: "Courage, we'll be back home soon." God, how desperately would we cling to that hope, expressed hurriedly, in passing! We simply lived on words like these.

I could not stand life in the hospital any longer. To witness how Jewish women were selected to be sent to the gas chambers was an ordeal, and I witnessed it daily or even every few hours.

An SS doctor used to come to the barrack, accompanied by women doctors (prisoners themselves). He looked around and shouted: "All Jews, get up!" Shadowy human forms then descended from their bunks. There were some Jewish women in the hospital who were not really ill, but who stayed on there thanks to their friends, just as I did. These women were sent to death, too, very often. Their eyes, wild with fear, seemed to implore help. They surely must have been sorry at that moment not to be in one of the work squads. The doctor was standing in the middle of the room and saying: "This one here, that one there," which meant this one for the chimney, that one could stay on in camp, perhaps a few hours longer. The words were not spoken aloud, and nobody really knew her fate up to the last moment. The SS man then looked at both groups and commanded a list of the camp numbers of those in one group; that meant they were to go to the crematorium. How could we look at those unhappy creatures in a moment like that? It was impossible to remain indifferent when witnessing such scenes. Human lives were in question.

The SS warden then blew her whistle, and all the nurses from the hospital came running. They interlocked their arms forming a circle into which Jewesses, whose camp numbers were on the list, were driven by force. They were taken to Block 25 which was isolated from the rest of the camp and surrounded by a high wall. After a short wait lorries began to arrive. Always strictly guarded, the Jewesses were crowded into the lorries and taken to the crematorium.*

While this was going on, everybody had to stay indoors. We were not allowed to look on. During the selection we had to lie in our beds at attention, and when the victims were being crowded into the lorries, we couldn't even budge. But we saw much through the crevices in the walls. The lorries started amidst despairing cries of the victims. An SS man sitting on top of the driver's cab belabored with his bludgeon the unhappy women who were already half-dead with fright and despair. There was some quiet in the morning, but a few hours later everything would start afresh.

Oh, to escape from here, to run away as quickly as possible. . . .

*Actually to the gas chamber located in the crematorium building.

16

Night and Fog

By far the largest women's concentration camp was Ravensbrück, located midway between Berlin and the Baltic; today the place is in East Germany. It was established in May 1939, first for German women and Gypsies. Soon it became an international prison for female "politicals" from all over Europe. The politicals—as distinguished from the "racials" such as Jews or Gypsies—were women who were considered dangerous to Nazi aims: members of the resistance movements in various countries or members of their families; secret radio operators and messengers; female parachutists; Socialists and Communists; patriotic women who harbored Jews, downed Allied pilots or other fugitives from German justice; women caught with illegal pamphlets in their possession or overheard expressing anti-Nazi opinions; women denounced that they had been listening to the London radio; hundreds of women accused of sabotaging the German war effort; and numerous innocent bystanders who happened to be at the wrong place at the wrong time and were swept up as visitors, neighbors or onlookers in the countless Gestapo dragnets.

There was also a sprinkling of professional criminals, murderers, thieves and prostitutes in Ravensbrück, and as in all camps, here too it was standard procedure to place them into positions of trusties. Only a small fraction of the 123,000 women who passed through the hell that was Ravensbrück were there because they were Jewish.

With the exception of the criminals and antisocial elements, their previous underground activities welded all nationalities into a tight-knit anti-Nazi sorority. Russian, Czech, German, Polish, Dutch, Belgian, Italian and even English women, were sisters in the hatred of their tormentors. This solidarity of instinctive sisterhoods and (brotherhoods) made it easier to suffer through indignities, tortures and the steady drudgery of daily and hourly existence.

From farmers' daughters to intellectuals, women were equal here, facing death at every step. Even Franciscan nuns were among the 14,000 Polish women who reached the camp in August 1944.

It was from Ravensbrück that in March 1942 a thousand seasoned inmates with their female SS guards were dispatched to establish the woman's camp at Auschwitz. It was also to Ravensbrück that SS women recruited for Krupp's slave labor camps were sent "to learn their trade."

As in the case of most concentration camps, so in Ravensbrück the last months of the war were the deadliest. As the SS sensed that their final hour was approaching, they all sought to drag down to destruction as many of their victims as possible. On January 28, 1945, for instance, 1,800 Polish women were killed in the so-called Jugendlager *or Youth Camp, which was a sham name for a place of genocide by various means. During February, women died by the scores: their rations were withheld until they starved; they were forced to take poison; they were executed by shooting. Among the executed were several German and Czech parachutists dropped from Russia to aid the underground movements resisting the Germans. Nazi fingers had a long reach: Olga Prestes, the German wife of the Brazilian Communist leader, was under Nazi pressure extradited by the Vargas regime and incarcerated in Ravensbrück. From here she was shipped with 1,600 others to the sanatorium for the mentally ill in Bernburg near Dessau and there gassed.*

Of the 123,000 women who passed through this vale of sorrow, 11,000 were alive there in early April 1945. After that, utter chaos took over. While the camp received a train load of inmates evacuated from the concentration camp Dora near Nordhausen (in Central Germany), it dispatched its own train of open freight cars to camp Sachsenhausen, near Berlin. It is known that sixty-two prisoners were executed in late April. When the Russians liberated Ravensbrück, all they encountered were about 2,000 disabled women.

Of the 10,000 French women whose misfor-

tune it was to enter these gates, a mere handful over 300 survived. Among them was Germaine Tillion (after the war a professor of anthropology at the Sorbonne), who had been arrested with her mother in August 1942 because they were involved in the Musée de l'Homme chapter of the French resistance network. Several members of this group had been executed six months earlier.

Tillon's case was marked NN. This was the designation of prisoners considered especially dangerous to the German Reich. NN stood for Nacht und Nebel, or Night and Fog. The expression came from Wagner's opera "Rheingold," in which Alberich could magically disappear. In SS parlance it designated prisoners whose investigations had been suspended for lack of time or evidence; yet, they were shipped to concentration camps, slated for disappearance.

In her memoirs, Tillion offers rare glimpses into life and death in Ravensbrück, where women worked at hard labor, draining marshes, building roads and slaving in the Siemens plant attached to the camp.

Aside from all her physical sufferings, the worst hardship she had to endure was encountering her mother in Ravensbrück and not being able to save her from death.

On August 13, 1942, I was arrested at the Gare de Lyon in Paris, where a traitor who had penetrated our "Musée de l'Homme" resistance network had arranged a meeting with the two of us. He was a priest and the vicar of La Varenne, the parish adjoining mine. His name was Father Robert Alesch.

At Alesch's trial in May 1948, his German superior Commandant Schaffer—the former deputy to Colonel Reile of the Abwehr*—was a witness. Schaffer testified that Alesch had signed on with the Gestapo as early as 1941, on his own initiative, and that he had been used by the Abwehr beginning in 1942. He sent scores of people to their deaths, including some very young ones from his parish youth organization, whom he incited to acts of resistance simply to be able to betray them. For this he was paid, in addition to certain "head bonuses," a fee of 12,000 old francs, plus 3,000 francs for his mistress and another 2,000 for someone named Claude; with his expenses, it all came to about 25,000 francs a month.

After my arrest, I was confined in the Santé prison in Paris (Division I, Cell 96), then—along with the entire section controlled by the Germans—I was transferred on October 13 to the Fresnes prison just outside Paris (Division III, Cell 326). I was interrogated seven times during August and October; not knowing at the time who had betrayed us, and fearful of telling too much to our enemies, I denied everything.

On Friday, October 23, 1942, a uniformed captain read to me the offenses I had been charged with; the officer who had usually questioned me—named Weinberger—provided a running translation. After each paragraph I was even allowed to make "corrections," which I did. Their attitude as they listened to me seemed sarcastic, but they recorded what I said; I listened to them attentively, politely, but rather gloomily. . . . The process was a long one and, except for the absence of an attorney, rather like the final interrogation in the presence of a "real" magistrate. Every now and then the captain stopped for a moment, looked at me thoughtfully, searching for words. When he had finished detailing the charges, he took on a solicitous air: "We are not like the French police, or the English. We are lenient with women. Very lenient. And, if we get a little help, we might even release a woman who has committed espionage. . . ." He broke off the sentence hesitantly, seeming unconvinced of what he was saying, while Weinberger translated. I made an effort to appear suddenly full of interest, and my reply literally made them gasp for an instant: "And those who have not committed espionage—what do you do with them?" Then they both laughed, nothing more.

My bill of accusations included five acts carrying a death sentence, one of which—"harboring English agents"—directly endangered my mother.

"Night and Fog" is from Germaine Tillion, *Ravensbrück* (Garden City, N.Y.: Doubleday, 1975), pp. xiv-xxiii. Translation copyright 1975 by Doubleday & Company, Inc. Reprinted by permission of the publisher.

*Abwehr was the German army counterintelligence.

Hearing the charges gave me some idea of the Germans' information about me—much of what they knew but, unfortunately, not everything. I still did not know how they had gotten whatever information they had, since I had not yet learned that Alesch was a traitor. Nor did I know that several of his accusations had been confirmed by an agent arrested along with me. Isolated in a cell later, he had denounced everyone he knew. My mother, arrested the same day, was kept in prison because of his confessions; she had denied everything, as I had.

I was not completely certain of my mother's arrest until January 12, 1943, when I was told by the German chaplain at Fresnes—who also gave me a small volume of *Imitation of Christ.* I still have the book today; in it I had recorded landmark dates of my imprisonment, which until then I had written with a nail on the walls of my cell.

My mother was imprisoned on the second floor, on the courtyard side; my cell was opposite hers, on the fifth floor.

Every day, when the soup was passed around and my door was opened, I tried to catch a glimpse of her cell. On April 11 our two doors were opened at the same time, and I saw her for the first time since our arrest. She waved at me and tried to smile; I waved back and tried to smile. The German guard (a woman) did not hurry me, allowing us a very long moment of reunion, and weeping as she watched us. We were still far from Ravensbrück.

On August 18, 1943, I learned that she was no longer at Fresnes, and for four days I foolishly hoped that she had been released. But my German floor officer told me on the twenty-second that she was at Romainville. Since I was no longer in solitary confinement at the time, I could receive parcels and send my clothes for laundering on the outside so we managed to communicate in various clandestine ways.

When I was deported on October 21, 1943, my mother was not on the train carrying about twenty of the "NN" prisoners, a group which included other women accused of "offenses" similar to mine. One week later, our convoy was joined by a second NN group at the Aix-la-Chapelle prison; we were sent together to Ravensbrück. I became hopeful again that my mother might have been released, and that hope made my own deportation easier to endure.

Our convoy was placed in quarantine as soon as we arrived at Ravensbrück, and almost all of us became very ill. In my case there were, in quick succession, diphtheria, double otitis, a serious incidence of bronchitis, complicated by an attack of scurvy. Two Czech deportees who did not know me—Zdenka* and Hilda—saved my life. I have no idea how long I was kept in the Revier (the infirmary), since during those first few months at Ravensbrück it was impossible to maintain anything near an accurate diary.

*Later identified as political prisoner Zdenka Nedvědová-Nejedlá, M.D., to whom countless prisoners were thankful for her help.

Then, on February 3, 1944, a convoy of 958 women arrived from France —the transport known as the "twenty-seven thousands"*—and my mother was among them. . . .

Soon afterward, during a roll call, I learned of her presence in the camp. The message was passed along in whispers along the almost silent rows as 18,000 or 19,000 women stood immobile. I think it was during a morning roll call, but I am no longer certain; I remember being almost paralyzed with grief, and I could see only darkness.

When we finally were able to have a reunion—and it was an emotional one—she did not seem to feel any sadness. Her convoy was lodged in Block 15, and, if I had not been an NN prisoner, I almost certainly could have moved in there unnoticed by the authorities, since no one in that block ever betrayed me. But the Blockova** of the NN block—Kate Knoll, a German prisoner—was vicious and untrustworthy, and I was NN.

The NN prisoners were not allowed to be placed in work Kommandos assigned to stations far from the camp, and for that reason were selected in sufficiently large numbers to form their own work column, known as Bekleidung (clothing supply), where the duties included unloading the trucks and rail cars crammed with some of the bizarre spoils accumulated by the German police in their pillages throughout Europe. Because of the Bekleidung—and despite the regular searches of the prisoners who worked there—a goodly number of useful articles filtered down to the prisoners, especially medicines. As for me, I managed to set aside by the handful enough odd bits of cloth to put together a pillow for my mother; she also received linens and warm underclothing.

From day to day my mother and I managed to learn almost everything the best-informed prisoners could find out about what was really happening behind the scenes at Ravensbrück. First—and throughout 1944—there were the executions and the "*transports noirs.*"*** Then, in January 1945, they created a sort of "annex" to Ravensbrück, where they exterminated selected prisoners. This "annex" was the small Uckermarck camp, which was more often known as "Jugendlager."****

Throughout January and February, the terror became more tangible day by day: there were increasingly frequent disappearances of prisoners not

*The figure refers to prisoners' numbers as they entered the concentration camp. Germaine Tillion's number, for instance, was 24,588; she arrived on October 31, 1943. Zdenka Nedvědová's number was 22,068; she arrived in August 1943. When the 27,000s were being admitted, however, there were only about 18,300 women actually in Ravensbrück; the rest were killed, died of various causes or were shipped elsewhere, as industrial slave labor or to extermination centers.

**Blockova—in several Slavic languages—or *Blockälteste*—in German—was a prisoner with seniority, often a professional criminal, who was in charge of a block or barrack.

****Transports noirs,* or black transports, were groups of political or racial prisoners, selected for genocide because they were old, weak or ill.

****Youth Camp, not necessarily for the young prisoners.

only from Uckermarck, but also from the infirmary of the main camp—the Revier.

Nevertheless, on March 1, 1945, I took the risk of going to the Revier because of an extremely painful abcess in my jaw, which for several days had kept me from opening my mouth. (I fed myself with scraps of stale bread soaked in water.) While I was in the Revier, the camp police moved in on several blocks, including the NN block, preventing any escape. All those caught inside were transferred to the Strafblock (the punishment section), my mother among them. I managed to get into the Strafblock that evening; I do not remember exactly how, but probably by saying—truthfully—that I was an NN returning from the Revier. Because of the police roundup, a majority of the Frenchwomen and most of the surviving Hungarian gypsies were, from that point on, isolated in the smaller confines of the Strafblock. The overcrowding was such that there was no possibility for normal sleep. My mother was very distressed and very tired, but did not complain; I too said nothing. And she wanted to remain sitting up throughout the first night.

The next day, two friends who "enjoyed" considerable seniority in the camp—Anička (Czech) and Grete (German)—arranged with the police* for me to return to the Revier for treatment. I was thinking that I would be away for an hour at the most, but before leaving I embraced my mother, and—because of our distress and all that we knew but would not say—I held her in my arms for a long time, as if it might be the last. And it was the last time.

While I was in the Revier, these same friends decided it was imperative that they get as many as possible out of the Strafblock, and they took out my mother and two NN comrades. They did the best they could for my mother, putting her in a "normal" block, number 27, "on a bed, near the door."

About one o'clock that afternoon, we learned at the Revier that there would be a new general roll call, lasting the rest of the day. I was taken under the protective wing of Grete Buber-Neumann, a German prisoner at Ravensbrück since 1940. She was well-educated and had been been a Blockova at one time. After removal from that post and a stay in the Strafblock, she became a secretary, working in a series of different offices in the camp. That day, she occupied a small cell—with a real bed. She took an enormous risk, hiding me at her feet, under the bedclothes. When Pflaum came in for the roll check, he noticed nothing and closed the door.

At five, when movement around the camp became possible again, my friend Danielle came to tell Grete in German that my mother had been taken away during the roll call.

*These police women were senior prisoners, often also professional criminals, who frequently were more brutal than the SS overseer women.

I can no longer remember how I managed to rejoin my block and relocate, one by one, my very efficient friends. But the next day I had one of them, an Austrian, take a final word of warning to my mother, to tell her to "hold out" as best she could. My friend also took a package no larger than a deck of cards—two or three sulfamide pills, a slice of bread, and the three sugar cubes and the biscuit my Czech friends had given me. On Monday (March 5) and on Tuesday, I persuaded another secretary to transmit a second and third letter, a second and third tiny package. . . . On Thursday, Miki returned the three packages and the three letters. It was foolish to hope any longer; I knew this, but I could not believe it. . . .

During this period, at all hours, the "hunts" were carried out throughout the camp to fill the ominous trucks which—quite openly by this time—shuttled among the various blocks, the Revier and the crematorium. The Revier nurses saw their patients taken away in hospital gowns, saw the trucks leave, and kept listening until they heard the trucks stop at the ovens. Then they saw the trucks return empty for a new load. One nurse clocked the time needed for a trip from the Revier to the crematorium, unloading and return: seven minutes. And—day and night—we could see the smoke pouring from the crematorium chimneys.

Even when I had lost almost all hope, I continued to search desperately for some trace, someone who might have seen my mother—just one woman from among the many penned up in the Jugendlager but still alive. I knew there were many who had not yet been killed, since from time to time groups came back down for work details, to make room for others, for any number of reasons.

Then, on Monday, March 19, I wrote: *France Odoul and Marguerite Solal, in Block 7* noticed Mother passing by on Friday evening. They did not even remember who was with her.*

* * *

On Monday the fifth I had undergone surgery by someone completely unknown to me—a pleasant woman, very young, and visibly terrified by the instruments in her hands. While she hesitated, Hellinger had passed through the room. This only worsened the distraction of my young surgeon, since I was there fraudulently to begin with, and Hellinger's only known function was to extract gold teeth from the dead—a task which insured that the living kept a respectful distance from him, as one would from a hyena or vulture. He stopped, came to look at me, even leaning over a bit to get a better view. I recall showing very little concern at the time; otherwise, he might have been more interested. . . . During the next several

*Block 7 was on the main road of the camp, leading to the Jugendlager, the place of extermination.

days, the nurses often dressed my wounds in such a way that I could be taken out quickly, since the Revier was then one of the most dangerous places in the camp. On March 15, I felt that I should try to walk, but my legs would not support me; my comrades took my temperature: 104°. The physical suffering was still intense, but at times it seemed almost a comfort, to the extent that it kept me from thinking.

Two weeks later, on April 2, 1945, 300 Frenchwomen were liberated through the intervention of the International Red Cross of Geneva, but the NN prisoners were not among them. On April 23, however, the NN were included in the liberation organized by the Swedish Red Cross and the negotiations of Count Folke Bernadotte.

The prisoners left with little more than the clothing they were wearing. Before the leave-taking there were, of course, innumerable searches by the Germans, but it was fruitless: the prisoners managed to pass from hand to hand those precious articles they wanted to keep. Thus two hidden "objects" somewhat more remarkable than the rest escaped the final inspection—the last two surviving French babies.* . . . .

For my part, I took out the notes I had taken during the last days, as well as the identities of the principal SS figures of the camp, vaguely coded and disguised as recipes. I also managed to hide a roll of undeveloped film showing the gangrenous legs of the schoolchildren who had been the subjects of Dr. Karl Gebhardt's experimental operations. I had kept the film in my pocket since January 21, 1944—always wrapped in scraps of filthy cloth to avoid its attracting attention during the searches.

The fact that I survived Ravensbrück I owe first—and most definitely—to chance, then to anger and the motivation to reveal the crimes I had witnessed, and finally to a union of friendship, since I had lost the instinctive and physical desire to live.

This tenuous web of friendship was, in a way, almost submerged by the stark brutality of selfishness and the struggle for survival, but somehow everyone in the camp was invisibly woven into it. It bound together surrogate "families": two, three, or four women from the same town who had been arrested in the same "affair," or perhaps a group formed within a prison cell or in a railroad car at the time of their deportation—all of them later clinging to one another to keep from being engulfed in the horrors of the prison camps. The major dividing line—more than nationality, political party, or religion—was language. But there were networks of mutual aid which functioned above these sometimes artificial divisions.

These invisible chains of communal aid among prisoners had a formidable counterpart: the organized networks of our captor-murderers. Systematic slaughter was not too easy outside of the organizations established

*As late as March 1945, thirty-two infants who had survived till then were gassed. The Russians liberated Ravensbrück on April 30, 1945.

specifically for that purpose—the "death factories" of Auschwitz and Lublin-Maidanek. While the extermination of prisoners at Ravensbrück was carried out by means one might call "inventive," our workshops continued to function, fed by a work force decimated by chronic famine, which was sufficient to do away with a certain number of prisoners without creating panic. And, while the number of cremations that could be accommodated by the ovens was not increased significantly, it is now known that a gas chamber with a capacity of about 150 persons was set up nearby. Why 150, and not 50 or 300? Was the number proportioned to the capacity of the ovens? Was the gas chamber installed in an existing structure? But the fact remains that it always functioned at the same time the other forms of organized murder were following their usual course—the more "personal" form, perhaps, of the terrifying "tête-à-tête" between the assassin and his victim. "Proper murder," like "proper torture," is a wild illusion.

There were, of course, thousands of individual journeys to a personal Calvary, but for only one of them was I able to mark every "station of the cross" with witnesses. That one terrible journey, which concluded in a merciful death, might help in finding the meaning behind the mere words of history.

Claire, a sweet and shy young woman was held in great affection by her comrades, partly because of her knowledge of poetry; I think she was a professor of literature. My mother liked her and often spoke to me about her. In March 1947 I sent an account of what I had learned about her death to the others who had known her: *Do you remember Claire? First of all she was cruelly bitten and mangled by a dog. Who set the dog on her? We do not know, but he was Claire's first assassin. She went then to the Revier, where she was denied treatment. Who refused her? We don't know for sure, probably Marschall. The second murderer. Her wounds did not heal, and she was sent to the Jugendlager. Who sent her? We don't know—probably Pflaum or Winkelman. The third murderer. Now that she was among the ranks of the condemned, who kept her from fleeing? An Aufseherin, or one of the police? Possibly both, possibly von Skine or Boesel. The fourth murderer. At Jugendlager, Claire refused to swallow the poison Salveguart had given her, and Salveguart, with the help of Rapp and Köhler, beat her senseless with a club and finally killed her.* *

Claire was only one woman among 123,000—one solitary agony. For this one victim, five bands of murderers. And for all the others there were the same assassins, or some like them; every victim was killed and rekilled. We were all caught in a terrifying cycle, with an assassin waiting at every turn.

*Elisabeth Marschall, chief nurse; Hans Pflaum, a "gross and bestial fiend," chief of the Ravensbrück labor force; Adolf Winkelman, M.D., camp physician; von Skine and Greta Boesel, Aufseherinen or supervisors; Vera Salveguart, prisoner ordered to administer poison; Rapp and Köhler, military medics. All but Salveguart were Germans employed by the SS. Other sources use different spellings of the names: von Skene and Salwequart.

17

Middle Ages Nazi Style

Just being incarcerated in a concentration camp and forced to do hard labor on starvation diets were sufficient to imperil the lives of women not used to such barbaric conditions. But this did not seem to satisfy the tormentors at Ravensbrück and the many other concentration camps. It is hard to find an answer to the question: how could once civilized people, camp physicians, for instance, condone what was going on in camps above and beyond the daily routines, bad enough as those were? The standard explanations forthcoming after the war were that they simply followed orders. It was the ancient "Maul halten and weiterdienen," "Keep your mouth shut and carry on," used once in the Austrian and German armies. Nobody wanted to rock the boat, nobody wanted to endanger his or her precious career in the Nazi hierarchy.

The nation that prided itself as being Kultur Träger, carriers of culture, selected especially fitting personnel to run the concentration camps. Many of the SS of both sexes, but definitely not all of them, were social outcasts, misfits and sadists, who gave vent to their base instincts especially in the women's camps. Ignorant persons with power in their hands are always dangerous. Given the green light and promised rewards for a job well done under camp conditions often made them into utter monsters. Lives of inmates meant nothing; they were expendable. There were always more where they came from.

Beatings were the order of the day for a dress too short or too long, even if both were issued by the camp in the first place; for standing or sitting; for talking at roll call or not answering loudly enough when addressed.

Are we doing injustice to the Middle Ages by calling some of the concentration camp practices medieval? It is fortunate that there were no windmills in Ravensbrück, or the SS would have tied more people to them for fun, as they did to some Jews in Holland. I heard from eyewitnesses of garrotting a prisoner on the ground by stepping on the two ends of a cane placed across his throat. In Ravensbrück supervisor Dorothea Binz placed her boot heels on one leg, her toes on another leg of a flogged prisoner, rocking back and forth on the woman; when she left, her boots were bloody.

The German writer Margarete Buber-Neumann tells us that Dorothea Binz also found an outlet for her bestiality in the Bunker, the dungeon of Ravensbrück. Buber-Neumann spent several weeks there in a dark, narrow hole, fed only occasionally. The physical and psychological consequences of such solitary imprisonment were devastating. Buber-Neumann, a disillusioned Communist —she had spent time in Stalin's gulag and was then handed over to the Gestapo—had an additional cross to bear. She and her inmate friend, the Czech journalist and fellow ex-Communist Milena Jesenská, the Milena of Franz Kafka fame, were taunted by the still faithful Communist inmates as "deviationists."*

There were countless executions, but often the prisoners found out about them only accidentally. Many Polish and French women met this fate at Ravensbrück. Several German and Czech parachutist women were among those shot, as were Communists, Soviet and Yugoslav partisans, all women. In reality, these were not executions in the legal sense of the word but murders.

Escape was impossible. The women who attempted it were recaptured and after horrible tortures killed. The Polish girl Genia managed to escape from the forest detail and live to tell about it. But her entire detail paid for her escape by two months in the punitive block, and the leader of the detail was sent to the Bunker, which amounted to a torture chamber with high chances for death.

The following partial description of the varied punishments comes from eyewitnesses who did time in Ravensbrück as political prisoners.

Dagmar Hájková and Hana Housková both returned from the women's concentration

*Margarete Buber-Neumann, *Kafkova přítelkyně Milena* (Toronto: Sixty-Eight Publishers, 1982), pp. 214-23. Original German edition: *Milena Kafkas Freundin* (Munich: Gotthold Müller, 1963).

camp of Ravensbrück and live, now retired, in their beloved thousand towered Prague. Dagmar Hájková was arrested by the Gestapo for her activities in the Czech underground at the age of twenty-five and spent almost five years at Ravensbrück. After the war she became editor of a publishing house.

Hana Housková, also a political prisoner, returned from Ravensbrück to a career as a journalist and home-maker. She has a son who is an architect and three grandchildren. She is also foster mother to an eleven-year-old Gypsy boy. Doing research at the Historical Institute on the resistance, she came upon her own Gestapo file, according to which she was supposed to have had a "Special Trial" on November 16, 1943—which was twenty-two months after her arrival at Ravensbrück! Such was the Nazi concept of justice. In spite of the hair-raising experiences she witnessed and lived through, she is a self-confessed eternal optimist.

Heavy punishment was meted out for "robbing" the camp: for stealing a raw potato or carrot—23 lashes by cane and the Bunker. . . . The mildest punishment was "Kostabzug," the denial of food; a woman thus punished had to stand for three to seven evenings in front of her barracks without dinner. This was often practiced for the whole block or for the entire camp. . . .

A much feared and dangerous physical punishment was brought to Ravensbrück by Himmler as his personal present at his visit in 1940. This was flogging, anywhere between 10 and 25 lashes, in harder cases 50 or 75 lashes, which were usually administered in installments of 25. It was carried out in the presence of the Kommandant, the chief woman supervisor and a physician. At first the whip had been handled by the female SS guards from the Bunker, named Binz and Mandel;* from August 1942 on this dirty work was given to the green** Anita Weiss. After the summer of 1943 the Germans always assigned Polish and Russian women to do the flogging. We did not understand the meaning of this then, but after liberation we read the circular that had been sent to all women's camps. According to this, Himmler had ordered the physical punishment of Russian women to be carried out by Polish ones, and of Polish and Ukrainian women by the Russians. Their rewards were a few cigarettes. The directive specified that "under no circumstances should a German prisoner be used to administer the flogging. . . ."

The pain from flogging was terrible; after the first four or five lashes it seemed unbearable. Most women were screaming with pain, many fainted and had to be brutally revived. The beaten parts of their bodies were dark blue like ink, with swollen bulges where the whip had hit. It took over three months for the pain to cease, and many were crippled for life.

Another punishment was transfer to the "Strafblock," the punitive barracks. . . . Here life was even worse than in the other blocks. The permanent residents were rough and raw elements, and decent women thrown in with them found themselves in a living hell. . . .

The worst times in the Strafblock were in 1942, when it was lorded over by the Stubova** Emma von Skene, a prisoner, nicknamed "the lame devil";

"Middle Ages Nazi Style" is by Dagmar Hájková in Dagmar Hájková, et al., *Ravensbrück* (Prague: Naše vojsko, 1961), pp. 79-86. Translation copyright by Vera Laska. Reprinted with the kind permission of the publisher and the authors.

*Maria Mandel, born in 1912 in Austria, without a high school education, was an early member of the Nazi Party. After Ravensbrück she was the head of the women's camp at Auschwitz; the prisoners referred to her as "the beast." For her share in the selections for the gas chambers and medical experiments and for her torture of countless prisoners, she was condemned to death in 1947 as a war criminal.

**"Green" was a prisoner wearing a green triangle in front of her camp number, designating a professional criminal. Politicals had red, Jews yellow, asocials black triangles. There were numerous other categories, color coded with thorough efficiency.

***The Stubova, an inmate with seniority, was in charge of a section of a block, serving under the *Blockälteste* or *Blockova,* also an oldtimer prisoner, was responsible for the entire block. Note that Tillion refers to Emma von Skine (sic) as an Aufseherin or supervisor (p. 208).

she terrorized her fellow inmates in a worse way than the SS supervisors. She was German, allegedly married to an Englishman.

Marie Pospíšilová will not forget Skene till her dying days. As a kitchen helper, she managed to give some tea to a sick woman and for that was sent to the Strafblock for half a year. She recalls her meeting with Skene: "Her eyes started gleaming with joy over her new victim. She ordered me to strip. . . . [When I hesitated] she called in two asocials who worked me over with their clogs until I fainted". . . .

Women in the Strafblock lived in strict isolation. . . . Their labor was the hardest. . . . In the evenings their hands were bloody, their fingers literally dripping with blood. The Strafblock had the roughest SS supervisors, beating the inmates at work with their fists or their whips. If a tortured woman lifted her arm to protect her face, she was accused that she had meant to hit her torturer. The SS supervisors had dogs that they sicked on women who did not work fast enough. Daily there were tragic scenes. One was witnessed by Marie Náchodská. When the Strafblock was detailed to clean out the swamps on a lakeshore, one girl fell face down into the mud. The supervisor placed her foot on the fallen girl and held her till she ceased to breathe. Such incidents were not exceptional. . . .

The hardest punishment in the camp was imprisonment in the Bunker. The Bunker was a jail in the jail, a prison in the prison. Once in the Bunker, it was hard to tell whether a woman would ever leave it alive.

It was a one story concrete building in the corner of the camp. It contained eighty four by six feet cells. . . . The place was strictly out of the Middle Ages. Hunger, cold, beatings and various instruments constituted the means of torture. One variant, a stream of water under high pressure, was more effective than beating; and besides, that was more tiresome for the torturer. . . .

The first weeks in the Bunker were spent in a cell where the windows were covered with iron blinds, so no light could penetrate. The inmate lost all track of time. . . . The women slept without a cover on the bare floor. The supervisors often would enter without any reason and take out their nasty moods on the imprisoned women. For supervisor Binz it was enough if one did not understand German, and she would lash out helter skelter beating up the victim. . . .

After five or six weeks, if the woman was still alive, she was transferred to a cell with a window and a cot, and fed daily. Here women spent months not knowing what lay in store for them; some had been already condemned to death, others were under investigation.

The women in the Bunker were tormented not only by cold but also by heat. The English Fanny Samson, who had been arrested in France as a member of the underground, was sent upon her arrival to Ravensbrück directly to the Bunker. She testified at the Hamburg trial [of Ravensbrück] that in the hot August days of 1944 the central heating in her cell was turned on full blast.

French Martha Desrumaux . . . saw a supervisor beat a girl with a chair, breaking it to pieces over her, then finishing off the poor creature with the leg of the chair. . . . She told of a drunken Kommandant who kept breaking champagne bottles over the head of a little Ukrainian girl, then kicked her bloody body under the table, where he then killed her with empty bottles. . . . She spoke of cell 60 that nobody ever left alive, about the dousings with cold, icy water, and the flooding of the cell while women, naked and half crazed, tried to climb the slippery walls to escape the rising waters until their fingers were bloody, and finally drowned. She witnessed women dragged by their hair over the steps of the Bunker. She saw wooden coffins with small openings into which women were placed while they were interrogated; they were gradually suffocated. There were all kinds of torture instruments there that would put the Spanish Inquisition to shame. . . .

Two Czech inmates working at the Revier or hospital, Hana Housková and Marie Svědíková, accompanied once an SS women to the Bunker. Hana Housková testified about what they had seen there:

> The small, gray yard with a tall wall reminded me of the Pankrác* yard, but that seemed like a dear, friendly place compared to the choking horrors that were oozing from every nook and crany here. A long, narrow corridor, cell doors on both sides, smaller than those at Pankrác, gray-green, with more modern locks . . . . Stairs leading down to the basement. . . . another corridor, narrower and more gloomy; cold, musty, mouldy air. . . . In a cell on the floor lay a naked, white body of a girl. She was lying on her side, with her head toward the door, arms outstretched, as if she had crawled in the dark instinctively toward the exit looking for help. She was dead. "Abholen," barked the guard, "fetch." We bent down to the corpse. Marie, a strong girl from Moravia, took her under the arms, I by the feet. We started lifting her, but we could not. . . . The guard was mad: "Los, los," "get going," she shouted. We pulled with all our strength. The body rigidly, heavily, hit our arms. On the floor where the girl's legs had been, were now parts of her skin. She had been frozen to the floor.

Many women got into the Bunker or the Strafblock innocently, simply by mistake. For instance in January 1945 the SS were looking for Božena Klečková and a Benešová, who were in secret communication with the outside. By mistake, through the similarities in names, the SS got hold of Božena Holečkova** and the wrong Marie Benešova. They were kept in a cell so tight that they could not even sit down. At the interrogation it turned out that they had nothing to do with the accusation. The SS located the right "culprits"; yet in spite of this, they sent both innocent women into the Bunker, where they spent four terrifying weeks. From the Bunker they were placed into the Strafblock. In February they were even put into a Gypsy transport that had some obscure destination. They were spared of that only through the help of friends who managed to hide them in the Revier.

*Prison in Prague where many of the Czech politicals were incarcerated before being shipped to concentration camps.

**One of the co-authors of *Ravensbrück*.

The SS justified this whole system of punishments as necessary for the maintenance of order. . . . But in reality it was part and parcel of the machinery for the liquidation of human beings. The food, the labor, the whole way of life in the camp, all served but one purpose: exhausting and annihilating the prisoners. Punishments were the means to accelerate the process.

And in spite of all this, hundreds of times a day we broke the camp rules; hundreds of times we risked being apprehended. It was impossible not to do so, not to violate the nonsensical and inhuman regulations of the SS "order." At times, with cooperation and aiding each other, it was possible to avoid punishment by simply not getting caught. Soon we became convinced that exactly this struggle against the stupid and malicious camp machinery not only did not weaken our strength, but on the contrary, it strengthened us and filled us with self-esteem.

18

The Stations of the Cross

Crude and at times phantasmagoric punishments, hard labor, constant hunger, the absence of legitimate medical attention, degenerate medical experiments including vivisection, executions by shooting or injections and mass murders by gas were the stations of the cross that the women had to walk once they passed over the threshold of Ravensbrück.

Mass gassing was "farmed out" because Ravensbrück did not boast permanent gas chambers. The management tried to rectify this deficiency in January 1945 by transforming part of a warehouse into a gas chamber, but capacity was a mere 150 or so a day, and the approaching front line made the SS abandon it in early April. Still, hundreds of women were liquidated this way. Among the last ones was a group of Czechs, singing their national anthem to the last minute of their lives, and an older German woman, who kept screaming at the SS that her three sons were fighting in the German army.

Hunger was a matter of course all the time, but toward the end of the war it reached such proportions that it was suspected that the corpses chewed up in some blocks were mutilated not by the rats but by humans. One woman was seen eating what another had thrown up. Yet after liberation the warehouses were found full of beans and other food.

Epidemics were frequent and took a horrendous toll. Without hygiene, baths or medicine, the women died like flies of tuberculosis, typhoid fever, spotted typhus, diarrhoea, scabies or simply of malnutrition. Rats and lice were rampant. A second crematorium had to be erected in 1944, and a new "corpse detail" (Leichenträgerkolone) *was established to gather the dead.*

The constant cross that the women had to bear was incessant labor, in long, mostly twelve-hour shifts, often at night. It kept draining the life juices of all. The women built roads and a railroad extension, the camp headquarters and homes for the SS guards; they moved bricks in a human chain, hands over hands, until they were bloody shreds; they carted cement, sand, also garbage and manure, on the run; they felled trees and labored in the fields.

A few "lucky" ones worked in the camp offices, kitchens and warehouses, with a chance to swallow a few extra scraps of food. Others were employed in the furrier workshops, transforming tons of fur coats taken from victims of transports to various concentration camps into army gloves, pilots' boots and uniform linings. By the spring of 1944, 4,500 women labored at the Ravensbrück branch of the Dachau Enterprises, making prisoners' striped uniforms and reconstructing army uniforms full of gunshot holes, blood and lice.

By far the largest number of women were employed at slave labor in various industries. Siemens had one of its factories directly at the camp (others at Buchenwald and Gross-Rosen, among others). Here 2,500 women manufactured munitions, electrical parts of submarines, field phones and parts of the V-2 rockets. Water was so scarce that they were not allowed to flush the single latrine; the German Kommandant had the exclusive right to do that!

Hundreds were working at branch camps at Neubrandenburg, Ganthin, Wansbeck and others. They were shipped out to over two dozen factories and estates as slave labor. They worked for companies like Patin, Grahl, Luftmuna, Heinckel, Junkers, AEG, Hermann Göring Werke, even for the V-Waffen Erprobungsstelle at Peenemünde, and, of course, for I. G. Farben which among others supplied their delousing powder that did not work, and the Cyclon B gas for the gas chambers that did.

The slightest slackening of the tempo was considered sabotage and could mean return to the punitive block in camp, the Bunker, or to the insane asylum, where gassing was on daily order. For stealing rubber bands to hold up their pants that were issued without elastic, twelve women were almost shot. For bringing garlic to the Siemens factory, thus endangering metal, two Ukrainian women were put into the Bunker and never seen again.

Interestingly, the SS collected daily wages for their charges, but the laborers never saw a penny of the two to four Marks they earned per day.

Such was the work situation of the Ravensbrück women. To round out the picture of their lives and deaths, read the following excerpts from eyewitnesses' testimonies about the medical practices in Ravensbrück. They included the sterilization of women who through the institutionalized barbarity of Nazi philosophy were considered "unworthy of reproduction" (fortpflanzungsunwürdig)*, and the vivisection of those most pitiful of all pitiful victims, the human guinea pigs nicknamed the "rabbits."*

Until February 1942 we had seen all kinds of horrors. But then we came face to face with something that could have been conceived only in the pervert minds of fascists. For the first time we became witnesses to mass murder.

Preparations had been under way already during January and at the beginning of February. Lists of incurable and seriously ill women had to be prepared. . . . At the same time the management of the camp launched a propaganda campaign that the selected women would go to some kind of an institution where they would not have to work. Many women believed that and volunteered.

One cold February morning trucks arrived with a commando of SS men. Their way with the sick was not exactly considerate. They grabbed the stragglers and were throwing them on the trucks helter skelter. The unfortunate women were tripping over their crutches and over each other on the floor of the truck strewn thinly with straw.

Thus the first one hundred and fifty left. The rest were awaiting their turn, hoping for some news about the place where they were supposed to go.

The news arrived before we knew it. It was on the third day after the transport had left. In the morning we went to work. In our warehouse a surprise was awaiting us: on the floor the clogs, underwear and dresses of the departed ones, with their numbers on them. But not only that; here were also the canes, crutches, artificial limbs, false teeth—all the things that sick people needed as long as they remained alive.

The trucks that had brought back this gruesome legacy carried off the next group of the sick, and on the third day the whole process was repeated. Altogether they removed 1,600 women; they were gassed in the sanitarium for the mentally ill in Bernburg near Dessau. . . .

In March 1942 a transport of 1,000 women left to "found" [the women's camp in] Auschwitz. It consisted of the entire punitive block and a few additional prisoners selected by the SS women transferred to Auschwitz.

In August 1942 it was the turn of the Jewesses. The whole Jewish block was sent to Auschwitz. By that time we knew quite well why the huge chimneys there were puffing smoke day and night. . . .

In February 1944 again lists were prepared of all women who were weak, old, sick or unable to work. . . . In two days chief nurse Marschall and doctor Treite,* sitting on top of the examining table at the Revier, selected

"The Stations of the Cross" is by Dagmar Hájková and Hana Housková in Dagmar Hájková, et al, *Ravensbrück* (Prague: Naše vojsko, 1961), pp. 95-112. Translation copyright by Vera Laska. Reprinted with the kind permission of the publisher and the authors.

*Chief nurse Elisabeth Marschall was a no nonsense German always "doing her duty" and "following orders." Percy Treite, the director of the Revier, was a talented organizer: he was less sadistic than most of his colleagues, but still performed sterilizations, selections and ordered poisonings. His mother was English.

over 800 women. Some of them were young; these were the daughters of the older women who did not want to be separated from them. . . . They were taken to Lublin and from there to Auschwitz. At the time Auschwitz was being evacuated in January of 1945, a handful of them returned to Ravensbrück. All the others had perished.

There were also smaller transports. For these they selected mostly sick, old, weakened, mentally ill and tubercular women. They were taken to other "liquidation centers." There were many of these. For instance I recall a transport of women with tuberculosis, which left in early 1944 for Barth, and a transport of French women from Paris, taken to be gassed in June of 1943.

In early 1945 transports were shifted back and forth under terrible circumstances. One transport from Ravensbrück to Reichow remained for four weeks without food, water and air, locked in cattle cars, often just standing on the railroad tracks. All women died.

In February 1945 a transport of 250 older women left Ravensbrück. By then all Germany was in an incredible chaos; not even the perfect SS and Gestapo organizations were functioning any longer. The women were carted all over Germany in closed cattle cars. Seventy-two of them returned; they were so eaten up by lice that the flesh was falling off their bones; their bodies were full of deep wounds, under which we could see the bones and tendons. In spite of the ministrations of a Soviet doctor, a prisoner who did all she could to save them, thirty more died.

It was not only the civilians who were being evacuated before the advancing Soviet army. Concentration camps were also being emptied. The horror filled "death transports" were criss-crossing all Germany.

In January of 1945 Auschwitz was being evacuated. Around 6,000 women embarked on a horrible march on foot to Ravensbrück. It was one of the worst marches. Along the way 2,000 perished or were shot. The sick were evacuated in closed cattle wagons. From among the several hundred, about 150 still survived the insane trip. Then in Ravensbrück they were gassed.

* * *

Dr. Treite, who had been a surgeon in a Berlin clinic, whence he came to Ravensbrück, started operating in the Revier, the camp hospital.

He had his periods. For instance he wanted to learn goiter operations. The Revier messengers were dispatched all over the camp to all blocks to report women with a swollen neck. . . . He then selected twenty or a few more, and for the following few days, every afternoon at two o'clock, there were goiter operations.

Once he felt he gained the needed routine and expertise in these operations, he turned to appendices. . . . Then came varicose veins, hernias, and gynecological cases. . . .

He trained prisoners as his nurses. First there was Isa Sicinska, a Polish medical student, a beautiful and intelligent girl, later the young Belgian Annette, and shortly before the end the Czech Hana Housková.

After he became handy with easier operations, he launched into large "scientific" ones on adrenal glands. This was a daring operation, transplanting a human organ, and he made careful preparations. He picked a woman suffering from asthma and another one who was healthy. Both were Russian. He removed the healthy woman's adrenal glands and implanted them into the woman with asthma. The operation was successful, but then both women died.

Then Treite rushed into gynecological surgery, and after that into kidney, urinary tract and stomach operations. The "stomachs" all died.

Encouraged by this example, and also fired by their own ambitions, other doctors, like Richter and Orendi,* started operating. Richter was also learning. He was not a surgeon, he did not understand surgery, yet he operated, unprofessionally but obstinately. He operated in the examining room.

The results of such operations? Just as it could be expected. Richter lost one of his first patients under the knife, the next one soon after surgery. The third one, a Pole, remained at the Revier for a long time, with a draining tube in her back, discharging a constant drip of thin yellow pus into a receptacle under her bed, before she died. The same was the case with a Belgian girl, who suffered for almost ten months before she died.

Orendi also discovered that he had great surgical talents. Perhaps he was just terribly bored because he ran out of money for his drinking bouts in the SS cantine, or because he lost out with the female SS supervisors, for competition was big. He killed a number of prisoners with his operations.

Dr. Orendi inscribed his name into the annals of Ravensbrück with still another "medical" exploit. In the early part of May 1944 the cubicle of the women in charge of Block 10 had to be cleared. The window was boarded up, and straw was spread on the floor. A new inmate supervisor was appointed in the person of Carmen Mory, a malicious pervert.** Then into this space of 9 x 9 feet Orendi placed mentally ill women . . . .

First there were only ten of them. Then more were brought in, and even with their high mortality rate, their number in this den of doom reached the fantastic number of fifty and finally eighty.

Here at this den, at a safe distance of course, often stood the spoiled brat Orendi and had a ball. This was his project! His "Orendi Express," or his "Shanghai Express," as he referred to it roaring with laughter.

In front of his eyes lay these unfortunate women; later on they only stood, pressed one against the other, their naked, emanciated, bloody, dirty bodies covered with feces, urine and rotten straw swaying in some insane waves or like stumps left after a forest fire. . . .

*Bruno Orendi was Dr. Treite's assistant; he had two years of medical school.

**Carmen Mory was a professional spy, possibly a double agent; she was sentenced to death for murder at the Ravensbrück trial in Hamburg after the war.

It was devastating. The terrible stench, the yelling, the inhuman screams like those of tortured animals, spread all over the camp day and night. The SS woman Binz, who after a successful career at the Bunker became chief supervisor, liked to bring the SS men here for some fun.

Nobody except Carmen Mory had the courage to enter this crazed whirl. They were scared of her; even in their confused minds they sensed her bestiality. The German prisoner nurse Paula also dared to go in among them; she was strong as a man. She was the one who bound the violent ones with leather belts.

The worst of it was that the doctors at times locked even normal women among these demented and raging creatures as a form of punishment, justifying it as "need for observation."

By the end of November they were all sent on a transport to Minsk, where they met their deaths. . . .

* * *

The harvest of death in Ravensbrück was growing with each month, each day. But that was not enough for the Nazis. Death had to be prodded on. Again the doctors took the stage. The first one to start the killings by injections was Dr. Rosenthal* in the spring of 1942.

One day at the Revier he stopped by a little Gypsy girl who had galloping consumption. He ordered her to a small room at the end of the corridor where the corpses were gathered until their number would justify a trip to the crematorium. The little girl, as if by premonition, resisted. . . . The nurse Gerda, who was an informer and secretly Rosenthal's mistress, carried her to the small room, followed by Rosenthal with the injecting needle in his hand. The little Gypsy girl was his first victim.

The deadly substance was evipan, used as an anaesthetic in minor surgery. Administered slowly it prevented vomiting. But injected all at once, it caused instant death.

After the first successful experiment this method of killing became standard procedure. Besides Rosenthal and Gerda, who killed this way also an old German political, these injections were administered by nurse Margarete Hoffman who killed seven Jewesses in one session.

Of course this insidious manner of killing could not be kept secret for

*Dr. Rolf Rosenthal was a practical man. At one time there were two German prisoners with similar names in the Revier; one died, but the death certificate was sent by mistake to the family of the other. Rosenthal calmly ordered his nurse to administer a deadly injection to the other one—and the problem was solved. He had an affair with his prisoner nurse Gerda Quernheim (the one who drowned newborn babies in pails of water), even performed an abortion on her; but when the affair was discovered, they were both sent to the Bunker. Milena Jesenská, who died in Ravensbrück in 1944 after four years of unspeakable misery, discovered that the couple, while trysting nights at the Revier, also killed women inmates and removed their gold teeth or fillings. (Buber-Neumann, *Kafkova přítelkyně Milena*, p. 212.)

long, and the prisoners were scared stiff of all injections. When some resisted and cried, they were first given a sedative and then were killed in their sleep.

But even that was not sufficient. Injections were too slow, and perhaps too expensive. So then they started killing with poison powder*. . . .

It started in Block 10 where there were 500 tubercular women. One evening Gerda distributed the "sleeping powder." With a nice smile she inquired who could not sleep at night. That first night about twenty "fell asleep". . . . the next day another five, towards the evening seven, and the following day about a dozen. The rest remained unconscious for two or three days, then came to. Since this whole affair caused quite a panic in Block 10, this "noble" procedure was moved to the Gypsy block.

The powder was administered also by Treite during his visits in the Revier blocks, his later denials in court notwithstanding. They were handed out also by Carmen Mory and Vera Salveguart, prisoners in the service of the Nazis. This method of murder was used most often especially toward the end of the war.

* * *

Sterilization was another "medical" activity in the camp, still another "contribution to science." . . . It was started in the spring of 1942 when Dr. Clauberg had requested permission for his sterilization experiments with a special substance. Himmler granted his permission for these experiments in Ravensbrück in a letter dated July 10, 1942 and marked "Reich secret,"** addressed to Clauberg:***

*In those years in Europe many medicines, including aspirin, were marketed in powdered rather than pill form, each dose packaged in a folded piece of paper the size of a bandaid.

**Letter written on Himmler's office stationery by Obersturmführer (Lieutenant) Brandt, transmitting the wishes of Reichsführer (Head of SS) Heinrich Himmler.

***Much has been written about the "angel of death" of Auschwitz, former physician Josef Mengele, who specialized in experiments on twins, dwarfs and Gypsies, and who was the person most instrumental in the selections at Auschwitz. Less is known about this professor Karl Clauberg, M.D. from Königshütte, who later pursued his experiments on live specimens in Auschwitz, where he had a much wider range of victims. Here he was one of the mainstays of the infamous Block 10, the only female block in the male camp of Auschwitz I, the mysterious block with boarded windows; from the slots the captive women could see the twice daily executions of both men and women in the equally infamous Block 11.

All kinds of experiments were carried out by different doctors here, among them castrations and sterilizations. The doctors made no bones about it that their purpose was to prepare for the sterilization of certain European nationalities, most likely Slavs, after the war.

Clauberg's sterilization project started with about 350 or 400 mostly Greek and Dutch women on December 18, 1942. He injected into their uterus consecutively iodipirin, F 12a, which was diluted novocain, and citobarium. He also subjected the women to x-rays. The process resulted in peritonitis, inflamation of the ovaries, and high fever. The ovaries were then removed, usually in two separate operations, and then sent to Berlin for further analysis. Most women who survived these experiments ended in the gas chambers.

". . . According to your judgement, go to Ravensbrück and there carry out the sterilization of Jewish women. . . . How much time is needed to sterlize 1,000 Jewish women? They should not know anything about it. You may use an injection during a general check up. The effect of the sterilization must be thoroughly tested. . . . by locking up together a Jewish woman with a Jewish man, and then we shall see the result after a while."

Thus one day an inconspicuous, polite and taciturn gentleman appeared at camp. He and Dr. Oberhauser* remained every evening in the examining room. They saw Gypsies, asocials, Jewesses and young Germans, imprisoned for illegal fraternization with the enemy, whose file from the Gestapo had been already marked with an order for sterilization. Even though they were strictly forbidden to talk, rumours started that they were sterilized. Then one day, almost a year later, the inconspicuous gentleman inconspicuously left.**

At the war crime trials in Hamburg and Nuremberg*** it was disclosed that he had fulfilled his task well; he reported personally to Himmler that he was capable of sterlizing 1,000 women per day "as required. . . ."

At the beginning of January, 1945 another gentleman arrived at Ravensbrück. It was the x-ray specialist from Auschwitz, professor Schumann.**** Now Gypsies between the ages of eight and eighteen were asked to report to the Revier, as well as Jewish women from last year's transport. These Gypsy children's mothers had to sign, mostly by three x-es, that they voluntarily

By July, 1943, Clauberg could proudly report to Himmler that under proper conditions he could sterilize, without an operation, as many as a thousand women a day. At the end of 1944 a new block was being built for experiments with artificial insemination, for the greater glory—and population—of Germany; but the evacuation of Auschwitz put an end to that. Clauberg left Auschwitz with over 5,000 scientific photographs in his briefcase.

Ota Kraus and Erich Kulka in their *Továrna na smrt* [*Factory for Death*] (Prague: Naše vojsko, 1957) quote testimonies of Sylva Friedmannová from Prešov, Czechoslovakia, Dora Klein, M.D., from France, and several others about this gruesome subject. See also Miklos Nyiszli, *Auschwitz* (Greenwich, Conn.: Fawcett, 1961).

*Dr. Herta Oberhauser was a "well bred" woman with a cultured background. Yet she killed prisoners with oil and evipan injections, removed their limbs and vital organs, rubbed ground glass and sawdust into wounds. She drew a twenty-year sentence as a war criminal, but was released in 1952 and became a family doctor at Stocksee in Germany. Her licence to practice medicine was revoked in 1960.

**He surfaced in Auschwitz (see footnote above).

***The Hamburg war crime trials dealt with crimes committed at Ravensbrück, those of Nuremberg (referred to here) with those of the physicians.

****Dr. Horst Schumann was a graduate of Auschwitz, where in 1942, in the woman's camp BIa, he had set up an x-ray station. Here men and women were forcibly sterilized by being positioned repeatedly for several minutes between two x-ray machines, the rays aiming at their sexual organs. Most subjects died after great suffering. The frequently following ovariotomies were performed also by the Polish prisoner, Dr. Wladyslav Dering. Dering once bet with an SS man that he could perform ten ovariotomies in an afternoon, and won his bet. Some of his victims survived. Dering was declared a war criminal but eluded justice and for a time practiced medicine in British Somaliland.

agreed to the operations on their children. Then the Gypsies and the Jewish women were taken in groups to the x-ray room, and soon the block resounded with the terrifying screams of the tortured girls. When they emerged, they were deathly yellow and white like ghosts. They were holding their tummies and wailing without end. The mothers had been waiting in front of the Revier, but the SS women were chasing them away with blows and kicks.

Some special substance and a solution of silver nitrate were introduced into the oviducts of each victim. This was sterilization by the so-called Clauberg method that had been tested by its inventor almost three years ago. The solution soon caused a violent inflamation, which in turn closed the oviducts, thus leading to permanent sterility.

It was unspeakable. Not only could these girls never become mothers but there was a great danger that the foreign substance would get into the gastric cavity and evoke inflammation there. This was exactly what happened with the first cases, and four girls died of peritonitis. Treite operated on two, but could not save either one. One died right after the operation, the other remained in the Revier. Pus was drained from her stomach constantly through an inserted tube into a basin under her bed. How could a poor little girl produce so much pus? Finally after three weeks of suffering she also died.

They called it also salpingography. After the war the committee that prepared the documentation for the Ravensbrück museum established that just between the 4th and the 7th of January, 1945 over 100 children were sterilized by this method.

Aside from children, adult women were also sterilized, mostly Gypsies. Dr. Treite carried out these sterilizations surgically, by tieing up the oviducts. The subjects of these operations were young German women who arrived to the camp already with this order for sterilization in their dossiers, Gypsies, Jews, and a few unfortunate creatures who were simply pulled out of the line at the time of office hours for this gynecological operation. Two of the first operated this way were Gypsy children on whom the previous method (by flooding the oviducts) did not succeed. They were kept in the Revier, and after the second x-ray check they were prepped for an operation. The doctors were so insensitive that they discussed the whole matter in front of the two children. . . .

* * *

In June, 1942, two men arrived in Ravensbrück. One was elderly, with graying hair and the noble visage of a scientist, the other one younger. Dr. Oberhauser ran out to meet them, and so did doctors Schidlauski and

Rosenthal. There was much polite welcoming. . . . Ten women from among the numbers 7700 and 7900 of the Lublin transport were called in for a special check-up.

Meanwhile we found out that these two men were not members of any commission, as we had first thought, but doctors from the SS hospital in Hohenlychen near Ravensbrück. Oberhauser boasted to us that it was professor Gebhardt,* the great scientific celebrity, Himmler's friend, who came to us to carry out scientific experiments. What an honor that of all places he had picked Ravensbrück. The other one, she said, was his assistant and right hand, Dr. Ernst Fischer.

The ten Polish women were brought in, and behind closed doors they were examined. It took a long time, and nobody was allowed to be even in the corridor. The next morning we found out that five of the Poles had been admitted to the Revier. Their room was under lock and key, and the SS nurse Erica Milleville was in charge.

Office hours were cancelled, everything was being disinfected, and all prisoners working at the Revier had to leave. But they forgot the office which was way at the end of the hall, or they had thought that nothing would be heard that far. Thus the girls in the office heard a terrible scream and then quiet, the kind of quiet that is always the foreboding of the greatest horrors. The quiet of a new, cunning death.

The first day they operated on two. Two days later on the three others. The screams never ceased from that chamber of torture. The Revier was full of them. The girls were not given any pain killers, so that the course of the experiment would not be impaired in any way. Dogs that had undergone the same experiments received strong doses of morphine for five days.

After a few days the first Pole, a girl of seventeen, died. Her leg was huge, swollen, monstrous, blue with red wounds, and the stench emanating from them was nauseating. The Poles from the Revier told that Gebhardt cut the leg off and took it with him.

Oberhauser was telling us that these were great scientific experiments that should solve a number of important questions in the treatment of shot wounds and other war injuries, and especially of gangrene and bone transplants. She also let it slip that for the first experiment in our camp they had used a man.

Live human guinea pigs! As a matter of fact, we never called those who

*Dr. Karl Gebhardt, Himmler's childhood friend, had a green light from him for his vivisection of women at both Ravensbrück and Auschwitz. In the former camp, he admittedly operated on 60, but survivors of Ravensbrück put the number closer to 100, mostly Poles between the ages of fourteen and twenty-five. He was an SS Brigadeführer (Major General) and stated in May 1943: "I carry the full human, surgical and political responsibility for these experiments." He was shot as a war criminal in 1948.

were operated on anything but "rabbits."* The first five were followed by another five in a few days. Gradually there were more and more of them. The moment that the Revier messenger came to the block with her list that so and so should report to the Revier, we knew what it was all about. . . .

There were two kinds of experiments. In the first type gangrene, tetanus or staphylococcic bacteria were implanted or injected into artificially cut wounds of healthy extremities. This happened in the case of the first five, who were desperately and hysterically screaming and who all died, one of tetanus, two of gangrene, one of blood poisoning, and one bled to death.

The other operations were called by the "scientists" bone, muscle and nerve surgery. In such cases, for instance, parts as large as two inches (5 cm.) were removed from the shin bone and replaced with metal supports or not replaced at all; in this case the doctors were waiting "how the organism will help itself." Muscles and nerves were removed and replaced by others, taken from another healthy woman.

The bone transplants were supposed to prove that without the periosteum** bones could not grow; muscle and nerve operations served research on regeneration of tissue. Such operations took two to three hours. They repeatedly removed from some women's hips and calfs larger and larger parts of muscles; naturally this resulted in the ever increasing weakening and deformation of the extremities. In order to carry out better and more detailed "research," they removed some women's entire hips, shoulder joints or the whole upper extremity together with the shoulder blade. Then the professor, or his assistants, also physicians from Hohenlychen, like Grawitz, Kogel and Schulz, wrapped these in sheets and carried them to their car. Naturally, the women thus operated on were immediately after the surgery killed by an injection.

Allegedly the doctors attempted to transplant these healthy limbs onto crippled soldiers whose crushed limbs had been amputated at the SS hospital in Hohenlychen.

According to the Hamburg trial with the Ravensbrück war criminals, it was Dr. Grawitz*** who issued the orders for certain operations, for instance those that were to determine the healing effects of sulphonamids.

*Derived from the German *"Versuch Kaninchen,"* meaning experimental rabbit or guinea pig. Of all the women martyred by the Nazis, perhaps the "rabbits" suffered the most excruciating tortures, although there were countless close seconds, incubated in the demonic minds of the prisoners' captors.

**Membrane of connective tissue that invests all bones except joints.

***Dr. Ernst Grawitz, SS and Police Gruppenführer (Lieutenant General) was the top doctor in the SS. He was the one who suggested to Himmler in the summer of 1941 gas chambers as means to the "Final Solution," i.e., the mass extermination of Jews. He knew of and kept an executive's eye on numerous other experiments with human guinea pigs at various concentration camps, for instance, body resistance to freezing, jaundice, typhus (research done for I. G. Farben), and the drinkability of sea water. He committed suicide in 1945.

Why test new compounds on guinea pigs or dogs, when they could be tested on humans safely and without any legal repercussions?

All the while that the vivisections on the "rabbits" were going on, the whole camp was buzzing with talk. Everybody wanted to help them. The agricultural details smuggled in pieces of fresh vegetables, or a crushed little bouquet of wild strawberries. . . . From the kitchen the girls were sending a little marmalade, a sliver of bread and even margarine. . . . If they could not "organize"* anything or were unable to smuggle it in, they sent at least at note, with primitive drawings of cities and villages, parks, streets and river banks, along which life was going on, or little poems about the sun in the sky, gardens in bloom, songs of rivers and meadows.

Later on the "rabbits" were no longer in one locked room but in several unlocked ones, and secretly we brought them pain killers; we were scared to death that the SS doctors would find us out; then they would take revenge not only on us but also on the poor "rabbits."

Clearly all these operations had terrible consequences, especially when the experiments were repeated on the same "rabbit" twice, three times, even six times, by both methods. If a wound caused by gangrene or some other suppurating infection healed, it was opened again and re-infected, or the limb opened at another, still healthy spot. New sections of bones were cut out, or other parts of nerves from the calf removed. As a result of putrefaction and excised muscle tissues, the poor women's legs became several centimeters shorter and of course weaker. Healthy, beautiful people were artificially transformed into cripples; healthy, beautiful legs became grotesquely twisted limbs of skin and bone. It was the more ghastly because in the majority of cases the victims were young girls.

This was how professor Gebhardt was earning his stripes. At first he had performed these operations with the assistance of dr. Fischer, and with the cooperation of doctors Oberhauser, a female, Rosenthal, Schidlauski and their helpers. Who helped them a lot was nurse Erica Milleville, their chief nurse, whom they evidently fully trusted.

And they earned their keep! Professor Gebhardt was rewarded by Hitler with the Gold Cross, Dr. Oberhauser with the Iron Cross.

Who were all these females serving "science" as guinea pigs? First of all the Poles who arrived with transports already marked by the Gestapo for the death penalty. They hung on to the hope that if they would undergo these operations "voluntarily," they would receive a reprieve and their lives would be spared. But the executions did not stop, and behind the camp the "rabbits" were also dropping under the salvos of their executioners. As we followed their cases, three of them were shot.

Altogether, according to the investigation commission, 74 Poles were

*"To organize" in concentration camp parlance meant to steal or to get by hook or crook; similar to the G.I.'s "to liberate," except under more dangerous circumstances.

subjected to the operations. . . . 13 either died or were shot. Thus of 74 Polish "rabbits" in Ravensbrück, 61 remained to give testimony after liberation about the incredible bestialities of the Nazis.

Besides the Poles there were other "rabbits," some mentally ill or incurable women; they were Ukrainians, one Czech and one Yugoslav, who was sent to Mauthausen and there went insane in the Bunker, one German professional criminal and a Russian, who had had polio. . . .

The operations continued until August of 1943. During this time the Polish women revolted twice. Once, when the first ten were supposed to be crippled for the second time, they refused. The procedure that followed was simple. The whole Polish block was locked, the windows boarded, and all the 400 women left there three days and three nights without food, drink or air. Naturally, after this treatment, the ten "volunteered."

The second revolt had worse consequences. That was in the summer of 1943. The Poles knew by then that not even the operations would save them from being shot. To be killed and before that be tortured and tormented? Ordered to report to the Revier, they simply did not show up. There were about twenty of them. Some remained in their block, others spread out and hid in other blocks.

They were caught by the SS women with dogs and forcefully dragged to the Bunker. Ten were jailed in the Bunker, and six were operated on in the cells, by force, dressed as they were, without any sterilization on the ground, where the SS men were holding them down.

That is how the last "rabbits" underwent bone operations. . . .

Of course their tormentors wanted to send them to the gas in the last moment. They did not want to allow such witnesses to remain alive. But the girls were well hidden. They were in different blocks, under other numbers and names (of deceased prisoners), in the Revier, even in the punitive block; they were handed from place to place, depending where the greatest danger was threatening. The entire camp supported them.

19

The Yellow Star of David

Zdenka Morsel spent several years at the camp of Terezín (or Theresienstadt in German). This small fortress town of 7,000 people, thirty miles north of Prague, was built in 1780, honoring the Empress Maria Theresa.

At the end of 1941, the "Protector" of Bohemia and Moravia Reinhardt Heydrich, and the man in charge of the "Final Solution" of the Jewish question, Adolf Eichmann, decided to relocate the Czech Jews to Terezín. The military garrison was transferred, the Czech civilians evicted, and what the Germans advertised as the "Paradise Camp" was ready for its occupants. The propaganda worked so well that some Jews bribed the SS to be shipped there!

Terezín was also to serve as an "old people's home" for German Jews who were war veterans, over sixty-five, disabled or decorated at least with the Iron Cross First Class, and for distinguished Jews whose disappearance could embarrass the Reich. At one time the Nazis also considered it as the "resettlement home" of the Jewish "parts" of mixed marriages. But about half of these privileged groups ended up directly in Auschwitz and other annihiliation camps, bypassing Terezín.

Relative to Auschwitz, Chelmno, Treblinka and other extermination camps, Terezín was indeed paradise. But compared with their lives before Terezín, the Jews found it hell on earth. Twenty-four women to a room in Terezín sounds frightful compared with a room of your own at home; but compared with 1,400 women to a room, three or four to a cot in Auschwitz? Food, lodging, and the way of life were all less punitive in Terezín than in the other camps. For Terezín was that strange mongrel, a hybrid of a concentration camp and a ghetto. And it did not have gas chambers.

Still, it was just a way station, a stopover on the way to sure death, mostly to Auschwitz. A few figures tell the story:

*Arrivals at Terezín:**

Czechs	73,608
Germans	42,832
Austrians	15,254
Dutch	4,897
Slovaks	1,447
Danes	466
Others	1,150
Total	*139,654*

In May 1945, at the time of liberation, there were 17,320 people in Terezín; 33,319 had died there. The rest had been shipped on to be liquidated. Of those who had left on these transports, fewer than 5 percent returned.

It is true that cultural activities were permitted. But the musicians who played the "Requiem" in concert one night might have been in a transport before the sun came up, especially since Eichmann was in attendance. The "Bartered Bride" or "Carmen" of one night might become ashes and smoke the next. Culture had its limitations: painters depicting the true face of Terezín were beaten to death or had their fingers crushed, as did the Czech Otto Ungar of Brno.

Terezín was a Potemkin village of the Nazis, the sham show place exhibited to pull the wool over the eyes of the outside world. When the Danish Red Cross visited in the spring of 1944, Terezín was spruced up: white table cloths, flowers, music, clean-scrubbed children were in view; less so were the tortured and crippled who had been conveniently shipped out. Dr. Paul Epstein, the German sociologist, was dressed up in tails and top hat to look as a proper mayor and was driven around with the guests in a limousine, with an SS officer posing as his personal chauffeur. After the Danes had left, the SS chauffeur put a bullet through "his honor's" head, and things reverted to "normal."

Zdenka Morsel's narrative is a factual, detached and rather understated testimony of

*Raul Hilberg, *The Destruction of the European Jews* (Chicago: Quadrangle Books, 1967), p. 283. Danish sources indicate 477 Danes.

her ordeal that included seven long years of separation from her husband and some extraordinary episodes attesting to her determination and courage. Her trip to Berlin was a more daring feat than she lets on; the offer of the SS man to smuggle her out of Prague to Italy is one of the most paradoxical—and exceptional—stories to come out of the Holocaust.

Being newlyweds, life in Prague looked all rosy for my husband Marek and me. Then suddenly, on March 15, 1939, the German army invaded Czechoslovakia, and in a single day my life changed.

In the most horror filled days I ruefully recalled the warnings of German Jewish refugees who had been leaving Prague for America. As they were making preparations, Marek and I were looking for furniture and an apartment. They were shaking their heads in disbelief. We on the other hand could not imagine that we in democratic Czechoslovakia would ever be in their predicament.

After the German invasion, we were suddenly confronted with the same ordeal.

In the following weeks we were busy visiting consulates to see which country would take us in. One day we heard that young men would be rounded up and deported to forced labor camps. Since Marek had a valid passport (I did not), I insisted that he leave immediately for any destination out of the German noose. I would follow whenever I could. On April 7th he left for Italy, and I found myself in Prague alone.

I did not realize then what impossible hurdles I would be facing. The registration of all Jews was only a beginning. We were ordered to leave our apartments and move into crowded quarters assigned to Jews. We were four women in one room. Hot water was so scarce that we had to take our baths in the same water. Our homes were taken over by the Germans.

Our identification papers were stamped with the letter "J" for Jude, Jew. We had to wear the yellow star of David on all our clothing. I wore it with pride. Our ration cards were also marked with a "J"; we could shop for food only in the late hours when most of the supplies were gone.

I had to deliver all my silverware and jewelry to the bank and got a scrap of paper as a receipt for them. Against orders, I kept two valuable rings that were heirlooms. My bank account was closed. Since I was no longer permitted to work as a secretary, I had to find another way of support. First I took in sewing at my room. Then a kind gentile woman gave me a sewing job in her shop. Here I had to remove the yellow star, for Germans were among her customers. This arrangement was of course dangerous not only for me but also for her and her other assistant; but these two kind women were willing to take the risk of harboring me.

I was deeply grateful for the friendly atmosphere and the encouragement, also for the warm shop. I earned a little money; the rest of my income came from selling off little by little my linen, my clothes, and my husband's stamp collection.

In the shop I also met a customer who was deeply concerned with the persecution of the Jews. Through her recommendation I got other sewing jobs that helped me survive. The same woman, when I was later arrested and

"The Yellow Star of David" is by Zdenka Morsel.

sent to concentration camp, took off her new boots and gave them to me, so that I could keep my feet warm wherever I would be taken. After liberation I was looking for her. I learned that she had committed suicide when her daughter and son-in-law had been hanged as members of the Czech underground.

All this time I was still trying to join my husband, but there was so much red tape involved that my papers never satisfied all bureaucrats. I managed to get an exit permit; but before I could receive a visa, it expired. Marek was also trying to move mountains from abroad, but there just was no chance to leave legally.

One day I had a visitor. An SS man in full regalia came to look for me. I almost fainted when I saw him. He told me to be ready the next morning for a trip. He had promised my husband to bring me to Italy. After the initial shock of being offered help by an SS man, I declined. That could have been my one chance to leave the realm of the Nazis; but I was afraid that my family would be punished for my disappearance, as we were all registered, and so I refused to go. Instead, I gave the SS man the two rings to take to Marek. He had met this man on the beach in Italy, out of uniform, and had no idea that he was an SS man until he brought the two rings from me, this time appearing in his uniform!

I had another frightful brush with two SS men. Marek had left his car in the garage, but I never used it. One day two SS men came and demanded the key to the car. Naively, I started arguing and fighting for my property. But the pair made the options quite clear: surrender the car or be deported to a concentration camp. I surrendered the car.

In 1940, my husband reached the Jewish refugee settlement in Santo Domingo.* With his help, I received a Dominican entry visa and once again I was ready to leave. I needed only an American transit visa. The U.S. consulate in Prague was closed, so in desperation I decided to get it in Berlin. Full of hopes and trepidations I reached the German capital.

The first difficulty was to find a hotel that would accommodate a Jew. When I finally located a room, I was asked daily when I would be leaving. The first night, during an air attack, I remained in my room; but the manager ordered me into the shelter, to a section segregated from the Aryans. I took my place behind some old furniture, where I was left alone. I spent part of each night there.

I went to the American Consulate daily, but was advised that I could not

*Zdenka's husband Marek, as thousands of other Jewish fugitives, was looking for a refuge outside the deadly circle of Nazism. He was shuttled between nineteen Italian and Balkan ports, his hopes and despair rising and falling with every passing week. Finally he reached New York, only to be detained on Ellis Island for four months, gazing at the Manhattan skyline in vain. He found refuge, ironically enough, in Santo Domingo, the fiefdom of a dictator. Here he spent the war years without any news of the life or death of his young bride.

be granted a transit visa. At that time there were sealed trains taking Jews from Berlin to Lisbon in Portugal, where the refugees were looked after by Jewish organizations. But as there was no direct connection from Lisbon to Santo Domingo, I could never get there without passing through the United States.

One day while waiting at the consulate for a miracle, I saw a man leaping to his death from a window, because he had been refused his visa. At this point I despaired; the suicide truly drove home the point that my situation was hopeless. I was physically sick. The guards were locking the building; I had to leave. Defeatedly I went to the railroad station.

Back in Prague at night, I walked to my lodgings. I was afraid to take the streetcar. I only hoped that I would not run into an SS man. The next day I started working again in my friend's shop.

In 1941 America entered the war, and the letters from Marek stopped coming. I heard nothing of him until after the war in 1945; he was also without any news from me until that time.

Soon after I had returned from Berlin, the first shipments of Jewish people started leaving Prague. In June of 1942 I was ordered into a transport. First I had considered this "resettlement" without fear, even though I had no idea where I would be taken. I presumed that we would be removed from the midst of Aryans in order to work somewhere. But as we were assembled at the Exhibition Palace and I saw how we were treated, I knew I had been wrong. We slept on the floor, received little or bad food. Men, women and children were herded together without the basic requirements for hygiene. It was a fearful omen.

In groups of a thousand people, we were being entrained. The cars were crowded beyond capacity, and I was standing for several hours. We got off at Bohušovice, from where we were marched to Terezín, carrying our meagre belongings. Later the Germans extended the railroad to Terezín, to make it more efficient for incoming and for outgoing transports. The men from the Terezín camp were used for this labor.

The arrival in Terezín confirmed my fears. We were billeted in military barracks. Our luggage was inspected, and soap, toothpaste, medicines, cigarettes and all new clothing were confiscated. My transport was only passing through Terezín to an unknown destination. While waiting for departure, some people were excluded from it and replaced by others already lined up. With German efficiency, the figures had to match: a thousand arrived, a thousand were leaving.

Without realizing the meaning of it then, I remained in Terezín. I was assigned to the cleaning detail, scrubbing halls, washrooms and toilets. Since I was a fast typist, two weeks later I was assigned to the Central Evidence Office, working the night shift. When there were no transports arriving or departing, we would work until 2 a.m.; when transports were leaving, we worked through the whole night.

The Germans demanded precise statistics, and we typed endless lists, recording who came with each transport, who died, who left in each transport.

I lived in one room with twenty-three women, sleeping on triple bunks. I came to bed when the rest were off to work. I had to get up to clean the room and to fetch our bread rations. Occasionally I was ordered to unload potatoes or sugar beets, which were welcome chances to steal a few potatoes or beets for a meal. We also tried to steal coal or wood to cook, heat water for washing or warm up the room a little. The morale in our quarters was high, and nobody would touch anybody else's food or property, such as it was.

Soon after me, my father was shipped to Terezín. I tried to look after him and make sure that he received his rations, since he could not stand in line for them; he was too old and too ill. Soon after he had arrived, I contracted scarlet fever and was transferred to the quarantine block, to live or to die there. I had no medication, yet, somehow, I survived. While I was in quarantine, my father took ill with dysentery.

The old people were housed separately, and most of them had no one to look after them. They were pitiful, sick and full of lice, dying fast. While I was cleaning and feeding my father, I could at least help a few others, give them water, cover them, or simply check whether they were still alive. The possibility of getting lice was terrifying. After each visit to my father I checked all my clothes to make sure that I would not infest my room.

Mercifully, my father died very quickly, but not before he saw my brother, whose transport remained in Terezín only overnight. I shall forever see my brother standing in the cattle car before the door was shut. The thousand people from this transport disappeared without a trace; there was not a single survivor after the war.

At the time my father died in February 1943, the mortality rate was between 100 and 120 a day. Several coffins were loaded on a pushcart and brought outside the camp for burial in a mass grave. The coffins were reused after each burial. I walked behind the pushcart carrying my father until I reached the gate; nobody was permitted to go beyond it.

A group of inmates were ordered to build a crematorium outside the camp. After cremation, the ashes were placed into paper urns and stored in chronological order in the casemates, so the Nazis would have clear evidence of how many Jews were dead.

One day, shortly before the end of the war, I was ordered to these casemates to be part of a human chain stretching to the river. We were removing the urns with the ashes, passing them from hand to hand, to be finally thrown into the river. For days upon end there were ashes floating on the surface. We all thought that the Nazis wanted to destroy the evidence, but actually they were emptying the casemates to turn them into gas chambers. The windows of the casemates were cemented, and there was a railroad car stationed close by. We found out later that it contained canisters of poisonous gas pellets. The camp commandant, Karl Rahm, reported this to the International Red Cross in Geneva. That saved our lives, as well as his, for after the war he was given a safe passage to Switzerland.

Life in Terezín was no bed of roses. Lodging was cramped as it would be when about 40,000 people had to live in a town meant for 7,000. Only the "prominents" like the Jewish Elders were allowed to stay with their families. Otherwise children, old people, the male and female labor force were all housed separately. Occasionally a couple got married, and their friends let them have a room for a few hours' honeymoon.

Food was lacking in nourishment and scarce. If once in a blue moon we were given meat scraps, it was horse flesh, and there was more bad smell from it in the room than meat in the gravy. Most meals were simply soups made of powder, with lonely potatoes or lentils swimming in them. Bread was rationed—one slice a day. Once a month or so we were given margarine and a little sugar.

No wonder women did not menstruate. This caused headaches and swollen feet. One remedy for this was blood letting, "to relieve the pressure."

There were hardly any babies or infants in Terezín. If pregnant, women were forced to abort. Only about two dozen infants born in Terezín survived.

Once a whole orphanage with children from Bohemia, Germany, Austria and the Netherlands was sent off in a transport to Auschwitz. In July of 1942 a thousand children arrived from Bialystok, Poland. They were dirty and full of lice. When they were taken to the showers, they put up a desperate resistance, screaming: "Gas, gas!" This opened some eyes as to the destination of those transports eastward. After several months of care in separate barracks, these children were also sent on a transport, together with their attendants.

All the good clothing of the arriving inmates was always confiscated and shipped to Germany for the "Winter Aid" of the bombed out population. We had to do with what we could find among the leftovers of those unfortunates who had left in the cattle cars. Our clothing was threadbare, and we looked everything but attractive. No wonder the SS men did not molest us sexually. Besides, it was dangerous for them, since fraternizing with Jews was drastically punished.

Aside from an occasional slap in the face or a kick and general chicanery, serious offenses were dealt with at the Little Fortress of Terezín. Torture and executions were frequent here. In early 1942 sixteen men were hanged for attempting to write letters to their families outside the camp. The Elders had to witness the executions.

As transports kept arriving with greater frequency, we were more and more crowded—and worried. My older brother and his wife also landed in Terezín and remained for a while.

During the High Holidays of 1944 the reign of terror started. One transport was leaving after the other. By this time we were aware of it that the deportations away from Terezín meant no improvements. Some people selected for transports did not show up, some got sick, some disappeared into hiding. The papers accompanying the transports had to be retyped over and over. In the chaos, the typists were ordered to the railway station, I among them. While some SS men were loading our people into the box cars, marking them off the lists, others kept threatening to put us on the train if we did not type fast enough. By the time the train pulled out, the few of us who were left behind were numb from cold and from fear, and I could never remember how I got back to my bunk.

Transports of thousands of people kept leaving Terezín. Included was my second brother, who died in Dachau, and most members of the Jewish camp council. Terezín was becoming a ghost town. I was so depressed that in my desperation I decided that I would volunteer for the next transport to put an end to my misery. That one had been planned but never took place, for the eastern front was approaching. We were liberated by the Russian army in early May 1945. All the SS men had disappeared during the night, yet we had no idea that we were free until the Russians arrived.

Because of typhoid fever and other diseases, we had to remain in Terezín for four weeks before repatriation started. I had no place to go, so I volunteered to work in the Central Evidence Office for a month. People were streaming in to find out the fate of their friends and relatives. We were mostly giving out sad information, based on the documents that we had been typing under the SS rule.

One day a soldier from the Svoboda army* came looking for his wife and mother. He was Marek's friend. He did not find his family, but told me that Marek's two brothers were in the army with him, and that one of them had already returned to Prague.

Getting in touch with my brothers-in-law filled me with hope. I started putting the pieces together. I wrote to my employer in Prague. The answer was heartwarming: I was welcome any time.

Then one day—a lucky day—two American servicemen walked into the office, seeking news of their families. I asked one of them how I could send a message to America to my husband's family or to him. One of the soldiers took my note** with the Prague dress shop as a return address.

When I returned to Prague, unlike many other deportees, I could move into my old apartment. All I brought with me was the yellow star of David that I had worn for over four years.

*The Czechoslovak volunteer army that fought the Germans on the Russian front; many of the soldiers and officers were Jewish. Similar Free Czechoslovak forces fought alongside the Western Allies.

**Some thirty years after the end of the war, visiting Fayetteville, North Carolina, I met a man who turned out to be one of the two American servicemen I talked to in Terezín. It was his friend who sent off my letter and helped me get in touch with my husband.

It took four weeks before the first cable arrived from Marek in Santo Domingo. I was anxious to leave Prague. In spite of the general rejoicing over the end of the war, I felt like I was living in a cemetery.

In January 1946 I left for France, New York, Cuba and Santo Domingo. After seven undescribably painful years, I was reunited with my husband. The following year my daughter was born, and one year later we moved to the United States to be with Marek's surviving family.

I will always remember the Dominican Republic with gratitude. We had a good life there. I heard that at the Evian conference for refugees it was the only country in the world willing to take in as many as 100,000 Jews. Unfortunately, in most cases like mine, those in need of a refuge could not take advantage of this generosity;* the Jewish organizations were unable to get the Jews out.

I had some good years after I joined my husband. Now with three grandchildren we again have a little family. The darkness of the Holocaust did not vanish and it casts its shadow over happiness. The memories remain, and I wish them to remain.

The yellow star of David hangs framed in my home to commemorate six million Jews murdered for being Jewish. I do not need a reminder of the Holocaust, I have my memories. But it should be a reminder for my family and for everybody else, now and for generations to come—a reminder of what happened to us and what could happen again.

*The Evian-les-Bains conference, held on July 6-15, 1938, was fruitless. Between 1933 and 1945 the Dominican Republic issued about 5,000 visas, which enabled many Jews to use them to settle in the free world. Only 705 actually came to the Dominican Republic.

20

A Mistaken Deportation

The case of fifteen-year-old Vera Keršovan of Yugoslavia was that of a mistaken deportation, or perhaps of malicious miscarriage of justice.

For two years she had resisted the forced Hungarization by the occupiers. She was consistently uncooperative with the Hungarian school authorities, until they placed her into the hands of a juvenile court.

Since she was no more communicative with the court than she had been at school, the judge decided that this child was a hopeless case. At that time Jews were being deported, but half Jews were exempt from deportation. Vera Keršovan's father was Jewish, thus she was half-Jewish, and for the time being safe from being sent off on a transport.

Perhaps the judge was not aware of the destination of the deported Jews. Perhaps he was anti-Semitic. Perhaps he simply took advantage of an easy way of solving a case that caused him nuisance. The Jews were leaving—why not make this annoying girl disappear with them?

Ironically, she was placed in the cattle cars with Hungarians whom she had been resisting in the first place. How this sheltered, pampered, mild-mannered child survived the horrors of Auschwitz and other dreadful experiences borders on the miraculous.

Today she lives in Yugoslavia. Her health was undermined by what she had to undergo during the war, so she had to give up her dream of studying medicine. She is now the manager of the Slovenian Philharmonic Orchestra in Ljubljana.

As my concentration camp sister, she is very dear to me, and we see each other in Yugoslavia or in the United States.

My name is Vera Keršovan. I was born in 1928, in the small town of Murska Sobota in Yugoslavia, near the Hungarian border. My father, a Jew, was the director of a small bank; my mother, a Catholic, worked in another bank. I was an only child. My parents brought me up with much love and care and taught me to honor all people and my country. I lived a very sheltered life.

I was thirteen when the war reached Yugoslavia. My father, a reserve officer, was called to service. My mother and I did not know where he was when first the Germans and then the Hungarians occupied our town. Eventually my father returned home, and we started to live as people without freedom have to live. First it seemed that at least we were to be allowed to live.

I was forced to go to a Hungarian school, where we were to be re-educated into Hungarians. This was very much against my grain. It contradicted all my previous schooling and my upbringing at home. My father became involved in the illegal resistance movement that worked toward the liberation of Yugoslavia from foreign occupation. This only reinforced my antipathy to the Hungarian school. In my own way I sabotaged the school; I would not follow instructions and would not even talk.

By the time I was fifteen years old, they took me to the police, then to the judge for juvenile delinquents. My father was arrested at the same time. The court made a very short process with me. Although I was only half-Jewish, and thus not subject to deportation, they stuck me into a Jewish transport and sent me off without much ado to concentration camp. I was not even allowed to say goodbye to my mother and father.

That is how I landed in Auschwitz-Birkenau.

This was the first time that I found myself without the protecting love of my parents. I was among strangers. I could not perceive what was happening to me and around me. I did not know a soul among the Jews in the cattle car that was whisking us into some unknown, bottomless abyss. We were locked into these cattle cars, without food or drink, for three days and three nights. There was a grandmother in the wagon with her grandchild; she took pity on me and shared with me some of their food.

After this endless hell, we finally arrived and could breathe some fresh air. They ordered us out of the wagons. Some German SS officers started barking orders at us. We had to line up before one of them, who sent the grandmother and her little grandchild to the left, but me to the right. I did not want to be separated from the only person who had been kind to me during the ordeal of the trip, so I ran after them, asking that I be allowed to go with them. But the officer grabbed me roughly by my arm and yanked me back to the right side, shouting at me: "Keep your mouth shut and obey orders, you!"

I found out much later that all who were sent to the left ended up in the gas chambers and within an hour were burning in the crematorium. Of the entire transport of about a thousand people, only 33 of us remained on the right side and alive. It was also much later that I found out who that high ranking officer was who almost pulled my arm out jerking me back to the right side; it was Dr. Josef Mengele in person, the mass murderer still sought today for his crimes.

I have often wondered what went on in his mind at that moment when he decided to select me and condemn me to life rather than to death? Why me? Could it be that for that split second the dormant human being had overcome the jaded, senseless animal?

It is true, in that moment Mengele saved my life; that does not diminish his sins. But this was not to be my only encounter with that monster.

Next our heads were shaved, our clothes taken away, and we were commandeered under showers with scalding hot water, after which we were lined up in rows of five, naked, in the cold outside the showers. After a couple of hours of standing and shivering, we were given some gray shirt-like dresses and wooden shoes like you see in pictures from Holland. Nothing fit; I could consider myself lucky that my "dress" was too big rather than too small; that was the only clothing we were given.

Then we were marched off to the barracks which were to become our sorrowful abode. Ours was Block 17. Sixteen of us were jammed on one of the tripple decker double cots. There was no space to stretch out nor to sit up; we were shelved there like sardines, waiting for God knows what, hungry, thirsty and shivering.

There were endless *Appells*, when we had to stand outside, lined up in rows of five, to be counted. At times we stood in rain or hot sun, waiting for the SS to get around to us. The worst thing was the constant dread. Animals must have this kind of instinctive fear before they are about to be slaughtered. You could never know when called for *Appell*, whether it would be for feeding, for a work detail, for a trip to the communal toilets, or the gas chambers. I do not understand how more people did not turn insane.

My nook was on the bottom bunk next to the wall. The place swarmed with bedbugs, and soon I was full of scabs because I could not resist scratching. My body was on fire from the bites and from the constant itching.

I was in this sorry state when we were standing *Appell*, and suddenly the order was given to undress. With dress in one hand and clogs in the other, we had to file naked by the SS female overseers. The same system applied as at the selection at the train station: some went right, others were shoved left. Since I was bitten by bedbugs and so full of sores all over my body, I was ordered to the left. After this *Appell* I was not returned to Block 17. With a group of other girls and women who were selected to the left, we were herded into a so-called *Schönungsblock*, which ironically means saving or protective Block.

Here the situation was quite different. Here were gathered the sick, the weak, the bodies covered with sores. Almost every second day we had to parade in front of the SS men who with the flick of their fingers separated us to the right or to the left. Here everybody knew that when Mengele or his henchmen came to the *Appell,* the left side meant the gas chamber or off to Mengele's domain for medical experiments.

A Polish *Blockälteste* (literally: the oldest of the Block) ruled here. Many of these supervisors were professional criminals who, while also prisoners, were given a free hand to lord it over the rest of the simple mortals in the Blocks. We were petrified when she started hollering and cursing and lashing out at us with her club. If possible, life—or existing—was even harder here than in Block 17. We were given just sufficient food not to die right away. I remember how thirsty and dehydrated we were, standing for hours in the scorching sun. Hunger was horrible and sheer torture, but thirst was a hundred times worse. The overriding feeling I had in this *Schönungsblock* was fear, absolute, undiluted fear, that permeated my body and my soul, that was draped around me as an ever tightening straight jacket choking me from the outside and an ever expanding poisonous gas that was expanding my body from the inside. I was scared of the *Blockälteste,* of the *Appells,* of Mengele. I was sure that he would not send me to the side of the living for the second time, not the skin and bone skeleton I was then, covered with disgusting and bleeding wounds. When he drove up in his car, I would jump through the window to hide in another Block or on the toilet.

In this Block was also a Greek professional singer. Every evening the *Blockälteste* ordered her into her cubicle and made her sing. Since childhood I was fond of music; I played the violin and the piano. When I heard the poor Greek girl singing Gounod's "Ave Maria" or the Italian song "Mama," I could not help crying. One night the *Blockälteste* overheard my sobs. She came out of her cubicle, looked at me for a long time, but did not say a word. I was quivering with fright at what she would do to me. But she did nothing; I had the feeling that for the first time there was no hatred in her eyes.

After this incident she used to stop in front of the line of five in which I was standing at *Appells.* She kept gazing at me. I did not understand what was going on and I was afraid. One evening she called me to her cubicle, and I could do nothing but obey. I was trembling and crying, but I had to go. The *Blockälteste* was seated at her little table and bid me to sit down. On the ramshackle table was a tin plate and a piece of bread with a touch of margarine spread over it.

"Eat," she said, "eat."

She kept questioning me; what was my name, where I came from, why I was here. She asked if I was afraid of her. I nodded, my mouth full of the precious bread ration.

"Do not be afraid of me any longer," she said. "I like you because you remind me of my son, you look just like he with your hair shaved off."

She went on talking, more to herself than to me, it seemed.

"I do not know where my son is, or if he is alive."

Then she told me that she would try to get me out of Auschwitz.

I hardly believed my ears. But the piece of bread was more important to me than idle talk about promises of escape from this purgatory.

Yet about a week later she roused me from my cot at dawn. It was still dark. She dragged me by my arm, I could hardly keep up with her long steps. She took me to another Block. Here she pushed me into a line of four and disappeared without a word.

"Vorwärts marsch!" I heard the order at the end of the line-up.

And the column started marching, not towards the gas chambers but in the opposite direction, towards the gate with the inscription "Arbeit macht frei," meaning "Work makes you free," which was one of the cruel jokes the Nazis perpetrated in Auschwitz. Another one was the women's orchestra that played at the gate every time the inmates were marched in and out to hard labor and back. One of the most heartrending songs they played was "In my homeland the roses are blooming."

This was my farewell from the living hell that could have been conceived only in a most sadist, sick mind.

On the other side of the electrified barbed wires, with the machine guns of the watch tower behind us, we boarded a train. Auschwitz receded into the night, only the flames of the crematoria chimneys sending their red and yellow tongues against the dark sky.

If you asked me for the definition of the concept of loneliness, I would say it was this disgruntling train trip. As in the cattle cars that conveyed me to Auschwitz, now again I felt the depression of loneliness, of being so absolutely alone in the whole world. Again I did not know a single soul. These women were mostly from Czechoslovakia and from Hungary. I hardly understood a word they were saying.

At one point the train stopped, and we had to get off. We waited until the morning for the next train. We were huddling in a flooded underpass. It was a cold night, and we stood in the drafty passage for hours. To share body heat, we moved together as close as possible; after a while, the outside circle facing the cold air would switch with those in the middle. But when my turn came to be in the middle, I was squeezed out to the rim. My teeth were chattering from the cold and my heart felt frozen from the injustice.

It was at that moment that I again realized how desperately alone I was in this nightmare, where I had no mother, no father, who used to protect me from the slightest hazard. But close upon this infinite despair came also the realization that if I wanted to stay alive, I would have to look out for myself, although I did not quite see how.

The morning train brought us to the town of Hirshberg, which was in eastern Germany, but now is called Jelenia Gora and is in Poland. We were told that now we belonged to the concentration camp complex of Gross-Rosen, but we were billeted directly at the textile factory in Zillerthal. The place was only about twenty miles from the Czechoslovak border and the Giant Mountains, and many of my fellow prisoners started dreaming and scheming of an escape. But without proper clothes and with shaven heads, not mentioning the ubiquitous SS guards with their dogs, it was pretty much an impossible dream. Soon the whole landscape was covered with deep snow, and that put an end to those hopes.

This place meant quite a switch from Auschwitz. This was a labor camp. We worked either in the spinning or the weaving departments of the factory, for twelve hours a day, from six in the morning to six at night. It was dark when we lined up in the traditional rows of five to march to work, and it was dark again as we returned to our barracks. But at least it was warm at the factory, for otherwise the machine oil would have frozen; and in the camp we even had a washroom with water. Miracle or miracles—there was space in the barracks so we slept only two to a cot. The straw in the mattresses was ancient and pulverized, but each pair of us had a blanket. As the season advanced, we even received coats, but their backs had two wide stripes painted on them with oil paint in the shape of the letter X, that was in no way removable.

In spite of the grueling labor, this life was a relief after what we had experienced in Auschwitz, mostly because there were no gas chambers or crematoria to remind us incessantly that our lives hung only on a thread or on the whim of an SS person.

Our caloric intake was still under 1,000 per day, we were still constantly hungry. We were dead tired from standing for twelve hours handling the spindles and tending the machines. Yet I remember much more clearly my life in this camp because in Auschwitz I do not think we were quite normal.

Here at Zillerthal we had female SS guards. I find it painful to say but these women were often more rude, cruel and sadistic than men. They were uneducated women, often from the gutter, who were given a uniform, a gun, and limitless power over other human beings, yet told that we were not quite human beings. Slaps in the face and kicks landing all over our bodies were still raining on us in great profusion. It was in this labor camp that we were given a couple of tooth brushes to scrub the floors of our barracks, and the SS women were standing over us laughing whenever we got splinters under our nails.

While we had no gas chambers, no crematoria, death was not far away. One woman had managed to conceal her pregnancy by hiding her body. But when her time came and her baby was born in our barrack, at dawn, her fate was sealed. By the time we returned from work, both she and her baby simply disappeared, never to be seen again.

I had a close call also when the flax combing machine caught my hand and made a bloody mess of it. I was taken to the factory dispensary and bandaged up. It was only by hiding my injury that I was not shipped out as a useless "piece" undeserving the investment of food.

In the factory there was a German civilian Meister, a foreman, who was way past retirement age, who at least did not holler or beat us. It was the German women who supervised us who were rather generous with vituperation and kicks who made our lives miserable.

It was in Zillerthal where I became acquainted with another prisoner, only a couple of years older than myself, but a mature person who knew what she wanted and who was the most intelligent one in our whole camp. I was quartered in another barrack but I was told that there was a girl who had lived in Yugoslavia and so spoke my language. I found her, and it was a great relief to me to talk freely with her. Her name was Vera; she was from Czechoslovakia.

I do not know, and I never have asked, why she took me under her wings. But she managed to have me transferred to her barrack, she took care of me and watched over me. I am thankful to her for many things, but most of all for my very life which she saved on several occasions.

Once I was in her barrack, I was no longer alone or lonely. She kept my spirit up. I had somebody to talk to and to protect me from the many greedy inmates who would steal my bread rations or otherwise abuse me. We shared scraps of food we "organized" along the road to the factory or from the garbage cans near the kitchen. A wilted leaf of cabbage or a rotten potato were treasures to us. But most importantly, once it became known that Vera was my friend, the bullies left me alone for they did not dare to tangle with her, and I no longer was the prey of my fellow inmates.

We spent Christmas 1944 and the New Year at Zillerthal. By then in the stillness of the night we could hear the Russian cannonade from the east. I must say, it was music to our ears and souls. Liberation was nearing. But nothing was so simple in the labyrinthine maze that was the Nazi mind.

In early January, we were suddenly marched out of Zillerthal. We were being evacuated west into the center of Germany. Even at this late stage of the war, the Nazi super-organization that was based on slave labor wanted to squeeze the last remaining ounces of strength out of a few hundred women. By train we were transferred to the Hartz Mountains. Here near the city of Nordhausen was the infamous concentration camp Dora and the Tunnel.

The Tunnel was a tremendous underground factory where among other things the V-2 rockets were manufactured. Of course we did not know it then, but these were the ultimate German secret weapons that were supposed to bring the Allies to their knees. Many of them rained on London in the last months of the war. Above and around the Tunnel were barracks of thousands of prisoners of war, political prisoners and forced laborers from many countries. With so many slave laborers who hated the Germans, no wonder that there were countless cases of sabotage. Our female contingent cheerfully contributed to that by any means we could. I recall my friend Vera instructing us in the proper work habits; we had to measure metal rings that went into the V-2. For each ring that went into the production line, she told us to discard two into the scrap bin as faulty. We also stole these rings, made buttons or belts out of them, or simply threw them away.

By the end of March the noose around the Nazi supermen was getting tighter. The British and the Americans were nearing from the west, the Russians from the east. And still the Germans would not give up on us. Thousands of prisoners were being evacuated from the Tunnel. Our detachment started out on foot, for the railways at Nordhausen were bombed to smithereens. Disorganization by now was rampant. We marched in snow and sleet, without food or drink, frozen to the bone in our scant clothing and ridiculous shoes. Many of the SS deserted but there were still enough left to guard us with their machine guns. It was a true hunger march.

If ours was a sorry lot, so was that of the German civilian population that was also fleeing, their possessions on carts drawn by themselves. Chairs, featherbeds, children and chickens were piled up on them, and families pushed them through the mire of the roads. At times a military vehicle would pass, forcing the columns of prisoners and the civilians off the road.

We marched for days. We passed through villages with only women and children. A few older women seeing us dragging ourselves along the road would throw us a piece of bread, when the backs of the SS women were turned.

Dozens of our transport died on this hunger march. Some stepped out of the line and were shot. Some simply lay down along the road, knowing that all stragglers would get a bullet, for the SS orders were to keep moving—although none of them really knew where. Aside from Auschwitz, this was the worst experience I had to live through. It was unbearable to move one foot ahead of the other. Without any nourishment for days, in freezing weather, fearing that around the next bend of the road we would be shot just to free our captors from their burden, we staggered on.

It was Vera who did not let me collapse and lie down along the road to be delivered of my sufferings by a merciful bullet. She prodded me on, coaxing me, ordering me not to give in.

"You would not give 'them' the malicious pleasure to shoot you like an animal, would you?" she said. "You would not want to miss the end of the war, would you?" she asked. "We MUST live just a few more days," she admonished me, "so we can live the rest of our lives."

"Whatever happens," she kept impressing on me, "do not move away from me. Stick to me at all times, for this confusion is made for escape."

One afternoon we reached a village. On the square the local women were boiling potato peels in a large cauldron to feed their animals. The smell of potatoes was permeating the air. In mass we broke our lines and descended in a heap on the hot stew of potato peels; we stretched our bony arms hoping to grab the food.

For that one moment I forgot Vera's words not to move ever from her side, not even for a moment. I extricated myself from the mass of tangled arms with a scalded hand clutching a chunk of potato peels. I looked for Vera to share it with. But I did not find her.

I saw her vault a fence, march along calmly on a field path, the telltale white cross on her coat covered by a potato sack thrown over her back. I wanted to run after her, but an SS gun stopped me.

After Vera's escape I was sure that now my number was up. I did not think I could make another step. But the instinct for survival somehow carried me on.

Our transport ended up in two other concentration camps. First we reached Mauthausen, another German paradise, where typhoid fever took the lives of many survivors of the death march. Rumors were about that concentration camp inmates from all over would be brought here, and the camp blown up with us inside. Somehow in the general confusion we were herded to nearby Gunzkirchen, where the Americans liberated us on May 4, 1945.

I was malnourished, to put it mildly, and sick from dysentery. I managed to survive because I wanted to see once more my parents and my country, and I had a craving to eat once more as much bread as I could stuff into myself.

After some adventurous traveling, I found my parents at home, and what is more, I had a sweet little baby sister, born in 1945. I also found Vera. We are friends. It is the kind of friendship only bonds of common suffering can form.

The first year after liberation was very hard. I kept having the most torturous nightmares about my days in the various camps and the hunger march. Gradually, however, with the loving care of my family, I started believing in the philosophy of buried memories. I made an effort not to think back, to relegate to oblivion all that had been painful. While this has never been totally possible, I concentrated my thinking on positive events and on people who had a kind word or a piece of bread for their fellow sufferers. I tried to erase from my memory hatred, for life with hatred in your heart is a life of misery.

Perhaps that is the reason why my tale does not even approximate the horrors I had been through.

21

Notes from the Camp of the Dead

Bergen-Belsen, south of Hamburg, was first a prisoner-of-war camp, where after 1941 thousands of Russians died of disease and hunger. By 1943, it was used by the SS who established there an anomaly, a residence camp (Aufhaltungslager) for 10,000 "privileged" Jews who were supposed to be exchanged for Germans interned abroad; 357 were actually exchanged. This was also referred to as the Star Camp (Sternlager), because the inmates had to wear the yellow star. Here families including children were allowed to remain together, which was quite unusual.

In another section was the Neutral Camp, with Jews from Portugal, Spain, Argentina and Turkey. From July to December of 1944, the Hungarian Camp section held 1,685 Jews, who were then taken to Switzerland, having been ransomed for $1.6 million. In the Tent Camp thousands of women evacuated from Auschwitz were kept without much of any kind of provisions after the winter of 1944.

But all these were just side camps. The original purposes of Bergen-Belsen were deleted as time went on, and it became a "normal" concentration camp, with all the expected trimmings of exploitation and abuse, slave labor, hunger and epidemics. It also became the living proof that even without gas chambers mass extermination was possible.

This became particularly evident after late 1944, when Bergen-Belsen was turned into a dumping ground for other camps. In open cattle cars in freezing weather, or via death marches, thousands of inmates poured in. In November, there were about 15,000 prisoners; by January 1945, there were 22,000, by February 41,000 and by mid-April close to 60,000.

In February, the camp administration for all practical purposes dissolved. The guards remained, but there were no more roll calls and there was no more food distribution to speak of. Yet transports kept streaming in. In the week of April 4 alone, 28,000 new victims arrived.

The death toll was enormous. In the last two months of the camp, 35,000 people expired of typhus, diarrhoea, malnutrition and hunger. Corpses were left decomposing among the living. Rats ran all over the camp. There were reports of cannibalism. The British arrived on April 15 and found 10,000 unburied corpses. For 13,000 inmates liberation came too late: they died as a result of the Bergen-Belsen treatment.

It was into this morass of humanity, ruled over by sadistic kapos and their patron saint, the SS Kommandant, that an individual of rare qualities and sensitive observational talents was tossed in the summer of 1944.

Hanna Lévy was born in Sarajevo and was a teacher in Cetinje, in the remote region of Montenegro. She joined the partisans and fought in their battles. She could have easily retreated into the mountains with them. Yet, after all Jews were registered, this "emancipated and assimilated" young woman opted to share their fate, for she did not want to jeopardize their safety by escaping the Nazi noose. Thus, she was transported to Bergen-Belsen and became one of the few survivors of that nether world.

The following excerpts are from her diary in which she noted not merely physical deprivations but also the wounds to the soul inflicted on those condemned to Bergen-Belsen. It is noteworthy that unlike eyewitnesses from Ravensbrück and Terezín, who report cooperation and empathy among most of the inmates, she saw in the cramped quarters and infernal conditions of Bergen-Belsen's Star Camp constant irritations and quarrels. This unique diary was previously translated from Serbian into Hebrew, French and German.

After the war, Hanna Lévy became a radio announcer in Belgrade and in 1948 moved to Israel. She was an early feminist.

August 19, 1944. People from all social classes are penned in here, but small town types prevail. One can find also a few capitalists in the real sense of the word, who are down on their luck. In general, all people exhibit petty, egoistic, narrowminded habits. This leads to endless conflicts and friction between opposing interests. Add to that the cases of hypocrisy.

It is hard to breathe in this atmosphere. It is not bad enough that people from all parts of the world were dragged here by force, and you can hear no less than 25 languages. If only there were bonds of a clearly defined common awareness. But that is not the case. This human mass is of all shapes and colors. It has been hoarded together by force in this dusty and damp room, it is compelled to live under the most undignified conditions and the most brutal deprivations, so that all human passions and weaknesses become unrestricted and at times take on animal form.

What a shame. What a sad picture. Common misery unites people who can hardly stand each other and who only bring into a sharper focus their very real misery through their lack of social awareness, through their spiritual blindness and the incurable diseases that isolate their souls. Certain egotistic instincts find here an ideal fertile soil, out of which they grow into grotesque shapes. Certainly it would be wrong to generalize. Still, the high individual qualities that I sense in some, their moral and intellectual honesty, remain in the shadow, powerless. . . .

August 20, 1944. I feel tired to the utmost and distant from all that is around me. My soul groans and hurts. Where are you hiding, beauty? and truth? Love? Oh, how just thinking of my whole life makes me suffer.

August 22, 1944. The utter lack of space and the difficulties to keep this place clean are just too much. Rainy days turn the whole floor into mud . . . and on top of that the incessant chicanery from our common enemy, the Nazis. This is only the first month, and I get depressed just to think of the endless misfortune ahead.

I should have moved with the others "up there,"* to the mountains. Without any doubt. Naturally, I would have encountered there also irregularities, small differences of opinion, minor inconsequent disagreements in some and a lack of firmness and principles in others. Perhaps that would have been even more painful, more bitter. But I would have at least felt like a human being who could think, talk and behave freely. And I would be surrounded by human beings, by real people, who talk a human language; I would be among people who today deserve respect and whose words and

"Notes from the Camp of the Dead" is from Eike Geisel, ed., *Vielleicht war das alles erst der Anfang: Hanna Lévy-Hass, Tagebuch aus dem KZ Bergen-Belsen, 1944-1945* (Berlin: Rotbuch Verlag, 1979), pp. 8-59. Translation copyright by Vera Laska. Reprinted with the kind permission of Harvester Press, Ltd., Brighton, Sussex, England.

*Fearful of mentioning in her hidden diary the word "partisan," Hanna Lévy is using the expression "up there" for the partisans in the mountains of her native Yugoslavia.

actions carry weight. Only "up there" could I have discovered my goal in life and my true worth, and what I really could offer or not offer.

Only "up there" makes suffering any sense. . . . Today I can say that if not absolutely but to a large degree I was created to be "up there," not here. . . . [Now] I know the enemy better and more thoroughly. . . . The knowledge I gained was worth it. . . .

August 24, 1944. I am saturated with fatigue and absolute loss of interest. What next? A world that is falling to pieces. A new, healthier world will replace it. I shiver with joy when I think of the new life, of the coming triumph of light and truth. . . .

August 26, 1944. One thing makes me lose my temper here: when I see that men are much weaker and less able to resist than the women. Physically and often morally. They can not control themselves and show such lack of spirit, that I feel sorry for them. Hunger is marking their faces and gestures in a more frightening way than in the case of women. In many of them it is either ignorance or lack of will power, or they are simply not capable to discipline their stomachs. It is the same story with thirst, fatigue and physical reaction to the most elementary privations. They lack the ability to adjust, the power to stand up straight. Some of them look so miserable that it hurts me more seeing their misery than their misery hurts them. In some the lack of discipline goes so far that in moments of greatest common grief and trials they react to their fellow sufferers only maliciously and with unveiled greed.

Is the whole male sex like this? That is not possible. What about those men who remain strong in the face of all trials and struggles? Who suffer and know how to remain silent with dignity, who control and are masters of their instincts because they are guided by much higher and human motives than their stomachs and other purely bodily needs. Naturally, what is taking place in front of my eyes, is only the natural continuation of the past. In the cases of most of these men they had been only too long used to satisfy the lowest instincts of their bodies and to coddle and fill their stomachs. . . . Few, very few stand up to the enemy with dignity and without cowardice.

August 28, 1944. I took on the task to care for the children. In our barracks there are 110 children of all ages, from three year old little ones to 14 and 15 year old boys and girls. It is not easy to work without any books. I have to write on small scraps of paper, dozens and dozens of them. . . . The children get paper and pencil wherever they can, they sell their bread ration or make other transactions, or they steal them from each other. . . . Teaching is often interrupted either by a roll call or an air raid or by the arrival of some committee that reminds us of our own visits to the zoo. . . . The children are wild, uninhibited, starved. They feel that their lives took an extraordinary and abnormal turn, and they react to this instinctively and brutally. In this atmosphere of general mistrust and anxiety bad habits spread quickly among the children. . . . but it is out of the question to lecture to them on morality. It would be ridiculous. . . .

August 29, 1944. I am sick because I do not have any books. I have the impression that my innermost being was killed. How many lost hours, how many missed, unreachable treasures. What a miserable, fruitless life—the spirit is wasting away. . . . I think with sorrow of real life, of the life of free people, of so much knowledge that I have gathered in the last years and even here, and the many gaps in my knowledge. . . .

August 30, 1944. Children who know no joy. Fear, nothing but fear. These poor, little, humiliated beings, who have to stand up straight for hours [at roll calls] with fear running through their whole bodies. . . .

September 1, 1944. Appell [roll call] was twice as long than normal today. Perhaps a child was late. . . . they let us stand often for hours. . . . It is a fall day. A steady soft rain, a gloomy day, humid air and a strong wind that reminds me of our "koshava," but it is blowing more. At roll call this morning the cold penetrated into our bones. . . .

Quarrels are unavoidable, especially among the women, either when beds are assigned or at the laundry. Everybody feels especially threatened or picked upon . . . without seeing that her neighbor is no less unfortunate. We are all slaves here and intentionally squeezed together without enough air to breathe. Intentionally "they" see to it that we should insult each other, get into scuffles and quarrels; they do want to make our lives unbearable, to turn us into animals, the better to deride us, humiliate us, torment us. The beasts. It became worse since they suddenly turned off the water.

September 4, 1944. Our barracks are like a madhouse. Only few can control themselves. The smallest incident leads to rude quarrels, offenses, threats and abuse. Everybody is highly irritable, quite ready to get involved and see a personal enemy in the next woman. . . . what a tragedy, what a tragedy. All these unfortunate faces from which I can read fright, hunger and animal fear . . . especially when food is distributed. . . . And all this time, during this desperate fight for a bowl of watery turnip soup you can hear the comings and goings. . . . chamber pots are carried from one end of the barracks to the other, they are being emptied and they are being filled. . . . And in all this hullabaloo, with the soup, smells and excrement around, and the brooms whirling up the dust, the grown ups are shouting and the children are crying, and the "traders" make their rounds. . . . exchanging trifles for bread. . . .

September 8, 1944. A few weeks ago I tried in vain to ignore all that was happening around me. Today I am fully aware of it that my life is inseparably bound to the life of the camp, and that we are all united in the same fate, for better or for worse, and in the same misery. . . . The ocean of suffering is endless. . . . More than once, at one or another point of our slavery. . . . I saw Dante's inferno before me, but not to enjoy literary reminiscences. Because the pictures of hell to which my imagination was used, were the only perceptions that my brain could register. I could not recall any other memories. . . .

September 25, 1944. New barracks are being built. For whom . . . ? As repercussions for sabotage, the Germans are reducing our bread rations daily. . . . An unknown epidemic seized the camp, especially the women and children. It manifests itself in high fever for two to three weeks, in fainting spells, absolute exhaustion and total loss of appetite. No pain. The doctors call it "camp fever. . . ."

October 17, 1944. In the neighboring barracks something is going on. Polish women are interned there, political prisoners or Jews, it is not clear. We only know that they are treated even worse than we are. Some of them are under special observation. It seems that they revolted today, or demonstrated or something. . . . Suddenly there came an order for all of us to return to the barracks. . . . the great gates were locked. General panic and absolute silence reigns all over the camp.

How the affair ended with the rebellious women, we never found out. However, one thing is clear: the Germans "restored order" in their own way and committed new crimes. The crematorium is working without interruption, as everybody can see. . . .

October 22, 1944. The men's distrust shows in sporadic outbreaks of personal hatred, curses and threats: "Thief, get lost, I'll show you, you. . . . " In the women's section it is the same, or almost. Sometimes there is even more noise here, you can observe hysteria, lamentations, curses, without anybody deciding to do something concrete and effective. In any case, perhaps because of the children, the women show at times signs of more practical and more collective tendencies. They make it a point to find a way, show real courage and if need be are ready for a sacrifice. . . .

October 23, 1944. Daily after 6:30 p.m. there is an alarm bell, and we spend the whole evening and night in the dark. . . . The complete darkness is used by thieves of all kinds. They are mostly after bread, the chief means of trade inside the camp and the only means that keeps you—at least for a while—alive. . . . The ration is smaller each week. The daily ration is measured by centimeters and today is only 3.5 cm.* You tremble for this little piece like for gold. . . .

November 6, 1944. These last days again a larger transport arrived, 1,700 women of various nationalities. . . . from Auschwitz. . . . The new arrivals are under a tent. They lie on a thin layer of straw, or rather, on the humid, naked earth. They look horrible, sick, gray, covered with abcessed wounds. . . .

Our barracks are daily inspected. It is a young SS woman, the "Gray Mouse. . . ." She dispenses cracking, impulsive, fast and sudden slaps in the face, without taking her glove off. She orders the bread or all food taken

*1.4 inches.

away from seven or eight inmates each time she comes, for no good reason. . . .

November 8, 1944. I would like so much to feel some pleasant and esthetic feelings, to awaken high and tender feelings, worthy emotions. It is hard. I strain my imagination but it does not work. Our existence is cruel, animal like. All that is human in us, has been reduced to zero. . . . The mind has been paralysed, the spirit raped. The damage to the soul goes so deep that your whole being seems to have withered away. . . . We did not die, but we are dead. . . . and to think that this is only the fifth month and that this camp, if one can believe the Germans, is not even among the worst ones. . . !

November 20, 1944. There is something extraordinary and horrible in the human capacity to adjust to everything: loss of dignity, degrading hunger, lack of space, stinking air, infections, washing yourself in front of others. . . . and we are sinking deeper and deeper. O horrors. This death, without dying, with a living body, slowly. . . .

November 22, 1944. For the last month, our daily food had dwindled to a cup of soup. Soup? A way of speaking, nothing else. They are turnips cooked in water. Nothing else. Turnips in water. On the ground, in front and behind the barbed wire. Everywhere. Wherever you turn, wherever you look—only turnips, endlessly. Mountains of turnips. Turnips. Turnips. Turnips. In wheelbarrows, in front of the big gates, the kitchen, in underground cellars, all over the place. They feed us this gray turnip, that is normally fed only to cattle.* . . . Germany, blessed land, land of the turnip, of "Ersatz" industries, of concentration camps, of slavery and of terrors. . . .

*December, 1944.*** I thought it was the end, there was nothing more I could note down. But there is no end, there is none. Days follow each other, black terrible, full of dread. I would not mind to see the end, whatever it may be. . . . As our female detail went to work yesterday, we saw potatoes on the road, they probably fell off a truck. . . . One of us bent down to pick one up. But in the same moment she had to let it drop, scared by the wild shouts of the guards who just could not tolerate such gluttony. . . .

December, 1944. The camp commandant has been replaced. The new one is a certain Kramer.*** Kramer was before the chief of the notorious camp Auschwitz. No further comments are necessary. The regime in the camp is getting worse by the day. . . . even God is powerless here. . . . We swim in a sea of microbes, lice and fleas, decay and stench. Since we lie literally one on top of the other, we are an ideal nursery for cultivating more lice. You can not destroy them. The labor of Sisyphus. . . .

*In many European countries turnips are used for cattle fodder only.

**Note that as time passes, the author loses count of the days, marking only the months.

***Josef Kramer, commander of Auschwitz II-Birkenau, including the women's camp, and of Bergen-Belsen, was executed for war crimes in 1945.

December, 1944. Kramer and his gang. He gave us a new commando, all Aryans, criminal inmates, Germans, Poles, French. . . . All sold their souls to the devil—that is Kramer—and there is nothing human left in them. They are cynical, cruel, sadistic; one has to see it to believe what perverse pleasure they get out of beating people. I have seen it clearly. They are animals in human form. The Germans did that to them, turned them into animals. And it seems that now they take revenge for it on us. These hardened criminals are now our masters, they dispose freely over our lives, our souls, our children. We are the slaves of these lowly slaves. What an infernal chain! The Nazi beast always gets new ideas to find still other ways to deprive people of their dignity, to "finish them." . . .

January, 1945. I managed to talk with a few women from the Auschwitz transport. Most of them are Jewish, from Poland, Greece and Hungary. They told us what they lived through in Auschwitz. During that time alone that they were there, from 1943 to 1944, hundreds of thousands of people were annihilated there. . . . They spoke of mass murder, of gas, of the 99 percent. . . .* The death factory worked with full speed, every day. Columns of hundreds or even thousands of men and women had to wait at times for their turn for the gassing in the large shower. And the crematorium chimney was smoking before their eyes, and they looked and knew exactly what it was all about.**. . . . The goal is the same, only tactics are different: there a quick, cynical procedure, mass murder by gas, and here the slow, calculated annihilation by hunger, use of force, terror and scientifically maintained epidemics. . . .

January, 1945. General undernourishment. It takes great effort just to make a move. Nobody is able to walk upright any longer. We all stagger, dragging our legs. Entire families die within days. . . . One nearsighted boy could not do anything against the vermin that was swarming all over his body and burrowed into his skin, sitting even on his eyelashes; his chest was all black from the thousands of lice and their nests. I have never seen anything like it. I could not imagine anything of the sort. . . . And the poor unfortunate boy looks almost like an idiot. They say that he used to be a very intelligent youngster, before. Today he is dragging his long, bony body slowly from one end of the barracks to the other. Everybody moves out of his way. His sister and brother are afraid of him, of his fleas. . . . On one of his last nights he dragged sadly his superfluous body from cot to cot begging people to give him a little space, but everybody refused with abhorrence. We all sleep two to a cot, and no partner for him was found. . . . Thus died young M., without encountering a spot where he could lay his body down. . . . His case is not unique. There are thousands of such cases in this camp. . . .

*Refers to transports of which 99 percent went directly to the gas chambers.

**Actually, there were four gas chambers working full blast at that time in Auschwitz.

February, 1945. Typhoid fever now started its reign. . . . Two little girls in a cot near ours died one "nice" day, very quickly, one after the other. Their mother, a simple and nice woman, watched over them and cared for them like a wolf for her cubs. When she saw that they were dead, she was so shaken by heavy grief, that her cries were tearing our ears. Then she started singing plaintive songs, inventing new verses with incredible talent, and talking with the small bodies softly, very softly. Now she is dragging herself around with unkempt hair, never takes her rags off, and is terribly neglected, with insanity sitting in her eyes. . . .

February, 1945. Everybody is thinking only of himself or herself. Nobody has any understanding for another. Many women simply let themselves go. Young girls, who do not know yet life and its rules, thoughtlessly seized the chances offered by the sad circumstances. They devour all they can find, they booze, flirt, dance, laugh, get clothes and silk stockings—all this kind of life offered by the kapos. . . .

February, 1945. On the 12th of this month it will be a year that we had been arrested down there, in Cetinje. . . . The hunger, the hunger; is there anything more terrible, more demoralizing for a human being? I become agitated by these faces of tortured animals who are desperately pushing and shoving toward a kettle with lukewarm, stinking, soured water, that is called soup. . . .

March, 1945. All I see here, and all that takes place before my eyes, causes me to begin to doubt the human qualities of my own being. Slowly a gloomier and heavier doubt sets in—the doubt of humanity. . . . On top of that I suffer of dysentery and all kinds of other ailments. . . . After all that we have lived through, could we ever live normal lives? Nearly impossible. It seems this is our end, an infamous, terribly infamous *finale* of our existence. . . . Is this all one great test? To establish how much ability we each possess to pull through? Is that it? The ability to pull through? The struggle against death, the survival instinct? Is that the criterion for individual strength and vitality? Must a human being go wild, become an animal, in order to save her life? Then it would follow that those of us who do not know how to fight that way and do not reach for animal like methods, are incapable of life and doomed for destruction? I don't know anything any more. . . .

March, 1945. We all got a typhus like fever, and we remain on our cots. Our barracks has been surrounded by barbed wire. We are quarantined. I had the fever for two weeks. . . . No medicine. . . . I had only felt that I was near death, very near, not only that death was in the general neighborhood but this time very near me. I felt its breath on my body. I was dying slowly, knowingly. My organism felt absolutely nothing and seemed to stop slowly its functions. Only the thought of death still lived on in me, stubbornly, obstinately. . . .

Nobody is able to help anybody else, the corpses remain lying in the cots, next to the living or the half dead. The living and the dead, all mixed together. There is almost no dividing line between one and the other, almost no difference. In the face of death and of the dead there is total indifference, it became an ordinary occurrence. One no longer thinks of liberation, nobody counts the days as before, it is not worth it knowing when the Allies would arrive, although allegedly they should be a few dozen kilometers from here. But there is little meaning in this. At this moment only death is our closest ally. . . .

The corpses, the real ones, are still with us, in our cots. . . . They are piled up also in the yards, one on top of another, piles of corpses, higher every day. . . . Nobody busies himself any longer with us, the Germans no longer show themselves. . . .

April, 1945. I am terribly ashamed that I have experienced all this. People are rotting and decomposing in the dirt. They say that in the next block there were cases of cannibalism. . . .

April, 1945. It is abominable what they had made of human beings. The darkest scenes of the Middle Ages and of the inquisition were repeated here, multiplied to the utmost. Their monstrous repetition will mark "civilized" and "cultured" Germany of the twentieth century forever with the sign of shame.

22

What of the Future?

Women who returned from the beyond of concentration camps after liberation had mixed feelings about their recent past. Those with hatred yearned for revenge. Those suffering from nightmares cried out for blissful oblivion. Some wanted to remember all forever as a warning to future generations. Others preferred to efface all from memory and remain silent about their experiences.

Micheline Mauriel, a French resistance fighter from Toulon, spent two agonizing years at the Neubranderburg concentration camp in northern Germany, working as a slave laborer in an airplane factory. She observed the gradual brutalization of the prisoners, the beatings by sadistic guards, the pettiness of human nature—but also its noble side, the endurance of the spirit against all odds.

Her query and her answer to "What of the Future?" is the expression of absolute sorrow over the past, yet not a denial of hope for the future.

Very few of the women who had been deported from Toulon came back. Mme. Armando was dead. I had to break the news to her husband.

The neighbors came from all over to meet the "deportee." I was the center of attraction. Cousins came from afar to visit me. At first I was very excited, I greeted everyone, I answered all questions. Then I became so exasperated that I shut myself in my room and refused to see anyone.

The questions I was asked were always the same: "Tell me, were you raped?" (This was the one question that was most frequently asked. In the end, I regretted having been spared this. Seemingly, by my own fault, I had missed one part of the adventure, to the great disappointment of my audience. However, I could at least tell them of the rape of others.)

"Did you suffer much? Were you beaten? Were you tortured? What did they beat you with? Were you sterilized? And the Russians, were they so awful? Do you mean to tell me you had no other clothing? How did you manage the periods? Tell me, truly, were there homosexuals among the prisoners? And just how did you manage to survive?"

I did not really know how to answer this last question, except to say that I had had Michelle's friendship, Sissy's scrapbooks to encourage me to keep writing. Kvieta's gifts, without which I would not have lived through the second winter, the intervention of Pani Irena to save me from the black journey into death, and then, of course, the solid fiber of my being that bore up under the blows of spade and club and booted foot.

But that question has another answer. Officially, it is true, I did return. But in a real sense, was it I who had come back home? That question may well be asked. Other people sensed this immediately and told me so as kindly as they could. For instance, I have a picture in my hand of a morning shortly after I had returned. My mother was bustling around the kitchen; two of my brothers and I were eating breakfast at table. My mother said, "What struck me most forcibly, when you first came home, was not how thin you were, not even the condition of your legs. Most of all, it was the look in your eyes—you had a crazed look."

"That's true," said one brother, "and you talked like a little child."

"You also didn't understand what people were saying to you," added the other with a disarming smile.

For a long time the concentration camp had a reality more true and more definite than the world I was in. I was haunted, and sometimes I still am, by the facts of Neubrandenburg—hundreds and thousands of faces, thin, twisted in pain, green with cold, full of hopelessness, attempting to smile, or wearing the permanent grin of death. I still instinctively feared a threatened blow, so that if someone moved too fast in my direction or brushed past me, I involuntarily winced and stiffened. In the voices from the street or

"What of the Future?" is from Micheline Mauriel, *An Ordinary Camp* (New York: Simon and Schuster, 1958), pp. 136-41. Reprinted with the permission of Georges Borchardt, Inc., New York.

from adjoining houses, I thought I heard remembered sounds: "Roll call!" *"Raus, schnell!"* or *"Schweine, kein essen."**

And then, too, the man I loved had found another woman.

Meat was rationed; rice was not to be found. My health was not returning. It was hard to do any work; at times it was out of the question. And yet there was enough to eat. I had no right to be unhappy.

During the seven years after my return, it often happened that I would have to live for several weeks on a daily crust of bread and nothing more, and to shiver in dismal rooming houses. I have been hungry and cold in Lyon, in London and in Geneva. I have watched the wealthy and successful passing by in the cities. Then I thought of Neubrandenburg. I had not the right to be unhappy, because I had left Neubrandenburg. But the camp was not yet just a memory.

In 1948, here in Geneva, I found, in a file of records "for the documentation of the history of the war," a volume full of photographs dealing with the concentration camps. In a mood of despair—or of lucidity—I wrote a sort of invocation which I have no wish to change, because others will doubtless find in it what they themselves have felt, and what, perhaps, they are still feeling:

"True God, let there be no more camps! I weep because there have been and there still are camps. Because there are people now who are preparing for war and for new camps and who do not know what this means. I would like to shout to them to keep silent, to make them destroy their bombs and all their armaments, to make them suddenly aware what war, what concentration camps really mean. But they would not understand unless they themselves had been in concentration camps.

"I weep because the human beings who were in the camps have never been freed. They have never known a joy which would make up for the suffering endured there. The deported are either dead or have brought back within themselves their camps, where no one has entered and very few have even tried to enter, where they are alone, wretched *schmustics,* **surrounded by the crawling crowd back there. Those who have come back vainly try to recapture the gift for happiness which other people have: the camp sets them apart from the world, just as it did when they were there. They cannot leave it. The past is still alive, the horrible past that cannot be destroyed.

"I weep for all those who died in the camps, because no one has ever understood or ever will understand what they suffered. For their sakes, I hope that their death is a total death. That they have no memory left. That

*"Out, quick!" or "Pigs, no food."

**The German *"Schmutzstück"* literally "dirty piece," referred to the walking skeletons. To the French it sounded like "schmoustique" or "schmustic." Another interpretation is *"Schmuckstück"* or "piece of jewelry," meant, of course, ironically.

even if they are among the Blessed, they cannot look back on those memories, those realities which remain real. I weep for all these too because they have been forgotten, or replaced, or maligned. And even when they have not been forgotten, there is nothing that can be done for them, since nothing can undo the horror of their life and of their death.

"A crime against humanity, a crime that never will and never can be avenged. It is of no avail to punish a few men who were only the tools. It is of no avail to punish an entire nation; other nations have done the same and others would do it. It is of no avail to punish; the harm is done. The camps did and do exist. And who should answer for so horrible a destruction of all human life, who should answer for it, if not God Himself?

"Confronted by this immeasurable, this irreparable, misery, the mind is shattered by rage and despair. No problem of evil, no philosophy, no religion can account for the suffering of the camps. No crime committed by men can justify it. No cause is great enough to warrant such stakes. No vengeance is possible or desirable. The only way to avenge would be to recreate the camps for those who made them, and it would begin all over again.

"To make up for so much suffering, for those millions of miserable creatures, motionless in the past or invisible beyond the horizons, who stare at us with horribly despairing eyes, it would take so much joy, O God, that even a bountiful and kindly God would not have enough. And where in life could there possibly be found enough joy to make up for this misery, when all the survivors together, since they have come back, have not found enough to make up for the suffering of a single one?

"Yet I believe that each deportee who has returned has felt, as I have in moments of annoyance or even of grief, that he has no right to be unhappy. For behind us is the multitude of the dead left at the camp, who fix us with crazed and envious eyes. Those millions of people envy us and wish they could shout, 'You fools, don't you see that you are happy?'

"Isn't it so?" What did we ask of the living when we were like the dead? To think of us? To pray for us? Yes, a little, in the beginning. But mainly to do all they could to send us material help, and then, when they had done all they could, oh, above all, to enjoy life to the fullest! We so often cried out to them, 'Be happy, be happy! Be happy, you who eat, and you who expect alms and receive them. Be happy, you who live in fine apartments, in ugly houses or in hovels. Be happy, you who have your loved ones, and you also who sit alone and dream and can weep. Be happy, you who torture yourself over metaphysical problems, and you who suffer because of money worries. Be happy, you the sick who are being cared for, and you who care for them, and be happy, oh, how happy, you who die a death as normal as life in hospital beds or in your homes. Be happy, all of you: millions of people envy you.'

"And we felt no anger against the 'civilians' who were happy but only against those who didn't realize their happiness.

"And yet, how can I be happy now, my poor comrades, when I find you again in photographs or in my memory, just as you were back there, as you were found, as you are, forever etched in the present? I feel that there is a staggering sum of suffering to be made up. I am torn by that suffering. I feel the camp around me. There is someone who walks in Geneva, who goes by my name: it is a phantom, a dream of the other me, the real me, who remains seated back there because she can no longer walk, holding out her empty bowl. My poor, my dear companions, all alike, all wretched, you the survivors and you the dead, I know it well: the camps have not been liberated. Each survivor had brought his camp back with him; he tries to obliterate it; he tries to stifle in the barbed wire and under the straw mattresses all those despairing *schmustics,* but suddenly a date or a photograph brings back the entire camp around him. He would like to run away, shielding his eyes with his arm in order not to see, howling in order not to hear. But the entire camp rises again slowly, for it has not been destroyed and nothing has made up for a single day of suffering."

III.

WOMEN IN HIDING

It is as if the whole world had turned upside down. But I am still alive, Kitty, and that is the main thing, Daddy says.

Anne Frank's diary

I made myself as small as possible.

Annie de Leeuw, 12, in hiding

23

Arisen from the Grave

After Hitler's attack on the Soviet Union in June 1941, the Germans soon overran the western part of the country. Special Strike Commandoes (Einsatzgruppen) started massacring the Jews along the way. With thoroughness and efficiency they combed through every village in pursuit of the Final Solution, killing over one and a half million people. At times even visiting American citizens were caught in the roundup and murdered.

The process of extermination was streamlined and standardized: men, women and children, stripped naked, were shot above their mass graves, their bodies conveniently falling into the pits. Babies were shot in their mothers' arms, their brains splattering over their mothers. Eichmann on one of his inspection tours complained that they damaged his coat.

Rivka Yosselevska was a young mother from the village of Zagorodski near Pinsk. She survived the years of doom hidden in a farmhouse. What is exceptional about Rivka, however, is not so much her torment during her hiding but the road, truly a calvary, that led to it. With her family she was lined up above their grave. Within minutes they were all dispatched into the bloody heap of victims below.

Miraculously, Rivka survived.

At the Eichmann trial in Jerusalem, on May 8, 1961, Rivka bore witness before humanity and God of her experiences that seem to go beyond the limits of physical and mental endurance. The following excerpt is from the court records.

Witness: . . . We were told to leave the houses—to take with us only the children. We were always used to leaving the ghetto at short order, because very often they would take us all out for a roll-call. Then we would all appear. But we felt and realized that this was not an ordinary roll-call, but something very special. As if the Angel of Death was in charge. The place was swarming with Germans. Some four to five Germans to every Jew.

Attorney-General: Then all of you were driven out, and were taken to this square, weren't you?

Witness: No, we were left standing in the ghetto. They began saying that he who wishes to save his life could do so with money, jewels and valuable things. This would be ransom, and he would be spared. Thus we were held until the late afternoon, before evening came.

Presiding Judge: And did the Jews hand over jewels and so on?

Witness: We did not. We had nothing to hand over. They already took all we had before.

Presiding Judge: I see.

Attorney-General: Yes. And what happened towards sunrise?

Witness: And thus the children screamed. They wanted food, water. This was not the first time. But we took nothing with us. We had no food and no water, and we did not know the reason. The children were hungry and thirsty. We were held this way for twenty-four hours while they were searching the houses all the time—searching for valuables.

In the meantime, the gates of the ghetto were opened. A large truck appeared and all of us were put on the truck—either thrown, or went up himself.

Attorney-General: Did they count the Jews?

Witness: Yes, they were counted. They entered the ghetto again, and searched for every missing person. We were tortured until late in the evening.

Attorney-General: Now, they filled up this truck. And what happened to the people for whom there was no room in the truck?

Witness: Those for whom there was no room in the truck were ordered to run after the truck.

Attorney-General: And you ran with your daughter?

Witness: I had my daughter in my arms and ran after the truck. There were mothers who had two or three children and held them in their arms running after the truck. We ran all the way. There were those who fell—we were not allowed to help them rise. They were shot—right there—wherever they fell.

When we reached the destination, the people from the truck were already down and they were undressed—all lined up. All my family was there—

"Arisen from the Grave" is from Martin Gilbert, *Final Journey, The Fate of the Jews in Nazi Europe* (New York: Mayflower Books, 1979), pp. 56-62. Reprinted with the kind permission of Rainbird Publishers, London, and of the author.

undressed, lined up. The people from the truck, those who arrived before us. . . .

There was a kind of hillock. At the foot of this little hill, there was a dug-out. We were ordered to stand at the top of the hillock and the four devils shot us—each one of us separately.

Attorney-General: Now these four—to what German unit did they belong?

Witness: They were SS men—the four of them. They were armed to the teeth. They were real messengers of the Devil and the Angel of Death.

Attorney-General: Please go on—what did you see?

Witness: When I came up to the place—we saw people, naked, lined up. But we were still hoping that this was only torture. Maybe there is hope—hope of living. One could not leave the line, but I wished to see—what are they doing on the hillock? Is there anyone down below? I turned my head and saw that some three or four rows were already killed—on the ground. There were some twelve people among the dead. I also want to mention what my child said while we were lined up in the ghetto, she said: "Mother, why did you make me wear the Shabbat dress; we are being taken to be shot"; and when we stood near the dug-out, near the grave, she said, "Mother why are we waiting, let us run!" Some of the young people tried to run, but they were caught immediately, and they were shot right there. It was difficult to hold on to the children. We took all children not ours, and we carried them —we were anxious to get it all over—the suffering of the children was difficult; we all trudged along to come nearer to the place and to come nearer to the end of the torture of the children. The children were taking leave of their parents and parents of their elder people.

Presiding Judge: How did you survive through all of this?

Attorney-General: She will relate it.

Presiding Judge: Please will you direct the Witness.

Witness: We were driven: we were already undressed; the clothes were removed and taken away; our father did not want to undress; he remained in his underwear. We were driven up to the grave, this shallow . . .

Attorney-General: And these garments were torn off his body, weren't they?

Witness: 'When it came to our turn, our father was beaten. We prayed, we begged with my father to undress, but he would not undress, he wanted to keep his underclothes. He did not want to stand naked.

Attorney-General: And then they tore them off?

Witness: Then they tore off the clothing off the old man and he was shot. I saw it with my own eyes. And then they took my mother, and we said, let us go before her; but they caught mother and shot her too; and then there was my grandmother, my father's mother, standing there; she was eighty years old and she had two children in her arms. And then there was my father's sister. She also had children in her arms and she was shot on the spot with the babies in her arms.

Attorney-General: And finally it was your turn.
Witness: And finally my turn came. There was my younger sister, and she wanted to leave; she prayed with the Germans; she asked to run, naked; she went up to the Germans with one of her friends; they were embracing each other; and she asked to be spared, standing there naked. He looked into her eyes and shot the two of them. They fell together in their embrace, the two young girls, my sister and her young friend. Then my second sister was shot and then my turn did come.
Attorney-General: Were you asked anything?
Witness: We turned towards the grave and then he turned around and asked: "Whom shall I shoot first?" We were already facing the grave. The German asked: "Whom do you want me to shoot first?" I did not answer. I felt him take the child from my arms. The child cried out and was shot immediately. And then he aimed at me. First he held on to my hair and turned my head around; I stayed standing. I heard a shot, but I continued to stand and then he turned my head again and he aimed the revolver at me and ordered me to watch and then turned my head around and shot at me. Then I fell to the ground into the pit amongst the bodies; but I felt nothing. The moment I did feel, I felt a sort of heaviness and then I thought maybe I am not alive any more, but I feel something after I died. I thought I was dead, that this was the feeling which comes after death. Then I felt that I was choking; people falling over me. I tried to move and felt that I was alive and that I could rise. I was strangling. I heard the shots and was praying for another bullet to put an end to my suffering, but I continued to move about. I felt that I was choking, strangling, but I tried to save myself, to find some air to breathe, and then I felt that I was climbing towards the top of the grave above the bodies. I rose, and I felt bodies pulling at me with their hands, biting at my legs, pulling me down, down. And yet with my last strength I came up on top of the grave, and when I did, I did not know the place, so many bodies were lying all over, dead people; I wanted to see the end of this stretch of dead bodies but I could not. It was impossible. They were lying, all dying; suffering; not all of them dead, but in their last sufferings; naked; shot, but not dead. Children crying "Mother", "Father"; I could not stand on my feet.
Presiding Judge: Were the Germans still around?
Witness: No, the Germans were gone. There was nobody there. No one was standing up.
Attorney-General: And you were undressed and covered with blood?
Witness: I was naked, covered with blood, dirty from the other bodies, with the excrement from other bodies which was poured on to me.
Attorney-General: What did you have in your head?
Witness: When I was shot I was wounded in the head.
Attorney-General: Was it in the back of the head?
Witness: I have a scar to this day from the shot by the Germans; and yet,

somehow I did come out of the grave. This was something I thought I would never live to recount. I was searching among the dead for my little girl, and I cried for her—Merkele was her name—Merkele! There were children crying "Mother!", "Father!"—but they were all smeared with blood and one could not recognize the children. I cried for my daughter. From afar I saw two women standing. I went up to them. They did not know me. I did not know them, and then I said who I was, and then they said: "So you survived." And there was another woman crying: "Pull me out from amongst the corpses. I am alive, help!" We were thinking how could we escape from the place. The cries of the woman, "Help, pull me out from the corpses!" We pulled her out. Her name was Mikla Rosenberg. We removed the corpses and the dying people who held on to her and continued to bite. She asked us to take her out, to free her, but we did not have the strength.

Attorney-General: It is very difficult to relate, I am sure, it is difficult to listen to, but we must proceed. Please tell us now: after that you hid?

Witness: And thus we were there all night, fighting for our lives, listening to the cries and the screams and all of a sudden we saw Germans, mounted Germans. We did not notice them coming in because of the screamings and the shoutings from the bodies around us.

Attorney-General: And then they rounded up the children and the others who had got out of the pit and shot them again?

Witness: The Germans ordered that all the corpses be heaped together into one big heap and with shovels they were heaped together, all the corpses, among them many still alive, children running about the place. I saw them. I saw the children. They were running after me, hanging on to me. Then I sat down in the field and remained sitting with the children around me. The children who got up from the heap of corpses.

Attorney-General: Then the Germans came again and rounded up the children?

Witness: Then Germans came and were going around the place. We were ordered to collect all the children, but they did not approach me, and I sat there watching how they collected the children. They gave a few shots and the children were dead. They did not need many shots. The children were almost dead, and this Rosenberg woman pleaded with the Germans to be saved, but they shot her.

Attorney-General: Mrs. Yosselevska, after they left the place, you went right next to the grave, didn't you?

Witness: They all left—the Germans and the non-Jews from around the place. They removed the machine guns and they took the trucks. I saw that they all left, and the four of us, we went on to the grave, praying to fall into the grave, even alive, envying those who were dead already and thinking what to do now. I was praying for death to come. I was praying for the grave to be opened and to swallow me alive. Blood was spurting from the grave in many places, like a well of water, and whenever I pass a spring now, I remember the blood which spurted from the ground, from that grave. I was digging with my fingernails, trying to join the dead in that grave. I dug with my fingernails, but the grave would not open. I did not have enough strength. I cried out to my mother, to my father: "Why did they not kill me? What was my sin? I have no one to go to. I saw them all being killed. Why was I spared? Why was I not killed?

And I remained there, stretched out on the grave, three days and three nights.

Attorney-General: And then a shepherd went by?

Witness: I saw no one. I heard no one. Not a farmer passed by. After three days, shepherds drove their herd to the field, and they began throwing stones at me, but I did not move. At night, the herds were taken back and during the day they threw stones believing that either it was a dead woman or a mad woman. They wanted me to rise, to answer. But I did not move. The shepherds were throwing stones at me until I had to leave the place.

Attorney-General: And then a farmer went by, and he took pity on you.

Witness: I hid near the grave. A farmer passed by, after a number of weeks.

Attorney-General: He took pity on you, he fed you, and he helped you join a group of Jews in the forest, and you spent the time until the summer of 1944 with this group, until the Soviets came.

Witness: I was with them until the very end.

24

Life Among the Partisans

Some victims of the Holocaust never reached the concentration camps or the gas chambers and ovens of the annihilation camps. There was no need to transport everybody over long distances; frequently, it was more efficient to liquidate them in situ. *This was the case with the family of seventeen-year-old Byrna Bar Oni, of whose nine members only she and her older sister survived by joining the partisans. Killed off by man and nature, typhus and hunger, of her original group of 370 only twenty-three lived to the end of their two years in the forest.*

Her hometown of Byten in Poland was first occupied by the Russians after the Nazi-Soviet Pact of 1939 and then by the Germans after their attack against the Soviet Union in the summer of 1941. Women and men were constantly abused and robbed by Lithuanian soldiers under German command. To meet repeated demands for gold, Jews had to have their gold fillings removed from their teeth. They lived in constant fear, confined to a ghetto behind barbed wire, squeezed as many as twenty to a room, and subjected to forced labor. Permeating their waking hours as well as their nightmares was the feeling that any day could be their last one.

Over three decades later, married and living in a Chicago suburb, Byrna still says: "I cannot forget those flames that consumed my faith in humanity. I cannot forget the past, the loved ones whom I have lost forever. Like a plant, a person uprooted this way cannot grow. The life that any refugee tries to build is without foundation."

On June 29, 1942, the ghetto in Slonim went through another liquidation. We learned of the details during the first days of July. This liquidation was no different from the others: first the ghetto had been blockaded; next the victims were taken in big trucks to the outskirts of town where gaping holes were ready for them; then they were shot.

Many Jews had tried to prepare for this day by digging hiding places under their vegetable gardens. The Germans knew this but were unable to find these havens during the short hours of the liquidation. So they set fire to the ghetto, burning alive many hundreds of Jews in their hiding places. Those who did come out leaped with their clothes flaming into the Szczara River.

There was more terror to come. On the banks of the same river stood a maternity hospital. The SS troopers marched into the hospital, grabbed infants by their feet, spread their legs until they were split in half and threw them through the windows into the river. That Friday the water of the river was red with the blood of Jewish infants. The mothers were shot in their beds. Later their bodies were burned in the inferno.

We in Byten knew that we were next in line. Diligently we prepared hiding places in the barns, cellars, caves, vegetable gardens and in the double floors and double roofs of the attics.

Father flatly informed us that he was not going to hide, that he would be the first to come out, for he welcomed death. Mother kept telling us that we should try our best to hide from our murderers, that, should we survive the war, we could join our brother or her brother and sisters in America.

Mother by now was quite ill and bothered by dizzy spells. She had been a heavy woman, about 180 pounds, and now she was only skin and bones. She had even shrunk in height and could hardly drag her feet. To the last minute, however, she tried to carry the yoke of the family. She would stand near the barbed wire and plead with passing farmers to bring her some flour or a little milk for her infant granddaughter in exchange for a dress, suit or a shirt. We children were so frightened that we accused her of not caring for our safety. Had the police caught her exchanging goods with the farmers, they would have killed her and the entire family.

Our White Russian neighbors were no more merciful than the German guards. For an egg or a little piece of cheese or a bite of bread, they took our last pieces of clothing. We were going to be killed anyway, they said; we would have no use for clothing. . . .

Friday, July 24, 1942. . . . when the workers returned they brought news that the local police had gathered farmers from three nearby villages and were forcing them to dig pits. The panic in the ghetto was overpowering. Each family inspected its hiding place. Rabbi Jaffe and Rabbi Lieberman conducted Friday night services, as usual, and chanted the part of the Torah that says, "*Nachamu, machamu ami*" ("Be comforted my people"). Sud-

"Life Among the Partisans" is from Byrna Bar Oni, *The Vapor* (Chicago: Visual Impact, Inc., 1976), pp. 45-71. Reprinted with the permission of the publisher.

denly several young men burst in, agitation reflected in their faces. They told the congregation to go home and prepare their hiding places. Our ghetto had been scheduled for liquidation. . . .

Later we learned that six trucks of police and one carload of Germans from Slonim, together with the gendarmes from Byten and our local White Russian police, had carried out the mission of liquidation. They had loaded 840 Jews on cattle trucks and beat them on the head to confuse them and prevent their resistance. The Jews were then driven to a big hole, where they were ordered to undress and lie down. They were machine-gunned from above.

Farmers from neighboring villages greedily hauled the clothes away, but not until the Germans searched pockets and linings for hidden diamonds or gold. The grave was covered with just a few shovelsful of dirt but the earth at the site wouldn't stop shaking. The pressure of blood oozing from the pit split the ground. . . .

* * *

We who escaped from Byten made our camp about three miles from Wolcze Nory on hilly and heavily wooded land. The first day we were shown how to build huts. We cut flexible twigs and bent them in a half circle. After firmly sticking the ends of the twigs in the soft ground, we braided more twigs for the top and sides. For the roof we peeled bark off the trees. Later we brought straw and spread it inside to protect against the dampness of the earth.

Men of our group went to neighboring villages and brought back food and utensils so we could start a communal kitchen. They also brought two milking cows to provide fresh milk for the children. Not always did the farmer give us food of his own free will. Often he did so because he feared our guns as well as our membership in the strong partisan movement.

Each day more and more groups of Jews came to the woods. Most of them came from Slonim, Kosov, Iwacewicze and Byten. With the group from Iwacewicze came a child from our group who had been lost in the woods. The six-year-old told us that she had fallen into a swamp and had not been able to get up. A few hours later, seeing people walk through the woods, she managed to drag herself out of the mud and follow them unnoticed. In the morning one of the Byten Jews recognized her and brought her to our camp.

Adjacent to our camp was Group 51, the pride of the partisan movement. Jews from Slonim, numbering about a hundred, they were all young men and heavily armed. Most of them had been employed by the Germans, sorting out weapons. It was they who smuggled military supplies to the partisans. . . .

We were Group 60. There were 200 of us and we were allotted the housekeeping chores. We worked in the communal kitchen, which served hot meals twice a day. We gathered firewood and made the fires, peeled potatoes and washed dishes. Women worked in the laundry, mended clothes and went to the fields every day to dig potatoes. Toward the end of the day, men loaded the sacks of potatoes and brought them to camp where they were stored underground for the winter.

One day, as we dug for potatoes, we suddenly heard gunfire and saw bullets overhead. Looking up I saw mounted police riding toward us. We all ran to the woods, but I was too far away to make it to cover. Seeing clusters of bushes in the middle of the field I crawled between the branches. I held my breath as the horsemen moved past me, but I was not noticed. After more shooting, the police left. They were a small group and did not dare enter the partisan stronghold. I ran back to the woods but lost my orientation; I did not find my group again until the next day. Luckily, no one had been killed.

It was difficult for us to come to terms with our new environment. The straw underneath didn't really keep us dry as we slept and we were covered by huge, white field-lice. They crawled into our long hair, which we couldn't cut for lack of scissors. We found it difficult to sleep nights because, though we were fully clothed, the lice managed to crawl all over us and bite us. Every night we made a fire, took off our clothes and held them above the flame until the heat made the lice drop into the fire. But it was a losing battle. As soon as we lay down, we were again covered with them.

My sister, Yentl, found the life particularly harsh. By nature delicate and sensitive, she could not even eat the food from the communal kitchen. Because she did not eat, she had no milk in her breasts for her son. The hungry baby sucked so hard that she would scream with pain. The lice made her break out in huge boils on her shoulders, her breasts and her feet. Yentl cried and blamed me for bringing her to the woods: "Byrna, you're responsible for my misery. It would have been easier to be killed by the Germans in the ghetto. We'll not survive the war—I nor my children. So why suffer? In the ghetto death comes quickly; in the ghetto you do not die alone, the community dies with you. Why should I live without my husband? My parents and so many who are dear to me have been liquidated." I would try to comfort her, to convince her to weather the hard times. "After the storm, good weather comes," I said. "You *do* have a reason to live—you have your son and daughter."

"No, we are all doomed. Look at Rochele. I can't shield her from her fright, from her longing for her dead father, from her fear that she might lose me, too. All the children in the woods are wise beyond their years. They don't cry, they don't ask for anything. The childish smiles have disappeared; their faces are lined with knowledge and cares that children should not have." . . .

By this time, our Group 60 numbered 370 Jews who had escaped from the Byten, Iwacewicze and Kosov ghettos. With us were six infants and 24 children. We organized a kindergarten and taught them songs and dances to make them forget, at least for a short time, the nightmare of their young lives. . . .

Our Group 60, with its many women, children and old people, was now called *"Semejner lager,"* the family group. Still, the partisan chief of staff sent us a Russian to instruct us in the use of weapons and a Russian supervisor named Seryosha who was our political leader.

More recent escapees from Byten told us the situation was so horrible that even the gendarmes had expressed pity.

As we later learned, the Byten Jews found an end to their suffering on August 29, 1942. At four o'clock that Saturday morning, the ghetto was surrounded by Lithuanians, who were stationed in Byten to give "protection to the city against the partisans." They entered the homes of the remaining inhabitants, dragged them out of their hiding places, clubbing them over the heads. Herding them in front of a Jewish home, they ordered the Jews to sit motionless in the street. They sat without moving until 10 a.m., by which time the murderers had found every last one of the 140 remaining Jews. The marched them down Church Street to the grave that contained the first 840. A man who had owned a liquor store before the war tried to run away and hid in the bushes. The gendarmes shot him down as he fled. On command, the Jews took off their clothes and lay down in the grave. A volley of bullets penetrated the convulsive bodies. The dead and the wounded were then covered with earth still soaked with blood of the victims of the first liquidation. Before they fired, the gendarmes took the best of the clothes. The rest were left for the farmers.

We received the news of the second liquidation with indifference. We had become conditioned to the idea that we were all marked for death. We had escaped into the woods but we gave ourselves little chance to survive the war. We only hoped that when our time came, we would die taking vengeance for the spilled Jewish blood.

Soon it was decided that our group would be subdivided according to military tasks. Two departments would be responsible for sabotaging the enemy and providing food for the entire group. The third department was to keep careful watch over the woods. Guard posts were set up in all the camps and on the outskirts of the woods. At any indication of suspicious activity or sign of danger, we were to fire three shots to warn the other partisans. I was the only girl in our camp who was assigned to guard duty. Every day I stood guard for eight hours. . . .

* * *

Early in the morning of Friday, September 18, we were summoned to a meeting by our political commanding officers. They read a radio message from the White Russian secretary of the Central Committee in Moscow, ordering the partisans to unite and to intensify their sabotage operations against the enemy. As we started to applaud the message, an airplane flying very low circled our camp. We were under close observation. At the same time we heard shooting just a few miles away. The officers ordered us to assume a defensive position. We camouflaged our food reserves, extra clothing and kitchen utensils. As the airplane came around again we dispersed to shelter. The rumor was that the Germans had launched a major attack against the partisans.

At two that afternoon we heard shooting from the direction of our patrol post, no more than a quarter of a mile from our camp. Seryosha, our political leader, ordered us to go deeper into the woods. As we lay flat beneath the foliage of the fallen trees, we saw partisans from a neighboring group running past, some of them wounded. It was the first group to be attacked: only 250 people to fight against thousands of Germans equipped with tanks and armed with machine guns and grenades. We later learned that 40,000 German troops had been ordered to fight the partisans in eastern Poland, White Russia and the Ukraine. With the retreat of one of our groups, the partisan opposition broke down and chaos prevailed. The central executive staff and its commander-in-chief left their camping place and disappeared deep in the woods.

Toward evening, our group of 350 gathered at a dry place, an island surrounded by mud and slime. It was getting dark and the shooting had quieted down. Seryosha told us we were to stay there for the night.

Yentl and her two children were overcome with fatigue. Rochele, the six-year-old, clung to her mother and cried that she was cold, wet and hungry. The infant, Matys, clung tightly to Yentl's dry breasts, sucking pus from her boils instead of milk.

Rochele had lost her shoes running through the woods and had cut her feet on the thorns. I took off my high-laced shoes and gave them to her to protect her soft feet as much as possible from the wild overgrown burdock and bramble. I was overcome with pain as I looked at my family, but I tried to comfort them: "Tomorrow it will quiet down; we'll go back to our camp and find food then." But all the while we smelled the smoke of our burning tents and huts. We slept little that night, praying that morning would never come, for we knew what awaited us.

At sunrise we heard the Germans shooting wildly. We gathered around Seryosha who was still calm, a trained soldier who had seen many battles. His instincts were quick and sensitive and he was able to endure stress, cold and hunger better than any of us. He not only knew how to use terrain for camouflage but he was an extraordinary night fighter. Calmly he listened, trying to pinpoint the German positions. The shooting seemed to get closer by the minute. Seryosha decided that we should divide into groups and that each group should move deeper into the woods, meanwhile keeping in contact with the others.

My sisters and I were in a group of about 100 people with Seryosha. We wandered through the woods the whole day. Everywhere we saw corpses of partisans. The boots of some of the dead had been removed and the pockets of their clothing turned inside out. Some lay on their backs with their eyes to the skies, as if they were saying: "See what you did to us!" I myself saw the bodies of friends with whom I had gone to school.

The weather was exceptionally hot and dry. Fear made us forget our hunger, but we could not overcome the parched feeling of our dry mouths. We were slowly dehydrating. The children cried with the last strength they possessed. Hearing their cries, the Germans stepped up their shooting and shouted, "Halt!" Seryosha, who had taken such devoted care of the babies and the small children, asked the mothers with infants to leave the rest of the group because they jeopardized the survival of all of us.

Yentl and her son joined five other women and their small children. They walked to a secluded area to stay overnight. Rochele did not want her mother to go and started to cry. I embraced her tightly and tried to assure her that next day we would all be together again.

The next morning, Sunday, the mothers came back to us carrying dead children. My sister was the only one whose baby was still alive. Rochele kissed and hugged her mother, but the reunion was not a joyful one. Yentl, her face the color of ash, lay bare the woes of the scene she had witnessed the night before.

We couldn't keep our children quiet. They felt our fear and our restlessness. The woods have a language of their own, and every murmur of the leaves, every sound of a squirrel running in the trees made us panic. We were sure the enemy had found us. Suddenly Golda, who was sick and distraught over losing her husband, began wrapping her child with her shawl. With a terrible blank look on her face, she choked her baby to death. The rest of the mothers tried to stop her, but then something happened: they too, became engulfed in some unexplainable madness—a kind of mass hysteria—and began to choke their babies to death.

I stood there confused. Was I dreaming all this? Or was I witnessing a madness beyond my comprehension?" She paused in her recital, then added softly, "Look at them, Byrna. At what price we buy life."

It was heartbreaking to see the mothers rejoining their families. One man took his dead child from his wife and kissed it fervently, covering the body with a torrent of tears. One young mother knocked her head against a tree while her husband stood in a stupor, his dead child in his arms. We had to do something before the Germans, hearing our hysteria, discovered us.

A few men took the dead children from their mothers and placed them close together under a fallen tree, covering them with leaves and branches. We left them hurriedly because again we heard shots and wild shouts of "Halt, halt!" The woods were no longer big enough for us; the low-flying airplanes kept the Germans informed of our exact position.

Monday, the fourth day of the siege, Yentl could no longer run. I took Matys from her arms; with my other hand I held my niece. As we ran, I kept calling my sisters to stay close and keep up with us.

We and the 15 people remaining in our group ran nearly 10 miles that day. Toward evening, when the shooting lessened, we stopped running and looked around to see who remained with us. Then I looked down to the baby in horror. He was black and blue, dead by suffocation. I must have held him too tightly. We cried and cursed the angry God who was not satisfied that the Germans, Lithuanians and White Russians were killing us but had to make us agents of death as well. I took off my slip and wrapped Matys in it.

With us was a pious man who kept praying no matter how great our suffering. He had a little hand shovel with him. I asked him to help us bury Matys, but he refused because it was not yet sundown and still Yom Kippur. I argued that it was more sinful to let a child's body be eaten by wolves than to help put him to his final rest. Finally he gave in, and under a huge old tree in the strange woods we buried Matys. Every year when I attend Yom Kippur services I pray only for forgiveness from my poor Matys. Before he had a chance to know life, he knew hunger, thirst, filth and a tragic death. All this, because he was born a Jew.

It was quieter the next day. We gathered berries, tried to dig for water with our bare hands and rested. Then we set out to search for others of our people. What we found were corpses. Some were tied to tree trunks, their tongues torn out, shoulders and arms wrenched from their sockets, hips bowed, knees turned inward, teeth clamped together, fingers bent in claws, faces contorted, eyeballs bulging and their private parts burned by fire. By these signs we knew that some of them had been captured alive. What we saw made us pray that if we had to die, it would be by bullet and not by slow torture. Many partisans kept loaded revolvers and were prepared to shoot themselves rather than fall into German hands.

In our wandering we came across a dead deer. Flies and vermin swarmed over the carcass and the smell was terrible. Still, we cut out its liver and roasted it over a little fire. Yentl refused to eat it; the sight made her nauseous. All of my pleadings did not help. Rochele's condition was almost as bad as her mother's. Her face was sunken, her body badly scratched by nettle weeds. . . .

[In a sudden ambush, Byrna lost her sister Yentl and her niece Rochele.]

Six months later my worst fears were realized. Moshe Witkow from Byten told me that, alongside the roadway leading to the village of Kochanowo, he had seen seven corpses in a pile, some of them women and children. I asked him to take me to this place. Among the seven skeletons I recognized Yentl by the half-rotted fur collar on her coat. Only one of her legs still had flesh. My little niece I recognized by the high-laced shoes I had given her. It looked at if all seven people had been caught alive and burned on a bonfire.

Moshe helped me dig a grave. We buried all seven in the one pit. As he chanted the *El Molei Rachamin,* I thought of the irony of that psalm which praises our merciful God. I stood there numb and without tears, feeling only that life means nothing. Life suddenly snatched away becomes only a troubling dream, a persistent vapor. I raised my eyes to heaven; the burning sun was shining in undisturbed glory on an earth soaked with human blood. The ancient trees murmured tales of tragedies they had witnessed.

25

A Refuge Above the Pigs

Marynia was one of eight children of a poor Jewish carpenter in Poland. At sixteen, she had just embarked upon a promising ballet career when the war broke out in 1939. Soon she was on the run from persecution.

She tried but failed to cross the border into Russia. She had been betrayed and humilated by Poles and Germans. Along her thorny calvary she married Wiktor, a young Jew also on the run, whom she later lost in the whirlpool of the Holocaust.

In the summer of 1942, the noose around her tightened, when the Jews in her town were being rounded up for deportation. By then she knew that most of her and her husband's extensive families were caught in the deadly net of the "Final Solution."

She managed to hide for a few months in farmer Drobinski's attic over the pigsty. Then she had to flee again, sleeping on park benches, even seeking shelter with an old German officer, who luckily for her was impotent. She ended up, with false papers, "volunteering" for labor in Germany as a Polish girl, surviving bombardments and close calls with Nazis visiting her place of work. She was a simple girl, and yet her resourcefulness repeatedly carried her over the hurdles of deadly dangers.

After the war she dispatched a letter to her uncles in America, addressed thus:

MAURICE ISAAC SILVERSTEIN
ROCHESTERNY AKRONOHIO
BECKAVE
CLIFFORDAVE
EDGEWOODAVE
NOBLEAVE

Postmaster: Please find my uncle.
Thank you.

The postmaster found both uncles, and in the summer of 1946 they welcomed her to America.

In the excerpt below Marynia tells of her hiding place over the pigsty.

Hiding a Jew endangered the entire Polish family. We had heard of instances when not only an entire Polish family was shot, but the farm completely burned out—everything, the house, the animals, the farm equipment. The Germans so wanted to make sure that no Polish farmer would dare harbor a Jew. . . .

Mr. Drobinski . . . had prepared a place for me to sleep—in the attic directly above the pigsty. It would be warm and comfortable, he said, and most important of all, no one would ever suspect anyone there. I was happy.

Later on, I climbed up the ladder to my new quarters. Straw covered the entire floor. In one corner, there was more straw than in the rest of the place. There was also a small pillow and a dark, wool blanket.

It was a warm night with not a breeze in the air and I didn't need the blanket. I rolled it up and placed it in the corner, hoping the war would be over before I would need to use it.

I lay on the soft straw, exhausted yet unable to sleep. The pressures of the day just past had been enormous for me to be able to just set them aside and relax. Everything that had happened that day came before my eyes for the second time. I actually recreated all in my mind and relived the entire situation, from the moment in which we were first notified of the newest anti-Jewish law issued by the Germans, to the panic in our house and subsequent separation. . . .

Many weeks passed. I still lay in the attic above the pigsty. Mrs. Drobinski sent up food to me once a day, sufficient to fill my stomach, but often the mashed potatoes were cold and dry, having a choking effect. Nevertheless, I was thankful for that. . . .

On rare occasions and under strict precautions, I was permitted to come down into the farmer's house. The windows were then covered carefully and our voices hushed. Occasionally, I even had my meal downstairs and this was a real treat.

Despite all, I didn't feel at ease there. I had been paying the Drobinskis for weekly keep, but I had the feeling they expected more. Soon they commanded me to work for them. Once Mr. Drobinski called me down from the attic and said that I had to scrub the floor in their bedroom and kitchen. I got on my knees and scrubbed till I was dizzy. The two rooms were very big, the floors made of long, porous wooden boards with many cracks in between them and mud filling the cracks.

I hadn't realized how weak a state I had been in, while lying on the straw in the attic. The realization came to me only now, every time I would bend my head down to scrub Drobinskis' muddy floors.

For the first time in a long time tears started flowing from my eyes, mixing with the hot scrub-water. I still remember, they were tears of despair

"A Refuge Above the Pigs" is from Marilla Feld, *I Chose to Live* (New York: Manor Books, Inc., 1979), pp. 124-40, 272. Reprinted with the kind permission of the publisher.

and dejection; tears of heartbrokenness and anguish; tears of anger and deep disappointment—all coupled with extreme loneliness. . . .

Time passed slowly without any sign of an end to the war. Lying in the attic afforded me sufficient opportunity for thinking and planning. I knew that this arrangement could not go on for very much longer. The farmers began to be restless, the risk was too great; no solution was in sight. . . .

A few weeks went by again. I was in Drobinski's kitchen, washing the dishes. Suddenly, Drobinski jumped at me and dragged me off into the bedroom. Before I could utter a word, I was pushed into a big wardrobe and locked inside. All I could hear Drobinski say was:

"If you let out one peep in there, so help me. . . I. . . I will kill you! Yes, I'll kill you! Your husband is coming here. . . ! Be quiet, you hear? Be absolutely quiet, I advise you!" There was determination in his voice.

Oh, my dear God! Wiktor was at the door already, before I even caught my next breath. I heard him ask for me.

"Mr. Drobinski, where is my wife?"

". . . Have no idea, Wiktor," said the farmer coolly.

"Please, Mr. Drobinski, help me. Marynia must be here. Let me see her please."

"Do you think me such a fool as to harbor a Jew?!"

"Where else could she have gone? She didn't know anybody! I beg you, let me talk to her. . . . I need her . . . I am so lost. . . " His voice broke, and tears streamed down his sunken face. His lips were quivering.

Broken up by intense fear for his life, Wiktor finally fell on his knees, begging the farmer:

"Oh please . . . I can't stand it any longer . . . I have no place to go to . . . Where is my Marynia? . . . She'll help me, I know . . ."

Drobinski was unmoved. There was too much at stake. Afraid of his own and his family's lives, he grabbed Wiktor's arm and pushed him out the door, saying:

"Go away, you are endangering us all, Jew! Disappear quickly!"

I heard some incoherent voices, then a short scuffle between the two men, and finally there was silence. I stood horrified and choked up inside the dark closet. It was surprising that I didn't suffer a heart attack right there. I began shaking violently. Although my pity for Wiktor was piercing my heart. I was in no position to help him. . . .

Little did he know how shaky my safety with the Drobinskis had been. As the weeks went by, they talked more and more about the risk they were taking in hiding me; that I didn't pay them enough money; that no one else would take such chances as they; it was too dangerous and that soon they would have to ask me to leave. . . .

Drobinski was meaner every day. I felt that he even resented having to bring my food to the attic every evening. I was getting increasingly scared of him.

Christmas came. I remember lying above the pigs, extremely cold, unable to fall asleep. The blanket was not sufficient to keep me warm. My head was against the thin boards that had parted from each other because of poor fit. The howling wind had easy access to my face and neck. There was no spot where I could hide from the wind.

It began to snow, and the wind was now blowing in snow flakes through the cracks in the wall, onto my pillow and my face. I pulled the small blanket over my head but I couldn't breathe very well and my feet were freezing. I curled up into a ball to keep warm.

Suddenly, in my distress, I heard singing and happy voices coming from the farmer's house. The Drobinskis were celebrating Christmas. . . .

I was above the pigs, cold and hungry, and dejected, and desperately afraid of being discovered. I cried and cried that night of Christmas Eve in 1942 more than any other time I can remember. Burning tears were running down my cheeks, sinking into the cold pillow. Before long, the pillow was frozen and I had to turn it over.

It must have been the music and the gaiety coming from the farmer's house that emphasized my own misery. The contrast and the irony of our lives, the farmer's and my own, was unbearable. All I could do was weep, while in the cracks above my head icicles were forming in silence.

Christmas came and went. . . . For me, every day was an eternity. . . .

I was forever so cold and underfed and, worst of all, so very lonely. The not knowing, the infinite uncertainty of what was in the future and how long my torture would last, nearly drove me mad. I really wanted to die.

Once as I was at the lowest ebb possible. I heard some noise in my attic. It was late at night, after midnight, and for a moment my heart stopped beating. But I soon recognized Drobinski who was tugging at my blanket and whispering:

"Come on down, little girl. Come into the house to warm up a bit."

I threw my arms around him, thanking him, and quickly followed him down the ladder. On the way to the house he explained that Mrs. Drobinski had left earlier that evening for Ludowny. She had to go to the doctor, some specialist. She wouldn't come back till the following evening.

We reached the kitchen, tiptoed into the bedroom. The Drobinski boy was sleeping in his bed. Drobinski pointed to the other bed where I was to get in. Almost simultaneously, he got in with me and placed his hand over my mouth, while whispering into my ear:

"Look, honey, you are frozen stiff, I want you to warm up. Don't be afraid of me, I really feel sorry for you, I really like you a lot . . . "

He pulled me closer to him, and I could not resist. My head was spinning. The noise in my ears was a stormy sea. I closed my eyes and called upon God to be witness to my mental anguish. For the first time in a long time, I was warm and comfortable and loved. I was completely helpless physically . . . and psychologically drained.

Before dawn, I returned to the attic above the pigsty. It was then that I made the decision to write a book someday. There were just too many traumatic experiences stored up within me. I knew that some day, I would have to tell about them.

It was then also that I seriously worried whether, if I should survive, I would be normal and sane. How much would I be blamed for, I wondered. Interestingly enough, I didn't feel as guilty as convention in those days would have me feel. That night with Drobinski, for instance, may sound awful. But I knew that I had been trapped and there was no use fighting off my attacker. I would have only aroused his son and endangered our lives, all three at once. Drobinski certainly could have put me outside in the snow, had I angered him.

As it was, Drobinski became nastier and angrier soon afterward. . . . I knew that he would not keep me much longer.

26

The End of a Love Story

Liliana was seventeen when the war ended in 1945, but her experiences add up to the life stories of several mature women. Between the German danger from the west and the Russians from the east, her Jewish family fled from place to place, ending up in the Warsaw ghetto. From there her grandparents and parents were taken away to concentration camps, and she never saw any of them again. She survived by working in a factory and being smuggled out into hiding by her family's maid Marysia.

At the age of fifteen she married Anek, a fighter for the Polish underground group that engaged in sabotage and in attacks on Germans and Polish turncoats collaborating with the Gestapo. A year later he was killed in the Warsaw uprising. Aided by Anek's sister Kazia, she survived with falsified documents, changing her hiding place several times, often under the noses of the Germans. At one point she helped cater a party for them. Liberation was no instant bed of roses for her.

After the war, Liliana moved to a Displaced Persons' camp in Berlin, and now makes her home with her engineer husband and two daughters in Maryland.

One beautiful, sunny, but very cold morning in January 1945 (we really had not noticed how beautiful it was because we were freezing in bed) we heard movement on the highway. It meant one thing: the Germans were withdrawing from Pyry and the surrounding areas. We ran out to look and ask questions. They were taking horses and wagons from the farmers, piling on them what they could, and running west. Heavy artillery, tanks, cars of all sizes and descriptions, everything was going west. That was it, the Russians were moving forward. The Germans passed through Pyry all day and all night, just a long line of people and machinery. The next day the high command left.

We sat around the table the whole night, waiting. The traffic on the highway stopped and we heard shots, but from far away. Now that the Germans were gone, the Russians would come without a fight. We heard that the division that had left Pyry was destroyed near Lowicz.

The next morning, around ten o'clock, we heard the sound of heavy wheels on the road, and after a few minutes the first Russian tanks entered Pyry. Everyone stayed home and watched from behind their curtains to see what would happen next. If fighting started, we were ready to run to the basement.

The tanks were enormous, looking more than two stories high. Suddenly they stopped, a few soldiers came out, talked to each other, and stamped their feet to warm up. A short while later, we heard a voice speaking very clearly in Polish. It was an order from the commander in the civilian population. We were not to go out on the streets for a few more hours, because they were unsure whether some Germans were not hiding in the nearby forest. Otherwise everybody was free and could go to their homes as soon as possible. Then he said that after the tanks moved ahead the Polish army was coming.

From afar we could hear the noise of the planes. In a few minutes we could see them coming out of the clouds. The soldiers stood by the tanks looking up because they were their planes. But suddenly the planes came down and started to shoot at them. Every one of the soldiers dived under the tanks, the planes flew away, then came back again once more and were gone. After a while the loudspeaker came on again and told us that the Russian planes had made a mistake, that it happened often when the front moved so fast.

In the early afternoon the tanks moved west and the infantry moved in. That is how the first day under Russian occupation passed. It was the first day I was free; I could go out and tell everybody who I was. No Gestapo or concentration camp hung over my head.

"The End of a Love Story" is from Liliana Zuker-Bujanowska, *Liliana's Journal, Warsaw 1939-1945* (New York: Dial Press, 1980), pp. 113-27. Reprinted with the permission of the publisher.

We waited a week before we decided to go to Warsaw and see if it was possible to live there. . . .

We could not use the highways; the soldiers said some were full of mines. We decided to go through the fields. Polish winters are cold, windy and snowy, this one was a little worse than some, or maybe we felt the cold more. We were undernourished and not properly dressed, even though we had put on layers and layers of clothes. The snow was deep and it was a slow walk. We were a little afraid to walk alone, so after a while we joined a group of men and women who were going in the same direction. Finally we came to the river, Wisla, but the two big bridges were gone. The Germans had blown them up before leaving. Only twisted metal and piles of rubble were left. They had even mined the ice on the river, but since then the river had frozen again and all of us decided to cross it. It would have been pretty easy if the ice had been flat, but the explosions had formed little mountains in the middle of the river and we had to walk zig-zagging. . . .

The city was in ruins. People returning had no place to live. The city had no water and no electricity. Everyone who lived in the city was required to work a specified number of hours cleaning the rubble from the streets so that traffic could be restored more or less to normal.

To get water we had to go to the pump two blocks away and wait in line. Sometimes I came home without the water because the pump had run dry. We melted snow and ice for washing and for the toilet.

The streets were full of people, but it was difficult to imagine where they lived. If it was barely possible to make a room habitable, people did it. Very few were as lucky as we were. All we had to do was board up the broken windows. We had beds, chairs, tables, dishes, a stove—all the necessities of life.

Most returning residents were forced to work for days before their repairs made their places livable. They searched the ruins for building materials, using old bricks and half-burned wood. We often saw a completely burned house with a newly built room somewhere in the rear where the family lived. The downtown was in ashes. Street after street was completely in rubble. It was very dangerous to walk close to the ruins because when the wind blew strongly, pieces of brick flew everywhere.

Shortly after we returned to the city, Kazia and I went to look for Anek's grave. We knew, more or less, where he had been killed. We began looking around the Plaza of Three Crosses and Mokotowska Street. The sidewalks and little gardens were full of graves. Some had crosses with names on them, some had nothing. The places where the fight had been bloodiest had the most graves. It did not take us long to find the grave we were looking for. It was in a small garden on Mokotowska Street and it had a cross with his name carved on it. We had no doubt that it was Anek buried there. We stood there in that quiet little garden for a long time. We did not talk; we just wept. People passed by, like us, looking for graves of their loved ones.

They thought we were lucky to find "our grave." Many of them would never know where their loved ones had been put to rest. Those who had died in the first days of the uprising were buried in the individual graves, but later, when there were more casualities and less time, they were buried in mass graves and often with no names.

The government informed the public that in the spring, families could dig up the bodies and take them to the military cemetery for burial. Graves without names would be taken care of by the government. Those bodies would be taken to a specially built mausoleum.

* * *

In the beginning of March Marysia and I decided to go to Kalisz to see what was left of my family's properties. Passenger trains were not running yet, but the military transport trains took civilians who wanted to go to their hometowns. There were hundreds of people waiting for this kind of transportation.

I said good-bye to Kazia, promising her that I would be back when it was time to move Anek's body to his final resting place. Words could not express what I felt. How could I just say thank you to her. How can you ever repay somebody who saved your life, at the same time endangering her own. We were both crying, but we were happy that we both had made it, and we were to be back together in a month or two.

We were lucky enough to get on a freight train. Before the war it had been a cattle train, during the war it had been used to transport soldiers, and now it was used for whatever was necessary. We climbed into a dark car that looked almost empty. Then we noticed a small iron stove with a few soldiers and civilians sitting around it. They looked at two helpless women and let us in. Marysia was terrified. We had heard about rapes taking place on the trains. It was cold in the car, and the men sat close to the fire without paying much attention to us. We did not look very interesting, with our bulky coats and heavy woolen shawls wrapped around us—anything but sexy. The trip should have taken about six to eight hours; it took two days and two nights. The train would stop for hours in the middle of nowhere, waiting for more important transports to pass by. After the first day, the trip grew worse by the minute. There was not enough wood to keep the little stove burning all the time. At night we sat close together to keep warm, afraid to fall asleep, keeping watch over our meager belongings. Our companions left the train at different stops, until finally we had only three soldiers with us. The bread we had with us was gone, we had to move around to keep warm, and we thought this trip would never end. Finally, after two days, very early in the morning, we arrived in Kalisz.

We had about a twenty-minute walk from the station to the Rypinek section of town, where, we were hoping, Marysia's cousin Janka still lived. We were chilled to the bone and hungry when we arrived in Kazimierz and Janka's house. Janka almost fainted when she saw us. They fed us a big breakfast, we talked a little, and then we went to sleep. We slept for twenty-four hours in a clean warm bed.

The city had not been ruined. The Germans had left in such a hurry that they had had not time to mine the roads or the buildings. However, they did take with them any movable objects from the houses they had occupied. In the time between their escape and the entrance of the Russians, thieves took the rest. Many of the naturalized Germans, the *Volksdeutsche,* stayed. They had no place to run to, and they were the ones people turned against. Most of them were put in jails, to be tried later.

Little by little, prewar residents began to return. The apartments evacuated by the Germans were occupied by the first arrivals, but after a few days the temporary government sealed empty apartments and houses. They were to be claimed by the rightful owners. If people could find their furniture, wherever it might be, they were entitled to a permit to move it to their dwelling.

My apartment had already been taken by someone, but our possessions were not there. I did not try to claim my apartment legally; it was too big for me anyway. I wanted the apartment where my grandmother Maria had lived. It had also been taken, but if I really needed it, I could legally get it. The people would have to move. The housing officials asked me if I would take the same size apartment one floor below. I agreed. It did not make much difference; both apartments had a few pieces of furniture, but none that had belonged to my grandmother.

It was a nice, clean place, full of sunshine. It was furnished with a bed, a little table, and a wardrobe in what became my bedroom, and an old sofa in the other room. The kitchen was in working order and the bathroom looked beautiful. . . .

Day after day we searched for the furniture from my family's apartment, or those of my grandparents, with no luck. Marysia remembered that we had left the sewing machine with a family that became *Volksdeutsche.* I went to their apartment and told them that I wanted the machine back. The man was afraid of his own shadow and gave it to me without an argument. He did not even ask if I had a permit from the agency to take it.

Before we had left Kalisz, mother had taken some curtains, linens, pillows, and blankets to the farmer we used to spend summers with. I rented a wagon and we went there, fourteen kilometers on terrible back roads. The farmer and his family had been certain nobody would return. When they saw us, they thought they were hallucinating. First they said the Germans had taken everything, and then that they had had to sell our things for food. After a long conversation they gave me back part of the things we had left. I was happy with what I received.

Some people we met gave us a table and a few chairs. Marysia's family supplied a few dishes, pots, and pans. And so we were settled.

Though I was busy with all these arrangements, I did not forget about the family's jewels buried on the grounds of the factory before we left Kalisz in August of 1939. I was afraid to go near the place immediately. I thought somebody might be spying on me and ready to kill for it. I wanted to wait a little, until life in town became more orderly and, most important, the earth soft enough to dig. Finally we went, Marysia and I.

The two large buildings were the same but everything around them had changed. All the little sheds and the garden were gone. The high wall and the janitor's cottage were gone. Where the garden had been was a new street. The two large buildings had been joined into one big paper factory. The doors were sealed now by the Polish government, and not a soul was in sight.

I was completely disoriented and had no idea where to look for the shed. I thought the place was probably where the street ran now. Marysia and I looked at each other and felt completely helpless. When I look back now, I think I gave up too easily. I was afraid to go to the police and tell them the truth. Who knows what would have happened. I did go to the office whose address was on the document tacked to the doors. I told them who I was, that I was the only survivor of the war, and asked what I could do to get the property back.

They told me that if I could open the factory and start production—paper was badly needed—I could be the manager of the factory. I knew I could not do it alone, but perhaps I could find some of the men who had worked there before the war who knew the machinery, and we could give it a try. I went to a lawyer, an old friend of the family, and told him about it. He advised me against it. He said that all I would have was a big headache. Even if I succeeded in starting the factory, it would eventually be nationalized. But perhaps the government would pay me something for the land and the buildings. I left him my power to represent me and that was the end of my dream of getting some money out of the factory. . . .

The dream of finding the little jar full of jewelry was gone. I had to do something to earn money.

The sewing courses that I had taken in school in Warsaw came in handy. With the sewing machine I had now, I started my own little business. Nobody had new materials, but everybody had some old clothes that needed to be made longer or shorter, larger or smaller, and I was there to do it. I was on my own and making a living for myself and Marysia.

* * *

About the middle of March, I received a letter from Kazia. She had obtained a permit to move Anek's body to the cemetery. . . .

The day after I received Kazia's letter, I packed a little bag with a change of clothes and went to Warsaw. Traveling conditions were much better. The trains were now passenger trains—not first-class Pullmans, but much better than the cattle train we had ridden to Kalisz. The train was full of smugglers who were buying food in small villages and taking it to Warsaw, where they sold it at enormous profit. The government tried to prevent this kind of profiteering, but with little success. Warsaw was a major market.

Kazia was very happy to see me. The following day, will all the necessary papers, we went to the cemetery to choose a place for Anek's final rest. In fact, it was not necessary, as we discovered when we arrived. Men worked day and night digging the graves, and as the coffins arrived, they were put in—that was it. There was no such thing as a better or worse place. A whole section of the National Cemetery had been set aside for victims of the uprising. As soon as the box was put in the grave, one man carved the name on the small wooden cross. They had stocks of them ready to be marked.

Another part of the same cemetery was set aside for unidentified coffins and there were many, many of those. In the middle of this section the government had plans to build a mausoleum to the unknown soldier.

When we had all the papers ready, we rented a wooden wagon—a wooden platform on four wheels—and we went to Mokotowska Street. We could see wagons with wooden coffins moving from everywhere toward the cemetery. The government was exhorting the people to do this grim job as fast as possible before the warm weather came. March this year was warm, and we could already smell the odor coming from the shallow graves. With the warm weather, the cleaning of the rubble started full scale and in almost every building people found more bodies, most of the time just a pile of bones.

We hired two men to help dig the grave. We were not sure whether Anek had been buried in a box or just wrapped in cloth, though we suspected that Jan had put the body in a coffin. We had a Polish flag to drape over it.

Some of the graves in the little garden were already empty. While we were there two other families came for their loved ones. The two men worked quickly though we thought it took hours. When the shovels touched something hard, we breathed a little easier: it was wood. We had both thought about the same thing: what would happen if there was no casket. We would have to pick up the bones.

The men lifted the long wooden box with ropes and set it on the ground. We were so nervous, so shaken, that we did not know what to do first. Kazia wanted to open the box, to be sure that it was Anek. She wanted to see with her own eyes that there was no mistake, that it was her brother in there. She told the men to open the coffin.

The men started to pull at the lid of the box. The rusted nails made noisy squeaks. The wood was almost black and looked partially decomposed. It took them a while to loosen all the nails. Finally the lid came loose but no one had the courage to open the box. Thousands of thoughts swirled in my mind. Maybe it was a mistake, maybe it was not Anek in that box, maybe he was somewhere in a German prison camp. I could smell the freshly turned earth, the odor of the decomposing wood, and felt as if I was going to faint. I clutched Kazia's sleeve in order not to fall. In that moment Kazia raised the lid a little. It was Anek, there was no doubt about it. He had on the same suit he had worn when he left home, though the color had changed some—it was darker. His hands were crossed on his chest. They were dark brown and there was no flesh on them. I was afraid to look at his face, but it was covered with a white handkerchief. On one side of him we saw a bottle with a white piece of paper inside. Kazia snatched it and broke it on a piece of stone. The noise was like a shot and the glass scattered everywhere. The wind blew the little piece of paper close to my feet, but I could not bend down to pick it up. I felt as if my arms were made from stone. Somebody picked up the paper and gave it to Kazia. On the paper, in Jan's handwriting, was Anek's name, birth date, the date of his death, and his pseudonym. There was no mistake; it was Anek.

The men closed the box, covered it with the Polish flag, and loaded it onto the wagon. We had not realized that a crowd had gathered around us. Two Russian soldiers stood looking at the box covered with the flag. Somebody took me by the arm and walked me out of the little garden. Kazia and I sat on the side of the wagon and held the box so that it would not slide during the long trip to the cemetery. The horse was trotting fairly fast, the streets were in terrible shape, full of holes from the bombs, and so the trip was far from smooth. When we arrived at the gate of the cemetery, four men lifted the box and carried it to the waiting grave. It happened so fast that Kazia barely had time to pay the men on the wagon. By the time we ran to the graveside, the box was already being lowered into the grave. We threw some earth on top of it and the sound echoed in our hearts. We waited until the grave was covered and the cross put in place. Slowly we walked out of the cemetery. We were the only family there to take Anek to his final rest. Jan was not back from the German camp yet and Rita had nobody to leave the children with.

Two days after the burial I went back to Kalisz.

27

A Happy Ending

Cyla Muller was married to the young architect Simon Wiesenthal in Lwow, Poland, when the war tore them apart. With his help she managed to procure false identity papers and hoped to survive under the name "Irena Kowalska," a gentile, residing at Topiel Street in Warsaw.

That entire street had been wiped out by German bombs, and all who had lived there were thought to have perished. Her husband heard about it while at Gross Rosen concentration camp.

The grieving husband, having miraculously escaped two firing squads, emaciated, heartbroken over the loss of his beloved wife, was eventually liberated at the concentration camp of Mauthausen. He started working for the American War Crimes Investigation Commission.

What followed was the wondrous "resurrection" of Cyla Wiesenthal.

After the establishment of the four military zones of Austria in 1945, Mauthausen became part of the Soviet zone. Our War Crimes group moved to Linz, in the U.S. Zone. Many of the former inmates of Mauthausen were brought to a Displaced Persons camp that had been set up in the public school in Leonding, a small town near Linz.

A little boy named Adolf Hitler had spent his first school days in this school. We slept on cots in a classroom whose windows looked out on a small house that was the former home of Hitler's parents. They were buried in the cemetery at the end of the road. I didn't particularly like the view from the room and moved out of the school after a few days. I rented a modest furnished room in the Landstrasse in Linz. Not much of a room, really, but from the window I could see a small garden.

I spent the mornings at the War Crimes office and the afternoons at the newly established Jewish Committee in Linz (later expanded into the Jewish Central Committee of the U.S. Zone in Austria), of which I became vice-chairman. The Committee set up a makeshift office in two small rooms.

The rooms were always crowded. In the months after the war our visitors were human wrecks who always seemed to be wearing somebody else's clothes. They had sunken cheeks and bloodless lips. Many said they had been at Mauthausen. We recognized each other by stories of SS men we all knew or by memories of friends who had died. Some of them acted like people who had just survived an earthquake or a hurricane and cannot understand why they have been saved while everybody else has died in the disaster. They would ask each other: "Who else is alive?" One couldn't understand that one had survived, and it was beyond comprehension that others should still be alive. They would sit on the steps to the office and talk to one another. "Can it be that my wife, my mother, my child is alive? Some of my friends, some of the people in the town where we lived?"

There was no mail service. The few available telephone lines were restricted to military use. The only way to find out whether someone was alive was to go and look. Across Europe a wild tide of frantic survivors was flowing. People were hitchhiking, getting short jeep rides, or hanging onto dilapidated railway coaches without windows or doors. They sat in huddled groups on haycarts, and some just walked. They would use any means to get a few miles closer to their destination. To get from Linz to Munich, normally a three-hour railroad trip, might take five days. Many of them didn't really know where to go. To the place where one had been with his family before the war? To the concentration camp where the family had last been heard of? Families had been torn apart too suddenly to make arrangements for the day when it would be all over.

In Jaroslav Hašek's immortal *The Adventures of the Good Soldier Svejk*

"A Happy Ending" is from Simon Wiesenthal, *The Murderers Among Us* (New York: Bantam, 1967), pp. 47-54. Reprinted with the kind permission of Opera Mundi, Paris.

the hero makes a date with a friend to meet him at a certain beerhouse in Prague "on Wednesday after the war is over." But the First World War had been a *gemütlich* affair compared to the apocalypse we had survived. And yet the survivors continued their pilgrimage of despair, sleeping on highways or in railroad stations, waiting for another train, another horse-drawn cart to come along, always driven by hope. "Perhaps someone is still alive. . . ." Someone might tell where to find a wife, a mother, children, a brother—or whether they were dead. Better to know the truth than to know nothing. The desire to find one's people was stronger than hunger, thirst, fatigue. Stronger even than the fear of border patrols, of the CIC and NKVD, of men saying "Let's see your papers."

The first thing we did at the Committee in Linz was to make up lists of known survivors. People who came in to ask for someone were asked where *they* were from. They were nomads, vagabonds, beggars. But once upon a time they had had a home, a job, savings. Their names were put on the list of some town or village. Slowly the lists grew. People from Poland, Czechoslovakia, or Germany brought us lists. We gave them copies of our lists. We worked long into the night to copy these lists. Early in the morning, the first people would arrive to look up names. Some waited all night to get in. Behind a man another waited for a glance that might mean hope or despair. Some people were impatient and there were brawls. Once two men began to scuffle because each wanted the same list. In the end they tore up the precious piece of paper. Another time two men started to argue, their eyes glued to the list in the hands of a third man. Each wanted it next. Suddenly they looked at each other and gasped, and the next moment they were in each others' arms. They were brothers and each had been trying to find the other for weeks.

And there were moments of silent despair when someone discovered that the person he was looking for had been there only a few days before, looking for him. They had missed each other. Where should one look now? Other people scanned the lists of survivors, hoping against hope to find the names of people they had seen killed before their very eyes. Everybody had heard of some miracle.

I hardly ever looked at the lists. I didn't believe in miracles. I knew that all my people were dead. After the Pole from Warsaw had told me what had happened to Topiel Street, I had no hope that my wife was alive. When I thought of her, I thought of her body lying under a heap of rubble and I wondered whether they had found the bodies and buried her. In a moment of illogical hope I wrote the the International Committee of the Red Cross in Geneva. They promptly answered that my wife was dead. I knew that my mother did not have a grave; she had died in the death camp of Belsec. I hoped that at least my wife might have a grave.

One night, when I had nothing else to do, I looked at a list of survivors from the Polish city of Cracow and found the name of an old friend from

Buczacz,* Dr. Biener. I wrote him a letter. I told him that my wife's body might still be lying under the ruins of the house in Topiel Street. I asked him to go to Warsaw and look at what was left of the house. There was no mail service to Poland, so I gave the letter to a man who specialized in getting things through Czechoslovakia to Poland.

I didn't know that a miracle had indeed happened. My wife told me all about it later. When the German flamethrower squads had closed in on Topiel Street, in the darkness and confusion my wife and a few other people had managed to get away. For a while they hid. After the battle of Warsaw, the few survivors were driven together by the Germans and assigned to forced labor transports for Germany. My wife was sent to a factory in Heiligenhaus, near Gelsenkirchen in the Rhineland, where they made machine guns for the *Wehrmacht.* The Polish laborers were decently housed and fed, and the Gestapo left them alone. The Germans knew that the war was lost.

My wife was liberated by the British, who marched into Gelsenkirchen on April 11, 1945. (That day I was lying on my bunk in the death block of Mauthausen.) My wife went to the British authorities and reported that she was Cyla Wiesenthal, a Jewish woman from Poland. Six women in her group turned out to be Jewish, but they had not known of each other. One of them told my wife that she was going home.

"Home?" asked my wife. "Where is home?"

"To Poland, of course. Why don't you come with me?"

"What for? My husband was killed by the Gestapo in Lwow last year. Poland had become a large cemetery to me."

"Have you proof that he's dead?"

"No," said my wife, "but . . ."

"Don't believe it. Now, suppose he were alive: where is he likely to be?"

Cyla thought it over. "In Lwow, I would think. We spent the years before the war there."

"Lwow is now in the Soviet Union," said her friend. "Let's go there."

The two women left Gelsenkirchen in June 1945. (At one point on her journey, we later discovered, my wife had been less than thirty miles from Linz.) After an arduous trip, they reached the Czechoslovak-Polish border at Bohumin. They were told that a train was leaving that night for Lwow. They got on the overcrowded cars and arrived in Cracow, Poland, in the morning. It was announced that there would be a four-hour stop.

At the Cracow railroad station somebody stole my wife's suitcase with everything she owned. That was her homecoming. To cheer her up, her friend suggested that they walk into town. Perhaps they would meet some-one they had once known. The beautiful old city of the Polish kings looked deserted and ghostlike that morning. Suddenly my wife heard her name

*The Wiesenthals' former hometown.

called out, and recognized a man named Landek, who had been a dentist in Lwow. (Landek now lives in America.) For a while they exchanged hectic questions and unfinished sentences, as always happened when survivors met. Landek had heard that Simon Wiesenthal was dead. He told my wife to talk to Dr. Biener. He might know more.

"Dr. Biener from Buczacz?" asked my wife, "Is he in Cracow?"

"He lives five minutes from here." Landek gave her the address and hurried away.

When they came to Dr. Biener's house, my wife asked her friend to wait downstairs. She walked up the stairway with a heavy heart. On the third floor she saw a sign reading BIENER and rang the bell. The door was opened. For a moment she saw Dr. Biener's face and heard a muffled cry. Then the door was quickly shut again.

"Dr. Biener!" my wife shouted, banging her fists against the door. "Open up! It's Cyla. Cyla Wiesenthal from Buczacz!"

The door was opened. Dr. Biener was pale, as if he were seeing a ghost.

"But—you are dead," he said. "I just got a letter. . . . "

"I'm very much alive," my wife said angrily. "Of course I *look* half dead, after spending the night on the train."

"Come in," Dr. Biener said hastily, and closed the door. You don't understand. Yesterday I had a letter from your husband. Simon writes that you died under the ruins of a house in Warsaw."

Now my wife got pale. "Simon? But he's dead. He's been dead for over a year."

Dr. Biener shook his head, "No, no, Cyla. Simon is alive, in Linz, Austria. Here, read the letter."

They called my wife's friend from downstairs. She was not at all surprised. Hadn't she told Cyla that her husband might be alive? They sat down and talked, and when they remembered the train, it was much too late. If my letter hadn't reached Dr. Biener the day before, if my wife hadn't met Landek, if Dr. Biener hadn't been at home, the two women would have gone back to the station and continued their journey to the Soviet Union. My wife might have been sent into the interior of the USSR, and it would have taken years to find her again.

My wife stayed in Cracow, and tried to get in touch with me. Dr. Biener knew several illegal couriers who would carry letters for a fee, with no guarantee of delivery. She wrote three letters and gave them to three men working different routes. I received one of them, from a man who had come to Linz by way of Budapest—which is quite a detour.

I'll never forget the moment when I saw Cyla's handwriting on the envelope. I read the letter so many times that I knew it by heart. I went to see the OSS captain for whom I was then working and asked him to give me travel orders to Cracow. He didn't like the idea of my going to Poland. He said I might never be able to come back. He suggested we think it over until next morning.

I didn't go to the Jewish Committee that afternoon. I was happy and perhaps feeling a little guilty at being a happy man among so many unhappy people. I wanted to be alone. I knew a peasant not far from where I lived who had a few horses. I thought of my summer vacations in Dolina, where I loved to ride horses. I asked the peasant to let me have a horse for an hour. I forgot that I was a little older and not yet in good physical condition. I mounted the horse. Something went wrong. I suppose the horse sensed at once that I was still weak. I was thrown and landed in a potato field with a broken ankle.

I had to stay in bed. That settled the matter of my projected journey to Poland. I asked a Jewish friend, Dr. Felix Weisberg, to go to Cracow and gave him a letter for my wife. He promised to bring her back to Linz. My OSS friends made out the necessary travel documents for her, so she would have no difficulty in getting into the U.S. Zone of Austria.

They were fine travel documents, but unfortunately my wife never received them. Crossing Czechoslovakia on his way to Poland, Dr. Weisberg was warned that there was an NKVD roadblock ahead, with "very strict controls." He got nervous; if the Soviet secret police found any American *dokumenty* on him, they might arrest him as a spy. He destroyed the documents. Too late he realized that he had also destroyed my wife's address in Cracow. As it turned out, the NKVD didn't even search him. In Cracow, he went to the local Jewish Committee and put a notice on the bulletin board. Mrs. Cyla Wiesnthal, the wife of Simon Wiesenthal, was asked to get in touch with Dr. Felix Weisberg, who would take her to her husband in Linz.

My wife saw the notice the next morning and went to see Dr. Weisberg. She was not the first visitor. Two other women were already there, each claiming to be the one and only Cyla Wiesenthal. A lot of people in Poland were trying to get to Austria, hoping they might later try to get to America. Poor Felix Weisberg had a trickier problem than the mythological Paris. Weisberg didn't know my wife. In all the excitement preceding his sudden departure, I had foolishly forgotten to give him her exact description. He faced the unpleasant possibility of bringing back the wrong Mrs. Wiesenthal. Weisberg told me later that he'd asked each of the three women to describe how I looked. Two seemed rather vague, but one knew a lot of details, naturally. Also, Weisberg admitted to me, he'd liked her best. He decided to take a chance and bought false travel papers for her in the black market.

One evening, late in 1945, I was early in bed as usual. My broken ankle still gave me a lot of trouble. There was a knock at the door. Felix Weisberg came in, confused and embarrassed. It took him quite a while to explain how he'd foolishly thrown away the American documents, and his dilemma over three women each claiming to be Mrs. Cyla Wiesenthal.

"I brought one of them with me. She's waiting downstairs. Now don't get excited, Simon. If she isn't your wife, I'm going to marry her myself."

"You?"

"Yes, my word of honor. You're under no obligation whatsoever. To tell the truth, I thought it safest to bring the one I liked best. That way, I knew even if she was not your wife, I would . . ."

But then she came into the room, and Felix Weisberg, God bless him, knew that he could not marry her.

Epilogue

The cataclysm called the Holocaust, the effort to exterminate the Jews and the rape of entire nations, was the ultimate evil, short of a nuclear holocaust, that part of mankind perpetrated against itself. If that premise stands, then *eo ipso* it was also the greatest challenge to Christianity. It failed, just as God failed in Auschwitz, looking away from the gas chambers and gallows and execution walls while God's children were being massacred.

The political opponents of the Nazis, the resisters, paid a heavy price in lives for their convictions. Yet those of them who emerged from the prisons and concentration camps could at least claim victory for their beliefs, for truth, in 1945 at least, had prevailed. The Jews, who had produced reformers like Jesus and Marx but declined to follow either, and whose losses were even larger, still await the Messiah who could convince the rest of the world to erase from their hearts the hatred against the "chosen people."

Life goes on. "Plus ça change, plus c'est la même chose," one of the escaped French prisoners of war said before he went off to die. Over twenty-four centuries ago Heraclitus stated that the only constant in life is change. I changed. Yet my memories did not change. They remain as a refrain that returns with the same tunes and images, with the same smell of scorched flesh and of bones that are glowing embers, with the same flames shooting toward a sky in search of God. In Auschwitz God, finding it impossible to cope, went on an extended vacation, as if replaced by a sign: "For the duration, this office is closed."

My memories remain unchanged. I cultivate them in solitude, for people around me nowadays would not comprehend them. I keep them as a bouquet of grotesque flowers, unknown on these happy and innocent American shores. They are called Auschwitz, Gross-Rosen and Dora-Nordhausen, and these are interspersed with weeds of cruelty, greed and malice. They are all of various shades of gray, and the ribbon holding them together is black sorrow. I am mourning millions I never knew and those few dozen whose lives touched upon mine and whom I called friends, who were lost in the complex cataclysm curtly called World War II.

My eyes have seen what cannot be expressed with words, ever. Yet

That one triumph the gods bestowed upon me,
That only wounded can a heart claim victory.*

*From the poem "Devisa" by the Czech poet Otakar Fišer, whose heart succumbed to the Nazi threat on March 12, 1938, the day of the Austrian annexation; he knew that Czechoslovakia would be next.

Just to die was a lark. It was the fear of dying, of steady, mental anguish visited upon us by virulent malevolence, that time whipped into an agonizing ordeal, keelhauling our souls day after day, night after night, without letup, that was so hard. What made us endure it? Partly moral support that we gave each other. The five of us who stood so many roll calls together were a closely knit unit. Olga, who managed to keep up her spirits and with it ours; her sister Alice, who often saved our sanity with her lovely voice, singing us into dreams of an esoteric past; Verice, who even at the gates of hell preserved her purity and never succumbed to malice. We are all alive, in Canada, Yugoslavia and the United States. Nothing can come between us.

The fifth member was our camp baby Ribizli from Rumania, all of twelve or thirteen years old, she was not sure. She had bright, lively eyes, our Pygmalion, whom I taught to read the clock in the dust. She did not know the multiplication table, yet would compute with lightning speed the chances of survival. She was the fastest "organizer," with the instinctive shrewdness of two adults. I meant to adopt her as my little sister after the war, but I lost her in the madness of the last death march. We know that she survived the end of the war, but she disappeared and did not report at the checking point we all had agreed on. Investigations in several countries were futile. She remains forever in our hearts as the breath of spring in our darkest winters.

How did I survive the physical and mental dehumanization? I believe through a fortuitous constellation of an originally healthy body, accidental luck, and above all a strong will, that constructive force that rules emotions and guides intuition and imagination, and channels sentiments and temperament into a disciplined personality. Those who despaired did not last long. Broken spirits could not protect abused bodies. Will power, determination, even hatred, positive thinking and mental energy were the life lines of endurance, hence of existence itself.

I see not much use philosophizing, interpreting or engaging in metaphysical speculations over the Holocaust. Such exercises limit the scope of communication to a select few. (That is also the reason why I switched from studying philosophy to the study of history.) What IS needed is the propagation of the stark truth, for facts are the clearest and most comprehensible carriers of the message, understood by all.

We who returned from those depths of hell, we the survivors, are trying to stand guard that history should not repeat itself. But there are too few of us. You, the present and future generations, have to be the sentinels of human decency and democracy, to prevent the recurrence of the obscenity that was the Holocaust.

Of the handful of us who returned to life, some are broken in body and spirit. A few others are luckier. I know what is thirst and hunger, cold and fear. I know what life is all about for I have tasted death. The experience did not break me; it made me stronger. While the black lace of sorrow will forever be draped over my heart, paradoxically I am capable of enjoying happiness more than those who did not savor the wages of fear. I gained the gift of knowing how to live life to the fullest, body and soul. I carry in me constantly the awareness that I want to see and hear and know as much and as many people as possible, for knowledge is power and knowledge is happiness. Those who resist partaking in knowledge are the beggars of the world, cheating themselves of their share of humanity's bounties and undeserving of the gift of life.

I constantly enjoy the sunrise at daybreak or the frolicking of the wind in the treetops. I rejoice over the laughter of a child and the beauty of a book. I am happy that I have food to eat and a clean bed to sleep in. I pity all those who do not know how to appreciate their plenties and thus shortchange themselves of so much gratification and pleasure. Above all I cherish my freedom to listen and to speak without fear.

To this day I have to force myself to use words like "worry" or "problem." The SS used to worry me; gas chambers were a problem. Dust on the furniture or lost keys are not. I have been liberated of many a burden of everyday life by having carried the ultimate cross. I am the living proof of the theory of relativity in practice.

Those without a conscience involuntarily taught me to deepen mine. The carriers of hate and evil elevated love and good into a sharper light. It is not enough not to be bad. Damn the neutrals sitting on fences not minding other people's sufferings, for they are the cowardly henchmen of evildoers. Praying at times and places prescribed by custom to the God of your choice does not make you your brothers' and sisters' keeper. Only by reaching out a helping hand and by actively opposing wrongdoing do we earn the right to be called human.

Celebrate life as much as you can, without hurting others, for too much of it has been wasted through sheer madness. Place flowers of sympathy and sorrow on the nonexistent graves of millions who were annihilated through cruelty and with malice aforethought. Keep in mind the victims of the Holocaust and their bones scattered all over Europe, unmarked with crosses or David's star. For lest you forget, their sacrifices will have been in vain, and humanity will tumble into the abyss of evil again. Honor the memory of those fallen and strengthen your soul against a repeated bereavement of mankind, so that you can look with a clear conscience into the eyes of your children.

Weep not for the survivors of the purgatory called Holocaust, for theirs is the ultimate glory in triumph: they outlived the evil of their tormentors, and by their very lives overcame it. Learn from them; for nobody, but nobody, knows how to savor the sunlight and the raindrops, the free flight of the birds and the smile of the flowers as those who were once denied dignity, beauty and the simplest things in life that make it worth living.

* * *

Here and now, in my fifth or sixth life, Gypsy the Kat, the personification of carefree contentment, dozes at my feet. My dear husband of many years is engrossed in the financial page, as if life depended on things material. Our world-wise son Tom paid with his life for the attainments of civilization, and that wound is deeper than even Auschwitz. Our son Paul, my sunshine, is darting by, nimble-footed, off to soccer practice.

A lovely afternoon. Spring is trying out its wings and is about to take off on its glorious flight.

Spring, and still another beginning.

Bibliography

The subject of the European resistance against totalitarianism is simpler to research than the subject of the Holocaust. Most source materials originate in the resisters' countries and are concentrated in a few libraries or archives. In all formerly occupied countries, there are organized groups of survivors of political persecution and of concentration camps. In France, for example, it is the Fédération nacionale des déportés et internés résistants et patriots. There are organizations of former inmates of various prisons and concentration camps. In some cases, as in Yugoslavia, where partisan resisters cooperated with the military, the Military Historical Institute maintains resistance records. Access to all of these varies, but other than personal visits prove frustrating. Familiarity with the appropriate language makes all the difference in facilitating research.

Much more has been written about the Holocaust, in the stricter sense of the term the Nazi attempt to exterminate the Jews, than about the resistance. The two subjects, as their victims, meet on the common ground of the concentration camps.

It is a physical impossibility to list here more than a handful of sources on both. There are nearly 10,000 known publications on Auschwitz alone. The bibliography that follows is by necessity of modest proportions. A more extensive bibliography comprising over 1,300 entries in twelve categories, including three on women, is Vera Laska, *Nazism, Resistance & Holocaust in W.W. II: A Bibliography* (Weston, Mass: Laska, 1982).

* * *

Yad Vashem Martyrs' and Heroes' Memorial Authority in Jerusalem is a depository of documents and memoirs on the Holocaust, mostly in German, Hebrew and Yiddish. It also issues the *Yad Vashem Studies on the European Jewish Catastrophe and Resistance.* The Centre de Documentation Juive Contemporaine in Paris and the Wiener Library in London are major sources of information. The Wiener Library's catalogue series published a bibliography, *Persecution and Resistance Under the Nazis* (London: Valentine, Mitchell, 1960). Addresses of the organizations of survivors in all formerly occupied countries might be obtained from their embassies.

In the United States the YIVO Institute for Jewish Research (1048 Fifth Avenue, New York, N.Y. 10028) houses several collections of ghetto documents and related primary source materials. It publishes the *YIVO Annual of Jewish Social Science.* Since 1960, Yad Washem and the YIVO Institute have been engaged in preparing a multivolume bibliographical series on the Holocaust; one of the volumes, Jacob Robinson, ed., *The Holocaust and After: Sources and Literature in English* (Jerusalem: Israel University Press, 1973), is most helpful.

The Anti-Defamation League of B'nai B'rith (823 United Nations Plaza, New York, N.Y. 10017) supplies teaching materials at reasonable prices, for instance *The Record—The Holocaust in History, 1933-1945,* published in cooperation with the National Council for Social Studies in 1978.

The Library of Congress and the National Archives are rich sources for researchers, containing among others the transcripts of war crime trials. This in itself is immense documentation; for instance, the Nuremberg Doctors' Trial of twenty-three defendants alone takes up 11,538 pages in nineteen volumes. Indexes can be consulted about various concentration camp trials. Helpful guides to the maze of countless concentration camps and their branches are: *Catalog of Camps and Prisons in Germany and German Occupied Territories, September 1st, 1939—May 8th, 1945,* 2 vols. (Arolsen, Germany: International Tracing Service, 1949-1950), a total of 821 oversize pages, and *Vorläufiges Verzeichnis der Konzentrationslager und deren Aussenkommandos sowie anderen Haftstatten under dem Reichsführer-SS in Deutschland und deutsch besetzten Gebieten, 1933-1945* (Arolsen, Germany: International Tracing Service, 1969). Both are in the Library of Congress.

Periodical literature almost all over the world may be scanned for articles on the subject. It yields a rich harvest especially in Russian, Polish, British, and American journals, as well as in the daily press, some of which is blessedly indexed.

Other organizations that are devoted to the topic of the Holocaust are the Jewish Book Council of America (15 East 26th Street, New York, N.Y. 10010), the United States Holocaust Memorial Council (425 13th Street N.W., Washington, D.C. 20004) and the Simon Wiesenthal Center for Holocaust Studies at Yeshiva University (9760 West Pico Boulevard, Los Angeles, California 90035).

The gigantic task of helping bring war criminals to justice is carried out by the Dokumentationszentrum des Bundes judischer Verfolgten des Naziregimes in Vienna, Austria. It is a modest office presided by Simon Wiesenthal. The progress of his work is summarized in a yearly newsletter sent to the supporters of the center for a voluntary contribution. Because of its limited staff, only the most serious scholars should address inquiries to this center.

* * *

A word of caution about personal memoirs of former concentration camp inmates. Most of them were acquainted only with that part of a camp where they were incarcerated, as free movement within the camp was strictly forbidden and the privilege of only a few. This is espcially true of gigantic camps like Auschwitz-Birkenau (Osvecim-Brzezinky). I learned more technical details *after* the war about the very camps in which I had been incarcerated, when as a member of the Czechoslovak War Crimes Investigation Team I saw the camp blueprints and read the hundreds of depositions prepared for the war crime trials, than when I was an inmate in those camps. It is therefore best to rely on the personal experiences of the memorialists. Even then, the pedantic researcher will discover seeming discrepancies, as, for instance, in the accounts of the first selections at Auschwitz: some mention that those selected for the gas chambers went to the right rather than to the left. This can be accounted for by the utter shock of a newly arrived victim or possibly the position of the train.

* * *

There were political resisters who ended up in hiding or in concentration camps, sharing the fate of the Jews in the Holocaust. Some men and women from both groups went through all stages: resistance, hiding, concentration camps. Their fates were often intertwined, and there is not always a clear line of demarcation between the two. A certain amount of overlapping is inevitable. It should be understood that most books on the resistance and on the Holocaust contain some information, general or specific, on women.

* * *

The entries in the bibliography are nonfiction. The reader who wishes to enter the arena of the resistance and of the Holocaust through the portals of literature may start with Tadeusz Borowski's *This Way to the Gas, Ladies and Gentlemen* (New York: Penguin Books, 1976), Jerzy Kosinski's *The Painted Bird* (New York: Bantam, 1972) or the writings of Arnošt Lustig, such as *Darkness Casts No Shadow* (New York: Avon, 1978), and of Elie Wiesel, notably *Night* (New York: Pyramid, 1961).

Abramowicz, Zofia. *Tak bylo* [*That's How It Was*]. Lublin, Poland: Wydawn. Lubelskie, 1962.

Adamovich, Ales, et al. *Out of the Fire.* Moscow: Progress, 1980.

Adler, H. G. *The Jews in Germany, From the Enlightenment to National Socialism.* Notre Dame, Ind.: Notre Dame University Press, 1969.

______. *Theresienstadt.* 2 vols. Tübingen: J.C.B. Mohr, 1955.

Ainsztein, Reuben. *Jewish Resistance in Nazi-Occupied Eastern Europe.* New York: Barnes & Noble, 1974.

Amicale de Ravensbrück. *Les Françaises a Ravensbrück.* Paris: Gallinard, 1965.

Apenszlak, Jacob, and Polakiewicz, Moshe. *Armed Resistance of the Jews in Poland.* New York: American Federation for Polish Jews, 1944.

Arendt, Hannah. *Eichmann in Jerusalem: A Report on the Banality of Evil.* New York: Viking Press, 1965.

______. *The Origins of Totalitarianism.* New York: Harcourt, Brace & Co., 1951.

Astrup, Helen, and B. L. Jacot. *Oslo Intrigue.* New York: McGraw-Hill, 1954.

Balicka-Kozlowska, Helena. *Mur mia dwie strony* [*The Wall Had Two Sides*]. Warsaw: Min. Obrony Narodowej, 1958.

Bar Oni, Byrna. *The Vapor.* Chicago: Visual Impact, Inc., 1976.

Bauer, Yehuda. *A History of the Holocaust.* New York: Franklin Watts, 1982.

______. *They Chose Life: Jewish Resistance in the Holocaust.* New York: American Jewish Committee, 1973.

Bauminger, Arieh, L. *Roll of Honour.* Tel Aviv: Hamenora, 1971.

Bayle, François. *Croix Gammée Contre Caducée.* [Neustadt (Palatinat): L'Imprimerie nationale, 1950].

Bellak, Georgina, ed. *Donne e bambini nei lager nazisti.* Milan: Associazione nazionale ex-deportati politici, 1960.

Berben, Paul. *Dachau 1933-1945, The Official History.* London: Comité International de Dachau, 1968, 1975.

Berg, Mary. *Warsaw Ghetto, A Diary.* New York: L. B. Fischer, 1945.

Berger, Alexander. *Kreuz hinter Stacheldraht: Der Leidensweq deutscher Pfarrer.* Bayreuth, Germany: Hestia, 1963.

Bernadac, Christian. *Les Mannequins nus.* 3 vols. Paris: France Empire, 1971-1973.

Bernard, Henri. Historie de la résistance européenne, La "quatrième force" de la *guerre 39-45.* Verviers, France: Gérard, 1968.

______. *L'autre Allemagne.* Brussels: La renaissance du livre, 1976.

Bertelsen, Aage. *October '43.* New York: G. P. Putnam's Sons, 1954.

Betrand, Simone. *Mille visages, un seul combat.* Paris: Éditeurs Français Réunis, 1965.

Bierman, John. *Righteous Gentile, The Story of Raoul Wallenberg, Missing Hero of the Holocaust.* New York: Viking, 1981.

Billig, Joseph. *Les camps de concentration dans l'économie du Reich hitlérien.* Paris: Presses universitaires de France, 1973.

Blatter, Janet, and Milton, Sybil, eds. *The Art of the Holocaust.* New York: W. H. Smith, 1981.

Blum, Howard. *Wanted! The Search for Nazis in America.* New York: Quadrangle Books, 1977.

Blumenthal, Ilse [Weiss]. *Mahnmal: Gedichte aus dem KZ.* Hamburg: C. Wegner, 1957.

Boehm, Eric H., ed. *We Survived.* New Haven, Conn.: Yale University Press, 1949.

Bradley, John. *Lidice, Sacrificial Village.* New York: Ballantine, 1972.

Braham, Randolph L. *The Politics of Genocide, The Holocaust in Hungary.* 2 vols. New York: Columbia University Press, 1981.

Brand, Sandra. *I Dared to Live.* New York: Shengold, 1978.

Bubeníčková, Růžena, et al. *Tábory utrpení a smrti.* [*Camps of Martyrdom and Death*]. Prague: Svoboda, 1969.

Buber-Neumann, Margarete. *Als Gefangene bei Stalin und Hitler.* Stuttgart: Action Verlag, 1958.

______. *Kafkova přítelkyně Milena.* [*Kafka's Friend Milena.*] Toronto: Sixty-Eight Publishers, 1982.

Bullock, Alan. *Hitler, A Study in Tyranny.* New York: Harper & Row, 1962.

Burg, J. G. *Maidanek in alle Ewigkeit.* Munich: Ederer, 1979.

Bürger, Kurt, ed. *Aus Hitler's Konzentrationslagern.* Moscow: Verlagsgenossenschaft ausländischer Arbeiter in der USSR, 1934.

Carré, Mathilde-Lily. *I Was the Cat.* London: Horwitz, 1967.

Chambard, Claude. *The Maquis.* Indianapolis: Bobbs-Merrill, 1976.

Chartock, Roselle, and Spencer, Jack, eds. *The Holocaust Years: Society on Trial.* New York: Bantam, 1978.

Chary, Frederick B. *The Bulgarian Jews and the Final Solution, 1940-1944.* Pittsburgh: University of Pittsburgh Press, 1972.

Chatel, Nicole, ed. *Des femmes dans la résistance.* Paris: Julliard, 1972.

Ciechanowski, Jan. *The Warsaw Rising of 1944.* London: Cambridge University Press, 1974.

Cohen, Elie A. *Human Behavior in the Concentration Camp.* New York: Grosset & Dunlap, 1953.

Conway, John S. *The Nazi Persecution of the Churches, 1933-45.* New York: Basic Books, 1968.

Cvetkova, Nadežda, et al. *V fashistskikh zastenkakh: zapiski* [*In Fascist Torture Chambers: Notes*] Minsk: Government Publications of BSSR, 1958.

Czech, Danuta, et al. *Auschwitz, Nazi Extermination Camp.* Warsaw: Interpress, 1978.

David, Janina. *A Square of Sky and A Touch of Earth.* New York: Penguin Books, 1981.

Dawidowicz, Lucy S. *The Holocaust and the Historians.* Cambridge, Mass.: Harvard University Press, 1981.

———. *The War Against the Jews, 1933-1945.* New York: Bantam, 1976.

Dedijer, Vladimir. *With Tito Through the War: Partisan Diary, 1941-1944.* London: Alexander Hamilton, 1951.

Delarme, Jacques. *The Gestapo: A History of Horror.* New York: Dell, 1965.

Delbo, Charlotte. *None of Us Will Return.* Boston: Beacon Press, 1968.

Derry, Sam I. *The Rome Escape Line.* New York: W. W. Norton, 1960.

Des Pres, Terrence. *The Survivor, An Anatomy of Life in the Death Camps,* New York: Oxford University Press, 1976.

Dinnerstein, Leonard. *America and the Survivors of the Holocaust.* New York: Columbia University Press, 1982.

———. ed. *Antisemitism in the United States.* New York: Holt, Rinehart & Winston, 1971.

Donanski, Jerzy, ed. *Oswiecim, malarstvo, rzezba, grafika.* Cracow: Wydawnictvo Artystyczno-graficzne, 1959.

Draenger, Gusta. *Pamietnik Justyny* [*Justyna's Diary*]. Cracow: Centralna żydovska komisja historyczna, 1946.

Duboscq, Geneviève. *My Longest Night.* New York: Seaver Books, 1981.

Dufurnier, Denise. Ravensbrück, the Women's Camp of Death. London: George Allen & Unwin, 1948.

Dunin-Wasowicz, Krzysztof. *La résistance dans les camps de concentration.* Warsaw: Panstwowe Wydav. Naukowe, 1972.

Eban, Abba. *My People: The Story of the Jews.* New York: Random House, 1968.

Ehrenberg, Hans P. *Autobiography of a Pastor.* London: Student Christian Movement Press, 1943.

Elkins, Michael. *Forged in Fury.* New York: Ballantine, 1971.

Elling, Hanna. *Frauen im deutschen Widerstand, 1933-1945.* Frankfurt am Main: Röderberg Verlag, 1981.

Fackenheim, Emil L. *God's Presence in History.* New York: Harper & Row, 1972.

Falconi, Carlo. *The Silence of Pius XII.* Boston: Little, Brown & Co., 1970.

Fein, Helen. *Accounting for Genocide.* New York: Free Press, 1979.

Feingold, Henry L. *The Politics of Rescue: The Roosevelt Administration and the Holocaust, 1938-1945.* New Brunswick, N.J.: Rutgers University Press, 1975.

Feld, Marilla. *I Chose to Live.* New York: Manor Books, 1979.

Fénelon, Fania. *Playing for Time.* New York: Atheneum, 1977.

Ferderber-Salz, Bertha. *And the Sun Kept Shining.* New York: Holocaust Library, 1980.

Ferencz, Benjamin B. *Less Than Slaves: Jewish Forced Labor and the Quest for Compensation.* Cambridge, Mass.: Harvard University Press, 1979.

Flannery, Edward H. *The Anguish of the Jews.* New York: Macmillan, 1965.

Flender, Harold. *Rescue in Denmark.* New York: Holocaust Library, 1980.

Foot, M.R.D. *Resistance: European Resistance to Nazism, 1940-1945.* New York: McGraw-Hill, 1977.

———. *SOE in France.* London: HMSO, 1966.

Fourcade, Marie-Madeleine. *Noah's Ark: The Secret Underground.* New York: E. P. Dutton & Co., 1974.

Francos, Ania. *Il était des femmes dans la résistance.* Paris: Stock, 1978.
Frank, Anne. *The Diary of a Young Girl.* Garden City, N.Y.: Doubleday & Co., 1952.
Frankl, Viktor E. *From Death Camp to Existentialism.* Boston: Beacon Press, 1959.
Friedlander, Saul. *Pius XII and the Third Reich: A Documentation.* New York: A. A. Knopf, 1966.
Friedman, Philip. *Martyrs and Fighters.* New York: Frederick A. Praeger, 1954.
______. *Their Brothers' Keepers.* New York: Holocaust Library, 1978.
Friedman, Saul. *No Haven for the Oppressed: United States Policy Toward Jewish Refugees, 1938-1945.* Detroit: Wayne State University Press, 1977.
Fromm, Bella. *Blood and Banquets.* New York: Harper and Brothers, 1942.
Fuller, Jean O. *Born for Sacrifice.* London: Pan Books, 1957.
______. *Madeleine.* London: Victor Gollancz, 1952.
Gallagher, J. P. *Scarlet Pimpernel of the Vatican.* New York: Coward-McCann, 1968.
Gallagher, Richard. *Nuremberg: The Third Reich on Trial.* New York: Avon, 1961.
Garlinski, Jozef. *Fighting Auschwitz.* Greenwich, Conn.: Fawcett Books, 1975.
Geisel, Erika, ed. *Vielleicht war das alles erst der Anfang.* Berlin: Rotbuch Verlag, 1979.
Gersdorff, Ursula von. *Frauen im Kriegsdienst, 1914-1945.* Stuttgart: Deutsche Verlags-Anstalt, 1969.
Gilbert, Martin. *Auschwitz and the Allies.* New York: Holt, Rinehart and Winston, 1981.
______. *Final Journey, The Fate of the Jews in Nazi Europe.* New York: Mayflower Books, 1979.
______. *The Holocaust, Maps and Photographs.* New York: Hill & Wang, 1978.
Gjelsvik, Tore. *Norwegian Resistance.* Montreal: McGill-Queen's University Press, 1979.
Gluck, Gemma LaGuardia. *My Story.* New York: David McKay, 1961.
Grant, Myrna. *The Journey.* Wheaton, Ill.: Tyndale Press, 1978.
Green, Gerald, ed. *The Artists of Terezín.* New York: Schocken Books, 1978.
Grossman, Mendel. *With a Camera in the Ghetto.* New York: Schocken Books, 1977.
Gurdus, Luba K. *The Death Train.* New York: National Council on Art in Jewish Life, 1978.
H., Janka. *W ghetcie i obozie: Pamietnik dwunastoletniej dziewczyny* [*In the Ghetto and Camp: Diary of a Twelve Year Old Girl*]. Cracow: Wojewódzka komisja historyczna, 1946.
Haag, Lina. *Eine handvoll Staub.* Frankfurt am Main: Röderberg Verlag, 1977.
Hájková, Dagmar, et al. *Ravensbrück.* Prague: Naše vojsko, 1960.
Hallie, Philip. *Lest Innocent Blood Be Shed.* New York: Harper & Row, 1980.
Hanser, Richard. *A Noble Treason. The Revolt of the Munich Students Against Hitler.* New York: G. P. Putnam's Sons, 1979.
Harel, Isser. *The House on Garibaldi Street.* New York: Viking Press, 1975.
Hart, Kitty. *I Am Alive.* London: Transword Publishers, 1961.
Hausner, Gideon. *Justice in Jerusalem.* New York: Herzl Press, 1978.
Heger, Heinz. *The Men with the Pink Triangle.* Boston: Alyson, 1980.
Hellman, Peter, ed. *The Auschwitz Album.* New York: Random House, 1981.

Herrmann, Simon H. *Austauschlager Bergen-Belsen.* Tel Aviv: Irgun Olej Merkaz Europe, 1944.

Hilberg, Raul. *The Destruction of the European Jews.* Chicago: Quadrangle Books, 1961.

______, ed. *Documents of Destruction.* Chicago: Quadrangle Books, 1971.

Hoess, Rudolf. *Commandant of Auschwitz: The Autobiography of Rudolf Hoess.* Cleveland: World Publishing, 1959.

Hoffman, Peter. *The History of the German Resistance, 1933-1945.* Cambridge, Mass.: MIT Press, 1977.

Homze, Edward L. *Foreign Labor in Nazi Germany.* Princeton, N.J.: Princeton University Press, 1967.

Horowitz, Irving L. *Taking Lives: Genocide and State Power.* New Brunswick, N.J.: Rutgers University Press, 1980.

Hyde, H. Montgomery. *Cynthia, The Story of the Spy Who Changed the Course of the War.* New York: Farrar, Straus & Giroux, 1965.

Igra, Samuel. *Germany's National Vice.* London: Quality Press, 1945.

International Military Tribunal. *Trial of the Major War Criminals Before the International Military Tribunal: Official Text.* 42 vols. Nuremberg, 1947-1949. [This is the Blue Series; see also Red and Green Series.]

Ivanov, Miroslav. *Target: Heydrich.* New York: Macmillan, 1972.

Janovská, Jarmila. *Osudy žen* [*Fates of Women*]. Zurich: Konfrontace, 1981.

Kaminska, Ruth T. *I Don't Want to be Brave Anymore.* Washington, D.C.: New Republic, 1978.

Kantor, Alfred. *The Book of Alfred Kantor.* New York: McGraw-Hill, 1971.

Karski, Jan. *Story of a Secret State.* Boston: Houghton Mifflin, 1944.

Katz, Alfred. *Poland's Ghettos.* New York: Twayne, 1970.

Kempner, Benedicta M. *Nonnen unter dem Hackenkreuz.* Würzburg: J. N. Nauman, 1979.

Kenrick, Donald, and Puxon, Grattan. *Destiny of Europe's Gypsies.* New York: Basic Books, 1972.

Kiedrzynska, Wanda. *Ravensbrück.* Warsaw: Academy of Science, 1961.

Kielar, Wieslaw. *Anus Mundi, 1500 Days in Auschwitz-Birkenau.* New York: Times Books, 1980.

Kirkpatrick, Clifford. *Nazi Germany, Its Women and Family Life.* Indianapolis, Ind.: Bobbs-Merrill, 1938.

Klarsfeld, Beate. *Wherever They May Be!* New York: Vanguard Press, 1975.

Koch-Kent, Henri. *Sie boten Trotz: Luxemburger im Freiheitskampf, 1939-1945.* Luxemburg: Imprimerie Hermann, 1974.

Koehl, Robert L. *RKFDV: German Resettlement and Population Policy, 1939-1945.* Cambridge, Mass.: Harvard University Press, 1957.

Koehn, Ilse. *Mischling Second Degree.* New York: Bantam, 1978.

Kogon, Eugen. *The Theory and Practice of Hell.* New York: Farrar, Straus, 1950.

Kohn, Nahum, and Roiter, Howard. *A Voice from the Forest, Memoirs of a Jewish Partisan.* New York: Holocaust Library, 1980.

Komorowski, T. Bor. *The Secret Army.* London: Macmillan, 1951.

Konzentrationslager: Ein Appell an das Gewissen der Welt. Karlsbad, Czechoslovakia: Graphia, 1934.

Korczak, Janusz. *Ghetto Diary.* New York: Holocaust Library, 1981.

Košutová, Olga, *U Svatobořic* [At Svatobořice]. Brno, Czechoslovakia: Družstvo moravského kola spisovatelů, 1946.

Kovály, Heda, and Kohák, Erazim. *The Victors and the Vanquished.* New York: Horizon Press, 1973.

Kovpak, Sidor A. *Our Partisan Cause.* London: Hutchinson, 1947.

Kraus, Ota, and Kulka, Erich. *Továrna na smrt* [*Death Factory*]. Prague: Naše vojsko, 1957.

Krausnick, Helmut, et al. *Anatomy of the SS-State.* New York: Walker, 1968.

Kühnrich, Heinz, ed. *SS im Einsatz, eine Dokumentation über die Verbrechen der SS.* Berlin: Deutscher Militärverlag, 1967.

Kulkielko, Renya. *Escape from the Pit.* New York: Sharon Books, 1947.

Kulski, Julian E. *Dying, We Live.* New York: Holt, Rinehart and Winston, 1979.

Kuznetsov, Anatoly. *Babi Yar.* New York: Dell, 1966.

Langhoff, Wolfgang. *Rubber Truncheon: Being an Account of Thirteen Months Spent in a Concentration Camp.* New York: E. P. Dutton, 1935.

Laqueur, Walter. *Guerrilla; A Historical and Critical Study.* Boston: Little Brown, 1976.

______. *The Terrible Secret: Suppression of the Truth About Hitler's "Final Solution."* Boston: Little, Brown & Co., 1980.

Laska, Vera. *Nazism, Resistance & Holocaust in W.W. II: A Bibliography.* Weston, Mass.: Laska, 1982.

Latour, Anny. *The Jewish Resistance in France.* New York: Schocken, 1981.

Le Chêne, Evelyn. *Watch for Me by the Moonlight.* London: Eyre Methuen, 1973.

Leiner, Isabella. *Fragments of Isabella.* New York: Crowell, 1978.

Lengyel, Olga. *Five Chimneys.* Chicago: Ziff-Davis, 1947.

Levi, Primo. *Survival in Auschwitz.* New York: Collier, 1966.

Levin, Nora. *The Holocaust.* New York: Schocken, 1973.

Lewinska, Pelagia. *Vingt mois à Auschwitz.* Paris: Nagel, 1949.

Liegeois, Constance. *Calvarie de femmes.* Ciney, Belgium, Editions Marsia, 1945.

Lorant, Stefan. *I Was Hitler's Prisoner: A Diary.* New York: G. P. Putnam's Sons, 1935.

______. *Sieg Heil, An Illustrated History of Germany from Bismarck to Hitler.* New York: W. W. Norton, 1974.

Low, Alfred D. *Jews in the Eyes of the Germans.* Philadelphia: Institute for the Study of Human Issues, 1979.

Lowenthal, Leo. *Prophets of Deceit.* New York: Harper & Row, 1949.

Macksey, Kenneth. *The Partisans of Europe in the Second World War.* New York: Stein and Day, 1975.

Margolis, Max L. *A History of the Jewish People.* New York: Atheneum, 1969.

Marrus, Michael R., and Paxton, Robert O. *Vichy France and the Jews.* New York: Basic Books, 1981.

Maršálek, Hans. Die Geschichte des Konzentrationslagers Mauthausen. Vienna: Österreichische Lagergemeinschaft Mauthausen, 1980.

______. *Konzentrationslager Gusen.* Vienna: Österreichische Lagergemeinschaft Mauthausen, 1968.

Massing, Paul W. *All Quiet in Germany.* London: Victor Gallancz, 1935.

Masson, Madeleine. *Christine-A Search for Christine Granville.* London: Hamish-Hamilton, 1975.

Masters, Anthony. *The Summer That Bled.* New York: St. Martin's Press, 1972.
Matussek, Paul. *Internment in Concentration Camps and Its Consequences.* Berlin-New York: Springer Verlag, 1975.
Maurel, Micheline. *An Ordinary Camp.* New York: Simon and Schuster, 1958.
Meed, Vladka. *On Both Sides of the Wall.* New York: Holocaust Library, 1979.
Meltzer, Milton. *Never to Forget, The Jews in the Holocaust.* New York: Dell, 1976.
Mendes-Flohr, Paul R., and Reinharz, Jehuda, eds. *The Jew in the Modern World.* New York: Oxford University Press, 1980.
Merkl, Peter, H. *The Making of a Stormtrooper.* Princeton, N.J.: Princeton University Press, 1980.
Michel, Henri. *La Guerre de l'ombre.* Paris: B. Grasset, 1970.
Michel, Jean. *Dora, The Nazi Concentration Camp.* New York: Holt, Rinehart and Winston, 1979.
Minco, Marga. *Bitter Herbs.* London: Oxford University Press, 1960.
Moreau, Emilienne. *La guerre buissonnière.* Paris: Sloan, 1970.
Morley, John F. *Vactican Diplomacy and the Jews During the Holocaust, 1939-1943.* New York: KTAV Publishing House, 1980.
Morse, Arthur D. *While Six Million Died: A Chronicle of American Apathy.* New York: Random House, 1967.
Moss, William S. *Ill Met By Moonlight.* London: Macmillan, 1950.
Mosse, George L. *Toward the Final Solution.* New York: Harper & Row, 1980.
Muser, Erna, and Zevrl, Vida, eds. *FKL žensko koncentracjisko taborišče Ravensbrück.* Ljubljana, Yugoslavia: Partizanska knjiga, 1971.
Neave, Airey. *The Escape Room.* Garden City, N.Y.: Doubleday, 1970.
______. *Little Cyclone.* London: Hodder and Stoughton, 1954.
Neumann, Peter. *The Black March.* New York: Bantam, 1967.
Nicholas, Elisabeth. *Death Be Not Proud.* London: Cresset, 1958.
Noble, Iris. *Nazi Hunter Simon Wiesenthal.* New York: Julian Messner, 1979.
Novac, Anna. *Les beaux jours de ma jeunesse.* Paris: Julliard, 1968.
Novitch, Miriam. *Sobibor, Martyrdom and Revolt.* New York: Holocaust Library, 1980.
Nyiszli, Miklos. *Auschwitz: A Doctor's Eyewitness Account.* Greenwich, Conn.: Fawcett Books, 1961.
Orska, Irena (Bytniewska). *Silent Is the Vistula: The Story of the Warsaw Uprising.* New York: Longmans, Green and Co., 1946.
Ourisson, Dounia. *Les secrets du Bureau Politique d'Auschwitz.* Paris: Amicale d'Auschwitz, 1946.
Papanek, Ernst, and Linn, Edward. *Out of the Fire.* New York: William Morrow, 1975.
Pawelczynska, Anna. *Values and Violence in Auschwitz.* Berkeley, Calif.: University of California Press, 1979.
Pearson, Michael. *Tears of Glory: The Betrayal of Vercours, 1944.* London: Macmillan, 1978.
Perl, Gisella. *I Was a Doctor in Auschwitz.* New York: International Universities Press, 1948.
Perl, William R. *The Four-Front War, From the Holocaust to the Promised Land.* New York: Crown, 1979.
Petrow, Richard. *The Bitter Years.* New York: William Morrow, 1974.

Poliakov, Leon. *Harvest of Hate.* Westport, Conn.: Greenwood Press, 1971.
Pore, Renate. *A Conflict of Interest: Women in German Social Democracy, 1919-1933.* Westport, Conn.: Greenwood Press, 1981.
Porter, Jack N., ed. *Jewish Partisans.* 2 vols. Washington, D.C.: University Press of America, 1982.
Presser, Jacob. *The Destruction of the Dutch Jews.* New York: E. P. Dutton, 1969.
Ramati, Alexander. *The Assisi Underground.* London: Sphere Books, 1981.
Rector, Frank. *The Nazi Extermination of Homosexuals.* New York: Stein and Day, 1981.
Reder, Rudolf. *Belzec.* Cracow: Wojewodska židovska komisja historyczna, 1946.
Reiner, Ella L. *Prisoners of Fear.* London: Victor Gollancz, 1948.
Reiss, Johanna. *The Upstairs Room.* New York: Bantam, 1979.
Reitlinger, Gerald R. *Final Solution.* New York: Beechhurst Press, 1953.
______. *The SS: Alibi of a Nation, 1922-1945.* New York: Viking Press, 1957.
Robinson, Jacob. *And the Crooked Shall Be Made Straight: The Eichmann Trial, the Jewish Catastrophe, and Hannah Arendt's Narrative.* New York: Macmillan, 1965.
Rose, Leesha. *The Tulips Are Red.* New York: A. S. Barnes and Co., 1979.
Ross, Robert W. *So It Was True: The American Protestant Press and the Nazi Persecution of the Jews.* Minneapolis: University of Minnesota Press, 1980.
Rubenstein, Richard L. *The Cunning of History: The Holocaust and the American Future.* New York: Harper & Row, 1975.
Saint-Claire, Simone. *Ravensbrück, l'enfer des femmes.* Paris: Tallandier, 1946.
Salus, Grete. *Eine Frau erzählt.* Bonn: Bundeszentrale für Heimatdienst, 1958.
Salvesen, Sylvia. *Forgive But Do Not Forget.* London: Hutchinson, ·1958.
Saphirov, Nikolai N. *Do poslednego dykhania* [*To the Last Breath*]. Moscow: Voen. izdatelstvo, 1958.
Schafranov, Sofia. *I Campi della morte in Germania.* Milan: Sonzogno, 1945.
Schellenberg, Walter. *The Labyrinth, Memoirs of Walter Schellenberg.* New York: Harper & Brothers, 1956.
Schoenbrun, David. *Soldiers of the Night, The Story of the French Resistance.* New York: E. P. Dutton, 1980.
Selzer, Michael. *Deliverance Day, The Last Hours of Dachau.* Philadelphia-New York: J. B. Lippincott, 1978.
Senesh, Hannah. *Hannah Senesh, Her Life and Diary.* New York: Schocken Books, 1972.
Sereny, Gitta. *Into That Darkness: From Mercy Killing to Mass Murder.* New York: Macmillan, 1974.
Seth, Ronald. *Noble Saboteurs.* New York: Hawthorne Books, 1966.
Smith, Bradley F. *Reaching Judgement at Nuremberg.* New York: NAL, 1977.
Smith, R. Harris. *OSS, The Secret History of America's First Central Intelligence Agency.* New York: Delta, 1972.
Smolen, Kazimierz, ed. *Reminiscences of Former Auschwitz Prisoners.* Osviecim, Poland: Panstwowe Muzeum, 1963.
Somerhausen, Christine. *Les Belges deportés à Dora et dans ses kommandos.* Brussels: Université Libre de Bruxelles, 1978.
Sosnowski, Kiryl. *The Tragedy of Children Under Nazi Rule.* Poznan-Warsaw: Zachodnia agencija prasowa, 1962.

Stein, George H. *The Waffen SS, Hitler's Elite Guard of War, 1939-1945*. Ithaca, N.Y.: Cornell University Press, 1966.

Steiner, Jean-Francois. *Treblinka*. New York: Simon & Schuster, 1967.

Stephenson, Jill. *Women in Nazi Society*. London: Croom Helm, 1975.

Suhl, Yuri, ed. *They Fought Back*. New York: Crown, 1967.

Ten Boom, Corrie. *The Hiding Place*. New York: Bantam, 1975.

———. *Prison Letters*. New York: Bantam, 1978.

Thomas, Gordon, and White, Max M. *Voyage of the Damned*. Greenwich, Conn.: Fawcett Crest Books, 1975.

Thyssen, Fritz. *I Paid Hitler*. New York: Farrar & Rinehart, 1941.

Tillion, Germaine. *Ravensbrück*. Garden City, N.Y.: Doubleday, 1975.

———. *Ravensbrück témoignages*. Neuchâtel, Switzerland Édition de la Braconnière, 1946.

Tokayer, Marwin, and Swartz, Mary. *The Fugu Plan*. London: Paddington Press, 1979.

Union of American Hebrew Congregations. *Spiritual Resistance: Art of the Concentration Camps, 1940-1945*. New York: Jewish Publication Society of America, 1981.

United Nations War Crimes Commission. *Law Reports on Trials of War Criminals*. 15 vols. London: H. M. Stationery Office, 1947-1949.

U.S. Office of Strategic Services. Research and Analysis Branch. *Concentration Camps in Germany*. Washington, D.C.: 1944.

Vechtomova, E. A., and Ivanov, V. V. *Liudi, pobedivshie smert' [People Who Conquered Death*]. Leningrad: Lenizdat, 1968.

Volanská, Hela, et al. *Hrdinky bez pátosu* [*Heroines Without Pathos*]. Bratislava, Czechoslovakia: Vydavatelstvo politickej literatury, 1967.

Volavková, Hana, ed. *. . . I Never Saw Another Butterfly. . . .* New York: Schocken Books, 1978.

Von der Lühe, Irmgard. *Eine Frau im Widerstand, Elisabeth von Thadden und das Dritte Reich*. Freiburg: Herder Verlag, 1980.

Vrba, Rudolf, and Bestic, Alan. *I Cannot Forgive*. New York: Bantam, 1964.

Waagenaar, Sam. *The Pope's Jews*. La Salle, Ill.: Open Court, 1974.

Waite, Robert G. L. *The Psychopathic God, Adolf Hitler*. New York: NAL, 1977.

Ward, Dana, *I. F. A. N. Y. Invicta*. London: Hutchinson, 1955.

Warmbrunn, Werner. *The Dutch Under German Occupation, 1940-1945*. Stanford: Stanford University Press, 1963.

Wasserstein, Bernard M.J. *Great Britain and the Jews of Europe, 1939-1945*. New York: Oxford University Press, 1981.

Webb, A. M., ed. *The Natzweiler Trial*. London: Hodge, 1949.

Weiss, Resha. *Journey Through Hell*. London: Vallentine, Mitchell, 1961.

Wiesenthal, Simon. *The Murderers Among Us*. New York: Bantam, 1967.

———. *The Sunflower*. New York: Schocken Books, 1976.

Wilborts, Suzanne. *Pour la France: Angers, La Santé, Fresnes, Ravensbrück, Mauthausen*. Paris: Charles Lavauzelle, 1946.

Wilkinson, James D. *The Intellectual Resistance in Europe*. Cambridge, Mass.: Harvard University Press, 1981.

Wolf, Lore. *Ein Leben ist viel zu wenig*. Frankfurt am Main: Röderberg Verlag, 1981.

Wynne, Barry. *The Story of Mary Lindell, Wartime Secret Agent*. Milton Keynes, England: Robin Clark, 1980.

Yoors, Jan. *Crossing, A Journal of Survival and Resistance in World War II.* New York: Simon & Schuster, 1971.

Young, Gordon. *Cat With Two Faces.* New York: G. P. Putnam's Sons, 1957.

Žak, Jiři, ed. *Buchenwald varuje: Dokumenty vzpomínky. svědectví (Buchenwald Warns: Documents, Reminiscences, Testimonies*]. Prague: Státní nakladatelství politické literatury, 1962.

Zassenhaus, Hiltgunt. *Walls, Resisting the Third Reich.* Boston: Beacon Press, 1976.

Zorn, Gerda, and Meyer, Gertrude. *Frauen gegen Hitler.* Frankfurt am Main: Röderberg Verlag, 1974.

Zuker-Bujanowska, Liliana. *Liliana's Journal.* New York: Dial Press, 1980.

Zywulska, Kristyna. *Wo vorher Birken waren.* Munich: Kindler Verlag, 1979.

Index

Numbers in italic indicate photographs.

About the Editor

VERA LASKA received her Ph.D. from the University of Chicago. She is Director of American Studies, Chairperson of the Division of Social Sciences and Professor of History at Regis College in Weston, Massachusetts. She is the author of *"Remember the Ladies," Outstanding Women of the American Revolution; The Czechs in America, 1633-1977; Franklin and Women; Benjamin Franklin, The Diplomat; Nazism, Resistance & Holocaust in World War II: A Bibliography*, and a column, "American History Reader," which appears in several local newspapers.

Recent Titles in
Contributions in Women's Studies

The Origins of the Equal Rights Amendment: American Feminism Between the Wars
Susan D. Becker

European Women on the Left: Socialism, Feminism, and the Problems Faced by Political Women, 1880 to the Present
Jane Slaughter and Robert Kern, editors

Toward the Second Decade: The Impact of the Women's Movement on American Institutions
Betty Justice and Renate Pore, editors

A Conflict of Interest: Women in German Social Democracy, 1919-1933
Renate Pore

The Second Assault: Rape and Public Attitudes
Joyce E. Williams and Karen A. Holmes

Oppression and Resistance: The Struggle of Women in Southern Africa
Richard E. Lapchick and Stephanie Urdang

Against All Odds: The Feminist Movement in Mexico to 1940
Anna Macías

Pariahs Stand Up! The Founding of the Liberal Feminist Movement in France, 1858-1889
Patrick Kay Bidelman

Separated and Divorced Women
Lynne Carol Halem

Female Soldiers—Combatants or Noncombatants? Historical and Contemporary Perspectives
Nancy Loring Goldman, editor

A Woman's Issue: The Politics of Family Law Reform in England
Dorothy M. Stetson

"Traitors to the Masculine Cause": The Men's Campaign for Women's Rights
Sylvia Strauss